# Insurrection or Loyalty

*Written under the auspices of the
Center for International Affairs,
Harvard University*

# Insurrection or Loyalty

*The Breakdown of the Spanish American Empire*

Jorge I. Domínguez

HARVARD UNIVERSITY PRESS

*Cambridge, Massachusetts, and London, England   1980*

Library of Congress Cataloging in Publication Data

Domínguez, Jorge I    1945-
    Insurrection or loyalty.


    "Written under the auspices of the Center for
International Affairs, Harvard University."
    Includes index.
    1. Latin America—History—Wars of Independence,
1806-1830.    2. Revolutions—Latin America.
3. Royalists in Latin America, 1806-1830.
I. Harvard University. Center for International
Affairs.    II. Title.
F1412.D67        1980        980'.02        80-24095
ISBN 0-674-45635-1

*To my parents*

# Preface

This book completes my research project on revolutions, work that has lasted almost a decade. The other results of the research are *Cuba: Order and Revolution*, published in 1978, and various articles on twentieth-century revolutions in Bolivia, Mexico, China, and the Soviet Union.* In them I address two general issues: flawed political orders and imperfect revolutions. As these terms suggest, the consistent scholarly and normative predisposition in these pages is toward criticism of the principal political alternatives discussed. I do not recommend this position for its pure pleasure or its ability to win friends; nevertheless, it is the one I reached as a result of my work.

In this book I examine the period prior to the revolutions in four Spanish American colonies and the processes of overthrowing the old order. My earlier publications concentrated more on the outcomes of revolutions. This book is concerned with events leading to revolutions. The book on Cuba is a historically informed case study and the articles are comparative but much less historically grounded. This study is both comparative and historical. The project as a whole encompassed both comparison and history even if that proved difficult to achieve in any one publication. The two books and the articles were written during the same time period, delaying the publication of each but informing one part of the research by the findings of the others.

I had several particular objectives in this book that were not pursued in

---

*Christopher Mitchell and Jorge I. Domínguez, "The Roads Not Taken: Institutionalization and Political Parties in Cuba and Bolivia," *Comparative Politics*, 9 (January 1977): 173-195; Jorge I. Domínguez, Nigel S. Rodley, Bryce Wood, and Richard Falk, *Enhancing Global Human Rights* (New York, 1979), pp. 66-85, on Mexico; and Jorge I. Domínguez, "Revolutionary Values and Development Performance: China, Cuba and the Soviet Union," in Harold Lasswell, Daniel Lerner, and John D. Montgomery, eds., *Values in Development* (Cambridge, Mass., 1976), pp. 20-54.

my other works on revolution. I wanted to study the one period in the history of Spanish America when the region was unquestionably engaged in a continental challenge to established political order. Never since has a political convulsion of such magnitude occurred. I wanted also to contribute to the dialogue between social scientists and historians, especially concerning areas and times where such dialogues have been infrequent. This reflects an autobiographical attitude, for my professional training began in history and moved later toward political science. I attempt to engage in open reasoning, that is, I not only present my arguments and evidence but also try to show explicitly why I reject alternative but plausible counterarguments. Although I did not discover this style of writing, I recommend it to the reader.

Two additional personal elements might be noted. Cuba is one of the four colonies studied in this book as well as the subject of my earlier volume. Years ago, I set for myself the task of exploring why the country of my birth had had such diametrically opposite experiences with revolution approximately a century-and-a-half apart. Moreover, as a person of an orderly temperament, I had wanted to explore simultaneously events during which some chose to side with the established order while others chose insurrection. None of the other revolutions I have studied present the complexity of loyalty or insurrection as richly as the cases studied here.

I have incurred many debts in writing this book. It was written, as were the other works in the project, at the Center for International Affairs, Harvard University, under the directorships of Robert R. Bowie, Raymond Vernon, and Samuel P. Huntington. The last-named, as well as Karl W. Deutsch, read critically and constructively the earliest version. I am grateful to these and to other colleagues for their comments and encouragement, even when they disagreed with many parts of my arguments. Different versions of this manuscript were typed by a number of people at the Center, but I especially want to thank the last of these, Andrée Brown, who worked and put up with me with skill and good cheer.

I am very grateful to Aida DiPace Donald and Marianne Perlak of Harvard University Press, who provided sound editorial advice and marvelous design work for both this book and for the book on Cuba. And, for this book in particular, Elizabeth Suttell gently but firmly edged me to make substantive revisions that improved the book and Ann Louise McLaughlin helped me to write more effectively about the subjects I had managed to confuse on my own. I also wish to acknowledge the kind permission of the *Journal of Interdisciplinary History* and the MIT Press, Cambridge, Mass., to reprint in Chapter 3 parts of an article of mine published in volume V (1974): 237-266.

Mary, Lara, and Leslie know that all my work is theirs too, and together we dedicate it to my parents.

J.I.D.

Cambridge, Massachusetts
June 2, 1980

# Contents

# TABLES

# Introduction

"All our contemporaries," Alexis de Tocqueville wrote in 1856, "are driven on by a force that we may hope to regulate or curb, but cannot overcome, and it is a force impelling them, sometimes gently, sometimes at headlong speed, to the destruction of aristocracy."[1] This idea, phrased differently, has remained basic to the study of the politics of large-scale social change. In a more general sense, the "decline of aristocracy" was the breakdown of central social and political institutions under the "force" of political participation. Tocqueville's *Old Regime and the French Revolution* identifies three problems: political participation, governmental response, and the ability of the existing political institutions to confront the challenge of political change by adapting to maintain civic life beyond transient crises. My book explores the breakdown of the Spanish Empire in America during the first quarter of the nineteenth century, concentrating on the burst of political participation in the first quarter of the nineteenth century in four colonies, the response of the Spanish colonial government, and the ability of political institutions to adapt to those events.

The breakdown of the Spanish Empire is a rare example of complex events that have been extensively studied but underanalyzed. There are many works on selected general aspects of the problem, studies of the successor states of the colonial empire, narrations of the events, and some interpretative essays.[2] However, social science concepts have yet to be applied to the richness of the data and the excellence of the historical sources. Political scientists have generalized about change mostly on the basis of the Western European and North American experience. Dissatisfaction with those early efforts has led to studies of the experiences of the newly independent countries of Africa and Asia.[3] My book engages in a dialogue between history and other social sciences. It examines the decline of a historical empire in America from the viewpoint of contemporary political science. The need for such a work has been presented by Deutsch and Merritt: "The analytical social sciences seemed shallow without the large processes and long series of data that are recorded by history, yet history seemed vague or chaotic without the help of more analytic disciplines."[4]

The key question of the Spanish American experience in the first quarter of the nineteenth century is why some colonies chose insurrection while others remained loyal — under the same prevailing international circumstances. Spanish rule on mainland America had ended by the close of the third decade of the nineteenth century. Yet this uniformity of outcome resulted from great variation in process. The Viceroyalty of Peru had to be forced to be free, invaded by armies from the north and from the south. Its first independent presidents became traitors in their own new state by defecting to Spain as the war of independence neared an end. Cuba, southernmost Chile (Chiloé and Valdivia), and western Venezuela (Coro and Maracaibo) remained bastions of Spanish rule until the bitter end. If such colonial capitals as Buenos Aires, Santiago, or Caracas were hotbeds of rebellion, viceregal Mexico City was a command post for the defense of Spanish rule. Modernizing elites in Cuba never broke with Spain; rather they modified colonial structures to accommodate accelerating change.

Why did wars of independence not occur everywhere, and why did the process differ so much that military conquest was required to expel Spain from America to the regret of so many of its former subjects who fought to save the empire? The political relations between elites participating in politics and the imperial and local governments responding to them were the decisive factors that led to insurrection or loyalty. The formation of political coalitions among formerly competing groups helped impel them in either direction. Social mobilization was not sufficiently advanced in Spanish America to serve as an explanation for insurrection, nor were the wars of independence extensions of mass revolts and protests that had been building up in the late colonial period. Elite political participation by itself or the development of a sense of national consciousness do not account enough for insurrection and loyalty. Attitudes toward or experiences with foreign trade were independent of decisions about insurrection and loyalty. Competition between the Spanish-born and the American-born did not lead everywhere or at all times to insurrection. Relative deprivation of individuals or groups played a role only in accounting for ethnic status conflicts, not as a general explanation.

The relation between political participation and government response was also crucial in shaping the actual conduct of the wars of independence and where they occurred, as well as in structuring the possibilities of political reconstruction. Government and insurgent strategies of political mobilization become the key elements. White fears of black or Indian revolts contributed both to elite cohesion and to loyalty to Spain.

Spain's American empire was a centralized bureaucratic political system that depended on a mix of traditional sources of legitimation and modern resources for war and wealth. The empire's preservation required balance and harmony, which were disrupted by Spain's program of government modernization and by international war. Yet even war, especially the Napoleonic invasion of Spain, was not a decisive enough event to explain the wars of independence. The colonies responded differently to war and invasion, as they had to the spread of Enlightenment ideas in the eighteenth century. The difference depended on political bargaining between government and elites and among the elites themselves, which varied from colony to colony.

The Spanish empire was characterized by the prevalence of neopatrimonial elite norms and by the presence of ethnic politics. Traditional forms of political participation included elite competition, ethnic status conflicts, social banditry, and various types of mass collective violence. The empire coped remarkably well with this array of behavior until the early nineteenth century.

## Approach and Countries

The theoretical purposes of this book require a comparative approach to isolate relationships among variables. Four cases are matched against each other, with certain variables held constant in order to study political behavior. Focusing on a single empire in a single geographic-cultural area with shared historical experiences reduces the variability that would have existed if the British, French, Dutch, or Portuguese empires had been included. The focus on a single empire ensures controls and commonalities; the focus on the colonies opens up possibilities for contrast.[5]

Four dependencies of the Spanish Empire were selected for study: Chile, Cuba, Mexico, and Venezuela. Spain's attention to them varied considerably. Between 1788 and 1795 Spain's Junta and Council of State discussed American affairs 401 times; 114 referred to particular colonies. The colonies at the vortex of interimperial politics — Cuba, Puerto Rico, Trinidad, Louisiana, and Florida — were responsible for two-thirds of the discussion. Attention to Chilean affairs was never recorded. Mexican affairs were the subject 11 times, the same number as for the other ancient viceroyalty, in Peru, and about twice as often as for Venezuela.[6]

The following criteria for selecting the colonies were established:

(1) At least one viceroyalty and several peripheral dependencies;

(2) At least one dependency that failed to have a large-scale revolt for independence, while most other dependencies were having such revolts;

(3) Dependencies with different kinds of agricultural, mining, and industrial production;

(4) Representation of the major population groups — Indians, blacks, American whites, and Spaniards;

(5) Dependencies with different degrees of direct involvement with countries other than Spain;

(6) At least one successor state able to reestablish institutionalized government relatively soon after independence.

Mexico, the Viceroyalty of New Spain, was Spain's most valuable colony in the late colonial period. One of the two original politico-administrative centers of the empire in America, it remained one of four viceroyalties. It was then, as it is today, a very complex country. Its population included all major population groups and all three types of economic production.

Two relatively peripheral countries were chosen: Chile and Venezuela. Chile was the first new state in nineteenth-century South America to reestablish capable institutionalized government. What experiences set Chile apart from those other countries so early in their national lives? Chile was also one of the most ethnically homogeneous dependencies and one of the most isolated from the extraimperial international system. Venezuela had a plantation economy with little mining or industry. It had relatively few Indians but a large free black population. Its political organization as a successor state relied heavily on charismatic leadership. Its international involvement was intermediate.

Cuba was the most important Spanish American colony that failed to revolt, remaining loyal in the end. Cubans did not fight for independence in large numbers until the last third of the nineteenth century. Its study poses most clearly the issue of loyalty to Spain at the time of independence for most of the colonies in the Spanish American empire. Cuba had the most direct extraimperial international involvement of any colony as well as a flourishing plantation economy. Some popular explanations of the wars of independence must be reexamined in the light of the Cuban case because they "overexplain" the wars. If they are correct, Cuba should have become independent in the first quarter of the nineteenth century.

*The Use of Statistics*

The statistical method, that is, the mathematical manipulation of empirically observed data, could be used only in an auxiliary capacity. Some of its tools, such as sample surveying, were not applicable. Others, such as regression analyses on time series, seemed unwise and unproductive because of serious problems of data validity and reliability. The collection of data for all dependencies of the Spanish empire for cross-national analysis at a point in time would have sacrificed the analysis of subtleties in these countries.

Statistics are used to a limited degree by lowering the expectation about the precision of the scales, shifting from interval to ordinal scales even though the data have the appearance of an interval scale.[7] Upper and lower scores are established for the variables under observation, and countries are ranked for comparison and contrast. This is a partial solution to the problem of reliability and validity. Sacrificing powerful statistical tools may seem a heavy cost, but only the illusion of precision has been surrendered. Although judgments about reliability and validity must be made, certain kinds of data can be used that could not otherwise have been employed because the demands placed on their accuracy are less stringent.

## The Wars of Independence in the Four Colonies

The conventional starting point for the wars of independence is the Napoleonic invasion of Spain. Charles IV and his son Ferdinand abdicated the Spanish Crown in favor of Napoleon in April 1808. On May 2 the people of Madrid rioted when the remaining children of King Charles were about to be removed to France. The Spanish war of independence began. First a Council of Regency and then a Supreme Central Junta were established to govern Spain in the King's absence. The Supreme Junta, housed in Seville, obtained pledges of allegiance from all the American colonies. When French troops overran Seville and most of southern Spain, the Junta was replaced early in 1810 by a Council of Regency in Cádiz protected by the British.

The colonies' responses to the news varied widely. A Supreme Junta was established in Caracas by the leading American-born citizens in April 1810; the governor, the justices of the Audiencia (supreme court), the intendant in charge of fiscal and military affairs, and the leading military officers were deposed. The Caracas Junta swore allegiance to the absent King Ferdinand VII, but not to any authority in Spain. The

Chilean elites, by contrast, had deposed the incumbent governor legally for abuse of power. Yet, when the Council of Regency in Spain appointed a new governor, the Chilean elites refused to accept him and established their own Junta in September 1810. They swore allegiance to the King and to the Council of Regency in Spain, even though its orders had been disobeyed. Revolt broke out in New Spain in September 1810, too, but it was not led by the colony's central elites. Instead, in the Bajío area, northwest of Mexico City near the cities of Guanajuato and Querétaro, Father Miguel Hidalgo revolted against the "bad government" of the Viceroyalty, pledging support for the King. The Cuban colonial government and the Cuban elites did not form a Junta and did not begin a rebellion, but pledged their allegiance to King and Council. Nor did they waver in their continuing loyalty to the imperial government in Spain through the next decade and a half.

The initial phase of the revolt did not fare well. The Venezuelans were the first to drop the fiction of loyalty to King Ferdinand, proclaiming an independent republic in July 1811. The war there, as in Mexico and Chile, soon became a civil war. Although the fortunes of insurgents and royalists varied, the Crown had won in Venezuela by the end of 1814. The patriot leaders there had been disgraced: Francisco de Miranda, the first revolutionary leader, capitulated to royalist forces; the eventual liberator, Simón Bolívar, had been defeated and exiled. In New Spain Hidalgo was defeated, captured, and killed in March 1811. The leadership of the Mexican revolt passed to another priest, José María Morelos, under whose leadership independence was proclaimed in November 1813. Morelos, too, was captured and shot in 1815. Chile, on the other hand, did not proclaim independence during the first phase of the war, although its government acted as if it had done so by 1811 when a Congress met. A provisional Constitution was proclaimed in 1812. The Viceroy of Peru, convinced that the Chileans were seeking independence, organized the reconquest of Chile for the Crown, and war developed early in 1813. Chilean patriots, led by Bernardo O'Higgins and José Miguel Carrera (who fought each other when they were not fighting the royalist forces), were decisively defeated at Rancagua in October 1814 and fled across the Andes. By the end of 1814 Chile and Venezuela for the most part had been pacified; New Spain's pacification was largely completed in 1815.

Ferdinand VII returned to the throne of Spain as an absolute monarch. The liberal parliamentary monarchy and the Spanish Constitution of 1812 established by the Cádiz government were abolished. Ferdinand sent thousands of troops to northern South America to complete its pacification. However, Simón Bolívar reorganized the patriot forces, with support initially from President Pétion of Haiti. The struggle was generalized throughout Venezuela and New Granada (Colombia). In August 1819 Bolíivar won at Boyacá and entered Bogotá. In June 1821 the Spanish Army was finally defeated at Carabobo; Venezuela was free, although pockets of resistance (Maracaibo and Coro) held out to the end for the Crown, as they had throughout the wars. Chile had to be conquered militarily with the support of the Argentine western provinces and the government of Buenos Aires. Buenos Aires' General José de San Martín organized the Army of the Andes that crossed the mountains in 1817. The royalist armies were defeated at Chacabuco in February and the patriots entered Santiago. Although the Chilean patriots were defeated by the royalists in March 1818 at Cancha Rayada, Chile's independence was finally won at Maipú in April 1818.

On January 1, 1820, General Rafael Riego led a liberal revolt in Spain. The Constitution of 1812 was restored and the Cortes, or parliament, called into session. The measures adopted by the Cortes were so radical and unpopular among the elites of New Spain that at long they preferred independence to continued loyalty. The commander of the royalist army of southern New Spain in 1820, Agustín de Iturbide, had been charged with defeating the remaining guerrillas led by Vicente Guerrero. Instead, Iturbide and Guerrero joined to announce the Plan de Iguala calling for independence, the establishment of the Catholic religion, and civil equality between American-born and Spanish-born. The Viceroy's recognition of Mexican independence was obtained in the Treaty of Córdoba in August 1821. Iturbide was proclaimed Emperor of independent Mexico in May 1822.

The first part of the book considers the period prior to the breakdown of the empire; the second part discusses the period of the wars. Each concentrates on mass and elite political behavior as well as on government responses to them. The puzzle of insurrection versus loyalty remains the book's central concern. Why did some choose to remain attached to the empire, while others were willing to break away from it?

# PART ONE

# The End of the Empire

# 2

# Imperial Legitimacy and Stability

Spain's American empire was one of several centralized historical bureaucratic polities. S. N. Eisenstadt has argued that these are political systems where "traditional, undifferentiated types of political activities and organizations coexisted with more differentiated autonomous ones, all closely interwoven in the major aspects of political activity."[1] In Spain's America, a traditional legitimation of rule remained in effect.

The unification of Spain and the conquest of America took place almost simultaneously. The American empire inherited the norms, procedures, and institutions of the Kingdom of Castile—that part of Spain directly responsible for its conquest and early settlement. Castilian political theory came to pervade much of the political theory of the unified Spanish state. The monarch claimed authority in the name of God and the pursuit of justice. The ruler was not accountable to the people or to the estates (Cortes) but to God, and only the monarch could interpret that accountability. Nevertheless, the basic constitutional instrument of Castile, the Siete Partidas, dating from the Middle Ages, included elements of medieval political philosophy that stressed the practical duties of the monarch to his people. There were injunctions against tyranny, against restrictions of personal or group liberties, and against economic, social, or educational mismanagement.

This strongly Christian, Thomist political theory believed in the sinfulness of all persons. Law was the manifestation of the will of God; but sinful persons were not likely to live up to the law. There was a gap, sometimes a chasm, between law as ideal and law as reality. This recognition of sinfulness in political theory affected both political inputs and outputs. On the output side, all subjects were obligated to acknowledge and obey the law as right and just. They were not obligated, however, to implement the law if there were special conditions, in a particular area or time, that justified a suspension of the applicability of the law pending royal review. On the input side, the distinction between obedience to and application of law required a differentiation within the role of the monarch. The monarch was not only the chief of state and the agent of God; he was also the chief administrative and political officer of the realm. His duty was to reconcile the gap between the moral ideal and the sinful reality. The monarch was an arbiter over his own edicts whose practical applicability had been suspended by subordinate officials.

This traditional theory of political legitimation, therefore, recognized the active role of the monarch as a political moderator or regulator among principles, groups, and individuals. This was essential for government flexibility. Communications and transportation were slow, and conditions varied widely in an empire that, at the height of its glory, spanned the world. Local officials had to be allowed discretion in law enforcement and applicability under the cover of the principle of centralized traditional legitimacy. This procedure was responsible to a large degree for the long history of the empire; knowledge of it is essential for understanding Spanish success in Cuba at the time of the wars of independence.[2]

As a centralized bureaucratic empire, there was in Spanish America only a limited distinction between the subjects' political role and other social roles; traditional ascriptive units and strata performed many political roles. On the other hand, these empires differed from other premodern political systems. The rulers had autonomous political goals. There was at least a limited differentiation between political activities and roles, and attempts were made to organize the political community into a centralized unit. Also, specific organizations for administration and politics developed. A critical issue was the growth of what Eisenstadt has called free-floating resources, those not embedded within, or committed beforehand to, any primary, ascriptive, particularistic groups linked to birth, sex, religion, region, language, or ethnicity. The chief sources of free-floating resources were those sectors of society that were less regulated by ascriptive and particularistic criteria. Such "pockets of modernization" were also the more articulated political sectors and could advance independent political goals and undermine the traditional legitimation of the rulers. To maintain the imperial political system the rulers had to regulate the more independent groups and their free-floating resources and link them to the more traditional groups.

The political system needed both traditional and free-floating resources, the former for legitimation and continued loyalty, the latter for expansion of the scope and domain of the authority of the political system. Scope refers to the number and kinds of issues affected by the political center, domain to the number and kinds of persons so affected. The paradox in the maintenance of the provision of free-floating resources is that they had to be adequate but limited. Change could be accommodated in this political system, provided that there was fundamental harmony between the modern and traditional pulls within it. Rapid growth would destabilize the system and lead to its breakdown.[3]

Although the Castilian influence was predominant in the Spanish theory of the state, another thread was traceable to the other major unit in Spain at the time of unification: the Kingdom of Aragon. Aragon's political theory legitimated the existence of independent political goals that the rulers pursued, internally or internationally, in America or in Europe. The rulers of Aragon absorbed the impact of Renaissance political theory more quickly and willingly than did those of Castile. The unified Spanish monarchy at the time of the conquest thus contained both a strong principle of traditional legitimation and a recognition of the autonomous political goals of the rulers.

The Spanish empire also had a neopatrimonial elite political culture, although Spanish America was not historically unique in this respect. Structurally patrimonial systems are much simpler than centralized bureaucratic empires. A patrimonial bureaucracy is so rudimentary that Max Weber called it a "purely personal administrative staff." The degree of social differentiation in the society is far too low to be compared with an empire; therefore, the Spanish American empire was not strictly patrimonial. Nevertheless, the attitudes, beliefs, styles, and policies of elite members, including those in the government, exhibited patrimonial characteristics. Because of this mix of structures and attitudes, this elite political culture will be called "neopatrimonial." In it, the government is highly interventionist, on behalf of the ruler, in all major spheres of the social system. In the economy, Weber noted that "the important openings for profit are in the hands of the chief and the members of his administrative staff." In more differentiated societies, such as the Spanish American empire, where there are such things as tax farming, and leasing or sale of offices, "there is an opening for capitalistic development, but it is diverted in the direction of political orientation."[4] There was intensive and frequent intervention by the ruler in the nonpolitical spheres that were politicized thereby. The ruler's intervention in Spanish America was based on his claim to personal, private, independent ownership of the realm and its resources in typical patrimonial fashion as a matter of law and right. Royal sanction was required to make any of a wide range of changes in most aspects of society, the economy, and the political system. The strong neopatrimonial element in the theory of the monarchy had also profound implications for political life in Spanish America. Grants of land or subsoil in the original settlement of Spanish America were royal concessions. The early grants, *encomiendas*, were not grants of land, but grants of the use of the land. Indians were distributed as wards of the state in the care of land users, to work under them and, theoretically, to be protected and Christianized by them. Indians were held as government tutees, enjoying the special protection of the Crown and of laws, regulations, courts, and officials distinct from the rest of the legal order. The Indian stratum thus became a sociological and a legal-moral fact.

The owner-monarch regulated the extraction and distribution of resources from his possessions. The monarchy's regulations and laws governed trade within and outside the empire, political appointments, and social relations, as well as the jurisdictions among the various sectors of the empire. The monarch's authority over competing jurisdictions was a key element of his regulative powers because administrative and judicial responsibilities were exercised by the same officials, often in competing ways, giving rise to many disputes. The practice of granting *fueros* — special privileges of separate jurisdiction for merchants, clergymen, Indians, and military men — further complicated the problem of overlapping and competing jurisdiction. The monarch and his personal delegates settled or compromised these disputes. In this way the king provided some harmony between the modern and traditional elements of the system to ensure that the level of resources available to him would be adequate but limited, and that they would be denied to other groups.

One problem in this neopatrimonial system is that the social structure induced changes in the normative orientation of the rulers. The modernizing Spanish monarchs of the eighteenth century sought to advance their autonomous political goals by stimulating the growth of the more modern economic sectors. But this required a reduction of the personally based, neopatrimonially oriented intervention of the government in the economy through the adoption of freer international trade and the recognition of private land ownership.

The breakdown or transformation of a centralized bureaucratic empire resulted from imbalance or disharmony in that system. Eisenstadt proposes a number of conditions for the transformation of these political systems into either more differentiated or less differentiated systems. They include transformation into prebureaucratic societies when there is limited social differentiation in some major spheres leading to the depletion of free resources, when there is intolerance on the part of the rulers of a high level of flexibility for social groups, and when there are significant elite groups with organizational capability and traditional orientations. On the other hand, there is transformation to more differentiated political systems when there is a great deal of existing economic and social differentiation and a high level of technological development and economic productivity. There must also be a strong emphasis on the economic strength and development of the state as a distinct goal of the political system. Universalistic values must be prevalent, and groups with such values must emerge with articulated political goals and organizations.[5]

The Spanish American empire fits neither type; it moved in both directions. Although the first condition for transformation into a prebureaucratic polity was not so prevalent, the other two were. The level of technological development and economic productivity did not even approach the level of Western Europe as it moved toward modernity, and ascriptive and particularistic values continued to be prevalent, even though universalistic values had emerged to a limited degree in some intellectual circles.

## Imperial Stability and Mass Participation

One key consideration for imperial stability is the nature of mass political participation. Men and women have often sought to shape the allocation of values in a society through political participation.[6] People participate in politics, in the final analysis, because they choose to do so. However, some political participants have internal, autonomous psychological sources for such participation. They can turn themselves on or off politically without depending on external agents. Although they may not always be political participants, they are always capable of becoming political participants. Other political participants rely more on external agents (leaders or organizations) to motivate them politically. They are not autonomous. When the external pressures cease, the political participation ceases. They are neither continuously involved in politics, nor continuously capable of becoming involved out of their own resources.

A second dimension rests on the experience of modernization. Modern political participation points to a total or partial break with historical commitments and patterns of past political participation. Traditional political participation, on the other hand, expresses continuity with the past. Even when traditional political participants protest, they often seek to restore preexisting conditions rather than demand new rights; they show low levels of political organization (such as food riots and peasant revolts), rather than more complex forms (labor strikes or political parties).

These two dimensions — the original source of participation and its historical context — are summarized by the social mobilization hypothesis. Karl Deutsch defined social mobilization as "the process in which major clusters of old social, economic and psychological commitments are eroded or broken and people become available for new patterns of socialization and behavior." Many scholars of different purposes and methods have supported this hypothesis.[7] The mechanism that dislodges traditional people from their accustomed commitments has several empirically observable components that are highly and positively correlated across time and national boundaries. Quantitative indicators for social mobilization include literacy, school enrollment, per-capita income, media exposure, urbanization, nonagricultural employment, and occupational mobility. The dependent variable is political participation. As the indicators of social mobilization increase, the probability of a break with previous patterns of politics and the launching of a new pattern is quite high. An increase in the scope and domain of political participation often follows an increase in social mobilization: more people participate in politics and are affected by politics; more issues are thought to be within the political realm.[8] Most studies of the social mobilization hypothesis define political participation as the capacity to participate, or the internal, autonomous ability to turn oneself on or off politically. It probably has a decisive impact on intervening variables, such as personalities, beliefs, and attitudes, that are the more proximate causes of political participation. Most studies also concur that this psychological capacity to participate is new — a break with historical feelings, orientations, and behaviors.[9]

We can draw three principal conclusions about the state of research on this venerable hypothesis.[10] Its essential features are still valid: education, income, and occupation have a significant and cumulative effect in propelling people into sustained political participation. Political participation of the sort affected by social mobilization is still the capacity to affect politics. Urbanization is now thought not to have an independent impact on political participation (even though it correlates highly with variables that do). There is little reason to assume an automatic politicizing or radicalizing bias to the process of migration to the city or to the urban environment. The political behavior of migrants results less from assumed widespread anomie and frustration and more from the attitudes and patterns of behavior that migrants bring with them from the countryside and from the active process of political socialization to which they are exposed in the cities. The critical issue is to specify the process of politicization — how the urban poor may be inducted into politics. There is renewed stress on the importance and independent impact of organizational involvement and political mobilization, even perhaps in the absence of much social mobilization, on the promotion of political activity. Organization-based political participation (in factories, unions, and parties) may differ from the behavior predicted by the social mobilization hypothesis. Relatively nonautonomous individuals participate in politics as a result of external pressures; they are motivated by leaders and organizations. Once this external mobilization declines or ceases, political activity declines or ceases, given the relative absence of effective social mobilization.

These considerations assume a significant amount of social mobilization. The research questions have been concerned with the effect of the speed of social mobilization and the mix between externally and internally motivated participation. However, two additional objections may be aimed not at the core of the hypothesis but at the range of its applicability. The logical structure of the social mobilization hypothesis indicates that there are circumstances where it does not apply. In order to argue that "old" commitments can be eroded or broken, it is necessary to envision a time when the "old" commitments were prevalent. The hypothesis cannot be used to explain all political participation at all times, but only a special kind: the internal, autonomous capacity of an individual to engage in sustained political participation. Second, the social mobilization hypothesis emphasizes a mass phenomenon. The utility of the hypothesis has been its stress on mass change beyond the elite, or beyond particular sectors that may have undergone modernization.[11] There has been an educated elite in many premodern political systems. The mere presence of such an elite, or of isolated pockets of modernization, is insufficient evidence of the existence of social mobilization. The hypothesis requires large numbers of socially mobilized people who are turning to new patterns of organization and behavior.

During the first quarter of the nineteenth century the Spanish empire in mainland America collapsed. One of the factors leading to the breakdown of the empire was a surge of political participation during the period of the wars of independence. Political demobilization or departicipation immediately followed, yielding little net social change. Can the social mobilization hypothesis explain political participation and lack of participation during and after the war period? The references of historians to the impact of the Enlightenment and to the clamoring for fewer restrictions on the evolving economic growth in cities and towns suggest that it may. In contrast to the early "black legend" views about Spanish lack of interest in education, revisionist historians have pointed to a richer colonial educational heritage; thus the social mobilization hypothesis may be a more efficient explanation of comparative political behavior — in secessionist and loyal colonies — than has been available in the past.

If social mobilization was at a relatively high level, subsequent research trying to connect independent and dependent variables would be warranted. But such a finding would make it more difficult to explain the lack of political involvement at the conclusion of the wars. If the probability of autonomous political participation was high, why was there such an apparent return to preindependence patterns of behavior in the mid-nineteenth century? On the other hand, if social mobilization was relatively low, other independent variables would need to be investigated to explain the wars of independence. Low social mobilization would also make it easier to explain political apathy at the conclusion of the wars. One would, then, expect that political participation during the wars would have been mostly of the traditional sort. And then the social mobilization hypothesis would simply be inapplicable. Spanish colonial officials have not been helpful; the nature of the evidence is fragmentary. Yet, a general picture of the level of social mobilization in the late Spanish colonial empire emerges.

### Assessing the Social Mobilization Hypothesis[12]

In 1810 the literacy rate of adults (persons over age fifteen) did not exceed 20 percent in any of the countries under study, and it was probably closer to 10 - 12 percent. The upper limit, perhaps approached by Mexico, was 14 - 17 percent. Fairly direct data on the percentage of school-age children actually enrolled were obtained for Chile and Cuba for 1810 and 1817, respectively; the level was 4 percent. Cuba (which experienced no war of independence at the beginning of the nineteenth century) and Chile (where the war was less severe than in other colonies) had surpassed Mexico (then ranking third) and Venezuela (at the bottom) by the middle of the nineteenth century in terms of school enrollment relative to the school-age population. By 1836 the proportion of free children of school-age actually enrolled was between 9 and 13 percent in Cuba; the proportion of all children of school-age actually enrolled in Cuba at that time may have been as low as 7 percent. One-fifth of the Chilean adult population was literate by 1854. In 1846, in contrast, only 7.6 percent of adult Venezuelans were literate, and only 3.5 percent of its school-aged children were enrolled in school in the 1846-47 academic year. The Mexican school enrollment ratio in 1844 was 4.8 percent, although before the outbreak of the wars of independence, it had ranked at the top.[13]

Quantitative and documentary analysis indicates that the Chilean, Cuban, and Venezuelan educational systems grew most rapidly during the eighteenth century, especially during its last third. Mexico made substantial educational strides in the sixteenth century following the conquest; after a long pause, its educational growth accelerated in the eighteenth century. The Royal and Pontifical University of Mexico was founded in 1553; the Universities of Caracas and Havana were established in 1725 and 1728 respectively; while the University of San Felipe began functioning in Santiago, Chile, in a limited way in 1747 and more fully only in 1756.

Educational opportunities were sharply affected by ethnicity. As late as 1836, 14.5 percent of the white males but only 2.3 percent of the free black males, aged five to fifteen, were in school in Cuba; the respective statistics for Cuban females aged ten to twelve were 7.3 and 1.6 percent. The enrollment of white students may have jumped 279 percent from 1816 to 1836, and the enrollment of free black students jumped 204 percent, in Havana province. Evidence of schools open to blacks in Venezuela was sparse and limited to a handful of schools mostly outside of the city of Caracas. Chilean education, too, belonged to the whites. Chile's failure to educate the Indians was perhaps more blatant than in the other countries, in part because the Spanish government had not militarily subdued the southern Chilean Indians, although efforts at educating the pacified Indians were also negligible. In contrast to the other countries, there was a serious effort in sixteenth-century Mexico to educate the Indians, although it came under attack. It would have opened the lower professions to the Indians. Partly to prevent this, the guild system was transplanted to New Spain, with provisions for exclusion of the Indians. Although not all Indians were excluded, the rise of the early, white, artisan, urban middle class in Mexico owed much of its success to the limitation of competition from Indian industrial and craft activities. This was an ethnic and an economic conflict. Some also feared that Indian education would destabilize a still precarious social system, as Indian alumni of some of the schools were among those who revolted against Spain. Thus the amount and quality of education available to Indians in Mexico was curtailed.

Urbanization, measured as the percentage of the population living in cities with 10,000 or more inhabitants, was between 20 and 25 percent in Cuba, 14 to 18 percent in Venezuela, about 10 percent in Mexico, and about 5 percent in Chile. Nevertheless, Mexico had developed a capital city unmatched for variety of urban life, a distinctive metropolitan center. The number of cities in Mexico was about twice that in Venezuela, while Cuba's and Chile's urbanization was concentrated in their capital cities. If cities with 10,000 or more inhabitants are tallied, the numbers total Mexico, seventeen; Venezuela, nine; Cuba, three; Chile, two. And if the distinctive qualities of life in metropolitan centers are stressed, the ranks are Mexico (Mexico City), Cuba (Havana), Venezuela (Caracas), and Chile (Santiago).[14]

Estimates of per capita income are available for only two colonies. Cuba's gross national product per capita in 1825, measured in 1950 United States dollars, was $170 — extraordinary for the age. There was considerable economic growth in Cuba in the first quarter of the nineteenth century, although it was based on an illiterate and oppressed slave labor force. The Mexican gross domestic product per capita has been calculated at approximately between 600 and 1,000 pesos in 1950 prices. Mexico's per capita product in 1950 United States dollars for 1803 may have been between $45 and $55.

Evidence of mass media exposure is drawn from the introduction and use of the printing press. The printing press was introduced into Mexico in the sixteenth century. Monthly newspapers appeared in the first half of the eighteenth century and daily newspapers began publication in Mexico City and Veracruz in 1805. Printing presses appeared in other cities of the Viceroyalty of New Spain in the eighteenth century. During the wars of independence there was a newspaper propaganda war in Mexico. The printing press came to Cuba in the beginning of the eighteenth century, and a weekly newspaper began publication in Havana in 1790. But the spread of the newspapers to the interior cities was slower in Cuba than in Mexico, where daily newspapers appeared first. Media exposure was extremely limited in Chile and in Venezuela. Although the printing press was introduced into Chile in the middle eighteenth century, Chile's first newspaper (a weekly) did not begin publication until 1812, after the war of independence had begun. Although there is some evidence of printing press activity in Venezuela in the eighteenth century, the first printing press whose existence can be validated dates from 1808. It was Venezuela's only press for some time and, most importantly, the first one with a significant social effect. Within a month of its arrival, Venezuela's first newspaper appeared. The press was important during the Venezuelan wars of independence, although less so than in Mexico.

Table 2.1 summarizes the ordinal scales. Urbanization is thus broken down into three components: the percentage of the population in cities of over 10,000; the number of cities of such size; and a ranking of capital cities. The date of founding of the universities is used to indicate the length of time during which elite professionals were produced by native educational systems. Table 2.2 summarizes the rank scores of each country on the six variables of Table 2.1. The combined rank of the countries is treated as a seventh variable in Table 2.3, which represents a matrix of Kendall's *tau-b* rank order correlations based on Tables 2.1 and 2.2.[15] These correlations measure the degree of association among variables, ranging from 1.0 where there is a perfect positive relationship to -1.0 when there is a perfect negative relationship; a score of zero indicates that there is no relationship between the two variables. If the social mobilization hypothesis is to be confirmed, the *tau-b* scores among the variables studied should approach 1.0.

Excluding variable 4, fourteen of the remaining fifteen correlations show *tau-b* values between 0.55 and 1.00; one other is 0.33. No single rank order correlation is very impressive when there are only four observations; rather, we are more impressed by their overall positive direction

*Table 2.1*  Social mobilization in 1810: Country rankings

| 1<br>Adult<br>literacy | 2<br>Universities | 3<br>Media<br>exposure | 4<br>Urbanization:<br>percent of<br>population | 5<br>Urbanization:<br>number of<br>cities | 6<br>Capital<br>cities |
|---|---|---|---|---|---|
| Mexico | Mexico | Mexico | Cuba | Mexico | Mexico |
| Cuba | Cuba | Cuba | Venezuela | Venezuela | Cuba |
| Chile | Venezuela | Chile | Mexico | Cuba | Venezuela |
| Venezuela | Chile | Venezuela | Chile | Chile | Chile |

a. Ties.

*Table 2.2*  Combined rank scores for social mobilization in 1810

| | Number of scores | | | |
|---|---|---|---|---|
| Countries | Rank 1 | Rank 2 | Rank 3 | Rank 4 |
| Mexico | 5 | 0 | 1 | 0 |
| Cuba | 1 | 4 | 1 | 0 |
| Venezuela | 0 | 4 | 1 | 1 |
| Chile | 0 | 1 | 1 | 4 |

*Table 2.3*   Kendall's *tau-b* rank order correlations

|   | 1 | 2 | 3 | 4 | 5 | 6 | 7 |
|---|---|---|---|---|---|---|---|
| 1 | — | | | | | | |
| 2 | 0.77 | — | | | | | |
| 3 | 0.71 | 0.55 | — | | | | |
| 4 | -0.24 | 0.18 | 0.00 | — | | | |
| 5 | 0.71 | 0.91 | 0.33 | 0.00 | — | | |
| 6 | 0.71 | 0.91 | 0.67 | 0.33 | 0.67 | — | |
| 7 | 0.71 | 0.91 | 0.67 | 0.33 | 0.67 | 1.00 | — |

and size. This would be expected from the social mobilization hypothesis. On the other hand, variable 4 clearly is not measuring the same things as the others. Its *tau-b* values range from *tau-b* $_{4.6}$ = 0.33 to *tau-b* $_{4.1}$ = $-0.24$. It is not an indicator of social mobilization for this period. The skepticism about this variable is supported by the theoretical discussion; the variable must be treated with caution.

Early-nineteenth-century Spanish American cities differed from those that had or would emerge in Western Europe and North America, and later in Latin America. Richard Morse has argued that the Latin American city was the point of departure for the settlement of the soil. The European city represented a movement of economic energies away from extractive pursuits toward those of processing and distribution. The colonial Latin American city was the source of energy and organization for the exploitation of natural resources. Its location was determined by political and strategic considerations arising from the needs of settlement. As the economic activities — agriculture and mining — of the urban dwellers drew them to the countryside, a political, "ruralized" city emerged. Throughout most of the colonial period, Morse believes, most cities propelled status- and fortune-seekers out into the countryside. The social organization of the town was often unstable; its very life was sometimes ephemeral. However, Mexico City and Havana began to attract population from outlying districts by the late colonial period, followed by Caracas and Santiago.[16]

In sum, it is likely that, other than the capital cities, even cities with 10,000 inhabitants, did not exhibit the quality of life associated with social mobilization. Neither their elites nor their masses altered their behavior very much. Even if they lived in cities or towns, their orientation was rural and nonindustrial. The correlations among variables which mark social mobilization, therefore, are stronger for adult literacy, university experience, media exposure, number of cities, and capital cities than for the percentage of the population in ruralized cities.

Deutsch has suggested that the threshold of significance for social mobilization is that level below which no significant departure from the customary workings of a traditional society can be detected and no significant disturbance appears in its unchanged functioning. He set that threshold at 60 percent of adult literacy.[17] That figure may be too high. Nevertheless, it is difficult to argue that the levels of social mobilization in the countries being studied, as measured by adult literacy, could have accounted for the "significant disturbance" and the "significant departure" of the wars of independence in three of the four. Moreover, if the social mobilization hypothesis were to apply, there would have been a revolt in Cuba (second in combined rank) probably at about the same time, and there might not have been a revolt in Chile, which ranked last. At these low levels the political implications of the rate of change of social mobilization are very marginal.

We must go far back into the history of the currently industrialized countries to find such low levels of social mobilization. In 1660 up to 30 percent of young rural males in England were literate; by 1770, 50 percent of young rural males in England were literate. The estimates of male literacy in Japan are 40 - 50 percent at the end of the Tokugawa period (1860s), when 43 percent of the young men and 10 percent of the young women were receiving some schooling. The United States census of 1840 reported only 9 percent of the white population over age twenty as illiterate.[18]

There are four conclusions. First, the rankings on social mobilization suggest considerable difficulty in linking the independent and dependent variables. If social mobilization were a significant cause of political participation during the wars of independence, one would have expected a revolt in Cuba and no revolt in Chile. Such was not the case; causes and consequences are not matched. Second, social mobilization is not a general, adequate explanation of political participation during the period. The levels of social mobilization in these colonies were far below the thresholds of significance that must be approached if the hypothesis is to be relevant. It is difficult to argue that social mobilization explains mass political participation during the wars. Third, there were enough educational institutions at the middle and upper levels to train the elite. Many of the leaders of the revolts were well-educated men. The concepts of the social mobilization hypothesis are useful in studying the elites. But the general utility of the hypothesis is that it stresses mass change beyond the elite. It requires large numbers of socially mobilized persons who are turning to new patterns of organization and behavior. This was missing in 1810. Fourth, the low levels of social mobilization suggest that the wars could not have been engendered by men and women who were psychologically independent and capable of self-generated political action. Political mobilization depended on leaders and organizations acting upon a fairly inert mass. Social mobilization stresses internal sources of political behavior. Political mobilization, in the relative absence of social mobilization, stresses external forces working to produce political behavior. When the external pressures cease, the political behavior ceases.

The social mobilization hypothesis, therefore, is valuable for the study of Spanish America after the wars of independence. It then would predict political demobilization or departicipation: only small, fragmented groups — the remnants of leaders and organizations — would remain once the grand challenge was met and overcome. Indeed, the wars of independence were not followed by sustained civic participation. The very fact that social mobilization does not apply to the onset of the wars allows it to provide an explanation for the failure of the wars to launch a fundamentally different, modern type of political system. But to explain the burst of political participation in the first quarter of the nineteenth century and to explain the breakdown of the Spanish empire, one must look to other hypotheses and independent variables.

## Imperial Stability and Traditional Political Participation

Political participation can be accommodated by a centralized bureaucratic empire provided the regulatory mechanisms for balance and harmony can keep it under control. One behavioral control was clearly effective: social mobilization was too low to pose a threat to imperial stability. What, then, are the characteristics of traditional or presocial mobilization participation, and what may be its relation to imperial stability?

Traditional political participation is not affected to any significant degree by social mobilization. Levels of education, literacy, and media exposure remain low; people are not psychologically receptive to new patterns of behavior. Old commitments remain; observed behavior displays striking continuity with the past. The source of the political participation is an external agent (leader or organization or group) acting on the potential participant; it is dependent, nonautonomous. Traditional political participation results from political mobilization by leaders and organizations that influence the masses. Modern participation results from mass action within organizations and upon their leaders.

Groups of traditional political participants are concerned with a limited number of issues. An urban mob may want bread; but its scope does not extend beyond that narrow goal. Revolting slaves may seek immediate freedom from their masters, without other economic, social, or political ends. A group of planters may seek a specific benefit, but might refrain from following the course of modern elites: to establish political parties concerned with a large number of issues. Such narrowness of scope is strongly affected by social structure: scope may be narrower for a peasant revolt than for merchant lobbying. For a given role in the social structure, scope is also narrower for traditional than for modern participants. A traditional peasant may revolt to achieve directly and promptly one or two specific goals (regain land, sell products). A modern farmer might join a farm federation to seek to achieve a wider range of goals.

Mass traditional political conflict is often fragmented rather than system-wide. Given social mobilization, political confrontation tends to be system-wide, as potential groups communicate with each other and form larger organizations. In the absence of social mobilization, political conflicts are more fragmented, with conflicts arising in some localities but not in others. If they appear in several places simultaneously, it is more by accident than by design, for the participants in the various localities are seldom in communication, nor have they designed common strategies. In the rare cases when a large coalition appears to have formed, its goals and methods are poorly integrated. Such large groups resemble a conglomerate more than a closely integrated party. Conglomerate participants may not have reconciled conflicting goals; each may be concerned with limited but different issues. Although each group may have a program, the conglomerate does not. The integration of structures is also low, and the struggle for advantage is often carried on at different and poorly integrated levels.

The goals of mass traditional political participants are typically backward-looking; they aim to restore or retrieve a condition perceived to exist in a real or idealized past, whether it be freedom for the slave, land for the peasant, food for the hungry, or prestige for a group fallen into decline. Revolts occur when something is lost, when value capabilities decline (while value expectations may remain constant). The goals of elite traditional political participants may be either backward-looking or adjustive. Elite groups often compete to incorporate gains into the existing system. Even when they seek something that they did not have before, it is within the context of existing procedures and organizations as a part of their continuing behavior. By contrast, more modern-oriented elites would set new goals of change, reform, or transformation of existing structures. Although some elites, especially in Cuba, were acquiring a more modern outlook, most of the observed elite behavior in the late colonial Spanish American empire was either backward-looking or adjustive.

Certain characteristics apply primarily to the lower ranks of the social structure in a traditional setting, as opposed to the same lower rank of the social structure in a more modern setting, but not to traditional elites. There is a generally low level of organization among lower-class mass traditional political participants. Their organizations, though very important, are transient, such as urban mobs or peasant revolts. Individual peasants or city dwellers are moved to do in these short-lived organizations what they would not do in isolation. Some organizations of this sort did not emerge from the creative acts of the poor and oppressed as, for example, some traditional caste organizations in India. The poor may be violent when they are organizationally creative; their paramilitary, highly improvised armies or militias may battle against the government. Yet the traditional poor have no political parties, labor unions, or peasant federations. On the other hand, a high level of organization in a centralized bureaucratic empire is often found at the elite level. Merchants, planters, priests, and soldiers have typically adjusted to the bureaucratic mode of politics; their guilds and other organized interest groups have an active and continuing life. Mass traditional participation is neither continuous nor periodic. In a more modern setting, lower-class organizations (parties, unions, federations, clubs) may have a more or less continuous existence, and lower-class participation results from this organizational life through reasonably periodic or cyclical elections or strikes or other participation. In a more traditional setting, mass political participation is recurrent but not continuous. Such actions frighten but do not surprise the elite; the cycles of mass explosions are more difficult to foresee. The time scale of traditional, mass political participation emphasizes short-term rather than long-term perspectives. Because the scope is narrow, the organization transient, and the goals backward-looking, long time frames into the future are rare.

The ruler's delicate balancing and harmonizing of the traditional and the modern, obtaining adequate but limited resources from the latter without undermining the former, was crucial for the maintenance of the imperial system. The level of social mobilization in Spanish America was so low that it could not have contributed meaningfully to the wars of independence; its low level, on the other hand, explains the ease of political demobilization after their conclusion. The wars of independence depended upon traditional political participants mobilized by external agents or organizations; in the absence of much social mobilization, mass political participation eventually declined. Traditional political participation, whether elite or mass, was congruent with imperial stability; it did not necessarily threaten the empire's continuation until new events — which will be examined — intervened.

# 3

# Ethnicity

Ethnic conflict could not provoke independence. It was a normal part of colonial life. Ethnic participation was one type of mass traditional participation that could be accommodated by the empire without threat to its stability under most instances. (The "accommodable" political participation has this meaning throughout the book.) The Spanish American empire was not ethnically homogeneous. Ethnic and cultural heterogeneity can spur the breakdown of centralized bureaucratic polities. Such empires must balance not only their modern and traditional sectors but also the different ethnic groups within the elite and different ethnic strata within the society. The balancing includes the preservation of the status quo and the provision of limited social mobility for the various groups and strata. Spain did this very effectively for centuries.

## The Ethnic Structure

Ethnic politics take different courses depending on the structure of group differentiation. In vertical or hierarchical systems, social class stratification is synonymous with ethnicity. Political and social mobility is often blocked by color. In horizontal or parallel systems, each ethnic community has its own criteria of social class stratification. Although one group may be relatively dominant, the groups are not usually ranked in relation to each other.[1]

In parallel systems ethnic groups coexist under conditions of mutual repulsion and disdain; each community considers its own honor highest. A hierarchical system, in contrast, brings about social subordination and an acknowledgment that the privileged groups deserve "more honor."[2] Thus, at certain points in their histories hierarchical systems may have "more social cement" and more normative justification than do horizontal systems. When the cement cracks, however, a social revolution may result. There may be intermittent conflict in horizontal or parallel systems, but it need not lead to major social transformations. Hierarchical systems typically result from conquest; parallel systems may result from incomplete conquest or migration.

The ethnic systems in Spanish America were shaped by conquest, a habit acquired before the discovery of America. During the half-millennium before Columbus' voyage, the history of Spain, especially of Castile, is the story of the Reconquista, the war to expel the infidels from the Iberian peninsula. By the middle of the thirteenth century the only non-Christian kingdom in the peninsula was Granada at the southern tip of Spain. The Castilian monarchs combined the consolidation of conquest with a settlement policy. The conquered territories had to be peopled with those loyal to the Christian God and the Christian King. Thus, settlement was added to military conquest as a continuing feature of Spanish life.[3]

Military values made conquest possible. According to J. H. Parry, "a gentleman was not primarily a man who held land by a particular kind of tenure. He was a man who owned a horse and was prepared to ride it into battle in his lord's support. His horse, no less than his sword, marked him off from the earth-bound peasant." The imageries of battle and militant religion rather than those of commerce, the arts, or government, dominated.[4] The conquerors were not won over to the tilling of the soil or those unlordly economic activities required to keep a transatlantic empire alive. Given the political and military insecurity of the first century after conquest, military and militant religious values seemed sufficient for the task at hand. Economic and politico-military requirements were reconciled by establishing a hierarchy of Spanish lords and Indian peasants; where the latter disappeared, black slaves replaced them. Ethnically different conquered peoples performed economic tasks under the lordly protection of their Spanish masters.

Thus a hierarchical system of stratification developed throughout most of Spanish America. Military force established the system, religion legitimized it, and the passing of time made it tolerable to most of the conquered peoples. The early, simple ethnic hierarchy was modified by sexual promiscuity and matrimony. White conquerors had children by Indian and black women. The result was the growth of ethnically intermediate groups which occupied (often but not always) intermediate positions in the structure of the political system.[5]

The rich ethnic diversity of the Spanish empire in America varied from one colony to another. The most generally accepted population total for the Viceroyalty of New Spain in 1810 is 6,123,354. The Creoles, American-born descendants of Spaniards, were largely white — or at least socially accepted as white — and accounted for about 18 percent of the population in 1810. The slaves were black; there were only about 10,000 left. Most of the 15,000 Europeans were Spaniards. Mexico's mestizos, the offspring of white and Indian and of black and Indian, made up 22 percent of the population. And about 60 percent of the population was Indian.[6]

The Captaincy General of Venezuela had about 898,000 people. Creoles accounted for 19 percent and Europeans for 1.3 percent. Mulattoes (the offspring of black and white) and free blacks were 49 percent. About 12.3 percent were slaves, and 18.4 were Indians, one-third of whom were so-called "marginal Indians," who neither were an active part of Venezuelan society, nor did they provide a continous threat to its existence.[7]

Because of the absence of a war of independence in the Captaincy General of Cuba, the population estimates of three censuses are shown in Table 3.1. There were no recorded Indians left in Cuba.

There is an inverse relation between the presence of Indians and the presence of black slaves. In places like Mexico, where, despite war, poverty, and famine, relatively large numbers of Indians survived, the need for slaves was small by 1810. Where the Indians had virtually disappeared, as in Cuba, the need for slaves for the labor force was much greater. Venezuela ranked between these two. The proportions of whites and, within this group, of Creoles and Europeans was remarkably similar in Venezuela and Mexico; Cuba's proportion of whites, on the other hand, was about twice as large.

Slave imports into Cuba, relatively moderate up to the last quarter of the eighteenth century, accelerated rapidly after 1790, except for a brief

*Table 3.1*   Estimates of Cuba's population, 1792-1827[a]

|      | Whites | Free blacks and mulattoes | Slaves | Total |
|------|--------|---------------------------|--------|-------|
| 1792 | 133,550 (49) | 54,152 (20) | 84,590 (31) | 272,292 |
| 1817 | 239,830 (43) | 114,058 (20) | 199,145 (37) | 553,033 |
| 1827 | 311,051 (44) | 106,494 (15) | 286,942 (41) | 704,487 |

*Source:* José M. Pérez Cabrera, "Movimiento de población," in Ramiro Guerra y Sánchez, José M. Pérez Cabrera, Juan J. Remos, and Emeterio S. Santovenia, eds., *Historia de la nación cubana* (Havana: Editorial Historia de la Nación Cubana, 1952), III, 344-348.

a. Percentages in parentheses.

*Table 3.2*   Estimates of slave imports into Cuba[a]

|  | Thrasher[b] | de la Riva[c] | de la Riva[d] (corrected) |
|---|---|---|---|
| 1521-1763 | 60,000 | — | — |
| 1763-1790 | 30,875 | — | — |
| 1790-1820 | 225,474 | 295,128 | 369,300 |
| 1790-1794 | 27,501 | 34,395 | 40,000 |
| 1795-1799 | 23,015 | 29,902 | 52,000 |
| 1800-1804 | 38,230 | 48,797 | 59,800 |
| 1805-1809 | 14,728 | 18,408 | 24,000 |
| 1810-1814 | 28,093 | 35,243 | 46,500 |
| 1815-1820 | 93,907 | 128,383 | 147,000 |

*Source:* Alexander von Humboldt, *The Island of Cuba,* trans. J. S. Thrasher (New York: Derby and Jackson, 1856), p. 218; Juan Pérez de la Riva, "El monto de la inmigración forzada en el siglo 19," *Revista de la Biblioteca Nacional José Martí,* 3rd. ser., 16, no. 1 (January-April 1974), 102-103.

a. The Pearson product-moment correlations (1790-1820) among the three estimates, using individual years as data points, are: $r=0.91_{1.2}$; $r=0.87_{1.3}$; and $r=0.95_{2.3}$.

b. Excluding 56,000 slaves smuggled into Cuba, 1791-1820. Thrasher's total estimate of legal and smuggled slaves is 278,940 for those years.

c. Based on existing historical sources, including smuggling. De la Riva's account for legal and illegal trade between 1791 and 1820 is 291,951.

d. Corrected by de la Riva to include other counts of smuggled slaves.

downturn as a result of the Napoleonic wars. The rapid growth after the Congress of Vienna is explained by the return of maritime peace and by attempts to beat the British-imposed deadline ending the slave trade by 1820. Cuba's slave population thus rose as a result of the slave trade, not from the natural birth rate. During the period under discussion the number of slaves increased from three-tenths to four-tenths of the population. White control over these black slaves had to rely more on physical coercion than on the weight of the past because these recently introduced slaves had experienced freedom earlier in their lives.

Chile's census of 1812 showed a population of about 900,000. There were between 25,000 and 32,000 (2.8-3.6 percent) blacks and mulattoes in Chile at the end of the eighteenth century, not more than 6,000 of whom were slaves. (There were only 4,000 slaves left by 1823, when slavery was abolished). The proportion or the Arauco Indians in the total population of Chile is estimated as between 19 and 25 percent during these years. In 1796 the Indian population of the Arauco region in southern Chile had been estimated at about 95,000. There is considerable debate about the size of that population in 1810 — from not much more than the 1796 estimate to more than twice as much. Outside of the Arauco region in central Chile, only 10 percent of the total population was classified as Indian and 12 percent as negro or mulatto by the 1770s; by 1813, 74 percent of the population of central Chile was called Spanish, and another tenth mestizo. Historians seem to agree that the population of Chile north of the Bío-Bíio river (excluding the Arauco region) was relatively ethnically homogeneous by 1810. Although degree of whiteness remained a status condition, the absence of a large Indian population, as in Mexico, or a large slave force, as in Cuba, had eliminated the bottom of the typical Spanish-American hierarchy elsewhere.[8]

Yet ethnicity was relevant in Chile. Parallel ethnic groups, with their own systems of stratification, engaged in intermittent conflict; this increased social cohesion within each group. Up to the eighteenth century, the wars between Spanish-dominated Chile and the Indians of Arauco had been a central feature of life. The actual fighting declined considerably during the eighteenth century, but the prospect of possible conflict remained. The Arauco Indians, unlike Indians in Mexico, Cuba, or Venezuela, were not subdued or eliminated during the colonial period. They lived in their own large, separate territory, over which they had undisputed actual control without tutelage. The Arauco wars of the 1720s and late 1760s kept the conflict alive.[9] Indians in Mexico had no more than limited local autonomy under Spanish tutelage; Indians in Mexico and Venezuela not under Spanish control were either marginal or controlled limited territory.

An indicator of the level of conflict is the relative size of Chile's army.[10] The larger the size of the military relative to the population, the greater the expectation of conflict may be; violent ethnic conflict was more frequent in Chile's parallel system. Chile can be compared to New Spain, because neither feared a direct European attack (unlike the two Caribbean colonies) and both faced Indians. Up to the 1760s the role of the regular army was very limited in Spanish America. In 1752 there were 1,279 regular troops in Chile, mostly because of the Arauco threat. The regular troops of the Viceroyalty of New Spain numbered 3,032 in 1758. By 1800 Chile had 2,358 regular troops; that same year the regular army of New Spain was 6,150; it rose to 10,620 in 1810. New Spain's population was 6.8 times greater than Chile's, so the regular troop militarization of Chile relative to its population was one and a half times greater than that of New Spain, even though the value of the former to Spain was but a fraction of the latter's. With slight variation, this proportion continued well into the late colonial period.

The degree of citizen concern can be estimated by the numbers joining the militias. Although by some counts there were only 15,856 militia forces in Chile in 1777, better statistics suggest as many as 29,639 militia forces in the bishoprics of Santiago and Concepción in 1775. New Spain had at least 23,812 in its provincial, urban, coastal, frontier, and replacement militia in 1800; other counts brought the number to 29,700 (including the so-called Internal Provinces to the north) or 30,685 (including some barely organized reserve units). If one takes the smallest estimate of the Chilean militia and the highest estimate of the New Spanish militia in 1810, the size of the militia in the Viceroyalty was 1.9 times the size of the militia in Chile, even though the population was 6.8 times larger. Chile's militarization, on the basis of militias relative to population, was at least three to four times greater than Mexico's. In fact, the size of the forces may have been the same in both countries, so that Chilean militia militarization relative to population may have been six times greater than Mexico's.

In Mexico the social order, including white domination over the Indians, was maintained by the weight of tradition. The unsubdued Indians, unlike those in Chile, were on the frontier, far from the major population centers, and their relative numbers were small. Considerable normative justification was provided for social relations based on hierarchical inequality in the core of Mexico. In Chile the Indians of Arauco remained unconquered and independent. In the hierarchical system of ethnicity of New Spain there was relative peace; in Chile's parallel system there was war.

These differences are important for the wars of independence. A social upheaval within Mexican society would also be an ethnic upheaval. A social upheaval within colonial Chile (exluding Arauco) would have few ethnic implications because of the relative homogeneity of that population. Ethnicity in Chile resulted in an expectation of continuous frontier conflict, which led to greater cohesion, not fragmentation, within the Spanish colonial framework.

## Ethnic Mobility and Conflict

The ascriptive aspects of the hierarchy differentiated broad strata of the population. Two major criteria separated the relatively free population from the relatively less free or unfree population, and the Spaniards and their descendants from those tainted with "bad blood."[11]

The first criterion was most obvious in the case of slavery: black slaves were at the bottom of all the strata in this hierarchical society. The stratum, which existed in virtually every major administrative unit of the empire, was especially important in the Caribbean basin. The first criterion was also manifested in the collection of the tribute, a personal or poll tax, paid by adult male Indians and free blacks regardless of income or property. It was the conquest tax. Resistance by black freedmen to the paying of tribute, however, made its collection less frequent in Venezuela and Central America.

Once the Spanish language began to spread, and intermarriage to increase, it was difficult to tell who was a pure Indian. The Indian was often defined by being in the tributary stratum; he was in that stratum, however, essentially because of ascriptive criteria of heritage and ethnicity. The life of the Indians was further limited by regulations that sought to protect or enforce their rights and their obligations to a separate and segregated existence, and that sought to extract from them services for the empire. Thus, the condition of the Indians, although possibly less oppressive than that of the slaves, was worse than that of mestizos, and even of mulattoes and black freedmen who were less encumbered by law and custom.

The second criterion required that purity of blood (*limpieza de sangre*) be proven in order to gain access to the professions, the craft guilds, the University, the Church, bureaucratic employment, and other major elite positions. Purity of blood required not only proof of whiteness but also of legitimacy and of prolonged adherence to the Catholic religion. It was a racial, a religious, and a status requirement, one that established an ascriptive barrier between the top stratum and the middle stratum.

The middle stratum of mestizos and mulattoes was made up of people who were relatively free but who did not have access to elite positions. The range of social class among mestizos and mulattoes was very wide, although the social "worth" of mulattoes was lower than that of mestizos. The ethnic criteria set upper and lower limits to those class and other status variations. How, then, did social mobility occur in this hierarchical system without destabilizing the empire? How was ethnic conflict contained?

One way to study Spanish American mass ethnic mobility is to compare it to another well-known hierarchical system, that of India. Although some features of the Indian caste system — closed endogamy groups with membership decided by birth, for example — do not apply to

Spanish America, the Indian and Spanish American systems share certain broad elements of hierarchical ethnicity. Moreover, the Indian caste experience permits considerable ethnic social mobility, notwithstanding other elements of rigidity in social stratification, without disrupting the basic traditional social or political order. This kind of mobility has been called "sanskritization" by M. N. Srinivas, who defined it as "the process by which a low Hindu caste, or tribal or other group, changes its customs, ritual, ideology and way of life in the direction of a high, and frequently 'twice born' caste." A claim is made to a higher position in the social hierarchy and the concession of such rank advancement may be forthcoming in a generation or two.[12]

Seven theoretical criteria identify sanskritization. (1) No "new" pattern of behavior results from social mobilization; the procedure reflects the flexibility and continuity of tradition. (2) The political system opened up possibilities for social and political mobility for those at or near the bottom of the hierarchy; it legitimized the desired change in rank. It channeled and regulated conflict: where low-status group mobility was resisted by high-status groups, the government balanced the goals of some versus the resistance of others. Systemic stability required government balancing competence. The social system was not frozen, thanks in large measure to the political system.[13] The claim to mobility, based often on a fraud, can only take hold because of political legitimation and enforcement.[14] This politically dependent type of social mobility, therefore, is not likely to disrupt the imperial political order. (3) The upwardly mobile assume the traditional perquisites of the high-status groups in the system. The structure of the system remains unaffected; even if there is conflict, change is positional only, not structural. This behavior can be accommodated within the traditional hierarchical political system. (4) Sanskritization responds to local conditions, challenges, and opportunities. No national or system-wide low-caste group seeks to be positionally mobile; only the local higher-status groups must adapt. There is no all-India movement by a single caste, often not even an all-language or all-region movement. The positional change process is thus fragmented. The appearance of national movements in contemporary India is not the result of sanskritization, but of modernization. (5) Sanskritization has mixed goals. It relies on a restored recognition of alleged ancestral high status; these are backward-looking goals. But because the status of other groups is changed, the goals seek also to adjust the balance of relations within the existing system. (6) The process is essentially an exchange of one status for another. Although its consequences may lead to more wealth, and some bribery may be involved in the recognition of the change in status, it does not depend on the legal, public purchase of higher status. (7) The caste must be organized to press its claims. It is a group rather than an individual process, and society's procedures must be seized upon to press those claims. These procedures were largely inherited from Indian history, and had the sanction of India's "great tradition."

Sanskritization differs a little from traditional political participation. Although the process is not universal, continuous, or periodic throughout the society, it tends to become so once it starts in a particular area. And the time scale typically emphasizes long-term perspectives before the recognition of the new status takes hold. Were there processes similar to sanskritization in Spain's American empire?

The major expansion of the Venezuelan economy took place in the early and middle eighteenth century. One effect of the expansion was the importation of more black slaves. In accord with Spanish practice, many of these became free, so that eventually about half of the Venezuelan population was composed of freedmen. Thus, the locus of political conflict between blacks and whites in Venezuela turned to matters of higher status.

The politicization of ethnic status conflict resulted from its regulation by the Spanish government. In a neopatrimonial culture the ruler regulates such status. The laws forbade black women to wear gold, silk, or diamonds or to cover themselves with cloth stoles. Black men were denied the use of pistols, swords, or umbrellas. Purity of blood was required for membership in elite organizations, the only routes to elite positions.[15] The Royal Decree of 1792 which established the Caracas lawyers' association (Colegio de Abogados), to which all lawyers had to belong, stated:

> We order and decree that, for any lawyer to be accepted into our *Colegio*, he must lead a reputable life; he must be capable of exercising his profession; he must be a legitimate son whose parents are known, not a bastard; and the petitioner as well as his parents and paternal grandparents must have been Christians for a long time, free of all bad blood of blacks, mulattoes, or other similar persons, and without a trace of Moors, Jews, or recent converts to our Holy Catholic Faith; and should any of these elements be missing, he should not be admitted.)[16]

This form was drawn up by Creole lawyers in Caracas, but it was fairly standard throughout the empire. Similar restrictions controlled access to municipal government, the University, or craft guilds and professional corporations, as well as positions in the Church. In 1766 marriages between whites and nonwhites were forbidden, although exceptions were permitted. In 1788 the Cabildo (municipal council) of Caracas petitioned the Crown to annul all marriages between whites and free blacks.[17]

One hallmark of Spanish imperial flexibility was the procedure in the royal order of *gracias al sacar* (grateful for deliverance), whereby a relatively well-off black or mulatto could purchase a royal dispensation from his blackness—a patent of whiteness. The Crown would declare this person "white," opening the doors to the corporations and organizations that required proof of purity of blood. Proof thus became independent of physical characteristics. Gracias al sacar was an institutionalized procedure, not a mere extraordinary occurrence. The royal order of February 10, 1795, established standard fees for seventy-one categories of gracias al sacar. Another royal deree, of August 3, 1801, raised the fee to be paid to purchase a patent of whiteness. The practice of granting patents of whiteness to blacks went back at least as far as 1773.[18]

Although this procedure operated within the bounds of the traditional system, it was a source of very serious conflict. In 1796 the Cabildo of Caracas protested against the royal tariff for gracias al sacar because it "exempted blacks and mulattoes from their condition and rehabilitated them so that they could otherwise fill the public offices of the commonwealth that are properly reserved for whites." The complaint added that blacks should be denied "the education that they have lacked up to now and that they ought to lack henceforth."[19]

In 1796 the Cabildo of Caracas protested against Spanish public officials and their "open scandalous protection given to mulattoes and blacks and to all despicable persons to reduce the prestige of the old, distinguished, and honorable families" of the city. Similar protests were reiterated in 1801 and 1808.[20] The goal of the elite was the restoration of rights of ethnic superiority and exclusiveness. It was not an effort to introduce new rights, but to restore old ones, and to block the access to higher status for competing individuals and groups who availed themselves of the flexibility of tradition.

Despite the general educational handicap of blacks, some of them were educated enough to petition for admission to the University. In 1797 and 1800 the Crown opened up the school, and profession, of medicine to blacks. But in 1803 the University Faculty still refused to admit a black applicant because of his skin color. The Faculty and the Bishop of Caracas protested against the breach of purity of blood, but they were temporarily overruled, and in 1806 the Crown upheld the University's exclusion.[21]

The proportionate decline of slavery in Venezuela had thus limited its utility as a criterion for social stratification. As many blacks became free, the main ascriptive barrier was purity of blood. The hierarchical ethnic system required "affirmative action" on the part of the political executive to provide for sufficient social mobility within the existing social framework. But such mobility stimulated further conflict, where the King sided with the blacks and the mulattoes, and the Creoles sided against them. The conflict involved access to public jobs, as well as to the professions, through the University.

Cuba's Indian population had effectively disappeared, leaving slavery as the ascriptive criterion at society's lower ranks. Nowhere in the four colonies was slavery so important as in Cuba, but there was some mobility within and beyond slave status. Four factors contributed to mobility through the lower ranks of artisan jobs. One was the lack of large-scale white immigration or white population growth during the first two centuries of settlement. The second was the settlers' desire to avoid manual labor. The third was the elimination of the Indian population, and the introduction of slaves to take their place. And the fourth was the need for heavy military fortification in Havana to defend Spain's major commercial port in the new world. From the sixteenth century on, blacks were engaged in masonry construction. Masters rented their urban slaves for many jobs. Humboldt estimated in 1825 that at least 28 percent of all Cuban slaves lived in cities and towns. Herbert Klein, perhaps with a touch of hyperbole, concluded: "Employed in every conceivable industry and profession in the urban centers and heavily engaged in a multitude of rural activities . . . the African Negro slave lived in a rich world of economic opportunity."[22]

The large number of Cuban freedmen, as in Venezuela, is evidence that manumission was an established practice. A majority of the freedmen in 1811 lived in towns and cities and were engaged in many jobs. (The ethnically restrictive craft guild system had broken down by 1861, when detailed quantitative ethnic and occupational evidence became available.)[23] Some free mulattoes had acquired small fortunes by the first third of the nineteenth century. The estate of Antonio José Oñoro (died 1836) included four houses, seven slaves, and no less than $3,000 in cash. That of José María Fuentes (died 1833) included six houses assessed at $7,533, ten slaves assessed at $2,500, and four slaves whom he had freed for $950. José Agustín Ceballos (died 1843) left an estate at $32,153; his weekly payroll had reached to $1,000 and his monthly income had been at least $400. He also lent money at interest to persons of all colors.[24] All three were mulatto foremen at Havana Harbor. The Cuban social system had a perverse adaptability: former black slaves, newly free, became slaveowners themselves!

The social system held the line at the elite professions. As in other colonies, the laws had prohibited the wearing of certain kinds of clothes by black and mulatto men and women. The University, the professions of law and medicine, and the Church continued to require purity of blood. The elite's position at the top of the ethnic hierarchy was preserved by these criteria; however, there was mobility within the bounds of the traditional system.

Despite royal opposition, at least seven blacks and mulattoes were ordained priests in 1732. There were at least three mulatto medical doctors in Havana in the early 1760s; efforts by local officials to prevent the exercise of medicine by two of the three were reversed by the Crown. There was at least one black lawyer in 1791. Although the bureaucratic job of *escribano* (scribe), requiring some legal training, was reserved for whites through the mid-eighteenth century, the bureaucracy was opened up by the end of the century. Gracias al sacar was also applied in Cuba. By 1797 the Poor Relief Office, the Quartermaster section of the navy, and the Royal Tobacco department had been opened to blacks. The proportion of freedmen was much higher at a subprofessional level. By 1834-1836, 40-43 percent of the 25 to 35 phlebotomists in Havana were free blacks or mulattoes.[25] The Cuban ethnic hierarchy thus rested on two ascriptive criteria: slavery at the bottom, and purity of blood at the top. But traditional social mobility, regulated by the government, kept the system flexible.

Gracias al sacar differs from sanskritization in three important ways. The former is an individual process, the latter a group process. The former is an exchange of wealth for status, the latter is in exchange of one kind of status for another that may then lead to more wealth. The former cannot rely on a claim to restoration of prior ancestry; the latter relies very heavily on such claims.

There are, however, several similarities between the two processes. First, no "new" pattern of behavior results from social mobilization; the procedures show the flexibility of tradition. Second, most laws and social conventions prevented mobility, but the political system made mobility possible by modifying and breaking through the legal obstacles and legitimatizing a fraud for the sake of a higher good. A neo-patrimonial political culture in Spanish America recognized the authority of the ruler to replace old status limitations with new ones. Third, as in sanskritization, the gracias al sacar black or mulatto took on the traditional perquisites of whites in the society. Low castes and blacks or mulattoes continued to be excluded from high status; only the newly found high caste or the newly found "white" had new status. The process resulted in change of position within existing structures, not in change of the structures themselves. Fourth, although the formal goals of sanskritization are restorative or backward-looking, its actual goals seek to adjust the current social relations between the claimant of new status and other high-status persons. The goals also remained premodern because there was no challenge to the classification or to the system requiring such classification. Thus, the difference in goals between sanskritization and gracias al sacar is modest. Fifth, gracias al sacar petitioners did not unite in system-wide challenges. Each petition was a discrete individual event. However, the white Creole elite had a system-wide response to these individual petitions, politicizing the ethnic system. Unlike sanskritization, the Spanish imperial procedure for traditional ethnic mobility was an individual rather than a group process; but the resistance to traditional ethnic mobility was an organized group activity in both India and in Spanish America.

The hierarchical ethnic system blossomed in Mexico. Unlike Venezuela and Cuba, the population of late colonial Mexico included Spaniards, Creoles, Indians, blacks, and mulattoes (though few slaves). Magnus Mörner has argued that "society in the Indies was the result of the transfer of the hierarchical, estate-based corporative society of late medieval Castile to a multiracial, colonial situation in the New World. The location of the existing ethnic groups within the hierarchical structure gave rise to [a] . . . pigmentocracy."[26] This applies best to the Viceroyalty where room was found for every shade of color.

The top of the social hierarchy was delineated, as in Venezuela and Cuba, by purity of blood. The bottom was delineated primarily by the system of laws and regulations that preserved the segregated identity of the Indians. Chief among these was the payment of the tribute, in principle a uniform head tax, although subject to variation in its implementation. The ordinance in 1786 classified as full tributaries all Indian males aged eighteen to fifty, exempting only chieftains and their eldest sons. The Indians were treated legally as minors; they paid tribute and were forced to supply their labor for private and public gain. Many laws denied them certain kinds of behavior and dress. They had a special tribunal to judge the laws that applied to them; they were outside the jurisdiction of the Holy Inquisition. They were exempt from direct taxes other than the tribute. Crown policy since the late sixteenth century sought to enforce residential segregation between Indians and non-Indians. Spaniards, blacks, mulattoes, and mestizos were forbidden to live in Indian villages, and sometimes mestizos were expelled from them.[27]

Indians could claim that their ancestors had had a glorious past in America and that certain perquisites of status, including exemption from tribute payments, had been granted by Spain to certain Indian peoples and chieftains at the time of the conquest. The Crown regulated the status system within the Indian stratum. It could grant or deny special consideration to recognized *caciques* (chieftains). An Indian could claim family descent from chieftains, demanding the restoration of rights. The chieftaincy petition and the governmental response were local, not system-wide, events. This Indian claim to higher status was a matter of right; and no money payment was required. It was an exchange of one status for another, although more wealth and safety might result. These factors (ancestral claim, localism, and no payment — although bribes were possible) distinguish a chieftaincy petition from gracias al sacar and render it closer to sanskritization.

For example, in the early nineteenth century José Jorge Cortés Chimalpopoca sought restitution of his family's ancestral privileges of chieftaincy. The petition was confirmed by the Viceroy in 1810. Many privileges were granted: (1) representatives of the people of the district would attend Cortés family funerals; (2) in community functions the chieftain would be seated separately in a chair bearing his name; (3) the chieftain was exempt from municipal service; (4) he was exempt from tributes and other taxes; (5) he was excused from compulsory Sunday worship and payment to the Church; (6) his servants could not be drafted for road repair; (7) the chieftain could not be imprisoned for debt, nor his house, arms, horses, oxen, clothing, or furniture be sequestered; (8) if imprisoned for a serious crime, he would be held in a royal household, not in the town jail; (9) when he visited the local Spanish official (*subdelegado*), the chieftain would be given a chair to sit in; (10) the chieftain's names would be included in the rolls of the nobility throughout the kingdom; and (11) the privileges would apply to his wives and widows.[28]

Efforts to win government recognition of chieftaincy pretensions apparently occurred with some frequency in the seventeenth and eighteenth centuries; at times they led to the fabrication of spurious documents. The number of chieftaincies (*cacicazgos*), according to Charles Gibson, increased through the centuries; and caciques came to be recognized by the government in communities that had never even had one before. Although as in the case of gracias al sacar, the extent of this type of mobility is difficult to establish precisely, this avenue for individual change clearly was used from time to time.[29]

In sum, despite several differences, there are broad similarities between gracias al sacar and sanskritization procedures. There are even more striking similarities between sanskritization and chieftaincy petitions. The crucial difference between the two is that chieftaincy petitions were individual acts, whereas sanskritization involved group mobility. In this respect, of course, gracias al sacar and chieftaincy petition procedures are the same. Therefore, the critical variable distinguishing traditional social mobility between the Indian and the Spanish American hierarchical ethnic systems is the mode of mobility: it is a group process in the former, and an individual process in the latter.

Social mobility was not achieved exclusively through procedures such as gracias al sacar or petitions for recognition of chieftaincy status. An erosion of purity of blood regulations took place, especially in the lower ranks of the corporate system — the craft guilds, established in Mexico since early colonial days. The guilds' purity-of-blood regulations for access to positions of master craftsmen sought to reserve these jobs for Spaniards and their descendants, even though some early efforts to prepare Indians for craftsmanship had been made. The needs of the country and the difficulty of supervision gradually eroded the craft guild system of purity of blood for mestizos. Thus, in Guanajuato in 1792 no craft was limited to an ethnic group, although wide imbalances existed from craft to craft. Evidence of both opportunity and discrimination is that 8 percent of the carpenters were mulattoes, though they were 32.6 percent of the work force; only 11.8 percent of shoemakers were whites, even though they were 34.6 percent of the work force. And in Antequera (Oaxaca) in 1792 mulattoes constituted 19 percent of the non-Indian work force, but accounted for only 2 percent of professionals and shopkeepers and 9 percent of high-status artisans.[30]

In contrast to blacks, the Indians' special position allowed legal openings. The King authorized the establishment of the University of Mexico for "the natives and for the children of the Spaniards"; the number of mestizos was limited to six by 1557. The Constitution of the University, drawn by Archbishop Palafox in 1645, excluded blacks, mulattoes, slaves, orientals, Jews, and Moors; but it remained open to Indians who could prove they were the children of caciques.[31] The University was ethnically segregated — and so, consequently, the professions and the Church — but the theory of segregation was less strict for the Indians than for descendants of Africans.

The case of the Reverend José María Morelos is a good example.[32] Morelos had to prove his purity of blood to be ordained a priest and to receive his bachelor's degree from the University of Mexico. There had to be some flexibility in the application of the purity of blood statute because his father at least was a mestizo. Yet even Morelos, who was to

succeed Hidalgo as the leader of the Mexican war of independence, sub-
mitted to the ethnic system without rebellion. Thus, prior to 1810 the
hierarchical ethnic system was an established and accepted sociolegal
practice.

## Status and Ethnic Conflict

The Spanish American empire had a hierarchical ethnic structure at its
core, including most of Cuba, Mexico, and Venezuela. At the frontiers,
however, there was a parallel ethnic system of intermittent warfare, as in
Chile. Where hierarchical ethnicity prevailed, a neopatrimonial ruler
sought to enforce stability, regulating relations among the various
groups and strata. The ruler also provided for the possibility of traditional social mobility. Individuals could petition the Crown for their
own and their families' advancement. This pattern of political participation, with the individual contacting public officials to obtain ethnic
status benefits, did not disrupt the traditional order of the empire.
Although traditional ethnic social mobility could be accommodated, ten-
sion was often severe enough to provoke conflicts between the Crown
and Creole elites. In hierarchical ethnic systems, the assignment of honor
to, and the acceptance of such assignment by, superior and inferior
ethnic groups is at the base of the system.[33] Some value stocks may be
perceived to be flexible and others to be inflexible in a society.[34] Wealth
is a value whose stock is often perceived to be flexible; there is a belief
that many groups and individuals, even though they compete against
each other, may be able to gain in wealth—a variable positive-sum
game. On the other hand, when value stocks in a society are perceived as
inflexible, a group's access to that value varies strongly and inversely
with the upward mobility of other groups on that value—where X's gain
is Y's loss. Status is a value whose stock is often perceived to be inflexible: there is only one group at the top.

When, in addition to absolute status, relative status is especially
valued, status typically becomes a zero-sum value. The more important
a status hierarchy is to a given society, the more critical this value will
become, and the more intense the competition. When the allocation of
status depends largely on the state, the allocation of the value is politicized. Relative status is very important in a hierarchical ethnic system
where the state allocates values. Ethnic mobility, accommodable though
it may be by the norms and structures of the political system, has an inherent destabilizing effect. It is accommodable in a centralized
bureaucratic empire only if it proceeds very slowly; any significant

perceived acceleration is likely to lead to elite fears of deprivation of relative status. Marginal changes in the ethnic system can bring about considerable consequences for the social and political system. The mechanism is often the inflation of ethnic demands — by those of lower ranks who wish to rise and by those of higher ranks who wish to block such elevation.

The inability to reconcile conflicting claims may cause ethnic group conflict to become incompatible with the maintenance of the political system. The system's failure to harmonize ethnic claims can lead to a breakdown.[35] Thus, the mere fact of traditional ethnic mobility did not have to lead to the wars of independence, provided the ruler was able to balance and harmonize the various claims.

One may argue that what is described here as ethnic conflict is simply class conflict. Actually it is very difficult to distinguish between class and ethnicity in hierarchical systems because they are so closely and positively correlated. Do these low-status groups respond more as low-income groups than as ethnic groups? One approach is to distinguish between the encompassing principle for social perception and the population it encompasses. Where ethnicity is important, there may be a transformation of perception such that it becomes the encompassing principle: where some X people are in Y occupation (or residential area, or educational level), the subjective perception may become that all X people are in Y occupation, or that all Y jobs are held by X people. The attributes of some X individuals are transferred to the whole Y collectivity, and hostility to some X soon becomes hostility to all Y, and vice versa. In these cases the encompassing principle is ethnicity, even if it is manifested in ways resembling those of social class. There are two ways of looking for the encompassing principle. One is identifying the target group: "where revolutionary violence expresses itself in the indiscriminate slaughter of members of a racial group, then the encompassing principle is race." The other is the character of precipitating events: impulses affecting racial differentiation and activating racial conflict must be distinguished from impulses which activate class conflict because they affect economic differentiation.[36]

The encompassing principle in the colonies being studied was ethnicity. Whites sought to exclude blacks and Indians because of their ethnic background. This exclusion had radical effects on the economy, education, and status. Yet the motivation seemed to be based more on ethnic group than class, although the two are closely related in a hierarchical ethnic system. The mechanism triggering the conflict was relative status deprivation on the part of the political leadership of the Creole elite

—a discrepancy developed between their expectations of high-status monopoly and the Crown's attempts to open up the social hierarchy and readjust status ranks.

Interethnic group competition can take place within very traditional bounds in a political system. Ethnic conflict is not a proof of modernization; much of it has been traditional behavior. Ethnicity is one source of political participation in the absence of much social mobilization. As Spain's example shows, centralized bureaucratic empires can cope with this form of participation. Independence movements would be strongly influenced by ethnic rivalries, but these occurrences were so common that they do not explain the break with Spain. When other factors appeared—and only then—a spiral of ethnic demands set in; continued accommodation of ethnic conflict proved difficult and contributed to the breakdown.

# 4

# Resistance to Change

Mass resistance to change has been a major type of traditional political participation. People with low levels of education, income, and media exposure and those who live in a rural environment may remain uninvolved and uninterested in what is occurring in the larger social system until it affects them directly. Then they sometimes respond, often in rage, to defend their interests, their life styles, and their culture through ad hoc resistance. Their struggle for food and shelter may be linked to large-scale political processes resulting from the intrusion of change into that premodern setting. Such political participation is likely to end when the external stimulus stops. This was a pattern of politics in the Spanish colonies — a troublesome but accommodable type of mass traditional political participation. But such mass violence did not have to lead to the empire's collapse.

## Social Banditry

Resistance to change can take several forms. The most primitive is E. J. Hobsbawm's "social bandit," found in rural areas and peasant societies. Social bandits emerge when certain actions not regarded as criminal by local social conventions are considered as such by the public authorities. Typically precapitalist and prepolitical phenomena, they also appear in response to early changes in the commercialization of agriculture. Social bandits attack the rich and the powerful. They are not necessarily politicized, but may become so if the mode of resistance changes. Social bandits are most likely to appear in periods of severe hardship (such as wars), or when modernity and the state are about to intrude in the life of rural communities. They differ from criminal bandits in that the former are regarded as "honorable" by the local population, the latter are not.

The greater the inclination to resist modernization, the more the social bandit blends into other types of resistance.[1]

Social banditry results from the activities of a leader who mobilizes support from the surrounding peasant population; peasant participation depends on social bandits and their bands. The scope of action of this mode of behavior is limited to the redress of local grievances. Goals may be backward-looking (to regain something) or adjustive within the existing system. Although social bandits may exist in different regions of a country, their activities are typically uncoordinated. Thus, social banditry may be endemic and at the same time not coordinated into an integrated movement; its level of organization, though important, is low. Social banditry, though a recurrent phenomenon, is not necessarily continuous, cyclical, or predictable; it rarely has a long-term perspective. The social bandit style of illegality can be accommodated by the political system. Bandits existed in virtually every Spanish colony in the Americas for long periods of time, but they did not pose a life-or-death threat to the empire.

One area where social bandits operated and eventually became politicized was the Bajío, north of Mexico City, whose urban centers included Guanajuato and Querétaro. Its complex economic structure relied mainly on mining, but also included agricultural plantations and manufacturing. These activities were incipiently capitalistic in orientation and mode of production. But the region also contained semi-independent farmers (rancheros), trying to make a living on marginal lands, whose precarious economic position often led to social banditry. When the Hidalgo revolt began in the Bajío in 1810, these social bandits readily participated in the plundering for personal gain that accompanied the Mexican war of independence.[2]

In Venezuela the main source of social banditry were escaped slaves, called cimarrones. By 1720 there were some 20,000 escaped slaves in the colony. Estimates for the beginning of the nineteenth century vary between 24,000 and 30,000, between 2.5 and 3.5 percent of the country's population. Many escaped slaves, in Venezuela as in Cuba, banded together in communities.[3] They plundered in order to survive, and their search for freedom was defined by the state as criminal. Their activities were political neither in goal nor in method but in effect. The cimarrones regarded themselves as honorable, and were admired by the slaves. They did not seek political power nor did they mobilize other groups; they did not even resist the intrusion of modernization into the plantations. Slave revolts, on the other hand, often resisted the intrusion of new, more modern methods of extracting gain from slave sweat and labor. Some revolts threatened the center of political power. They engaged the slaves directly in participation — not vicariously through identification with a social bandit. Therefore, most slave revolts are classified as defensive collective violence, while the activities of the escaped slaves remain cases of social banditry on the margins of politics.

The number of known communities of escaped slaves increased in Venezuela from three in the sixteenth century, to nine in the seventeenth century, to thirty-seven in the eighteenth century. Perhaps the most notable was the sixteenth-century community in Nirgua. These cimarrones were so resilient that, in order to end their plunder, the Crown legally freed them in 1601, recognized them as loyal subjects, and granted them political autonomy. Thus the empire's political flexibility and responsiveness accommodated even social bandits by creating a new niche for them: a republic of escaped slaves within the colony.[4]

By the second half of the eighteenth century escaped slaves were a recognized, integral part of smuggling. Smuggling suits social banditry very well because it results from government-initiated restrictions on trade rather than from anything intrinsic in trade. The social bandits were integrated into Venezuela's network for internal and international trade with countries other than Spain. But because a good part of the smuggled merchandise was obtained by plundering the cocoa plantations, planters, especially in the 1790s, made serious efforts to eradicate the communities of escaped slaves. By 1798, with the help of the Consulado (the guild of merchants and planters), the planters had established permanent patrols to combat the activities of the escaped slaves.[5]

An important element of social banditry is that the local population regards such actions as honorable. This was the case in Venezuela's Tuy River Valleys between 1771 and 1774. The cimarrón leader Guillermo was actively supported by black slaves in the plantations; they mentioned him admiringly in the presence of their masters, threatening retaliation from Guillermo if slaves were ill-treated. The social bandit's "honor" was important to gain the support of and provide for the self-defense of those who admired him.[6]

Venezuela was not an idyllic, peaceful place. Social banditry was a recurrent, perhaps increasing, part of life there. Escape was one of the few avenues open to slaves who wanted to be considered as individuals rather than pieces of property. When the unhappiest and more adventuresome slaves left, those left behind were less likely to revolt. And when the wars of independence broke out, many communities of escaped slaves joined the fighting.

In Cuba a type of social banditry developed at the end of the eighteenth century when many tobacco lands were deliberately destroyed to open up new land and provide labor for the then-beginning sugar and coffee boom. Not all tobacco farmers became sugar or coffee workers; some responded to modernization not by revolting against it, or adjusting to it, but by becoming bandits. Their previous life had been destroyed; they had been pushed outside the law. Some turned to highway robbery, others to stealing slaves and selling them to other planters. Many became *rancheadores*, hunting down escaped slaves and returning them to their masters for a fee.[7] These bandits, too, were useful to the social system, for they supplied slave labor to plantation owners and checked the process of slave escape. Criminal in many ways, agents of the rich in others, these were honorable men in the community of tobacco farmers, and some of their activities were directed against the rich.

Communities of escaped slaves were more prevalent in the eastern part of Cuba where government control was weakest. They survived by trading with neighboring plantations, and at times with foreign merchants. As in Venezuela, long-established communities of Cuban escaped slaves received legal sanction from the Crown. In April 1800, as the sugar and coffee plantations multiplied, the Crown freed the community of slave descendants in Cobre (eastern Cuba) from both slavery and punishment. However, the fight against escaped slave communities in Cuba accelerated during the first half of the nineteenth century as more labor was needed for the plantations.[8]

Communities of escaped slaves posed no more than a limited threat to the viability of a colonial system. To survive, they had to be located in almost inaccessible areas, far from the economic, social, and political centers of the colonies. Because slaves recently arrived from Africa were the most likely to escape, being the least acculturated, the social bonds between escaped slaves and those remaining enslaved were often weak. Escaped slave communities resembled African societies more than Spanish American societies.[9] They posed a threat only when they became very large (as the African Kingdom of Palmares in seventeenth-century Brazil).[10] In general, such communities did not threaten imperial stability.

Criminal, not social, banditry prevailed in Chile where, with a bit of statistical license, the estimate of those making a living from theft was as high as 12,000. Stealing cattle was an important activity. But criminal banditry was accommodable within the social system, and despite periodic efforts by the authorities to suppress the bandits, landowners and cattleowners often protected them. Some purchased stolen cattle from the bandits; others relied on them for violent attacks against competitors. During the Chilean war of independence, criminal bandits were employed as irregular or guerrilla forces by both sides.[11]

Banditry was pervasive in the four countries under study, social banditry in all but Chile, but bandits did not threaten the empire. Although social banditry is only partly a political activity, it is a form of traditional, accommodable mass political participation because it puts pressure on the government, forcing it to divert resources to maintain law and order. It provides the poor and the oppressed with a means of obtaining freedom and wealth by stealing or by dealing with merchants and landowners. It differs from defensive collective violence in that it does not engage the oppressed directly, only vicariously, in making demands on the government.

## Defensive Collective Violence

Defensive collective violence refers to events whose participants usually were reacting to some change considered to be depriving them of rights they once enjoyed. Included are urban food riots, peasant land-retrieving revolts, or many (though not all) slave mutinies. These are backward-looking or, at most, adjustive explosions. Their level of organization was very low, often transient or ephemeral, yet that minimal level of organization changed isolated nonparticipants into forceful, often violent, and sometimes effective participants. Defensive collective violence stems largely from crises of local conditions responding to the pressures of social change. Many such local crises may occur at once in any political system, but the explosions are typically unintegrated and fragmented, not system-wide. Defensive collective violence is not new behavior. The oppressed participate directly (unlike social banditry). Its scope is typically limited to the achievement of one or two immediate goals; its perspective is of very short range. It may be endemic and recurrent, but not continuous, cyclical, or predictable.

Modern collective violence has greater organizational complexity. It strikes out for rights that the participants perceive are due them, but are not yet enjoyed. Its scope is often larger, its time perspective longer; it may be coordinated as national, system-wide strikes, or closely integrated national revolts. In the search for new rights, it entails a break with the past. Revolutions belong to this second type of collective, organization-dependent violence. They are characteristic of the process of modernization and can only be sustained in societies in which there has already been a significant amount of social mobilization. A localized peasant revolt is linked with other social groups, especially in the cities, and including elite offshoots. Thus, whether a defensive parochial rebellion turns into a broader revolutionary movement often depends on factors beyond the local setting. It is this second feature that makes a revolution so difficult to cope with.[12]

Defensive collective violence has been a favorite method of political participation for the poor and the oppressed, for those who must worry about not getting enough food and shelter or who want to cling to ancestral religious beliefs and customs. Their needs are pressing, the time is now. But precisely because it is such an old, recurrent method, traditional elites (though frightened) have learned to live with protestors, to repress them or to compromise with them. They have been fundamentally accommodable. This variant of political participation is disruptive only when it is transformed by modernizing revolutionary elites. They can be, but rarely are, the dynamite for revolution.

Rebellions in the Viceroyalty of New Spain illustrate this point. If we consider all violent political turmoil from 1520 to 1809 — reported conspiracies, Indian wars, urban riots, and similar events — no less than four and as many as twenty such rebellions were begun every quarter-century, and at least one rebellion was begun every decade but one. Most revolts were brief, lasting less than a year, often only a few days. Their frequency and duration have been closely related.[13] There was no major Indian revolt in the decades prior to 1810 in the core of the Mexican Viceroyalty where the hierarchical ethnic system flourished. Most of the Indian wars were fought in the north of contemporary Mexico. Virtually all the revolts were localized explosions, for narrow goals, typically seeking the restoration of lost land, or the removal of a new policy, or the reversal of a decline in the food supply. They were anguished cries for food, shelter, personal dignity, and tradition. They were also poorly organized short-range explosions that did not look forward to the establishment of new changes and rights, but harkened to an idealized past.

An analysis of some of the most important revolts that broke out closer to the beginning of the wars of independence — the revolts of the 1760s, the peak in the frequency of revolts — supports this conclusion. Several economic, fiscal, and political reforms were introduced in New Spain in the 1760s. By July 1766 some 6,000 persons in Guanajuato, the main city of the Bajío region, tried to storm the treasury building crying "Long live the King! Death to bad government!" They were protesting against the new taxes on maize, flour, meat, and wood; against the new government monopolies and their poorer service; and against being drafted into the militia. Moreover, the Count of Regla, owner of the Real del Monte silver mine, had tried to cut the daily wage of his peons by 25 percent and to reduce the share of the ore received by his pickmen according to customs dating to the Spanish Middle Ages. The workers went on strike and murdered the local magistrate. The government intervened and restored the wages to their previous level. In 1767, in response to the government's expulsion of the Jesuits, perhaps the largest urban riot in the history of New Spain took place, again in Guanajuato. Mine workers, the Indians of Pátzcuaro and Uruapán, and people from the city of Guanajuato rioted for three full days demanding the return of the Jesuits. They again stormed the treasury house and the office buildings of the tobacco and gunpowder government monopolies. This riot was subdued by the ruthless application of military force. There were also protests by miners in Cerro de San Pedro, San Nicolás and San Luis Potosí, demanding payment for wages owed to them.[14] All of these protests were defensive collective violence opposing religious secularization, fiscal reform, and the violation of custom.

These incidents highlight the role of miners in collective protest, one they have played throughout the world.[15] Miners are highly susceptible to unemployment; their work is dangerous. In the early history of mining, they were often induced or coerced to leave farmlands for the mine fields, so they are among the first socially uprooted persons in a premodern setting.

Miners are also among the first of the poor whose work brought them into contact with broader national and international perspectives because of links to refineries and marketing. Some of their leaders may seek to expand those connections. The mining output is usually of sufficient political significance that miners learn to apply political muscle to obtain results. Although typically paid more than peasants, miners may not feel that they are much better off. In a premodern setting, miners are not likely to be much more literate than the peasants, but they are more apt to feel relatively deprived for this reason. Their expectations to be literate may be increasing as a result of their contacts, while their condition remains unchanged. In addition, the higher wage may only compensate for a higher risk of accident on the job that workers have to absorb on their own in the absence of insurance.

Early miners may retain relatively traditional orientations. They may not want to exchange some of their values for others. Previous experiences with broken elite promises and with coercion from mine owners may have made them skeptical. Miners are likely to resist giving up old rights and privileges and to claim those which had been taken from them, thus participating in defensive collective action. The probability of protest increases with a mine's size and importance to the government. Large, wealthy, and productive establishments have higher concentrations of miners, more contacts with the outside world, and are objects of more state interest.

The miners' behavior begins to resemble modern protests only much later in the process of modernization. Miners and their organizations have played crucial roles in the organization of modern political participation; yet not all of their political activity has been "modern." In fact, the evidence of miner defensive collective behavior can be traced through Western European history. Many early protests by British miners were characterized by riots, recklessness, and desperation. Protests were often oriented, not against employers, but against outside forces such as food suppliers; and when they focused on the employers, it was to redress perceived violations of custom. Modern protest requires that the workers be convinced of the righteousness of their demands and of the new means to enforce them.[16]

Miners in New Spain, volatile and prone to protest, resisted change. When protests were addressed against employers, the goal was not to gain new modern rights, but to restore preexisting wages and privileges. Some of the more important protests were aimed at external forces, seeking to prevent violations of customary religious practices. The protests were poorly organized — violent explosions lasting a few days, with a minimum of ephemeral organizations.

The actions of the Indians in the north of Mexico were not true revolts, but the continuation of the Indian-Spanish wars by Indians who had been barely pacified. The northward march of miners, missionaries, and soldiers in the seventeenth century was marked by an acceleration of these so-called Indian revolts. Northeastern Mexico — contemporary Coahuila, Nuevo León, Tamaulipas, and eastern Chihuahua and Durango — was peopled by nomadic Indians prior to the conquest. Their so-called revolts were more frequent in areas of more intensive Spanish settlement. The Indians thought those lands belonged to them and had been usurped by the Spaniards.[17] These struggles are typical of those of horizontal or parallel ethnic systems. The northern frontier of New Spain, therefore, resembled the southern frontier of Chile. But Mexico's north was far too distant from the core of the Viceroyalty, or even from the mining area of the Bajío, to affect ethnic relations much in the rest of the territory. Thus, the Indian wars in the Mexican north were unable to induce the kind of core area homogeneity that the clearly perceived common threat from the Arauco Indians engendered in central Chile.

Chile stands out as the colony least troubled by defensive collective violence – aside from the Arauco Indian wars. Considerable conflict dealt with the restoration of lost rights, or the readjustment of existing positions of advantage, but they tended not to be violent. The prevalent political culture of colonial Chile emphasized the channeling of conflict and of protests against imperial policies through existing organizations, such as the Cabildo or the Governor. Thus, the government responded cautiously to violence. In 1776, for example, the government pushed through a number of fiscal reforms aimed at raising revenue in Chile. Taxes were to be collected more thoroughly, the baselines on which to levy them were reassessed, and tax loopholes were reduced. The increase in the effective rate of taxation led to an increase in prices, as producers passed costs on to consumers. There was a public protest in the streets of Santiago, and the Cabildo called an open meeting. But there was mostly talk, not rebellion. The reforms were suspended for about a year, and then only partly reinstated. In 1781 the government suspended the application of new measures to raise revenue to prevent a possible protest, another example of the flexibility of imperial governing procedures.[18]

Cuba's best example of nonslave defensive collective violence was the revolt of the tobacco farmers in the early part of the eighteenth century. In 1717, to increase government revenues, the Spanish government established a government monopoly (estanco) for the manufacture and marketing of tobacco. Tobacco farmers were forbidden to sell their products to anyone but the monopoly officials. The farmers revolted in 1717 and 1723; they burned the farms of those who collaborated with the government and marched on Havana, clamoring for the restoration of the preexisting situation. They were crushed.[19]

Revolts against governmental monopolies, established to centralize and rationalize the marketing of major crops, also occurred in Venezuela. The Crown had chartered the Compañía Guipuzcoana de Caracas in 1728. The Caracas Company had a monopoly over the import and export trade between Spain and Venezuela, including the lucrative cocoa trade; the only foreign outlet it did not control was trade between Venezuela and New Spain.[20] Defensive collective protest against the Caracas Company was one of the most significant outbursts of rebellion in Spanish American colonial history. (Because of the strong elite participation, it will be discussed in Chapter 7). The company was a target of social bandits. The most successful theft and pillage was conducted by a black-Indian social bandit, Andresote, and his bands. They also engaged in extensive contraband with the Dutch and traded with Venezuelan white plantation owners in the 1730s.[21]

Another example of defensive collective violence against the company was the urban riot in the town of San Felipe in 1741. A recently appointed leading town official had sought to eliminate the contraband trade that injured the company's monopoly. The town revolted and the appointment was revoked. Thus, in contrast to social banditry, a specific political event in need of redress engaged the participation of those affected. In contrast to more modern protest, the goal was to restore the preexisting situation. The town's revolt was organized by the local elected public officials, but this organization did not last beyond redressing the wrong; only the local elite participated, seeking backward-looking goals.[22]

*Slave Revolts*

Slave revolts were another manifestation of defensive collective violence in Cuba and Venezuela. Despite many rumors of vast conspiracies reported by scared planters and government officials, most slave revolts were localized and fragmented, not system-wide. One of the largest reported conspiracies, even though there was no revolt, was alleged to have existed in Venezuela's Tuy River Valleys in spring 1749. Evidence of the extent of the conspiracy comes entirely from slave confessions obtained by torture — not the most reliable source of evidence. The effort, which was limited to that region, sought to engage the slaves directly in revolt for their freedom, not to rely on social bandits. It had a peculiarly restorative or backward-looking goal: the slaves confessed rather uniformly about their belief in the existence of a royal decree granting their freedom. This was not absurd, because the freeing of slaves was institutionalized in the empire. Some slaves may have thought the King had freed them, but bad masters had disobeyed the law. These beliefs were thus widespread in the empire's closing decades. Had these rebellions succeeded, they would have enforced that "law."[23]

Most actual slave revolts, in Venezuela as in Cuba, had even narrower goals. Many of these frequent revolts occurred not in response to daily oppression, but to protest a new effort by the master to exact more labor. They resulted from a deterioration of existing conditions and sought a return to preexisting conditions. The slaves often proposed only to redress specific wrongs without calling for their freedom.

Slave revolts where "freedom'" was the goal were rare and did not often entail a further political or social program. Even the goal of "freedom" was often peculiarly backward-looking, conceived as the restoration of status prior to enslavement in Africa, especially when the slaves who revolted were Africans recently arrived in America. Most slave revolts had limited political significance. They were expected, traditional, and accommodable; they were localized, fragmented, barely organized, barely political.[24]

Yet there were differences. There was a slave and freedmen revolt in the Venezuelan region of Coro in 1795 that was not defensive collective violence, but perhaps Venezuela's first modernizing revolt. Coro (population 26,509, only 3,771 of whom were white) was the area of Venezuela where, under the impact of economic growth, the slavery system had moved furthest toward tenancy.[25] In Coro (west of Caracas) slaves worked for their masters only for the time necessary to harvest the crops; the rest of the time they worked their own land under a tenancy arrangement. By 1760 some slaves owned as many as one hundred head of cattle. Daily slave work paid in kind for the use of land; the slave-tenants also paid in produce once a year. Because they were not responsible for their slaves' physical sustenance, the masters' costs were reduced while their labor supply was ensured; at the same time, the marginal freedom and level of income of the slaves increased.

Two factors converged to bring about slave-tenant protest. Their agricultural production became subject to taxation through the *alcabalá* (sales tax). This was the first time that many of them had produced enough on their own to be confronted by the tax collector. Their expectations of income and freedom were curtailed by an external agent that they had not encountered before. Second, fiscal reforms of tax collection in the early 1790s stressed payment in cash, not in kind; but these new producers had very little cash. The convergence of their entry into the taxable market and the fiscal reform provoked a clash. The better-educated black freedmen knew about the nonimplementation in Venezuela of the milder royal slave code of 1789, as well as the successful rebellion of the slaves in Haiti. The 11,566 black freedmen constituted a plurality of Coro's population (there were 7,911 Indians).

On May 10, 1795, there was a revolt in Coro involving two hundred to three hundred people. Its social bases can be estimated roughly on the basis of attendance at meetings where the revolt was planned. Of fifty-nine leaders or cadres identified as having attended such meetings, 47.5 percent were black slaves, even though black slaves were only 12.3 percent of Coro's population; 39.5 percent were black freedmen (43.6 percent of the population); and 13 percent Indians (29.8 percent of the population). There were no white rebel leaders. Therefore, the rebellion was most important for the black slaves, most of whom were from the rural areas of the Coro district, rather than from the city itself, and therefore more likely to have been affected by the economic and fiscal changes of the 1790s.[26] The publicly stated goals of the rebellion were the abolition of slavery and the elimination of taxes, specifically the alcabalá on slave-tenant production. This was also an explicitly anti-white movement.

Although no system-wide revolt occurred elsewhere in Venezuela, the more modern elements of this slave revolt set it apart from defensive collective violence. Rural modernization in Coro had gone far beyond that of other areas, so that the form of political participation resembled modern lower-class participation. Several dozen persons had attended a number of meetings to plot the rebellion. Their crude (and eventually ineffective) military plan reflected a level of organization far superior to an urban riot or a simple defensive slave revolt. Their time perspective was also longer because they envisioned what they would do after they revolted. The goals were not just backward-looking or adjustive. They proposed to kill the whites and seize political power. The top leadership was familiar with the ideology and programs of the French Revolution and, more important, with the Haitian uprising. The revolt proclaimed not only freedom for the slaves and the suppression of taxes but also the "law of the French," including a republican government and social equality. The rebels claimed a new right: the right to govern. These rights were due them, but not yet enjoyed, to transform the social and political system. The Coro revolt was not a mere local peasant explosion; it was an alliance of urban and rural people from two social strata. Although black freedmen were at the top, there were more slaves in the leadership ranks. The slaves' contacts with the market system and the tax collector alerted them to the government structure and to those in Haiti who had changed such a structure. Coro's social and economic modernization permitted the slaves a broader political world view that loosened their chains.

Internal economic changes could lead to political and ideological changes and, eventually, to revolt. In the absence of these changes, other slave revolts failed to be modernizing and failed to integrate coalitions drawn from different strata. In the Coro coalition, even the taxation goals of freedmen and slaves could be integrated because both had had experiences with the tax collector. Isolated slaves could not have done that. The Coro revolt differs because of the broader scope, greater degree of forward-looking goals and structural integration in a multistrata coalition, and more extensive political organization, planning, and sustained participation, culminating in an actual uprising, than was the case in other slave revolts. Yet even this modernizing participation depended on political organization and political leadership — not on autonomous participation. It had not yet made a full transition to modernity.

Mass politics were often violent in the late colonial Spanish American empire; but still accommodable. The empire's survival was not threatened by escaped slaves who acted like social bandits, or a violent urban mob demanding the return of the Society of Jesus, or by slave revolts against brutal masters.[27] The empire could withstand such demands, and did so throughout the centuries. These movements were not precursors of independence, but an integral part of normal colonial politics. The explanation of the wars of independence does not depend only on mass politics. As traditional participants, these various groups and strata could — and would — provide the dynamite that ignited the wars, but they were not the arsonists who lit the fuse.

# 5

# The Record of Economic Growth

There was impressive economic growth in Chile, Cuba, Mexico, and Venezuela in the eighteenth century and the first decade of the nineteenth, although its starting point differs from country to country.

## Chile

Chile was the first of the four to undergo large-scale economic expansion. For complex economic, ecological, and natural causes, Peruvian wheat production declined sharply during the second half of the seventeenth century, and Chile rushed to supply the needed wheat.[1] By the late 1690s the Chilean wheat boom was under way (therefore, the data below underestimate the magnitude of the growth).

The most dramatic increases in wheat production took place in the last quarter of the seventeenth century and the first quarter of the eighteenth, as the following figures[2] indicate:

| period | quintals |
| --- | --- |
| 1698-99 | 71,385 |
| 1700-10 | 110,000 |
| 1787 | 193,707 |
| 1788 | 198,271 |
| 1789 | 149,050 |
| 1790 | 145,516 |
| 1793 | 159,140 |
| 1795 | 161,280 |

Sharp variations in wheat production from year to year brought considerable hardship and conflict by the late 1780s. Mining production also increased in response to continuing imperial demands for such production (Table 5.1). Copper exports rose from 1,330 metric tons in the late 1780s to 2,035 metric tons in the early 1790s.[3] The result was a period of unquestioned economic growth.

## Venezuela

The second colony to embark upon a process of economic growth was Venezuela, which depended mostly on cocoa production. While Chile exported wheat, copper, silver, gold, and other agricultural products, cocoa accounted for 75.1 percent of all Venezuelan exports in 1775, 62.8 percent in 1786, and 62.1 percent in 1793.[4]

Cocoa exports had begun to increase at the end of the seventeenth century (Table 5.2). Under the guidance of the Caracas Company, they increased sharply once again beginning in the 1730s. After the demise of the Caracas Company in the 1780s, exports doubled from the company's average in the 1750s and 1760s to the peaks in the 1789-1794 period (detailed data for the years after 1800 are unavailable). According to reports to the king by the Consulado of Caracas in 1799 and 1804, exports ordinarily remained approximately at 100,000 fanegas until the beginning of the wars of independence, without much change in production levels.[5] The decline of the late 1790s and the sharp drop of 1804 resulted from international war rather than problems internal to Venezuela.

Humboldt claims that Caracas province produced 150,000 fanegas at the end of the eighteenth and beginning of the next centuries.[6] However, his annual statistics (Table 5.2, column 2) indicate a level of cocoa exports of 70,000 to 111,000 fanegas between 1794 and 1797. One possible

*Table 5.1* Growth of Chilean mining production (annual averages)

| Period | Copper (metric tons) | Silver (kilograms) | Gold (kilograms) |
| --- | --- | --- | --- |
| 1701-1720 | 100 | 50 | 400 |
| 1721-1740 | 250 | 950 | 400 |
| 1741-1760 | 750 | 1,500 | 800 |
| 1761-1800 | 1,000 | 3,750 | 1,500 |

*Source:* Hernán Ramírez Necochea, *Antecedentes económicos de la independencia de Chile* (rev. ed.; Santiago: Universitaria, 1967), pp. 51-52.

explanation for such a large discrepancy between production and exports could be domestic consumption. The most direct data are from 1720, when only 5.5 percent of all cocoa production was consumed domestically.[7] Even if that percentage had increased slightly with population growth and improved living standards, it is obviously insignificant. A more probable explanation is contraband. Humboldt, who was aware of the leakage of production through contraband, deliberately increased his production estimates from the level of official exports presented in the table. He indicates, too, that the level of production of the late eighteenth century continued at least through 1806. It reached a plateau, but it was the highest of Venezuelan history.

Venezuelan economic growth had been impressive throughout the last century of Spanish rule, and it finished with a flourish in the final quarter-century. Yet the importance of war cannot be totally discounted. Exports for 1804 were a disaster. As will be shown later, Venezuela's international economic problems were worsened by cocoa's relative price and supply inelasticity.

There was a remarkable growth in Venezuela's indigo exports in the last quarter of the eighteenth century, as the following figures[8] show:

| period | pounds |
| --- | --- |
| 1774-78 | 20,300 |
| 1784 | 126,233 |
| 1785 | 213,172 |
| 1786 | 271,005 |
| 1787 | 432,570 |
| 1788 | 505,956 |
| 1789 | 718,393 |
| 1792 | 680,229 |
| 1794 | 898,353 |
| 1796 | 777,966 |

Indigo's share of exports rose from less than 1 percent of the value of exports in 1775 to 19 percent in 1786 and 29.2 percent in 1793.[9] Indigo production remained secondary to cocoa in its importance for the economy, despite the cocoa crisis at century's end. However, indigo exports crashed in the commercial crisis of the late 1790s. Exports dropped from an annual average of 738,991 pounds from 1793 to 1796 to an annual average of 198,303 from 1796 to 1800.[10]

Table 5.2  Venezuelan cocoa exports (fanegas)[a]

| Silva Michelena | | Humboldt | | Brito Figueroa[b] | | Depons | | Arcila Farías | |
|---|---|---|---|---|---|---|---|---|---|
| Year | Amount | Year | Amount | Period | Amount | Period | Amount | Year[c] | Amount |
| 1630 | 946 | 1763 | 80,659 | 1691-1700 | 12,527.1 | 1793-1796 | 83,595 | 1750 | 58,793 |
| 1640 | 3,352 | 1789 | 103,655 | 1701-1710 | 14,632.8 | 1796-1800 | 54,355 | 1751 | 48,231 |
| 1650 | 4,148 | 1792 | 100,592 | 1711-1720 | 14,848.0 | | | 1752 | 60,756 |
| 1660 | 7,486 | 1794 | 111,133 | 1721-1730 | 22,170.7 | | | 1753 | 48,384 |
| 1671 | 3,499 | 1796 | 75,528 | 1731-1740 | 41,474.0 | | | 1754 | 70,061 |
| 1680 | 10,960 | 1797 | 70,832 | 1741-1750 | 33,342.0 | | | 1755 | 40,989 |
| 1690 | 9,120 | | | 1751-1760 | 49,588.7 | | | 1756 | 59,442 |
| 1701 | 20,721 | | | 1761-1770 | 50,312.3 | | | 1757 | 60,986 |
| 1721 | 34,017 | | | 1771-1780 | 42,666.5 | | | 1758 | 66,367 |
| 1731 | 33,000 | | | | | | | 1759 | 56,527 |
| 1750 | 58,793 | | | | | | | 1760 | 56,819 |
| 1760 | 56,819 | | | | | | | 1761 | 64,817 |
| 1764 | 66,118 | | | | | | | 1762 | 36,667 |
| 1775 | 58,923 | | | | | | | 1763 | 80,661 |
| | | | | | | | | 1764 | 66,118 |
| 1816 | 30,000 | | | | | | | 1804 | 48,000 |

*Table 5.2* (*Continued*)

*Source:* José A. Silva Michelena, *The Illusion of Democracy in Dependent Nations* (Cambridge, Mass.: MIT Press, 1971), p. 283; Alejandro de Humboldt, *Viaje a las regiones equinocciales del nuevo continente*, trans. Lisandro Alvarado (Caracas: Biblioteca Venezolana de Cultura, 1941), p. 174; Federico Brito Figueroa, *Historia económica y social de Venezuela* (Caracas: Universidad Central de Venezuela, 1966), I, 103; Francisco Depons, *Viaje a la parte oriental de tierra firme* (Caracas: Tipografía Americana, 1930), p. 340; Eduardo Arcila Farías, *Economía colonial de Venezuela* (Mexico: Fondo de Cultura Economica, 1946), p. 257; "Solicitud de libertad de comercio entre la provincia de Venezuela y las naciones neutrales durante la guerra de España con Inglaterra," in Eduardo Arcila Farías, ed., *El Real Consulado de Caracas* (Caracas: Universidad Central de Venezuela, 1957), pp. 243-244.

a. Fanegas are taken to weigh 110 pounds, but these weights varied somewhat through time (1 quintal = 100 pounds, and 1 fanega = 110 pounds).

b. Fanegas are annual averages; 1691-1780 includes only the exports to mainland Spain and to New Spain.

c. 1750-1764 includes all exports.

## Mexico

Third of the four colonies in starting its economic growth was Mexico. The Mexican economy was the most complex of all under consideration, for it was the only one to exhibit an incipient industrial development, in addition to mining and agriculture.

From 1796 to 1820 bullion accounted for 74.9 percent of all exports, cochineal for 12.4 percent, sugar for 2.9 percent, and other products for the rest.[11] Silver and gold production increased sharply between 1700 and 1800 (Table 5.3). Silver production grew throughout the eighteenth century; gold recovered from its seventeenth-century decline and reached new heights in the 1760s and 1770s. The silver production average per decade was 5,624 metric tons in 1781-1800 and 5,538 metric tons in 1800-1810; the real decline began in 1810 with the outbreak of the wars of independence. Gold production peaked in 1800-1810; its average

*Table 5.3* Mexican mining production, 1521-1850

| Period | Silver (metric tons) | Gold (kilograms) |
|---|---|---|
| 1521-1540 | 68.34 | 4,200 |
| 1541-1560 | 253.6 | 3,400 |
| 1561-1580 | 1,004 | 6,800 |
| 1581-1600 | 1,486 | 9,600 |
| 1601-1620 | 1,624 | 8,440 |
| 1621-1640 | 1,764 | 8,020 |
| 1641-1660 | 1,904 | 7,420 |
| 1661-1680 | 2,042 | 7,265 |
| 1681-1700 | 3,204 | 7,380 |
| 1701-1720 | 3,276 | 10,470 |
| 1721-1740 | 4,615 | 13,600 |
| 1741-1760 | 6,020 | 16,380 |
| 1761-1780 | 7,328 | 26,170 |
| 1781-1800 | 11,249 | 24,580 |
| 1800-1810 | 5,528 | 17,630 |
| 1811-1820 | 3,120 | 10,710 |
| 1821-1830 | 2,648 | 9,760 |
| 1831-1840 | 3,309 | 8,640 |
| 1841-1850 | 4,203 | 19,940 |

*Source:* Diego López Rosado, *Historia económica de México* (Mexico: Universidad Nacional Autónoma de México, 1963), pp. 93-94; Manuel López Gallo, *Economía y política en la historia de México* (Mexico: Solidaridad, 1965), pp. 59-60.

per decade rose from 12,290 kilograms in 1781-1800 to 17,630 kilograms in 1800-1810. There were dramatic drops in both silver and gold production during the wars of independence. Gold production did not recover the late colonial level until the 1840s; silver production had not reached that level even then.[12]

From 1744 to 1812 the minimum value of any one year's mining production was 10,932,172 pesos. That was higher than the maximum value of any one year's production for either the 1690-1732 (9,745,870 pesos) or the 1813-1852 (9,276,009 pesos) periods. The value of mining production per year was as high as 27,175,880 pesos in the late colonial period and as low as 161,730 pesos in the postindependence period. Mexican mining did not recover during the first half-century of independence.[13]

The increase in production of the scarlet cochineal dye peaked in the 1770s (Table 5.4), when overproduction resulted in a price drop. From 1764 to 1773 the price per pound of cochineal fluctuated between 32 and 18.5 reales, with an average in the low 20's. From 1774 to 1792 the price was steady but lower (between 15 and 18 reales per pound); between 1793 and 1795 it collapsed to a level between 10.5 and 13.5 reales. Then a fairly steady price recovery began, because the supply of the dye had declined when producers cut production back: by 1799 the price rose to 19.5; by 1805 it was 23. Between 1806 and 1811 the price fluctuated between 27 and 29 reales, reaching 33 in 1809.

In sum, first, there was a production and price boom which peaked in the 1770s. Second, overproduction drove the price of cochineal down to touch bottom in 1794 and production was cut back drastically. Third, the cutback in supply was so severe that the price rose again to new heights; Table 5.4 shows the period 1798-1807 with lower production but

Table 5.4  Mexican cochineal production and value

| Period | Production (pounds) | Value (pesos) |
|---|---|---|
| 1758-1767 | 8,413,874 | 18,157,924 |
| 1768-1777 | 9,809,540 | 27,122,413 |
| 1778-1787 | 7,911,812 | 16,452,162 |
| 1788-1797 | 4,513,512 | 8,136,268 |
| 1798-1807 | 3,869,162 | 10,428,180 |
| 1808-1817 | 3,383,764 | 11,661,339 |
| 1818-1826 | 3,025,674 | 7,857,798 |

Source: Brian R. Hamnett, Politics and Trade in Southern Mexico, 1750-1821 (Cambridge: Cambridge University Press, 1971), p. 171.

higher value than the previous decade. Producers increased their annual production threefold and steadily from 1805 to 1810.[14] Although production did not reach the levels of the 1770s, cochineal production finished the colonial period in a production and price boom. As in the case of mining, both the production and the value of cochineal fell as independence arrived, reaching an all-time low between 1818 and 1826. The combined declines of mining and cochineal values were responsible for the economic depression in Mexico's first years of independence. Agricultural production grew sharply in late-eighteenth-century Mexico, aided by substantial price increases which served as incentives to production. For example, maize prices, which were fairly stable from the 1720s to the late 1770s, doubled between the late 1770s and the first decade of the nineteenth century. In that period the value of agricultural production almost tripled and, for the first time, surpassed that of mining production.[15]

The Mexican economy had an important industrial sector, primarily for domestic consumption. From the beginning of colonial days the city of Puebla experienced three waves of textile production. As each ended, the city adapted itself to the new one, so that it remained engaged in textile manufacturing throughout the colonial period. From the conquest until 1634 Puebla was one of New Spain's three silk production centers. When silk production was banned by the Crown, the city shifted to wool textiles. When, before the middle of the eighteenth century, this industry decayed, it was replaced by a cotton textile industry, composed primarily of small shops of artisans organized in guilds. The cotton industry's period of greatest prosperity coincided with the international wars; these wars prevented the importation of many foreign textiles, and domestic production was de facto protected. However, between 1800 and 1810, the Puebla textile industry entered into a period of crisis as a result of overproduction during the earlier period and the few but recurrent relaxations of the imperial trade restrictions that permitted trade with neutral countries. It lost the de facto protection of the wars and the de jure protection of imperial trade restrictions in the midst of excess supply.[16]

Another area with several manufacturing centers was the Bajío, northwest of Mexico City, whose complex regional economy by the 1790s included industry, mining, agriculture, and trade. Farmers made up only 49 percent of the 110,993 reported working population; industrial workers, artisans, and day wage-earners accounted for 41 percent of the regional population, and miners for another 8 percent.[17] Much of industry concentrated on textiles. In 1793 there were 1,500 workers in 215 shops in the city of Querétaro; by 1804 there were 18 factories (*obrajes*) and 327 workshops (*trapiches*) in that city's textile industry, producing ponchos, blankets, serges, serapes, hats, and similar goods. In 1803 the official estimate of spinners and weavers in Querétaro was 9,000.[18]

Manufacturing contributed 29 percent of the estimated 190 million silver pesos of New Spain's national income in the late colonial period (mining accounted for 15 percent, and agriculture for the remainder). This is evidence of an economy that had gone beyond mere primary production, even if many of its industries were technologically backward.[19]

## Cuba

Cuba's period of economic escalation did not begin until the 1790s. The volume of sugar exports grew fairly steadily after 1790. From 1788 to 1793 these ranged between 1.1 and 1.4 million long tons; after 1796 no year was below 2 million long tons. The figure, which rose to about 3 million long tons a year for the first fifteen years of the nineteenth century, never fell below 3 million after 1813, nor below 4 million long tons after 1821. Thus, there was rapid growth from the 1780s to 1800; a stable plateau for fifteen years at a rough annual average of 3 million tons; and renewed rapid growth from 1816 to 1830. In a forty-five-year period the volume of sugar exports tripled in the first third, held steady for the second, and doubled in the last third.[20]

Coffee exports also increased, though with much year-to-year variability. Coffee exports rose from 7,411 arrobas in 1790 to 69,369 in 1805. The level did not fall below 250,000 arrobas after 1809; after 1817 it did not fall below 500,000 arrobas; and after 1825 it did not fall below 1 million arrobas for several years. Despite variability, the growth trend is evident.[21]

Coffee and sugar accounted for the bulk of Cuban exports (tobacco still had a role, which increased later in the nineteenth century). They were the dynamic elements in the Cuban economy. Although some sugar and coffee was consumed domestically, most was exported. Sugar accounted for 18 percent, and coffee for 9 percent, of the estimated product of Cuba's aggregated enterprises, calculated at 49,662,987 pesos in 1827. Tobacco accounted for 1.4 percent, and other technologically primitive agricultural enterprises, very important for domestic consumption, accounted for the remainder.[22]

There was impressive economic growth in the closing decades of Spanish imperial rule. Venezuelan cocoa and Chilean wheat appeared to have reached a plateau — but it was the highest of their economic histories.

Cuban sugar and coffee, Mexican mining and cochineal, and Chilean mining continued to do well. Venezuelan indigo and Mexican industry were in trouble. On balance, the economic growth of the empire was impressive, although signs of structural constraints on further growth were appearing. The relatively mature export economies as well as Mexican industrial production needed structural changes to continue or renew their growth.

# 6

# International War
# and Government Modernization

Spain's eighteenth century opened in misery. The last Hapsburg king, Charles II, presiding over the decay of his empire, died childless after a long and unfortunate reign. The new Bourbon king, Philip V, spent over a decade establishing his internal and international legitimacy through the war of the Spanish succession. During the course of the eighteenth century Spain fought in wars that heightened sensitivity to security threats and to the need to modernize its political structures to meet the challenge. The mixture of direct and indirect threats to the empire predisposed the monarchy in behalf of modernization. Modernization of government required the rationalization and centralization of authority. This would eventually create new problems of legitimacy and power for the Crown and its subjects.

## National Defense and Government Modernization

The structure of a centralized bureaucratic empire is fragile under conditions of change. The political system requires balance and harmony; it can accommodate some carefully regulated change. At times, however, the rulers themselves may seek to bring about political change, at a high risk, in the name of national security. War or some indirect threat can make a country aware that it lags behind in the development of war capabilities. If a rival's economic growth surpasses, the ruler may seek to hasten economic growth.

The Spanish empire responded to security threats in the eighteenth century with political modernization. This involves the rationalization of political authority, and the replacement of traditional religious, familial, and ethnic political authorities with a single, secular, national political authority. Power grows and is centralized in that new or revitalized authority. The scope, domain, range, and weight of the power of the ruler are increased. Regional and local authorities must bow to the central authority; law is man-made, not the product of God or nature. New political functions are differentiated and new specialized structures to perform them are developed. Participation in politics by social groups increases throughout the society.

Under these conditions the ruler may claim a new and different legitimacy that may challenge the foundations of the preexisting political system. This appropriation of legitimacy at the center of the system, at the expense of other elite groups, may trigger counterclaims by the latter against the former. Elite groups are likely to resist the ruler's selective political demobilization. The modernization of government institutions and the centralization of power often bring about the demise of the autonomous organizations that had had considerable authority and access to government. Conflicting claims of legitimacy develop between ruler and elite groups. The overarching compact about the legitimacy of the imperial political system is dissolved, and new groups and individuals compete to appropriate and enforce new bases of legitimacy. Notwithstanding the ruler's modernization, elite political participation often remains traditional, as backward-looking elites try to regain or retain access to government, reinstating old customs and privileges. The ruler's new policy may also result in new and different claims to legitimacy by elite groups.

Although industrialization is the typical economic response to security threats, there are important political institutional differences in the response to economic inferiority. The roles of the state, or of intermediary institutions, in the mobilization of resources for industrialization are important in a poor country. For example, industrialization in nineteenth-century Germany, France, Italy, Switzerland, Belgium, and the western parts of Austria-Hungary — in contrast to England — relied heavily on intermediary financial institutions, especially banks. Where backwardness was very pronounced, acts that were essentially political — such as the emancipation of the serfs in Russia in 1861 — had to be taken.[1] Spain's experience probably was closer to that of Russia.

The state became the primary agent in economic change, deriving its interests from national security requirements. To achieve necessary changes the government had to subject people to severely oppressive measures. Such modern oppression differed from previous oppression; it was more pervasive and efficient. External circumstances had changed the political system. What may have been traditional behavior turned disruptive under the new conditions. Simultaneous radical political and economic changes may turn ordinary political participation toward more disruptive ends (traditional or modern). A state engaged in political modernization may encounter elite resistance or defensive collective violence. The ethnic balance may be disrupted.

King Charles III defined the purpose of the Ordinance of Intendants for New Spain and of his policy of government modernization as an instrument "to unify the government of the great empires that God had entrusted to me."[2] The Crown sought to systematize, rationalize, and centralize political authority. An Ordinance of Intendants was issued for Spain in 1718. Revoked in 1721 because of opposition by the traditional forces in the kingdom, it was reinstated in 1749, as pressures on the empire continued. The tendency to centralize in Spain was not inevitable, but responded to external demands that had to be met, even at the cost of internal opposition.[3]

Intendancies came to America, too, because of international political pressures on the empire, not from an abstract desire to modernize the internal structures. The first intendancy in Spanish America was established in Cuba in 1764 to oversee finances and war-making capabilities. Great Britain had conquered a part of the island in 1762, holding it for a year. Spain sought to rationalize and centralize government in Cuba; economic growth would be promoted and military fortifications built. Cuba's elite protested; the Captain General or Governor asked that the Ordinance be revoked. Spain held firm — but delayed implementing the policy elsewhere.[4]

The next intendancy was established (December 1776) by gathering together the provinces of Cumaná, Guayana, Maracaibo, and Margarita, the first three loosely supervised from Bogotá, and placing them under the direct authority of the Caracas colony. This created an enlarged Captaincy General and Intendancy of Venezuela, ruled from Caracas, the predecessor of today's Venezuela. In 1786 an Audiencia was established in Caracas, segregating Venezuela's juridical problems from Santo Domingo and Bogotá. During the same period religious centralization was achieved by placing the bishoprics of these provinces under the see of Caracas.[5] Finances and military policies were centralized first; government, law, and religion followed. The external threat to these five provinces of the southern Caribbean was also severe, for British colonies in the central Caribbean were bases for possible military attacks. Internal motivation to unite these provinces for both external defense and internal reform also was strong. Despite the opposition of traditional elites, the Crown held fast in Venezuela.

Increasing commitment to reform and the new measures introduced in the Caribbean were greatly influenced by the revolt of British colonies in North America. Spain followed France in supporting their war against

Great Britain. As war approached, the Spanish Crown embarked upon a frenzy of reform. In 1777, even in the absence of a statute (forthcoming in 1782), an intendant of Buenos Aires was appointed. An intendant in the frontier province of Louisiana was appointed in 1780. By 1784, through the period of Spain's war with England, intendancies were established in Chile, Peru, Puerto Rico, Chiapas, Nicaragua, Camayagua, Quito, and Nueva Granada (Bogotá).[6] In 1785 an intendant was appointed in Concepción, in southern Chile, to protect the frontier against Indian attack and from other possible threats.[7]

The intendants centralized all revenue collections and provided for uniform administration, replacing private collectors to whom taxing collection rights had been leased. They were appointed by the Crown directly and were usually Spaniards. Many were among the first professional administrators of the empire. Centralization, rationalization, and efficiency within their respective jurisdictions became paramount.

A long debate over the reform program took place in New Spain. A plan of intendants for New Spain was approved in principle in 1769, and one was appointed for Sonora in the north, where the military threat to Spain from unsubdued Indians was greatest. But the protests of the Mexican elites, including the Viceroy, halted the program in New Spain.[8] This was the only example in America where the intendancy system was stopped for a number of years. The reason was not the lack of reform but the success of reforms other than intendancies. A long series of fiscal reforms had raised New Spain's revenues enormously,[9] as shown in pesos:

| | |
|---|---|
| 1712 | 3,068,400 |
| 1763 | 5,705,876 |
| 1764 | 5,901,706 |
| 1765 | 6,141,981 |
| 1766 | 6,538,941 |
| 1767 | 6,561,316 |
| 1773-1776 | 12,000,000 |
| 1777-1779 | 14,000,000 |
| 1780 | 15,010,794 |
| 1781 | 18,091,639 |
| 1782 | 18,594,412 |
| 1783 | 19,579,718 |
| 1784 | 19,005,574 |
| 1785 | 19,770,000 |
| 1789 | 19,044,000 |
| 1792 | 19,521,692 |
| 1802 | 22,200,000 |

The elites used this revenue increase as an argument to oppose other political reforms that might have curtailed their political power and raised revenues further. Revenues increased threefold from 1767 to 1781 as a result of the rationalization and the centralization of revenue collection. Until the middle of the eighteenth century the Crown had contracted with private merchants, leasing the rights to collect royal revenues in return for a fixed payment to the treasury. The shift toward direct royal administration and collection of sales taxes and excise revenues began in 1754; it was complete by 1776 in all the leading towns of New Spain. A lucrative source of new revenue was the establishment in 1768 of a government tobacco monopoly whose profits went directly to the treasury in Madrid.[10]

Thus, fiscal reform was achieved in New Spain without the introduction of intendancies. It was not a reform without problems; examples were given in Chapter 4 of defensive collective violence aimed at the new fiscal burden in New Spain and elsewhere. There was also concern in New Spain over the use to which the new revenue was put. By the end of the eighteenth century some 6 million pesos out of total gross revenues of about 20 million pesos were remitted to Spain, and another 3 to 5 million were sent as foreign aid (situados) to the Caribbean islands and the Philippines. In short, at least one-half of the revenue raised went abroad. New Spain contributed 6 to 7 million pesos per year to Madrid between 1800 and 1810, a period during which all the American colonies together contributed between 8 and 9 million pesos. New Spain thus was responsible for most of Spain's American revenues.[11]

Despite delay and conflict, the Ordinance of Intendants for New Spain was issued in 1786, bringing the jewel of the empire in line with the rest of the colonies. Twelve intendancies were established in the Viceroyalty. Conflicts and protests continued, however, and the intendancies were less successful than had been hoped. Reform was thus limited to the urban sector. Because fiscal reform had already taken place, the intendants concentrated on law and order. Internal conflicts within the bureaucracy continued, and centralization in the viceregal office increased. Flon, the first intendant of Puebla, noted in 1803 that his achievements were limited to the city of Puebla. He had eliminated riots and public disorders, built a municipal granary and a prison, and cleaned up and paved the city. Yet he did not make regular inspections of the provinces, and he did not try to stop his provincial deputies from engaging in trade, contrary to law. Extreme injustices in the countryside had become easier to correct because the intendant could monitor complaints and punish abuses based in Puebla, whereas before this had to be done from Mexico

City. He complained that the Church limited his effective jurisdiction and that too much authority had been centralized in the hands of the Viceroy in Mexico City.[12]

The unmistakable effect of the intendancy system in Cuba and in Venezuela was centralization; in Chile the establishment of an intendancy in Concepción provided better frontier defense, but also decentralization vis-à-vis Santiago. In New Spain the form of the intendancy system at first might suggest decentralization; in fact, King Charles III sought centralization in the area immediately under an intendant. The formal decentralization of executive authority away from Mexico City was necessary to achieve effective centralization of executive authority in the other cities of the Kingdom. Mexico City had been so distant that its effective authority was limited, even though its formal authority was vast. Although the intendancy system had the appearance of decentralization, it was in fact the penetration of the royal bureaucracy deep into the country, in many cases for the first time. The intendancies brought unprecedented government control over the people. The office of the Viceroy was also strengthened, even if it appeared to be formally weakened. The Viceroy became the chief executive officer, the commander in chief of army and militia, and the superintendent of finances, including the directorship over the mercury monopoly. Such power, exercised through a more aggressive, professional, and efficient bureaucracy, also was unparalleled.

## The Military: A Case Study

The international system was an important reason for Spain's desire to modernize its American empire. Fear of political, military, and economic defeat spurred the Crown toward change. Resources and personnel committed to the military increased. The empire's policies were reflected by the military, including ethnic mobility and the search of private gain through political access typical of a neopatrimonial culture. The military would play a complex role in a society where military-aristocratic values had always been important.

Military strength increased during the second half of the eighteenth century, coinciding with imperial political modernization, with international wars, and with economic growth. The size of the regular army in Chile doubled from 1,279 in 1752 to 2,358 by 1800; in Mexico it rose from 3,032 in 1758 to 10,620 in 1810. In Cuba the increase from 3,591 in 1770 to 15,000 by 1830 resulted from Spain's retreat from the continent of South America. Spain maintained that level of regular troops in Cuba for the next three decades. The size of the militia rose in Mexico from

10,698 in 1766 to 30,685 in 1810 (the peak militia strength was 34,717 in 1784). The militia's size also doubled in Cuba from 8,076 in 1770 to 15,000 in 1830. Militia strength in Chile reached at least 29,639 in the late eighteenth century.[13]

Military participation ratios (see Table 6.1) are far greater for Chile than for Mexico. Chile's rate of regular army participation is 1.5 times Mexico's; for the militia, it is over six times greater. Cuba's rate of militia participation is just under Chile's for the early nineteenth century, but its regular army participation ratio was almost four times greater (Table 6.1). This reflects Cuba's strategic importance for Spain, and Chile's horizontal or parallel ethnic system.

Although no time series is available for Venezuela, it had 918 regular troops and 13,136 members of the militia by 1800.[14] Its regular army participation ratio was lower than Mexico's, much lower than Chile's and Cuba's. Its militia participation ratio was not quite three times that of Mexico, thus a bit lower than that of Chile and Cuba. By the standards of 1960, the rate of militarization of Chile and Cuba falls somewhere between that of Israel and North Korea, higher than France's during the Algerian war.[15] Venezuela is at the level of Czechoslovakia or Spain; Mexico's level was similar to that of Canada. In short, Chile's and Cuba's rates of militarization were extraordinary.

These military participation ratios are explained by international politics, or by the characteristics of ethnic systems; they differ from social mobilization measures. The rank order correlation (Kendall's tau-b) between the ranked military participation ratio and the composite ranked scores for social mobilization (see Table 2.2) is −0.67. However, military participation ratios are not accurate indicators of repression. Spain had a total military force of about 125,000 men in America in 1808, but the overwhelming majority of these were not regular troops, but militiamen — citizen soldiers who were mostly Americans.[16]

Military participation in a neopatrimonial elite political culture served to maximize elite political access for private gain in wealth, status, and power. The chief mechanism was the *fuero militar*, military privilege.[17] This removed the military from the jurisdiction of the ordinary court system and established a separate system of military courts with their own privileged jurisdiction. The principle was, in part, the same as that justifying mercantile or mining courts with their own jurisdictions: mercantile courts handled mercantile cases and mining courts handled mining cases, but military courts handled all sorts of cases, military or not (with exceptions to be noted). This was the key to maximizing political access. The fuero permitted members of the regular army to enjoy

*Table 6.1*  Military participation in 1800

| Country | Regular army | Militia | Total military | Military men per 1000 persons | Rank order[a] Regular army | Militia | Total |
|---------|-------------|---------|----------------|-------------------------------|----------------------------|---------|-------|
| Chile | 2,358 | 29,639 | 31,997 | 36 | 1.5 | 6.6 | 5.3 |
| Cuba[b] | 3,591 | 8,076 | 11,667 | 32 | 5.7 | 4.5 | 4.8 |
| Venezuela | 918 | 13,136 | 14,054 | 16 | 0.6 | 2.9 | 2.3 |
| Mexico[c] | 10,620 | 30,685 | 41,305 | 7 | 1.0 | 1.0 | 1.0 |

*Source:* Francisco Depons, *Viaje a la parte oriental de tierra firme* (Caracas: Tipografía Americana, 1930), pp. 179-182; Francisco A. Encina, *Historia de Chile* (Santiago: Nascimiento, 1946), V, 60-61, 73, 162-169, 529-534; Herbert S. Klein, *Slavery in the Americas: A Comparative Study of Virginia and Cuba* (Chicago: Quadrangle, 1971), pp. 218-219; Lyle N. McAlister, *The "Fuero Militar" in New Spain, 1764-1800* (Gainesville: University of Florida Press, 1957), pp. 53, 73, 93-99; Christon I. Archer, *The Army in Bourbon Mexico, 1760-1810* (Albuquerque: University of New Mexico Press, 1977), pp. 22, 110-111, 240; Marcello Carmagnani, "Colonial Latin American Demography: Growth of Chilean Population, 1700-1830," *Journal of Social History* 1, no. 2 (Winter 1967): 183-185; and Timothy E. Anna, *The Fall of the Royal Government in Mexico City* (Lincoln: University of Nebraska Press, 1978), pp. 83-84.

a. Ratios of military personnel per population computed with reference to Mexico whose score was set at 1.0.

b. Estimates are very conservative because the 1800 population was extrapolated at 362,129 from 1792 and 1817 censuses, but military statistics dated from 1770.

c. Mexican data for 1810.

military jurisdiction in civil and criminal cases as well as in strictly military matters. The rights were extended to wives and dependent children, widows and surviving children, and to their domestic servants. They were often passive rights, exercised only when the army officer or soldier was a defendant.

The fuero for militiamen varied according to whether a unit was urban or provincial, on active duty or not. When urban or provincial militia units were mobilized, they enjoyed the complete fuero of the regular army. When provincial units were not on active duty, the officers and their wives and dependents still enjoyed the complete fuero. But enlisted men in inactive provincial units enjoyed only the criminal fuero; they were subject to the regular court system for civil cases. The variation in the inactive urban militia was greatest. There was a difference between officers and enlisted men, but the degree of privilege while inactive is difficult to specify. Some enjoyed full privileges, some criminal privileges only, and some none at all. Militia fueros were also passive rights, except that the militias of Cuba and Yucatan had the active fuero. The latter gave those who enjoyed it the right to bring actions in their own military tribunals against persons of another fuero. This concession illustrates the Crown's preferential policies toward Cuba.

*Preeminencias*, immunities, assured that officers and men of the regular army and their dependents could not be called to discharge municipal duties against their will. They were exempt from providing transportation, lodging, or subsistence for army, church, or civil officials in transit. They were exempt from special money aids to the Crown. They could not be imprisoned for debts, and their arms, horses, or clothing could not be attached for the settlement of private debts. The militia enjoyed the same immunities, except those concerning debts. Upon retirement, regular army and militia officers and men could petition that these immunities and fueros be granted for life, to an extent varying by rank, length of service, and circumstances of retirement.

There were general exceptions to military privileges. Cases dating before entry into the service were not privileged. Actions in mercantile law and those related to entailed estates and inheritances were excluded. Malfeasance in public office, sedition, fraud against the treasury, and similar actions were also excluded. These privileges were extended to the military in America in the last third of the eighteenth century because the Crown needed a larger army for imperial defense. The privileges and immunities of the regular army did not pose serious problems because the regular army was small, and lodged in barracks or deployed to remote posts on the frontier. The militiamen, however, because they were more numerous and dispersed throughout the empire, created jurisdictional disputes and enjoyed the fruits of privilege.

The preeminencias provided immediate and direct benefits; the benefits of the fueros were procedural and substantive. Jurisdictional disputes between military and other courts often occurred. A military man of the regular army or militia who was guilty, or who had lost a civil action, benefited from the delay created by the jurisdictional dispute. Military courts often treated military men more leniently than other courts would have; it was a decided advantage to have one's case tried in courts biased in one's favor. The growth of the military establishment and the efforts by military men to extend the military jurisdiction were serious sources of conflict during the closing decades of the empire. Militia officers in the countryside were often landowners who benefited from courts predisposed in their favor. In the cities many militia officers were medium- and small-scale merchants who benefited greatly from militia privilege.[18]

The military reflected imperial policies and structures in providing a stimulus to the mobility of blacks by providing a means for advancement and for the development of a black elite. The military reflected the larger society by institutionalizing the structural inequality of ethnic groups at the same time that it provided for the advancement of the ethnic strata at the bottom of the social structure. For example, a white sublieutenant's monthly salary in Venezuela was 32 pesos per month; that was higher than a mulatto or black captain's monthly salary (30 and 28 pesos respectively). For each military rank, whites earned approximately twice as much as blacks. For instance, a white captain earned 60 pesos per month, a black 28; a white lieutenant earned 40 pesos, a black 22.[19] On the other hand, mulattoes and blacks in the officer ranks gained status, power, and absolute wealth, although they lagged relative to whites.

The chief reward of black military participation, too, was the enjoyment of privileges.[20] Black militiamen typically did not enjoy fueros of any sort when they were inactive, but they enjoyed the full civil and criminal fuero when on active duty. Because of the nearly continuous state of war in the empire after 1790, many black militiamen enjoyed the full fuero most of the time. There was also a regional variation in the likelihood of mobilization into active duty, and hence in the likelihood of the full enjoyment of the fuero. Cuba, coastal New Spain, and coastal Venezuela were most likely to be on alert, so black militiamen in these areas frequently enjoyed privileged jurisdiction.

In order to stimulate black enrollment for imperial defense, the Crown stipulated that black militiamen would be exempt from the payment of the tribute while they were in service. This was especially relevant in New Spain, where such a tax was extensive. Because of treasury protests of loss of revenue, the tribute exemption was limited in the early 1780s: the full exemption was allowed every black in every unit on active service; when they were inactive, only the older, more established provincial militia units continued to enjoy the tribute exemption, not the urban units. However, all militia units on the coast of Veracruz continued to enjoy this exemption at all times because they were frequently on alert. Because these units included most of the black militiamen, relatively few blacks were actually affected by the formal change in the law.

White militiamen had more privileges than black militiamen; Indians were excluded from the military altogether. Therefore, the military reproduced and institutionalized the inequalities of the social structure. Yet it was a crucial instrument for social mobility within the established political system by providing privileges for blacks. Such privileges made military service attractive to blacks and mulattoes and allowed many of them power and status that many whites did not have.

About two-fifths of all militiamen in Cuba and Venezuela were blacks; in Mexico, the proportion rose during the 1770s to at least one-third,

*Table 6.2*  Black participation in the militia

| Country[a] | Total militia | Percentage of blacks | Year |
|---|---|---|---|
| Cuba | 8,076 | 42.2 | 1770 |
| Venezuela | 13,136 | 41.8 | 1800 |
| Mexico | 10,698 | 17.6 | 1766 |
| Mexico | 34,717 | 34.2 | 1784 |
| Mexico | 23,812 | 33.6 | 1800 |

*Source:* See Table 6.1.

a. Low estimates for Mexico. Assumed (same proportions across time) that only about 90 percent of the militia units on the Pacific and Gulf coasts and of the Lancers of Veracruz were composed of blacks, and that two-thirds of the militiamen in New Galicia-Guadalajara were black. All personnel enrolled in units identified as composed of blacks were added.

before stabilizing at that level (Table 6.2). Thus, a large share of Spain's military force in these colonies was contributed by the black population. The blacks were important to the defense of the empire; and the empire, by welcoming them into military ranks, was important to blacks because it opened up avenues for mobility. Black percentages in the Cuban and Venezuelan militia were about the same. But there were many more free blacks in Venezuela than in Cuba, so it had a lower rate of militarization than the island. Consequently, every third free black adult male in Cuba, but only every twenty-fourth in Venezuela, was enrolled in the militia. The rates of militarization for Venezuelan and Cuban whites were comparable: one out of eight. But this meant that Cuban whites were only about one-third as militarized as Cuban blacks, while Venezuelan whites were three times more militarized than Venezuelan blacks.[21] Cuba's free blacks were far more likely to have been coopted in the imperial system as a result of their direct access to government resources.

Many Cuban blacks were either slaves, or members of the military which sustained and defended a slave system. This ethical paradox was noted in Chapter 3, where it was pointed out that some successful free blacks became slaveowners. From the government's point of view this reduced the probability of a coalition of free blacks and slaves in Cuba. Black free men in the military improved their access to job, power, and status, often at the expense of black slaves. In this respect, they were no better — and no worse — than Cuba's white population.

From a comparative point of view, Cuba's high black military participation ratio removed many free black male adults from the active job market and from competition with whites for upper- and middle-income jobs. In Venezuela the army did not serve this function: it absorbed too few free black adult males to affect the upper- and middle-job market. Given Venezuela's large free black population, competition for these jobs was far more severe than in Cuba, and the white elite of Caracas expressed alarm that blacks might take over jobs in the government reserved for whites. Black pressure for political access in Venezuela was continuous; in Cuba it was diverted to the military. Venezuela, therefore, had a manpower surplus for upper- and middle-income jobs, and a manpower shortage for plantation jobs. The Cuban colonial government coopted freedmen by means of military jobs, giving them income, status, and power, far more than did the Venezuelan colonial government. Cuban black militiamen defended the empire that made their mobility possible. This function was performed less well in Venezuela.

Although the imperial military establishment was an army of Americans, it was not so equally everywhere. In Venezuela only about one-fifth of the military was Spanish. In Chile the bulk of the soldiers and half the officers were American Chileans.[22] In Mexico, Americans accounted for 76 percent of all enlisted men in the regular troops in 1790, rising to 95 percent in 1800. However, Spaniards held a far higher proportion of the officer ranks than was warranted by their share of the population, thus increasing conflict between Creoles and Spaniards. In 1788 Spaniards filled 11 of the 17 slots at the rank of captain and above in the Regiment of the Crown, and 38 of its 62 slots at or above the rank of first sergeant. In 1800 Spaniards filled 10 of 13 officer jobs in the Guanajuato infantry battalion, and 7 of the 9 colonel and lieutenant colonel slots in the Bajío militia regiments. Only 3 of the 45 senior regular army officers of the Army of New Spain were from New Spain itself at the end of the eighteenth century.[23]

The military establishment in America grew out of international threats to the security of the empire. Its growth reflected the social system within which it developed. The military exhibited the neopatrimonial characteristics typical of other elite institutions. Maximizing political access for private gain was pursued relentlessly. The rate of general militarization varied from colony to colony; its maximum growth is explained by international factors, whether in response to major European powers in Cuba or Indians beyond Spanish control in Chile. The military reflected the structural inequality and flexibility of the empire's ethnic systems. It did so differentially, for the coopting of black freedmen in Cuba went furthest and had the most widespread effects. In the final analysis, the military establishment reinforced existing trends. It accounted for more government responsiveness to freedmen in Cuba, and it responded to Cubans far more than to other colonials. Its effect on Mexico may have worsened existing elite ethnic differences among officers.

# 7

# Elite Competition

Competition among elites is a key factor for understanding the closing decades of the Spanish empire. It had a continuing impact on government policy. Although members of the elite exhibit some of the demographic characteristics of the socially mobilized, Spanish American elites rarely exhibited "modern" orientations. They were often divided, but they shared certain general attitudes and orientations.

Elite competition occurred within a neopatrimonial political culture even during periods of economic growth. The elite sought access to government for personal economic advantage. As Max Weber notes: "in patrimonial systems generally . . . all government authority and the corresponding economic rights tend to be treated as privately appropriated economic advantages."[1] The neopatrimonial model stresses the centrality of the monarch who dispenses favors; openings for capitalism exist, but they have a political orientation. Economic elites petition the public authority for favors that further their private advantage. An alternative model might be that of bargaining activity by autonomous producers in a market; the neopatrimonial model stresses the dependency of producers on politics and the key role of access to the political center.[2]

## The Impact of Economic Growth

Social change is not a uniquely modern phenomenon.[3] Certain processes in premodern but relatively socially differentiated political systems — centralized bureaucratic empires — change the system so that otherwise accommodable traditional political participation may no longer be contained within it. This can lead to disruptive traditional political participation. Sometimes certain modern elements of political participation also arise.

Economic growth, or its absence, is one such process. The relation between economic change and political order is complicated. Certain kinds of economic change may increase the well-being of a people, thus supporting the political order. Other kinds of economic change, especially in premodern settings, may contribute to the breakdown of political order. Traditional political participation may be transformed through the rapid commercialization of agriculture in a centralized bureaucratic polity. The diffusion of capitalist, or semi-capitalist, principles of economic organization turn land, labor, and wealth into commodities. In premodern societies land is typically encumbered by an array of social and communal ties. Commercialization breaks through the social ties that prevent a capitalist use of the land. The consequences of such radical restructuring are not merely economic. There is a broad cultural encounter in which different world views face each other. What is new about commercialization is not the beginning of exploitation — that is a time-honored human endeavor — but that the ties of custom, mutual service, protection, and dependence, and the face-to-face relations of the precapitalist order were eroded or broken. The ownership of the land, often communal even if used individually, was to change too. Commodity formation is impersonal; the new elite is less able to respond to the traditional social cues of the affected population.

To be disruptive, the process must take place quickly and be associated with the centralization and increase of the government's power. It is the sharp *joint* shift in economics and politics that is destabilizing. And it is the absence of higher levels of social mobilization, of intellectual, political, economic, social, and religious elites with modern orientations, of a modern industrial sector of some size, and of modern, forward-demanding orientations by the middle class and workers that distinguishes the challenge to the Spanish American empire from the major historical revolutions. The forces of tradition may be the catalyst, but whether they serve a modernizing instrumental purpose depends on a substantial presence of individuals, groups, and structures that are already modernizing.[4] Spain's empire did not have enough of these. There were three major sources of protest. First, some elite groups had an economic interest and/or a normative-affective attachment to the precommercialization status quo. For example, the navy might wish to conserve forests to guarantee the supply of lumber for naval construction; therefore, it would oppose the commercialization of politically encumbered land on the grounds of national security. The lands of the churches and other charitable institutions grow over time through wills and other donations; the commercialization of land would break through these religious encumbrances. Likewise, under precommercialization conditions, the landowning elite was often more interested in the mere possession of land for prestige and power than for its monetary exploitation; commercialization may thus involve also a displacement of landed elites.

Second, the commercialization of agriculture may also lead to the rise of social bandits or defensive collective violence by the displaced peasants. Commercialization changes legal and moral norms in the countryside, redefining the behavior of some individuals or very small groups as banditry, even though most of the local peasantry, abiding by custom, would not so consider it. If the pressures of commercialization are even more severe, whole communities may resist and clamor for a return to the preexisting normative and economic order. The most typical peasant protestor is the "middle" free peasant. Very poor or enserfed peasants are usually so deprived that efforts to redress the wrong done to them may appear futile, but those who are relatively well-off may be coparticipants in the new, more efficient government policies. At the same time middle, free peasants may be the target of much of the political and economic change, in which case they will resist efforts to confine them to traditional molds and will object to paying the costs of modernization. Unlike serfs, they are not destitute or devoid of means of struggle; but if they object to being dispossessed of their land and related necessities and oppose the breakup of communally owned land, they may even attempt to reestablish the old order.[5] Elite and mass protests often were not linked in the Spanish American empire because of imperfect social communications. When they were, however loosely, their common concerns usually were defensive and backward-looking.

A third different source of protest results from slow and insufficient change. The critical strategy of the ruler in a centralized bureaucratic empire, it has been argued, was that free-floating, unencumbered, modern resources had to be adequate but limited. The ruler would promote the development of the modern sector so long as it was compatible with traditional, legitimate purposes. More modern, developing, economic elites, generating their own momentum, may want to dispense with traditional limitations faster than the rulers judge prudent. And yet, given the persistence of a neopatrimonial elite political culture, this new sector often wants to retain and enhance its access to government at the expense of its more tradition-bound elite rivals.

Commercialization of agriculture or an increase of mining production may bring about a surplus for export. In a neopatrimonial context, the new, more modern elites in a relatively backward or peripheral area in a centralized bureaucratic polity would petition the Crown, not for unfettered foreign trade, but for a Crown-induced political opening into a secured and guaranteed market located in some other niche of the empire. Similarly, in a more modern, economically developed central area, these new commercial elites would petition, not for unfettered foreign trade, but for a new share in the control of the imperial commercial monopoly. New, more modern elites might try to break up a politically organized monopoly over a wide geographic area into two monopolies, each with its own carefully delimited jurisdiction, or to establish new rules of political and economic privilege for a new emerging sector. However, some of these elites may break out of traditional political participation and develop a new type of political participation and political goals. This happened in Spanish America — but mostly in Cuba, the colony which failed to revolt.

The economic gains or profit of traditional elites depend on their ability to maneuver in the political sphere. They might use their government connections not to effect change but to work within existing structures. The elite normative orientation curtails the dynamism of economic growth. Elite behavior seeks to adjust claims of access to the political center, not to set forth new claims typical of modern economic, social, or political elites. Neopatrimonially oriented elites, unwilling to stand on their own in the economic, social, or religious spheres, calculated their advantage on the basis of their access to government and resisted changes impeding that access.

Inadequate commercialization may also affect the masses. When commercialization is introduced, some changes must occur among peasants. Some labor has be to freed from its traditional duties and obligations to work in commercial agriculture. However, a ruler of a centralized bureaucratic polity may seek to prevent the complete modernization of these "liberated" workers. The Crown may attempt to reimpose traditional rules and customs, which may trigger resistance. This differs from modern resistance because often it seeks only to preserve the status quo — not to establish new rights but to defend existing ones.

Under conditions of insufficient change, an elite group (economic, intellectual, religious, political) may claim political legitimacy, breaking with the old regime (perhaps by proclaiming independence). Such political participation is no longer accommodable but disruptive. In classic neopatrimonial fashion, it may also adjust government policies to provide the victors with new access to government for private gain, while other elements of the social structure remain frozen. There is, in short, maximum political advantage to a given elite group and minimum large-scale social change. An elite claim to political legitimacy breaks with custom at long last and does not seek the restoration of the preexisting order, though the mechanism remains conservative, preserving the existing social structure. Elite competition turned into an elite seizure of legitimacy.

More modern, nonagricultural sectors may also develop in what remains basically a premodern setting. Manufacturing takes place in artisan shops; the civil service is meritocratic, but barely so. These sectors also suffer from insufficient modernization. The imperial bureaucratic ruler may prevent certain kinds of manufacturing in some parts of his realm, but foster it in others. He may reimpose traditional customs on some industrial workers; he may want to limit the scope and domain of nonagricultural activities. The elite and masses in these sectors may exhibit similar strategies. Worker protest may seek to defend existing rights. The neopatrimonially oriented elite may maximize new paths of government access by establishing new monopolies or gaining a significant share of the old ones. And certain elite groups may move toward radical politics with conservative social aims.

In sum, more modern economic growth is necessary for the development of centralized bureaucratic empires. Yet the traditional sources of legitimation of such empires require the containment of these forces. Protest may result from either expansion or containment. Too much change in any direction may challenge and disrupt the hybrid legitimacy of the political system. Internal economic changes can agitate elite competition or provoke resistance to change. When nothing more happens, the variants of political participation may be accommodable.

There are four characteristics of traditional elite competition. First, elite individuals and groups compete for access to the political center to gain advantage in the private nonpolitical spheres; struggles between groups such as planters or miners and merchants are strongly politicized. Thus, there is a predisposition in a neopatrimonial political culture toward praetorianism or the general politicization of all social forces. A neopatrimonial norm, latently praetorian, is held in check by the other norms, structures, and policies of the political system. When the system breaks down, the praetorianism may flower. Second, rulers often sought to limit the elite's access to the political center; this was bitterly resisted by the elite.[6] Third, the Spanish American empire's colonies were not only hierarchically subject to Spanish authority but also hierarchically related to one another. Elite struggles often were not just internal but involved groups from two or more colonies and the metropolis itself. Thus, elite competition was manifested on a continental and transatlantic canvas. Finally, ethnic groups often had — or were perceived to have — occupational specializations, so the mix between social class and ethnic factors was not only a social problem but also specifically an elite problem.

Traditional elite competition, seeking access to government, is an age-old form of behavior. Because the government is usually the most formally organized aspect of a society, elite competition must depend on a high level of organization. Elites can compete through guilds or other corporate organizations; their participation is apt to be organizationally dependent, as are other forms of traditional political participation. Although the scope of traditional elite participation is broader than that of other groups in the social structure, it is more limited than the scope of modern elite participation. Although traditional elite participation is more often system-wide than traditional peasant participation is, it is usually less so than modern elite participation. Traditional elites are more likely to recognize corporate, guild, or regional boundaries to their political participation. In contrast to other forms of traditional participation, traditional elite participation is continuous and characterized by longer-range perspectives.

The goals of traditional elites are adjustive, or restorative, or resistant; they differ from those of a forward-looking elite. A forward-looking elite lays claim to something new that it had not claimed before. It is willing to tear down old structures and build new ones — not shore up existing ones or bring back older ones. A modern elite may wish to reduce government influence in its sphere, or it may harness government support for the process of change. A modern elite can be autonomous; if associated with the government, it seeks to change existing structures — to break them down and create a new process based on new claims. The least traditional of the traditional elites — the adjustive elites — seek changes in their relative position within existing structures, while modern elites (in coalition with government or against it) seek changes in position and structure.

A transformation of accommodable into disruptive, but still traditional, political participation may result from a loose linkage between defensive, backward-looking elites and masses which, for different reasons, concur in the need to reestablish some element of the preexisting order. It may also stem from a need to defend existing conditions. These group may be small, and the elite groups among them may remain neopatrimonial; yet the effect often challenges political legitimacy. A group may even appropriate legitimacy for itself. Such a radical political outcome, nevertheless, need not change economic and social policies.

## Accommodable Competition

### Chile

Chilean elite behavior, with few exceptions, fits the neopatrimonial elite competition model, even up to the wars of independence. The competition was both internal and international, involving not only conflict within the colony but also conflict between Chilean and Peruvian elites. An example is the crisis of the 1750s, probably the most severe of the century. The Viceroy of Peru established a policy of equality of wheat purchases, from internal producers in Peru and from Chile, through import controls in 1752. This curtailed Peruvian imports from Chile, hurting Chilean producers and Peruvian shippers. The shippers closed ranks, as they had in the past, limiting their purchases in Chile and purchasing together at a common fixed price. Given the high level of Chilean wheat production and the limits imposed independently by the Viceroy and the shippers on purchases, the price of Chilean wheat collapsed. There was a fixed, low demand and a high, variable supply.[7]

Chilean elites mobilized their access to government. The Cabildo of Santiago fixed the price of wheat at a high 52 pesos per fanega; the supply of wheat which could enter the port of Valparaiso was set at 130,000 fanegas, and a permanent deputy was appointed to enforce these laws. The price of wheat per fanega then was only 25 percent of the Cabildo's proposed fixed price. The Governor of Chile supported the Cabildo. The Viceroy of Peru claimed jurisdiction and revoked the Chilean measures in 1754.[8]

The Chilean effort to limit the supply and fix the price failed because of viceregal intervention and because the wholesalers of Valparaiso were opposed to a reduction of their business. The wholesalers did not want to alter their own bargaining power with the Chilean wheat farmers, and they wanted to supply the Peruvian shippers. This local Chilean elite coalesced with a local Peruvian elite to defeat another fragment of the Chilean elite.[9]

The shippers and wholesalers sought a return to the past from both the Peruvian and Chilean colonial governments; they were backward-looking. The Peruvian and Chilean wheat farmers, on the other hand, had used their access to their respective political centers to adjust and maximize their private gains within the existing, restricted trade structure. The public authorities had concurred to increase their own political power — the Viceroy sought self-sufficiency, the Governor to defend the wealth of his realm.

In 1775 the Viceroy ordered Peruvian wheat to be preferred over imports; he banned the importation of Chilean wheat until the stocks of Chilean wheat then in the Callao and Lima stores and the Peruvian wheat currently being produced had been consumed. This coalition between the Viceroy and Peruvian wheat farmers, maximizing their position, was met by a combined coalition of Peruvian shippers, Chilean wholesalers, Chilean farmers, and the Chilean Governor, who appealed to the King, challenging the Viceroy's authority to institute such a policy.[10]

These and similar crises were resolved in various ways, but attempts to adjust and maximize private gains and position by mobilizing access to government are present in all. The goal was to establish a privileged monopoly or other colonial privileges within the existing, restricted trade policy and structure. The traditional elites, though politically restless, were accommodable.

Chile and Peru also clashed over fiscal policy. Until 1786 the Chilean colonial government received Peruvian funds to help defray expenses. Peru also supported the military garrisons at Valdivia and Chiloé, defending southernmost Chile, until the end of colonial rule. This was the so-called situado, an early form of foreign aid whereby one province was responsible for the costs incurred by another. Imperial defense was the justification for these transfer payments among colonies. In the closing years of imperial rule, Peru was also in charge of collecting funds from Chile to pay for Spain's international wars.[11]

Competition between Chile and Peru continued, as it did between elites within each country, over the distribution of existing trade rewards. Chilean protests to the King to act in their favor were fervent and repeated, arguing for more Chilean control over their economy. In the long run, this became mixed with the movement toward independence: the desire to nationalize economic decisionmaking.[12] However, in the period up to and including the outbreak of their wars of independence, the Chilean elites carefully distinguished between pressing the government for their private advantage vis-à-vis Peru and not pressing for free foreign trade.

Free trade would have liberated the Chilean merchants and producers from their dependence on the government, permitting them to expand and sell to other countries. Modern, forward-looking elites might have pressed for this, or for a combined government-private sector venture outside the empire. They did not. A test of attitudes on free trade came in 1778, when the empire became a free trade zone. Imperial free trade meant that goods could be brought into Chile from virtually any other colony or port in the metropolis. The colony was flooded with imports, lowering prices and bankrupting many merchants. The removal of intra-imperial tariffs exposed Chilean industry to competition. It, too, collapsed. To pay for the new imports, Chilean currency was extracted, provoking a liquidity crisis that affected the entire economy.

An anguished outcry from Chilean elites protested that imperial free trade was ruinous to the economy. In 1789 Governor O'Higgins called for an adjustment of economic relations with Peru (including a fixed price for wheat) and charged that imperial free trade had resulted in economic disaster. Anselmo de la Cruz, Secretary to the Consulado in the last years of the colony, also argued for the need to facilitate Chilean wheat exports. Yet, when it came to unfettered trade outside the empire, he argued in 1807 that "there is no doubt, sovereign protection is definitely favorable to us." Nor is there evidence that Chilean landowners requested freer trade.[13]

Chilean neopatrimonial elites were sheltered and protected politically, and they treasured that protection more than an economic transformation that might be accompanied by uncertainty. Political access and security were maximized, even at the expense of possibly greater profits under more uncertain conditions. The elites wanted to adjust relative positions in the imperial structure, not break out of it or establish new structures. Chile's economic difficulties derived less from economic overproduction than from cautious, traditional politics.

Some proposals were made for freer, extraimperial trade — though not unfettered free trade. Manuel de Salas suggested expanded trade beyond the empire in 1799, only to be rebuked by the Consulado. A similar modest proposal, as already indicated, came from Anselmo de la Cruz in 1809. In 1810, after initial steps to sever ties with Spain were taken, the need arose to raise revenue for the young national treasury. The Consulado opposed free trade when the new Junta formally proposed it, fearing another liquidity crisis with the extraction of currency. They worried also that the remainder of Chilean industry, if left unprotected, would founder. Some elites feared the implications of a further break with Spain; most opposed the diffusion of heretical or anti-religious doctrines through free trade.[14]

In early 1811 the Junta's revenue needs were so pressing that free trade became a necessity (some obviously also thought it would be a good forward-looking goal to implement). Import duties were set at 30 percent. Before 1811 import duties on goods from Spain had been only 13 percent; duties on foreign goods transshipped through Spain to Chile were higher because they had been taxed upon entering and leaving

Spain.[15] Thus, the new measure probably did not result in changed protection. The chief difference was that revenues formerly collected in Spain would accrue to Chile. The free trade decree of 1811, therefore, was a compromise. Trade with all countries was facilitated; exchanges would be direct. Trade no longer had to go through Spain; its volume could be expected to increase. Both the revenue and protective purposes were to be served by a high tariff.

Traditional Chilean elite political participation was highly organized through the Cabildo or Consulado, over issues of narrow scope, though lasting over a century.[16] Political participation depended on external mobilization, not autonomous motivation. The behavior was by no means new; it was continuous and predictable. Coalitions formed with Peruvian shippers and Valparaiso wholesalers were transient; the goals and methods were not well integrated. Most importantly, goals were adjustive or backward-looking and elites relied on political access within a neopatrimonial culture.

## Mexico

A similar though more complex pattern of elite competition emerged in Mexico. There was a sharp increase in mining production during the second half of the eighteenth century. The Mexican mining elite responded to it putting forth adjustive claims: the establishment of privileges for the mining sector. Discussions about the organization of the mining sector had continued throughout the eighteenth century. In the 1770s the mining elite of New Spain petitioned the Crown for the granting of fueros, privileges, and in the royal decrees of 1783 the King authorized the reorganization of mining. The first two articles of title V of the Ordenanzas of 1783 established ownership relations: Article 1 stated that "the mines are properly of my Royal Possessions"; article 2 that, "without separating them from my Royal Patrimony, I concede them to my vassals in property and possession." The local mining elite would elect a deputation in each mining district; it would control the government's mercury monopoly and distribute mercury (essential for refining of silver through the widely used amalgamation method). In short, the miners utilized their political access, founded on the importance of bullion, by persuading the Crown to devolve to them a government monopoly in which they had a crucial stake. The private group that had most to gain would manage this public monopoly.[17]

The deputation was also in charge of all other local mining affairs, including judicial affairs. The deputation thus became a guild of the mining elite and a mining court, with private jurisdiction over litigation, including the settlement and arbitration of disputed claims to ownership, demarcation of mining boundaries, and labor-management relations. This combination of a private business association and judicial power, in the absence of any other impartial arbiter, opened the way to abuse of power. One of the more serious abuses was committed in Guanajuato in 1791, where a deputy used his public authority to advance his private fortune at the expense of another mineowner. The aggrieved party appealed to the Viceroy, who intervened. The Guanajuato deputation protested that the Viceroy had no right to invade their private, privileged jurisdiction, referring to their fueros and to rights derived from the medieval Siete Partidas, which governed such privileged jurisdiction. As the dispute grew more complicated, the Audiencia stepped in, and eventually it was settled by negotiation. The jurisdictional dispute was settled by a royal reprimand against both the Viceroy and the Audiencia for having interfered in a privileged mining case.[18]

In addition to the local deputations, there was a mining court in Mexico City, some of whose duties were judicial, some legislative. Like the local deputations, it was far more than a court. It was also chartered as a bank in 1784, though, as the result of many thefts by its officials, the bank was closed down in bankruptcy two years later. The court also established the Mining School and diffused technical knowledge; despite serious shortcomings, these were perhaps the only modernizing achievements of this bundle of private privilege. The court — the public voice of the mining interests — was also a lobby. It opposed new taxes (as in 1778) and supported miners' petitions for tax exemptions for difficult undertakings. In 1793, as a result of the deputations' problems with the administration of justice, the mining court of Mexico City became a court of appeal, with jurisdiction over all mining cases. It could reverse local judgments and guarantee that the private, privileged jurisdiction of miners would remain inviolate. The court became the head of the industry, defending it against claims from the Viceroy or Audiencia.[19]

The response to economic growth of Mexico's most dynamic economic sector, therefore, was to petition the Crown for new privileges and status in neopatrimonial fashion. Instead of impartial justice for all mineowners, to standardize contracts, reduce costs of litigation and bribes, and facilitate further growth, miners opted for an increase of private influence and politics in the administration of justice. They chose the traditional methods they knew best: politics and protection. Instead of breaking up a costly public monopoly over mercury, they petitioned the Crown for a share in administering it. Instead of the honest and efficient administration of a bank to promote growth in mining, they stole the funds. They knew the politics of lobbying and played them to the hilt. When they needed a model of organization, they turned to the medieval rules of King Alphonse X rather than to Adam Smith.

Economic growth in the mining sector can be traced to the Crown's economic policies, and to entrepreneurship—not to political participation. The attempt of the mining elite to advance its position within the traditional structure brought about a great deal of conflict, which was both accommodable and accommodated. It did not entail a change in existing structures, or new and distinct claims unknown to the imperial political framework. Government was not harnessed for an institutional revolution. Rather, the existing structures were used. The empire was thoroughly attuned to this style of petition. The miners wanted a privileged niche in the existing framework—not modernization. They got what they wanted.

The merchants of Mexico City were perhaps even more traditional in their political participation. The Consulado of Mexico City, chartered in 1592, was in continuous existence after 1594. The miners tried to emulate it in the latter part of the eighteenth century. The Consulado was a private association of merchants, a chamber of commerce, a political and economic lobby. It was also a court with exclusive privileged jurisdiction over mercantile disputes. It was even favored by a special tax, whose proceeds it administered mostly for public works. This privileged guild, and separate judiciary, served as one cornerstone of the system of restricted trade that characterized Spain's American empire.

There are many examples of the Consulado's backward-looking goals and of its traditional approach to politics. It resisted all efforts to establish other consulados in the Americas (except in Peru, chartered in 1593), lest they threaten its privileged economic, political, and social position, and until the 1790s it succeeded. The public interest paid dearly for this privilege. In 1781, for example, twenty-three merchants of Veracruz petitioned the Crown for a consulado, pointing out that it took time and money to travel to Mexico City to plead rights and submit controversies. In addition, Veracruz had a specialized interest in shipwreck claims, and the city wanted to construct its own public works. Similarly, in 1791, Guadalajara merchants complained about the distance to Mexico City where they had to go to settle disputes, and about the tendency of Mexico's Consulado to spend all its funds for public works in the capital city. Mexico's Consulado fought these petitions—but lost in 1795 when consulados were chartered in these cities.[20]

However, the behavior of the provincial merchants was no less traditional. If the scope of issues had been broad, they might have challenged the system of monopoly and restraint to change the existing structures. But they wanted only to divide the vast monopoly of Mexico's Consulado into several regionalized monopolies, each with ancestral privileges, and thus better their own position in the system. The charters of the consulados of Veracruz and Guadalajara exemplified the creation of privilege and the combination of private and public purposes in the same organization, as it had always been done.

The policies of the old and new consulados were remarkably similar. The Consulado of Mexico City resisted efforts to liberalize trade, opposing not only extraimperial free trade but even an imperial free trade zone. In 1786 it demanded the restoration of the monopolies of the cities of Cádiz and Mexico and the reestablishment of the long decaying system of convoys and fleets. The Veracruz Consulado defended its port monopoly against other claimants: it opposed the Crown's decree of 1797 permitting trade with neutral countries and was bitterly hostile to the first ships that came from the United States to trade in 1799.[21] Its first secretary criticized trade with neutral countries because he believed it would weaken the colonial ties to Spain. Veracruz merchants fought to improve their position, rather than for structural, modern change.

Landowners, on the other hand, were in a more ambiguous position. They wanted more export opportunities, but they were fiercely protectionist against agricultural imports.[22] Industrialists had increased production, especially of textiles, when war prevented importing from Europe; they wanted to protect these products after the war.[23] The cochineal trade exhibited similar traditional characteristics with regard to political participation. The structure of cochineal marketing is a classic example of the importance of political access for private gain. The local government officials appointed by Spain to oversee and protect the Indians were the Alcaldes Mayores and the Corregidores. These officials were responsible for collecting the tribute and were required to post a bond (*fianza*), an advance guarantee, of the revenues they would collect. Their salaries were low and they were forbidden to engage in trade, so financial pressures led them to violate the Laws of the Indies. The cochineal trade flourished under a system of deliberate, widespread corruption. Merchants of the Consulado of Mexico covered the fianza and contributed to the financial support of the local official in exchange for a contract whereby the latter guaranteed them delivery of a certain amount of cochineal. Cochineal came from small Indian farmers, via the local government, to the merchant. As middleman, the official provided the Indians with cash, commodities, or equipment on the merchant's account and managed the merchant's business with these producers. The middle step was formally illegal, but the process guaranteed an important part of Spain's fiscal revenues and exports.

The Church and government reformers opposed the cochineal trade structure, for it weakened respect for the laws of the central government and exploited the Indians. Religious paternalism and modernizing centralization combined to produce the Ordinance of Intendants of 1786, abolishing the old local government posts and banning trade through a government middleman. A fresh corps of intendants and their subdelegates, paid higher salaries, would take over in a reform intended to centralize administration and reduce corruption.

The reform came under immediate and continuous fire from some subdelegates, who wanted to revive the old practices; from the Minister of the Royal Treasury of Oaxaca (the core area of production), who claimed that Indians turned to ignorance and vice without the coercive pressures of local officials with a vested financial interest in production; and from the merchants of the Consulado of Mexico, who found it personally ruinous. The Crown yielded somewhat in 1794 and authorized the Viceroy of Mexico, at his discretion, to suspend the prohibition against local officials' engaging in private trade. This led to uneven enforcement and more conflict. The Crown yielded further in 1804, and the cochineal trade gradually returned to its old structure. Certain merchants had benefited through the elimination of the local government middleman, reducing costs while maintaining supply levels. These forward-looking merchants sought to move through the capitalistic opening that the central government had exposed. However, they were few and poorly organized, and they were often blocked by the local government officials defending their prerogative to engage in corrupt activities.[24]

Mexican economic and political elites behaved typically in traditional, accommodable fashion. Well organized, they participated in politics through guilds and maximized political access. They won often enough, forcing the Crown's ministers to back down.[25] They sought changes in their position within existing structures rather than changes of the structure. The scope was narrow and the goals were adjustive or backward-looking. The future of the empire seemed safe.

## From Accommodable to Disruptive Elites: Venezuela

The Venezuelan elites showed a mix of traditional and incipiently modernizing political participation. Until the very end of the empire, both orientations coexisted: one did not replace the other; they continued in a fused elite political culture.

The effect of the Caracas Company on defensive collective violence was discussed in Chapter 4. The Company enjoyed a monopoly of all import and export trade between Venezuela and Spain. In 1749 its attempt to extend its control over the supply of cocoa (including the suppression of contraband) was met by a revolt led by Juan Francisco de León. The rebels, a broad mixture of elite and mass, seized Caracas. The Cabildo of Caracas, which included the city's economic elite, endorsed the protest, accusing the Company of importing too few goods at a high price and exporting too little cocoa, for which it paid the producers a low price. The rebels sought a return to the trading system that had existed prior to the granting of the royal monopoly to the Caracas Company. That system of trading, whose domain was the empire, was highly restricted, although less so than a pure monopoly situation. The elite withdrew during the more violent parts of the rebellion, and in its final stages it became defensive collective violence without elite support.

The rebellion was defeated, but certain changes were made in the operation of the Company. In 1752 an open meeting of the Cabildo petitioned the Crown to allow the Company to sell shares to Venezuelans. With royal consent, the Company did so. Thus, the Caracas elite was accommodated in typical fashion by being given a share in the existing monopoly. The elite shifted from a backward-looking goal, in the first phase of their protest, to an adjustive goal in the second. No attempt was made to change the basic structure of restricted trade. The elite was accommodated and co-opted by reopening the political access the Company had closed. Other changes in the Company's procedures ensured a fairer share for the Venezuelan planters but, on the whole, the Company continued operating with little change — except that its monopoly was shared a little more widely.[26]

Another serious protest erupted between July and October 1781 in the Andean region of Maracaibo province, now western Venezuela. Sales taxes (alcabalá) doubled in 1778, and two years later the government established a tobacco monopoly to raise revenues. As a result of these and other measures, the province's tax collections increased fivefold. The revolt broke out in many towns as protests against such measures occurred in neighboring colonies. Although this so-called comunero (community) revolt involved large numbers of people, local town elites soon took control of most of the town governments affected by this insurrection. Of the twenty-three top insurrectionary town officials (capitanes de pueblos — town captains), at least twenty-two were white; fourteen of the twenty-three were among the richest men in the town, and four others were rather well-off. The revolt sought to roll back taxes and to eliminate the tobacco monopoly. Its leaders appealed to the King to redress the wrongs committed by bad governors in his name; instead, the revolt was speedily crushed.[27] This tax protest, although more broadly based than previous ones, was similar to many in the empire's history.

By the late 1770s Venezuelan elites began to petition for an end to the Company monopoly. Maracaibo province, with the most modernizing elites, was most insistent in this demand. The Company lost its monopoly in 1781; it was dissolved in 1785. During the struggle for independence of England's rebellious Thirteen Colonies, Spain permitted Venezuela to trade with allies and neutrals, but this permit was revoked in 1783. In October 1797 war in Europe led Spain again to allow trade by its colonies with allies and neutrals. The colonial government in Caracas anticipated this decision, authorizing such trade in April 1797.[28]

As already noted, the consulados of Santiago, Mexico, and Veracruz opposed trade outside the empire and opposed it in particular during 1797-1799. The Consulado of Caracas favored extraimperial trade and protested the suspension of the permit in 1799. Trade with neutral and allied countries was considered necessary for Venezuela's economic well-being. The restricted system was rejected, and the Consulado of Caracas, in contrast to others, sought a fundamental change of the trade structure.[29]

To be accurate, the Venezuelan elite was divided. In 1797 a group of merchants in Caracas had protested the permit of trade with allies and neutrals, while a group of planters promoted the case for such trade. Yet the dominant group, speaking through the Consulado, favored a change in the trade structure. The elites of Mexico and Chile were also divided. Some Chileans and Mexicans favored structural change, but the dominant groups in those elites were overwhelmingly adjustive, if not backward-looking. Thus, the policy views of the Caracas Consulado point to a different balance of social, economic, and political forces in this colony. The trade modernizers had the upper hand in Venezuela; the trade traditionalists in Mexico and Chile.

In 1801 the Consulado of Caracas again petitioned the Crown to permit trade with neutrals and allies, asking the Intendant of Caracas to allow it pending a royal decision. After much hesitation, the Intendant did so; a confirming royal order permitted trade beginning in 1801, to be revoked in 1803. In 1805 the Consulado once again petitioned the Crown and the local government authorities for permission to trade with allies and neutrals; officers voted nine to four in favor.[30] The social identity of one of the four negative voters cannot be identified. Six of the remaining twelve voters were merchants and six were planters. It is statistically necessary for the winning group to include at least one-half of the planters or one-half of the merchants. Empirically, at least three merchants and two planters were known to have favored the proposal. Theoretically, most of the planters should have supported the proposal, since they were the ones under direct economic pressure, with least to gain from a price drop if the supply of cocoa.built up. The merchants, on the other hand, could benefit either by the price drop (thus would oppose the proposals) or by new opportunities for trade (thus would favor the proposal). Merchants who had traded with Spain opposed free trade; merchants who traded elsewhere favored it.[31] Historically, a convention of planters had favored the proposal in 1797, and a convention of merchants had opposed it. Comparatively, merchants in Chile, Cuba, and Mexico were more likely to oppose freer trade than planters; Cuban planters were free traders.

Thus, the Venezuelan merchants were probably divided, with about half in favor of freer trade. The modernizers, therefore, had support from the two main elite groups.[32] This recruitment of the merchants into the modernizing outlook contrasts with the situation in Chile and Mexico. The freer trade orientation of the Caracas Consulado was not the result of the capture of the Consulado by the planters, but of a broadly based alliance of modernizers within the elite which cut across group boundaries.[33] The government reacted in a very limited way to the demand of the Venezuelan modernizing elites for a changed trade structure. The Caracas government's initiatives in 1797 and 1801, granting permits on its own authority, only anticipated Madrid's decisions; and the royal permits for 1797-1799, 1801-1803, 1805, and 1806-1809 were examples of government responsiveness to free traders, but they pale before government responsiveness to Cuban elite demands. Trade with neutrals and allies was granted to Venezuela briefly in 1805, and again in 1806, to be revoked in 1809.[34] As in 1797-1799, this, too, was common throughout the empire.

The imperial government and the colonial government in Caracas encouraged a degree of modernization so that modern resources should be adequate. As Venezuelan demands for freer trade and modernizing structural change increased, Spanish bureaucratic resistance stiffened. The latter's support for modernization to make modern resources adequate turned to resistance to such modernization to prevent structural change. Had the bureaucracy not limited modernization, there would have been a structural modernizing transformation, as happened in Cuba.

Spanish support of black mobility had been resisted by the Caracas elite. Modernization does not necessarily and simultaneously spill over from one issue area to the next. Modernizing orientations began to prevail in Venezuela in trade matters, while backward-looking orientations continued to prevail in race relations. Government and elite split in the two areas, although for different reasons, accelerating elite-government conflict.

The problem of plantation manpower supply links the elite's modernizing views on trade structure and their reactionary views on black status. When the Venezuelan growth rate accelerated late in the eighteenth century, a severe plantation labor shortage seems to have developed. The 1789 permit for free slave trade (which can be traced directly to Cuban planter lobbying) was also extended to Venezuela.[35] But Venezuela did not "benefit" from free slave trade as much as Cuba did. The formal decree permitting free slave trade was renewed twice during the 1790s, and then again in 1804. However, the governor prevented publication of the royal order of 1804 in Venezuela, thus formally ending the free slave trade, and in January 1807 the Crown confirmed this decision.[36] Actually the Venezuelan slave trade had ended earlier; no slaves were imported after 1797. The importation of slaves during the earlier 1790s was also limited. The government feared the repetition of a "second Haiti," and the Coro revolt lent credence to that view.[37]

Although the Caracas elites may have feared a slave uprising, they were more concerned with manpower shortages.[38] Unlike Coro and Maracaibo, they had not experienced serious black conspiracies or revolts; unlike Cuba, they had fewer French planters. They were accustomed to the social banditry of escaped slaves. They had few political fears, but their economic fears were widespread. The chief executive officer (*prior*) of the Caracas Consulado wrote about the "agricultural decay caused by the labor shortage," when, in December 1801, he noted the decline in exports and production as a result of international war and trade restrictions (see Table 5.2). He continued, "even in the limited state of production one cannot find adequate manpower," and proposed a forced labor draft of all without demonstrable occupation. After satisfying the needs of the urban labor market, the bulk of the labor draftees would be sent to work in the fields.[39]

The labor shortage had drastic effects on individuals. The freedman Juan de Jesús Ponte, a blacksmith, was seized in 1792 because he could not prove he was free. The freedman Agustín Baquero had similar difficulties in 1796. That same year Pedro Pablo Leyba was in custody for six months until he proved he was free.[40]

The plantation labor shortage in Venezuela arose out of the joint effects of economic growth and the curtailment of the slave trade. Even as production declined in the late 1790s, the labor shortage remained acute. As the Caracas elite, through the Consulado, considered a forced labor draft, elite and government perceptions continued a diverge. The government promoted the mobility of free blacks and stopped the slave trade. The elite was outraged by the labor shortage and by its loss of relative status vis-á-vis free blacks. At least as painfully, the elite knew that

Madrid treated other colonies differently. In December 1804 the Consulado of Caracas wrote to its agent in Madrid, requesting information about the royal decree of April 1804 that extended free slave trade — that which the governor of Venezuela had refused to publish. The agent responded in July 1805 with copies of the relevant documents, stressing the King's solicitude for the Cuban economy which was generously supplied with slave labor.[41] The Caracas elite could add jealousy of their Cuban brothers to their list of injuries.

Problems arose even when the Crown wanted to assist the Caracas elite. The Royal Decree of 1804 exempted coffee, cotton, sugar cane, and indigo from Church tithes, sales taxes, and other duties under certain circumstances. The colonial government, however, needed these tax yields and, notwithstanding the protests of the Caracas Consulado, years after the Royal decree was issued, refused to implement it.[42]

## Institutionalization and Imperial Survival

A decisive factor in the breakdown of the Spanish American empire was the introduction of new political, social, and economic organizations and procedures in the last quarter of the eighteenth century. When challenged by the domestic and international environment, these organizations and procedures were neither stable nor valued. They were not adaptable. Institutions are stable, valued, recurring patterns of behavior; organizations and procedures may be more or less institutionalized.[43] In a political situation the level of institutionalization, the process by which organizations and procedures acquire value and stability rests on the complexity and coherence of its organizations and procedures as they lead to adaptability and autonomy.

Complexity involves the multiplication of organizational subunits and their internal differentiation. Functional adaptability (the dropping of certain functions and adoption of others) is more likely to occur in complex organizations. Adaptability is the capacity of organizations and procedures to meet new challenges. Coherence involves a high degree of consensus on the functional boundaries of an organization and the procedures to resolve conflicts within those boundaries. The probability of autonomy increases with organizational coherence. Autonomy is the extent to which organizations and procedures are independent of other social forces and modes of behavior. Autonomous organizations have values distinguishable from those of other organizations and social forces.

Imperial legitimacy was challenged toward the end of the eighteenth century as groups began to claim political legitimacy, threatening the autonomy of organizations and procedures. Although similar challenges had been met in the past, the general level of institutionalization had declined with a loss of adaptability and autonomy, and social, economic, and political change had accelerated. The convergence of international war, internal changes, and the decline of institutionalization shaped the breakdown of the empire. The level of institutionalization did not decline uniformly. The increase in institutionalization in Cuba, despite the same international war and many profound internal changes, seems to account for Spanish success in maintaining control there. Statesmanlike decisions spurred the adaptability of the Havana government and its autonomy with regard to Spain, while maintaining a distance from internal Cuban social forces. This institutional factor was decisive in the containment of modernization and political participation in Cuba.

## Accommodating Modernization: Cuba

The dominant sectors of the Cuban elite were modernizing, and colonial government institutions adapted to the changes successfully. The story of Cuban modernization and institutionalization dates from the British seizure of Havana in 1762. This advanced post of Spain's American empire, guarding the naval routes to New Spain, could not be allowed to fall again into non-Spanish hands; it had to be strengthened militarily and economically. The motivation was imperial defense, but the results would be far-reaching. Beginning in the 1760s, the government launched an extensive program of reform, along with a build-up of military fortifications.[44]

Cuba's value was not intrinsic for Spain, but derived from its geographic-strategic position. The island has been a relatively backward colony that could not be expected to pay for the military fortifications, so New Spain had assumed a large part of that burden through situado transfer payments. New Spain contributed to the Cuban treasury, as well as to those in Trinidad, Florida, Louisiana, and the Philippines. Its situados were raised from Mexican taxes. From 1766 to 1774 New Spain contributed 21.6 million pesos to Cuba; from 1775 to 1788, 36.1 million; from 1788 to 1806, 50.4 million. The grand total was 108.15 million pesos from 1766 to 1806, when is was discontinued because Cuba was wealthy enough. Cuba's total internal revenues, in contrast, amounted to 13.5 million pesos from 1775 to 1788. Both Cuba's fiscal effort and New Spain's foreign aid increased during the war of independence of thirteen of Britain's North American colonies, which were supported by Spain. The foreign aid increase as a result of this war was far greater than the

Cuban internal contribution; except for 1777 and 1787, foreign aid received always exceeded Cuba's annual internal revenues.[45]

The money, although allocated for military fortifications, stimulated the rest of the Cuban economy. Skilled and unskilled labor had to be hired to construct the fortresses. Materials had to be transported and assembled. Money entered the financial community, giving rise to an early banking system. Some of the money was diverted into agricultural and sugar mill investment through corruption. The productive capacity of sugar mills increased, jumping from 3,772 arrobas per sugar mill in 1761 to 5,063 arrobas per sugar mill in 1792, making evident the need for a further expansion of the labor supply.[46]

The military and aristocratic values of the Spanish settlers were not oriented toward agricultural work, and because the government and the elite were committed to preserving this status, servitude appeared in every Spanish colony. However, Cuba's distinguishing feature was the presence of abundant capital as a result of foreign aid and relatively low numbers of slave labor. The rate of importation of slaves into Cuba had been low before 1790. Spain had restricted the slave trade throughout the colonial period, as it had restricted all trade. In the 1780s the Cuban planter elite sought to end these restrictions. Repugnant though it may sound, this was a a modernizing elite, trying to break out of imperial laws that restricted economic growth by curtailing the labor supply.

A far more dramatic example of modernization would have involved the transformation of cultural values. This test was met by no elite of Spain's American empire. But the Cuban elite of the 1780s did go one step beyond the others in demanding something new and distinct to promote economic growth: free slave trade. This was a frontal attack on the old structure of restricted trade. Faced with the Cuban lobby and its ties in Madrid, the Crown granted freedom of slave trade in the Caribbean, opening a new chapter both in its responsiveness to the Cuban elite, saving Cuba for Spain in the long run, and in an increase in human suffering and oppression far beyond anything Cuba had known.[47] Modernization from these conditions of severe backwardness was associated with an increase in the modernity of oppression.

Legal slave imports jumped at least from an average of about 1,000 per year from 1763 to 1790 to an average of about 7,500 per year for the next thirty years (see Table 3.2, first column). During the 1790s the rate was about 5,000 per year, and it was slightly higher than that during the first decade of the nineteenth century. Although there would still be manpower shortages in Cuba, they were nothing like Venezuela's. Spain had responded to the Cuban planters' demand for labor with the blood and sweat of Africans, while neglecting Venezuelan planters. The difference can be traced in part to very capable Cuban leadership and lobby by men such as Francisco de Arango y Parreño. More importantly it can be traced to Spain's perception of the greater strategic importance of Cuba than Venezuela. Cuba was not more economically important than Venezuela at the time; if anything, the latter might still have had a slight edge.

Unlike other colonial elites, the modernizing Cuban planters challenged another pillar of the imperial structure: the Church. While remaining nominally loyal in theological allegiance, they weakened its political and economic power. Religion remained strong throughout the wars of independence in Chile and Mexico, supported by all, attacked by only a few; though some of the Venezuelan leadership was skeptical, there, too, religion remained strong.

Each plantation in Cuba had a chaplain to minister to masters and slaves; it was the planter's obligation to pay his salary. By the 1780s the custom was being challenged by the cost-cutting planters, and by the end of the century chaplains were phased out. The planters also obtained an exemption from the slaves' Friday meat absention, so they could feed them cheap jerked beef every day. Protesting that transporting dead slaves to church cemeteries was costly in time and money, over church protest the planters established their own cemeteries. By the 1790s they had begun to fail to observe compulsory rest on Sundays and holy days; by 1817 the Bishop of Havana agreed.[48]

A struggle ensued between the church and the planters over tithing (church taxes). In 1796 the Consulado of Havana requested that new sugar mills be exempt from tithing. In 1798 church tax collectors asked to see the account books of all planters; the Consulado refused. The conflict continued for several years, until the Church lost. The Crown exempted coffee production in 1792 from tithes for ten years; this exemption was made permanent in 1804, when it was extended to all new sugar mills. Part of the production of existing mills was also exempted. Church tithes had reflected the increase in agricultural production. In the Havana diocese they amounted to 260,082 pesos in 1794; when the conflict peaked in 1798 they were worth 399,432 pesos; and when the exemptions were granted in 1804 they were worth 466,143. A year later they had dropped to 392,030, and, with the exception of the 1814-1818 period, they remained below 400,000 pesos for the next quarter-century.

Though the planters ruined tithing, they transformed the economic basis of the Church. It served as the easy-term banker of the economic boom, deriving interest on its loans and deeply committed to the profitability of agriculture. Seminaries, convents, and religious orders financed the sugar and coffee boom. Capitalist modernization undermined the economic basis of the traditional Church, laid the economic foundations for the new Church, and subverted its value premises by associating it with the slave-based boom.[49]

The power of Cuba's modernizing coalition can best be examined through its foreign trade. Like other Spanish colonies, Cuba benefited from trade with allies and neutrals during the war of independence of thirteen British colonies in North America; but in contrast to them, Cuba was authorized to trade again with allies and neutrals, especially the United States, in January 1790. The slave trade was an important, though not the only, component of this trade. Sugar, too, flowed north. Spain's permit remained valid until January 1796, and Cuban exports grew. In 1797 the Crown permitted all the colonies to trade with allies and neutrals, but the permit expired in 1799 (to the delight of Mexicans and Chileans and the consternation of Venezuelans). At that time the colonial government in Havana assumed a historic role. Already in 1793, as war was generalized in Europe, Governor Las Casas and Intendant Valiente had extended Cuba's freedom of extraimperial trade beyond the provisions of the royal permit of 1790; their actions were confirmed by the Crown for a twelve-month period. In 1799 the Consulado and the Ayuntamiento of Havana asked the colonial authorities to exercise their discretion to disregard the revocation of the free-trade permit. Governor Someruelos and Intendant Valiente agreed. Trade with the United States continued uninterrupted.

In the earlier 1790s both the imperial and the colonial public authorities had supported freer trade for Cuba. That degree of generalized government responsiveness to modernization was not equaled in Venezuela; in other colonies the government was reasonably responsive in being restrictive. In 1799, as the imperial government retreated from free trade, the colonial authorities showed continued and independent responsiveness to the Havana elite — still in contrast to Venezuela. Cuban authorities exercised their right under the institutionalized imperial procedure whereby a local public official can suspend a royal decree, pending further royal decisions. Cuba differed from Mexico and Chile in its commitment to modernization through public and private cooperation. It differed from Venezuela in the commitment of the local colonial government to respond positively and boldly to elite initiatives toward modernization.

The Crown formally authorized trade with neutrals and allies in January 1801 — a trade that had never ceased in Cuba. This new permit was suspended at the end of the year. However, once again the Cuban authorities disregarded the imperial prohibition (the Venezuelan authorities did the same until 1803), and free trade continued. A new, sharper prohibition against trade with foreigners issued in 1804 interrupted the trade briefly. As war broke out in Europe in 1805, trade with neutrals and allies was renewed. Orders to cease trading with neutrals were promulgated again in 1808, 1809, and 1810.[50] They were disregarded by the Cuban colonial officials. Venezuelan officials, in contrast, waited until 1806 to receive formal confirmation of a trade permit and closed down trade in 1809.

For nineteen of the twenty-one years between 1790 and 1810 Cuba enjoyed trade with all but Spain's enemies. (The exceptions were 1796-97 and 1804-05.) Venezuela traded "freely" for about seven and a half years during the same twenty-one years, the other colonies less. The Cuban colonial authorities acted on their own, responding to local elite demands for freer trade in 1793, 1799, 1801, 1805, 1808, 1809, and 1810. In all but the first and fourth of these years, they suspended the application of an imperial decree in Cuba. The Venezuelan colonial authorities acted in similar fashion only in 1801, in anticipation of an imperial decree. In Chile and in Mexico this never happened in the area of freer foreign trade. There is perhaps no better indicator of government responsiveness in Cuba, where foreign trade was essential. Cuban officials coopted the elite and joined in changing basic structures. They sacrificed obedience to a distant government without challenging its overarching legitimacy: they relied creatively on an existing institutionalized colonial procedure, in the long term saving Cuba for Spain.

What were the social bases of these policies in Cuba? As in the other colonies, the planters tended to favor freer trade, and the merchants, many of whom were Spaniards, restricted trade, especially in the 1790s. However, the shift toward a general modernizing orientation depended not on a planter capture of economic policymaking, but on the establishment of a modernizing coalition between most planters and many merchants. Consensus on the need for modernization was essential. The modernizing coalition was stronger in Cuba than in Venezuela, for modernization went further and faster in the former than in the latter. By 1811 the resolutions of the Consulado of Havana demanding free trade with the United States and with other foreigners were supported unanimously by member planters and merchants.[51] Thus, on the question of free trade, Cuba stood at one end, Venezuela in the middle, and Chile and Mexico at the other end.

Not all Cuban elites favored modernization. There was merchant opposition in the 1790s, and Church opposition for a longer time. The planters demanded the removal of privileges over land and forests which accrued to the Royal Navy. The planters sought wood for energy and land for sugar and coffee; the Navy needed trees for shipbuilding. In 1805 planters won the right to cut trees on their own property, but the Navy retained principal authority over other forests. This was understandable, when war raged in the Atlantic. Traditional landowners, who owned land for prestige and consumption rather than for the market, resisted modernization, successfully opposing fragmentation of their land before the onslaught of commercialization. In short, the battle for modernization moved ahead in Cuba through the beginning of the nineteenth century, but it was far from over. There were still successful backward-looking elites, with narrow scope and purposes.[52]

In conclusion, political participation by an organized elite was widespread in Cuba. Elites lobbied as members of organizations for their own private gain, even if the private gain came to imply the modernization of some structures. The neopatrimonial norm, though weakened, remained; the personal corruption of officeholders continued unabated. Change in values proceeded more slowly than change in structures. The degree of change in norms and structures toward modernization, however, was unparalleled in the rest of Spanish America. The scope of issues was broad, the domain expanded, the perspective was long term, the goals were forward-looking, the ideology of change had taken hold. Action was system-wide, not fragmented; the behavior was decisively new. Ethically, however, modernization in Cuba illustrates the ordeal of change, for the process was built on the dehumanization of four-tenths of the population. Slavery in Cuba took a turn for the worse around 1790. Modernization and the intensification of slavery in the sugar sector were closely correlated.

## Elite Ethnicity

A number of important conflicts existed within the elite in America: some concerned economic issues, others ethnic issues. Differentiation within the elite had been strongly shaped by economic disputes as well as by the spread of education by the late colonial period. However, the most persistent source of intraelite differentiation was ascriptive: place of birth. Were whites born in America or in Spain? The acceleration of economic growth increased elite competition and added to the salience of these ascriptive differences.

The Creole or American-born white element was overwhelmingly larger than the Spanish-born element in Venezuela and in Mexico by twenty to one. The maximum number of Spaniards in Chile was 15,000,

1.67 percent of the population (according to the 1812 census). The number of Spaniards in Cuba is more difficult to determine, for as many as 20,000 Spanish troops and exiles from the mainland were in Havana in 1821. However, the Creoles were also the overwhelmingly preponderant element in Cuba's permanent white population.[53] The Creole-Spaniard conflict was more severe in Venezuela and in Mexico than in Cuba and Chile, although it was an important factor in all four colonies.

The process of elite differentiation was shaped by the practices of the Crown. Lower-level jobs were largely open to Creoles. Most top elite government jobs were reserved for Spaniards, including 98 percent each of 170 viceroys and 602 captains-general and presidents throughout Spanish America. The Church permitted slightly more access to Creoles, with "only" 85 percent of the 706 bishops born in Spain. Comparing Spanish domination of elite jobs with their proportion of the population, the discrepancy is staggering. Lucas Alamán, the conservative Mexican historian, argued that the "division between Europeans and Creoles was the cause of the revolutions."[54] Though an overstatement, there is little doubt that this was an important issue in the late colonial period, especially in Mexico. Representations to the Spanish government after 1810, even by Mexicans still loyal to Spain, highlighted the problem. The following elite jobs were held by Spaniards in Mexico in 1808: the Viceroy and his main advisers, the Dean, the Regent of the Audiencia and most of the justices, the three prosecutors, the directors of the Mining and of the Alcabalá offices, and all but one of the intendants. Thus, in the top elite civil bureaucracy, only some justices of the Audiencia, one intendant, and the director of the Lottery were Creoles. The Archbishop of Mexico, seven of the eight bishops, all the members of the Holy Inquisition and their secretaries and treasurer, the chaplains and chief officers of the Archbishop, the Nuncio, and the Vicar General were also Spaniards. In the top elite ecclesiastical bureaucracy only the Bishop of Puebla and some of the canons were Creoles. And, as shown in Chapter 6, Creoles held very few top military jobs.[55]

The Creole-Spaniard differentiation for elite positions in government, Church, and military is an example of an ascriptive criterion at the top of society that went beyond purity of blood. In 1771 the Cabildo of Mexico City protested against the Crown's practice of appointing only Spaniards to the leading positions in the civil bureaucracy. The event that instigated this was the fact that Creoles had secured far fewer elite jobs in running the Royal Tobacco Monopoly on behalf of the King than they thought they deserved. The Cabildo argued, more generally, that Creoles were capable of governing America, while Europeans were not. They claimed that those born in Spain were not acquainted with the local environment and its customs. Hence the probability of poor government increased when Spaniards were appointed instead of Creoles, who were more sensitive to the local situation. The Cabildo also argued that the high personal transportation expenses incurred by Spanish appointees increased the likelihood of corruption in office to recoup their losses.[56] The Cabildo of Mexico City in 1771 was presenting ethnic concerns as if they were national concerns. The seeds of disruption were sown as Creoles began to claim legitimacy. Spaniards and Creoles had been similar for a long time, but their experiences had begun to diverge. The Cabildo's argument focused on these differences in experience, which would become disruptive in the long term. The faculty of the University of Mexico also protested to the King in 1777 that the most prestigious jobs were nearly monopolized by Spaniards. The faculty showed special concern that its Creole graduates would suffer discrimination. The Cabildo of Mexico City protested again in 1792, in terms similar to those of its 1771 protest; in two decades it had perceived no improvement.[57]

In fact, the Creole share of public offices in New Spain declined during the last quarter of the eighteenth century. Between 1778 and 1793 the number of Creoles in the Guanajuato Ayuntamiento dropped from eleven to six and the number of Spaniards rose from six to eleven. Although the Guanajuato Ayuntamiento in 1809 was back at the level of 1778, there had been no net improvement.

There was also a turn in the composition of memberships of the Audiencia of Mexico City between 1769 and 1779. The number of members born in America fell from eight to four and the number of those born in Spain rose from three to ten. But the change should not be exaggerated. For example, there had been a Creole majority in the Audiencia of Mexico City in 1715. More importantly, eleven of the Creoles were born in New Spain, and they alone constituted a majority. Spaniards had regained the majority by 1725, and the number of Creoles born in New Spain had dropped to three. If the decline in Creole shares of top elite roles, such as Audiencia memberships, was a decisive factor in provoking independence, a war should have occurred a century earlier. Even the significance of the drop from the 1760s to the 1770s can be exaggerated. Only two of the Creole Audiencia members in the 1760s were born in New Spain. The others were born elsewhere in the Americas; they were also foreigners in New Spain. The share of native-born Creoles in the membership of the Audiencia of Mexico City remained virtually unchanged (between zero and three) from 1720 until independence.[58]

More troublesome may have been the fact that the number of non-natives with confirmed local ties -- married a native woman or entered a local business—fell from seven between 1755 and 1770 to never more than two after 1785. Thus proportions of Audiencia members with roots in New Spain, regardless of place of birth, declined indeed. Creole membership in the Audiencia was certainly a political issue, but one which the empire had accommodated well. The Crown once had even succeeded in reducing native-born Creole membership. The problem in the early nineteenth century was that the context within which disputes occurred had changed, so that formerly accommodable issues turned disruptive.

Creole access to Mexican bishoprics before independence was also below the colonial average. Of the total of 171 bishops in New Spain from 1519 to 1821, 32 (18.7 percent) were Mexican-born, while only 1 of the 9 bishops (11.1 percent) in 1810 was Mexican-born.[59] This hispanization of the elite contrasted with the americanization of those on whom imperial defense depended. The average proportion of Mexican-born regular troops in Mexico was 75.8 percent in 1790; by 1804 it had risen to 94.9 percent.[60]

The modernizing ministers of the late eighteenth century preferred men born in Spain for high public office in America. The government itself came to appropriate systemic legitimacy for the Spaniards, reversing earlier, more multinational policies of the empire. Americans had considered themselves subjects of the Crown; the Bourbon modernizers thought of them as subjects of Spain and of Spaniards. Creole protests were thus backward-looking. Although they began to issue forth claims of their own—claims to be the exclusive legitimate embodiment of the Spanish nation in America—these were reactions to the change of imperial appointments policy. What made these Creole claims disruptive was that they were not limited to a call for a return to previous conditions, to the multinational access to public office, but had moved to demand an exclusive access for Creoles.

Chile was a strong contrast. In 1802 the commandant of the frontier army facing the Arauco Indians was a Creole. In 1808 two of the six justices of the Audiencia were native-born Creoles. A Creole headed the Customs House, and another the *Casa de la Moneda* (the mint). Between 1699 and 1807 three of the bishops of Santiago had been Spaniards, two had been Chilean Creoles, and five had been Creoles born elsewhere. Between 1711 and 1805 two of the bishops of Concepción had been Spaniards, three had been Chilean Creoles, and two had been Creoles born elsewhere (another's birthplace has not been established). In 1810 the Bishop of Santiago was a Creole and the Bishop of Concepción a Spaniard.[61] Chileans ordinarily occupied the top posts in the six religious clerical orders operating in Chile, in part because of the scarcity of Spaniards. The main exception were the Franciscans, who alternated Spanish-born and American-born Superiors toward the end of the eighteenth century.[62]

The Bourbon reforms had a modest effect on Chilean Creole access to office. The Audiencia of Santiago had eight members in 1759, of whom two were Spaniards, two were Chilean-born, and the others were Creoles from other colonies. All five justices were Americans (two Chileans) by 1776, but this was very unusual by previous standards. Thereafter, the Crown began to appont Spaniards to the Santiago Audiencia, limiting Creole appointments to those not born in Chile. Chileans were not appointed to the Santiago Audiencia again until 1794. Between then and 1810, however, there were at least two Chilean-born justices in the Santiago Audiencia out of a typical total of six justices. Notwithstanding the loss of participation for two decades, through marriage links and other associations Chilean elites were able to coopt Audiencia members born elsewhere. Barbier had noted that "there is no evidence that this process of cooptation was stymied by the Bourbon reforms."[63] By the start of the nineteenth century Chilean elites had recovered their pre-1776 level of Audiencia participation.

Compared to Mexico or to the empire as a whole, Creoles in Chile, whether born there or elsewhere, had significant access to elite positions. The subjective perception of Chilean Creoles that independence was either desirable or necessary had developed little, if at all, before 1808, resulting in part from the greater openness of the social system to Creoles.[64] Eyzaquirre has argued, for example, that "the jealousy between European Spaniards and Americans, which became a constant throughout the New World, lacked in Chile the hateful elements which were found elsewhere."[65]

But there were less salient but real and increasing conflicts between Creole and Spaniard in Chile for control of religious orders and the Cabildo of Santiago.[66] The issues were similar to those in Mexico, but their frequency and intensity were less. What was once a single Chilean elite, with common traditions, learning, and outlook, gradually became internally differentiated and split because of different experiences, the increase of elite education, and the policies of the Crown.[67]

Venezuela stood in between those two. In the Cabildo of the city of Coro, the Creoles had refused to comply with the decree of 1776 mandating a Spanish mayor every other year. The Cabildo of Caracas was controlled by the leading families of the colony. By the eighteenth century the ecclesiastical council (cabildo eclesiástico) was also Creole-controlled. Francisco de Ibarra, Archbishop of Caracas in the late eighteenth century, came from a distinguished Creole family. The Rector, chancellor, and professors of the University were mostly Creoles. Creoles could rise up to the rank of colonel in the armed forces.[68] However, the Creole-Spaniard conflict was stimulated when the Spaniard-controlled Audiencia intervened repeatedly to ensure Spanish participation in the Cabildo. Before 1810 there were no Venezuelan-born Creoles in the Audiencia, nor were the foreign-born Audiencia judges as well connected locally.

### Relative Deprivation

Relative deprivation results from a perceived discrepancy between expectations and capabilities. The consequence may be a disposition to aggressive action. Such discrepancy has political consequences if the deprived believe that violence against government is justified normatively and is potentially useful to defend or enhance their positions. The patterns of deprivation may vary. There may be a net loss of capabilities, even if expectations change little. There may be a rise in expectations, even if capabilities change little. Or there may be a simultaneous rise of expectations and capabilities, followed by a leveling off or decline of the latter, while the former keeps rising.[69] The relative deprivation hypothesis may help to explain political conflict.[70]

Relative deprivation may also explain ethnic rivalries within the elite. Creoles, especially in Mexico, protested their relative deprivation during the late eighteenth century. Their expectations were rising but their capabilities were declining. This was the result of a broad shift in imperial policy. Loyalty to the government came to be defined by Spain increasingly in ethnic or national origin terms: only Spaniards could be trusted. Creoles were not absolutely deprived of access to office; but they had less than they considered their rightful due, and in some colonies they had less at the beginning of the nineteenth century than they had had in the past. This relative deprivation apparently was felt by individuals as well as by groups, and served powerfully to turn Creoles away from loyalty to the Crown.

## Contrasting Individual Leadership Success in Chile and Cuba

Manuel de Salas was born in Santiago, Chile, in July 1754.[71] His father was the prosecutor (*fiscal*) of the Audiencia. Manuel studied at the University of San Marcos in Lima and became a lawyer. In 1775, at the age of twenty and one-half years, he was elected Mayor of Santiago by the Cabildo; the following year he became its solicitor general (*procurador*). Thereafter he spent seven years in Madrid. Salas united the colonial authorities in Chile and the Creole elite during the last quarter-century of imperial rule. Trained in the tools and beliefs of the Enlightenment, he was at home with Spain's last governors in Chile, including O'Higgins, Avilés, and Muñoz de Guzmán.[72] Yet he was also deeply respected by the Creole elite, for he was one of them, playing an active role in the government of the colony.

Salas was the syndic or attorney of the Consulado of Santiago from its founding in 1795; he was responsible for important public policy recommendations. He recommended unsuccessfully to Governor Avilés and the Creoles that an Economic Society should be established in Chile. He tried again under Governor Muñoz de Guzmán in the early nineteenth century, but failed again. He argued in 1799, as the imperial permit for freer trade was ending, that Chile should be permitted to engage in extra-imperial trade with allies and neutrals.[73] He was soundly rebuked by the Consulado. He tried to develop the textile industry in Chile, but to no avail. He may be best known for success in the least politicized of all his proposals: the establishment of a trade, craft, and applied science professional school, the Academia de San Luis.

By the last days of the colony Salas was one of the Creole leaders who sought greater autonomy for Chile. He was a member of Congress in 1811 and 1823. Although always a strong supporter of the Chilean Junta, his erratic posturing between 1810 and 1815 makes it difficult to define precisely his views toward independence. Salas had been a loyal subject of the Crown. He despaired of good government, like so many Chileans, between 1808 and 1810. It is understandable that he sought to do away with the last colonial governor, García Carrasco, and that he favored greater autonomy; but he remained loyal to Spain until at least 1808.[74]

Salas wrote his *Diálogo de los porteros* in 1811, envisioning reconciliation between Chile and Spain's Ferdinand VII, on Chile's terms -- except for a renewed imperial link. He seems to have proposed several times that reconciliation with the Viceregal government at Lima be attempted, but, in classic fashion, he failed. Despite full awareness of grievances which he had articulated loudly, Salas still hoped for reconciliation after 1810; the thought of a final break with Spain was still "unthinkable." During the brief Spanish reconquest of Chile, 1814-1817, he, along with other leaders of Chile's elite, was exiled to Juan Fernández Island.[75]

What judgment can be made about Manuel de Salas? Chilean historians have been generally kind, calling him a precursor, anticipating the future, ahead of his times. Yet his ideas met an unreceptive audience.

As a leader and political mobilizer, Salas was unsuccessful. Even the coming of Chile's independence was a defeat for him, for it meant that enlightened, colonial government, linked to Spain — the government to which Salas devoted the best years of his life and with which he sought reconciliation — was over. And yet Salas is an enormously attractive figure precisely because his task was so difficult. He tried to awaken a sleepy colony; he tried to modernize it along the canons of emerging European liberalism. Salas was noble in his failure.

Francisco de Arango y Parreño was born in Havana, Cuba, in May 1765, into an aristocratic and rich family.[76] He, too, became a lawyer. In 1787, at the age of twenty-two, he was appointed agent (apoderado) of Havana's Ayuntamiento in Madrid. He became a Justice in the Audiencia of Santo Domingo in 1793, at the age of twenty-eight. He became the syndic or attorney without term of the Consulado of Havana in 1794, a post he held until 1809. He became acting superintendent of the tobacco monopoly in 1804. He became a Minister of Indies, and deputy at large to the Spanish Cortes in 1811, and was elected Cuban deputy to the Cortes in 1813. From 1814 to 1817, he was a full member of the Royal Council of the Indies. He was an arbitral judge on the international mixed commission on the slave trade from 1819 to 1821. He became a member of the Royal Council of State in 1820, and again in 1833-1834. From 1824 to 1825 he served as Intendant of Cuba. The Council of State empowered him in 1825 as its plenipotentiary for the reorganization of Cuban education. A member of the Order of the Cross of King Charles III, an honorary member of the Audiencia of Mexico City, and Prócer (titled "Great Man") of the Kingdom, Arango was without question the leader of the Cuban elite and was recognized in Madrid as a statesman of the empire.

Arango's crucial contribution was the modernization of the Cuban economy. He was the agent of the Cuban elite in Madrid when free slave trade was won. His discourse on Cuban agriculture in 1792 laid the groundwork for trade with the United States and reduction of taxes (including Church tithes) to stimulate the Cuban boom. The key to the discourse, however, was the accelerated introduction of slave labor. Arango knew that capital had been infused through Mexican foreign aid; what was needed was a steady labor supply. He argued that the introduction of slaves in Cuba was justified because Spaniards treated slaves better than Frenchmen did. Leaving nothing to chance, he proposed also a systematic program of repressive laws and the exclusion of black freedmen from the militia. He steadfastly opposed all plans for the abolition of slavery during the crucial period of Cuban economic expansion from

1790 to 1815. Economic growth from severe backwardness would go hand-in-hand with oppression. He battled in Spain against the abolitionism found among many Spanish and Spanish-American liberals.

Unlike Salas, Arango did not lean toward independence; most of what he sought could be found within the structure of the modernized empire. Like Salas, however, he proposed more autonomy for Cuba at a critical moment. In July 1808, Arango and seventy-two other members of the Cuban elite asked the Cabildo to ask the governor to establish a Junta to govern the country in union with Spain during the absence of the King. This, although done with the Governor's knowledge, did not gain enough public support and was dropped.

Arango was the leading Creole who cooperated with the Governor and the Intendant in pursuing an autonomous trade policy for Cuba within the empire. His ideas were supported by the Cuban elite, and many were written into law. He was esteemed by his peers and by the imperial authorities, who showered honors upon him. His programs worked. Cuba experienced an economic boom unparalleled in its history, thanks to the abundance of capital and slave labor, tax inducements and free trade. The economic structure was modernized beyond anything experienced elsewhere in Spain's American empire.

Because of his undoubted and impressive achievements, Arango has been hailed as one of Cuba's great historical figures. He set his course early in life and achieved it, while transforming his country. Marxist historians have criticized his role in the development of a Cuban capitalism based on slavery. But it does not take a Marxist to recognize that Arango's system was based on the deprivation of life to many who did not want to be enslaved or remain enslaved; that it was based on the absence of personal liberty for four-tenths of Cuba's population; and that it was growth and luxury for a few at the expense of death or misery for many.

Much elite behavior was traditional and could be accommodated within the existing structures of the empire in all four colonies; this was especially true in Chile and New Spain. In matters of foreign trade (but not race relations), modernizing elites were rising, despite internal opposition, in Venezuela. Such elites had clearly taken the upper hand in Cuba, setting in motion a far-reaching transformation. The Cuban case was an example of modernization within the context of institutionalization. It was, therefore, not disruptive. The accommodable features of elite behavior in Chile and in New Spain were also not disruptive. The only colony where elite behavior was dangerous was Venezuela.

Elite competition over economics and status contributed to internal differentiation within the elite and to conflict between elite and government, especially in Venezuela and to an important degree in Mexico. In Chile the conflict appeared primarily in its relations with Peru. Important elite groups in all four colonies sought to nationalize the power to make decisions in matters concerning them. They reached out toward autonomy. This was accommodated successfully by the colonial government in Cuba, but not in the other three colonies.

# 8

# The Impact of
# the International System

Sustained economic growth in the export sectors of the economies of Chile, Cuba, Mexico, and Venezuela throughout the eighteenth century, and especially in the few decades immediately preceding the wars of independence, responded to international demand. Gold and silver production increased in New Spain and Chile to meet Spain's rising need for bullion to pay the costs of wars. Venezuelan cocoa production increased in response to changed international income and tastes demanding a new luxury product. Venezuelan and Mexican dye production (indigo, cochineal) increased responding to the European industrial revolution in textiles. Chilean wheat production increased to satisfy Peruvian demand, as wheat production there fell, and subsequently to meet Spanish demand as well. Cuban sugar and coffee production increased after the collapse of Haitian production. Commercial export growth resulted from international rather than internal needs. The international dimension, therefore, is vital to the explanation of changes in the Spanish American empire. However varied the international causes and the sources of demand may have been, the chief consequence was the same: a dramatic long-term increase in production for export. This had significant internal economic, political, and social effects.

Foreign trade has an important impact on centralized bureaucratic empires. An imperially channeled and monopolized foreign trade confirmed and sustained the imperial hierarchy and colonial dependence established initially through political and military means. The Spanish American territories were linked to Europe only through Spain, and there was no imperial free trade until the last quarter of the eighteenth century. The trade monopoly was concentrated in Seville and Cádiz; no other cities—in Spain or any other country—could trade directly and legally with Spanish America. Non-Spaniards had to ship their goods to Spain, whence they were transshipped to America. Spanish American territories traded with each other in a circumscribed fashion. There was trade along the imperial trade routes to Spain. Trade was also authorized between particular colonies; for example, there was active trade between New Spain and Venezuela. Although intercolonial trade was one of the empire's bonds, there was no imperial free trade until after 1778, when prohibitions against most intercolonial trade were lifted. (Venezuela and New Spain did not join this imperial free trade zone until 1789.) The ties linking colonies to each other, however imperfect, preserved a common polity especially during the long interruptions of trade with Spain as a result of war.[1]

Foreign trade had modernizing effects when Spain opened the imperial channels. Foreign trade can provide material means and capital, foster competition, and disseminate knowledge, technology, skills, and managerial talent. Its long-term economic transformative effects, however, depend very much on its "educative" effect. If premodern peoples learn new ways, they can use the other benefits of foreign trade to transform themselves.[2]

Although modernization varied from most in Cuba, followed by Venezuela, to much less in New Spain and Chile, it existed in all four colonies. Some elites welcomed it, some denounced it. Three questions arise in foreign trade policy. Why did elite norms and attitudes toward structural change in foreign trade policy shift more quickly in some colonies than in others? What was the impact of foreign trade policy in provoking conflict with Spain? What was the impact of capital infusion through foreign trade and aid on the centralization or pluralization of the political and social systems?

## Political Consequences of Commodity Characteristics

World demand for tropical crops increased rapidly in the eighteenth century. Many of the crops that came to be cultivated in Venezuela and Cuba could be grown only in the tropics. Cocoa, for example, is strictly a tropical crop, thriving in a hot, rainy climate within 20 degrees of either side of the Equator. The tree requires an average temperature of at least 23 degrees C, humidity between 80 and 90, and 50 or more inches of rain annually — conditions met best in tropical lowlands. Sugar cane grows little when the temperature falls below 22 degrees C. These and a few other crops require a high minimum temperature for growth; rain is also important, although irrigation can be substituted. Some crops, such as fruit trees, are not suited to the tropics because they need a cold period during the year. A few crops, such as tobacco, maize, and rice, can be cultivated under a much wider variety of climatic conditions.[3]

These ecological characteristics combined with a high price for the relatively new and scarce crops, under low technological conditions, and limited substitutability of relatively fixed factors of production, to lead to a tropical crop export boom. The comparative advantage of tropical areas for such production was considerable.[4] Foreigners liked to invest in the export sectors of tropical countries because their domestic markets were small, and the Crown provided incentives to mobilize resources for such production.

The social effects of crops vary from commodity to commodity according to the elasticity of supply. Other things being equal, annual crop producers (such as Chilean wheat growers) can respond to price changes more quickly than perennial crop producers. Two characteristics of perennial crops cause a delay between price changes and output response: the time lag between planting and crop production often lasts several years; and once the plant starts to produce, the grower must stay with it and with its production for a long time. If a war were to prevent the export of perennial crops, production could not be cut back easily other than by destroying the plants or discarding the production. And, unlike minerals, agricultural products can rot if low levels of technology have not developed methods of preservation.[5]

Perennial crops differ. The cocoa tree blossoms the third or fourth year after planting, bears in about five, and reaches full production in the eighth year. The coffee tree begins to yield after three or four years; it peaks fifteen to eighteen years after planting, but its annual yield is highly variable. Both trees have an economic lifespan of over thirty years. Sugar cane, in contrast, starts to produce within eighteen months after planting. Its economic lifespan, under good growing conditions, is between eight and ten years; when sugar cane is planted initially in fresh soil, those first plants may yield as many as fifteen good harvests.[6]

Producers of short-term perennials such as sugar cane, therefore, can respond more easily to price increases. Whereas war or economic recession can hurt all perennial crops, short-term perennials suffer less and can benefit more quickly from improved market conditions than longer-term perennials. Thus, price and marketing fluctuation problems may be more severe for a country that emphasizes long-term perennial crop production than for one that concentrates on annual or short-term perennial crop production.

The adaptability of mineral production resembles that of annual rather than perennial crop production. Yet an annual crop such as wheat can be consumed in the domestic market, while minerals are not likely to be consumed domestically under conditions of low economic development. Internal consumption is also relatively low for nonessential foodstuffs like cocoa and coffee. To conclude, the probability of international economic disruption is least for a government whose country specializes in annual crop production of essential foodstuffs that can be consumed domestically in a crisis, and greatest for long-term perennial crop producers of nonessential foodstuffs. Minerals and short-term perennial crops are in an intermediate category.

Chile produced wheat (annual crops, essential foodstuff) and minerals; thus potential disruptive effects were low. Mexico produced minerals; its industrial production was for domestic consumption. Cuba produced sugar, a short-term perennial; its coffee production (long-term perennial), though increasing rapidly, would not become important until after the Napoleonic wars. Mexico and Cuba, therefore, were at middle levels of potential disruption, with Cuba being more vulnerable. Venezuela produced cocoa, a nonessential foodstuff and a long-term perennial crop; its shift to coffee did not reduce its high potential vulnerability to sharp international market change.

For example, Venezuela's domestic consumption of cocoa in 1720 (a better-than-average year for production and exports) amounted only to 5.5 percent of production. At a comparable time domestic consumption of wheat in Chile amounted to 72.9 percent of production. Even assuming that all of the increase in Chilean wheat production in the later part of the century was exported, and that the population growth in Chile resulted in a decline in per-capita wheat consumption, domestic consumption of wheat in Chile would still amount to 58 percent of production by 1800.[7] The foreign market was essential for the Venezuelan economy. It was important for Chile, too, but much less so. The Venezuelan elite after 1790 sought more far-reaching and faster structural change in trade — in contrast to Chile — because of economic and ecological pressures. The Venezuelan elites, with much more to lose from a restricted system of trade than the Chilean elites, had to plunge into freer marketing: they could not have done otherwise, given the increase in production at the end of the eighteenth century and the interruption of trade with Spain as a result of war.

A comparison can be made also between the importance of exports for the more diversified Mexican economy, and for the more specialized Cuban economy. Between 1800 and 1810 the average annual Mexican exports were 15.8 million pesos, about 8.3 percent of national income. The average annual Cuban exports between 1826 and 1830 amounted to 14 million pesos, about 28 percent of gross product.[8] Although the external market was important to both colonies, it was much more so to Cuba. The Cuban elite after 1790 sought more far-reaching and faster structural change in trade than did the Mexican because exports were much more important to it. The Cuban elites had far more to lose than the Mexican elites, given production increases and interruptions of trade with Spain.

The attitudes of the Venezuelan and Cuban elites toward free trade differed little: both favored a structural change to permit it because of economic and/or ecological reasons. But the difference in their achievements was considerable. The Cuban elite and colonial government, in defiance of the Crown, opened Cuban ports to extraimperial trade. Modernization and institutionalization developed simultaneously in Cuba; in Venezuela they did not. Spain responded favorably to the Cuban elites because of that colony's strategic importance. Cuban trade prospered, Venezuelan trade crashed. Venezuela faced a problem that did not affect the other countries: rotting produce. The chief executive officer of the Consulado of Caracas noted in 1801 that cocoa was piling up because of the difficulty of exporting it.[9] The full Consulado, in its 1799 petition for freer trade, indicated that the "precious cocoa production . . . cannot be preserved because of its characteristics . . . though the climate is suitable for producing it, it is not so for preventing it from rotting." Speed in exporting was essential. The majority coalition of the Consulado, in panic by 1805, stated that freer trade was necessary "not so that the country would flourish, because this would only result from a long period of peace, but so that it would not sink into complete ruin; so that its abundant and desirable crops should not decay and rot and so that agricultural decay would not set in." Even opponents of freer trade admitted that its only justification was "the inability of the planters to sell their harvest and especially cocoa, which rots, and which is consequently suffering more."[10] Venezuelan perennial crop producers did not benefit from sharp and short-lived price rises caused by wars. The time lag between tree planting and tree production kept them from taking advantage of sudden price increases; and their perennial trees kept producing, their fruit rotting, even when the price declined.

Chileans complained that their production was too high in comparison to the needs of the Peruvian market and, as a result, the price of wheat was too low; in order to control the supply, not all their productive land was producing wheat.[11] These serious complaints illustrate the greater flexibility of Chilean production. The problem was low price, not spoilage. Chilean producers could cut back annual production before it would rot; Venezuelan planters could not.

In sum, economic and ecological factors explain differences in elite normative orientation. The specific kind of economic growth created the pressures for structural change under unstable international conditions. Those pressures were greatest in Venezuela and Cuba, less so in Mexico and in Chile. The Cuban colonial government was responsive, the Venezuelan colonial government was not. Thus, Venezuela faced the most severe problem.

Elite normative changes, however, occurred everywhere to some degree. All four colonies had reached a level of economic maturity such that Spain's policies were becoming oppressive. For example, though most of the Chilean elite recoiled at the thought of unfettered foreign trade, they were aware of serious difficulties in their economy: given the existing structures, future growth was unlikely. Because they were not as badly off as the Venezuelans, they were slower to change their outlook. Their subjective perceptions had not been modernized, although the structure of their economy probably had. A characteristic of a neopatrimonial elite political culture is that there is a gap between norms and structure. The normative orientations and the social structure eventually catch up. This occurred faster in Cuba and Venezuela than in Chile and Mexico, but it was incipient in all four. The objective conditions for beginning modernization had probably appeared; the normative orientations to modernize had appeared only in some colonies.

## Rejecting Alternative Explanations: The Enlightenment and Elite Norms

It could be argued that the social mobilization of the mass of the population put new pressures and demands on the elite in selected countries. More income from exports would be needed to meet such new demands; cheaper imports might be required. The social mobilization hypothesis has already been shown to be inadequate, because aggregate, country-wide levels of social mobilization were far below recognized thresholds of significance for it to apply. This hypothesis can be rejected on other grounds. It is disproved by the fact that one of the less socially mobilized countries (Venezuela) should have encountered the most acute pressures. Also it fails to explain why these pressures did not develop to the same extent in New Spain. The hypothesis underpredicts the Venezuelan case and overpredicts the Mexican.

It might also be argued that the impact of the Enlightenment and the French Revolution accounted for the normative shifts of the elites. The rise and diffusion of new political ideas in the eighteenth century en-

gulfed the Western world, including Spanish America. The ideas informing the French and American revolutions were well known to the Spanish
American elites.[12] They were used to some degree as part of the
rhetorical justifications for most of the wars of independence.[13] It would
have been surprising if these transnational ideas had not reached the
Spanish colonies and been used to justify rebellion.[14] But it is another
thing to specify the causal connection between these ideas and the wars
of independence. Many of the French Enlightenment ideas are not pre-
scriptions for revolution.[15] A great deal of selectivity must take place
before they can be incorporated into such actions. Moreover, the
behavior of many revolutionaries is difficult to square with the ideas of
progress, liberty, equality, and fraternity.

The spread of new political ideas can be considered a permissive condition for independence; they are not a sufficient reason. It is difficult to
explain why the uprisings did not take place sooner than they did, even
though the ideas were present. But these ideas were at times irrelevant to
independence. When independence came to Mexico and Venezuela, the
ideas of the French Enlightenment and Revolution were in retreat in the
face of conservative notions of independence.[16]

Ideas and ideologies are difficult to contain. Enlightenment and
revolutionary literature could be found in all colonies. Prominent
Spanish American leaders were exposed to the new ideas in Europe.
Baron Humboldt, who visited Mexico, Havana, and Caracas (not Santiago), indicates that "this (intellectual) progress is indeed very remarkable at the Havannah, Lima, Santa Fé, Popayán and Caracas." He adds
that "at Havannah, the state of politics and their influence on commerce
is best understood," and that "no city of the new continent, without even
excepting those of the United States, can display such great and solid
scientific establishments as the capital of Mexico."[17] Humboldt seems to
rank Mexico and Cuba at the top, followed by Venezuela, on exposure to
the Enlightenment (a perfect match with the social mobilization rankings
of Chapter 2). It is, therefore, impossible to explain why there should be
differences among the colonies at all, causing Venezuela and Cuba to
press for freer trade, but not Mexico and Chile. Venezuela is under-
predicted, Mexico overpredicted. The causes and the consequences are
matched in Cuba only. The economic-ecological hypothesis remains a
more adequate and comprehensive explanation of changes in elite norms.

## Conflict and Political Economy

Impressive economic growth had occurred prior to the wars of the
Spanish succession and the Napoleonic wars. By the beginning of the

nineteenth century each of the four colonies had reached a degree of objective economic maturity that had outgrown many of the restrictive colonial structures. The specific characteristics of the economic growth had accelerated the catching-up process between structural and normative change in some colonies more than in others. All colonies had to grapple with a new political economy; some sought for freer trade. When the international crisis of imperial legitimacy struck in 1808, their foreign trade difficulties were compounded by political crisis. Four plausible hypotheses concerning the impact of foreign trade policy on elites should be considered.

Venezuelan cocoa exports peaked in the early 1790s, as has been seen. In the later 1790s, and in 1804, exports apparently declined to the level prior to the export boom, but production remained at about the same level. Venezuelan elites asked for, but did not get, freer trade. The severity of the crisis was increased by the inelasticity of supply. Accordingly, one may hypothesize that a decline in the level of exports leads to the rise of a conscious, subjective elite desire for freer trade, challenging the existing structure. The views are so irreconcilable that the movement toward independence begins. Therefore, a conscious, subjective demand for structural change in trade is a necessary and sufficient condition for explaining the wars of independence. This first hypothesis must be rejected on the basis of the evidence presented in Chapter 7. There were wars of independence in Chile and in Mexico. In contrast to the Caracas Consulado, the consulados of Santiago and Mexico opposed freer trade. A conscious, subjective elite desire for freer trade in Cuba did not result in a revolt. Thus, this hypothesis is neither a necessary (Mexico, Chile) nor a sufficient (Cuba) explanation of the wars of independence. The same cause—desire for freer trade—had opposite consequences in Cuba (loyalty) and Venezuela (insurrection). Opposite causes—protectionism versus free trade preferences — had similar consequences in Mexico, Chile, and Venezuela (insurrection).

Second, one may theorize that an objective decline in exports, regardless of the level of elite consciousness, is a necessary condition for explaining the revolts. However, the value of Mexican exports increased from the 1790s to the following decade, except for 1805 (Table 8.1). Therefore, the decline of foreign trade value is not a necessary explanation for Mexican drives toward independence. Opposite causes—export rises and declines—had still similar consequences in Mexico and Venezuela (insurrection).

Third, it could be argued that a drive toward independence occurs whenever an objective export decline appears, even though not all the wars of independence can be explained by a decline in foreign trade value

*Table 8.1*   Value of exports in Cuba and New Spain (pesos)

| Year | Cuba | New Spain |
|------|------|-----------|
| 1769 | 615,664 | |
| 1770 | 759,426 | |
| 1771 | 786,003 | |
| 1790 | 10,775,664 | |
| 1791 | 12,806,122 | |
| 1792 | 7,281,169 | |
| 1793 | 12,308,952 | |
| 1794 | 18,277,050 | |
| 1795 | 16,771,085 | |
| 1796 | | 9,308,387 |
| 1797 | | 1,423,077 |
| 1798 | | 3,371,328 |
| 1799 | | 8,715,956 |
| 1800 | | 5,968,470 |
| 1801 | | 1,970,573 |
| 1802 | | 38,447,367 |
| 1803 | 8,108,678 | 14,482,918 |
| 1804 | 8,165,736 | 21,457,882 |
| 1805 | 5,830,886 | 573,572 |
| 1806 | 6,364,036 | 5,478,762 |
| 1807 | 5,498,184 | 23,578,658 |
| 1808 | 3,843,397 | 15,525,099 |
| 1809 | 9,180,526 | 29,248,256 |
| 1810 | 7,903,700 | 16,568,887 |
| 1811 | 7,308,890 | |
| 1812 | 4,015,920 | |
| 1813 | 6,142,657 | |
| 1814 | 10,985,642 | |
| 1816 | 8,363,135 | |
| 1823 | 12,329,170 | |
| 1824 | 7,380,350 | |
| 1825 | 8,181,244 | |

*Source:* Ramón de la Sagra, *Historia económico-política y estadística de la isla de Cuba* (Havana: Viudas Arazoza y Soler, 1831), pp. 152, 164; Jacobo de la Pezuela, *Diccionario geográfico, estadístico, e histórico de la isla de Cuba* (Madrid: Establecimiento de Mellado, 1863), I, 37; and Hira de Gortari and Guillermo Palacios, "El comercio novohispano a través de Veracruz, 1802-1810," *Historia mexicana* 17, no. 67 (1968): 447.

or by elite consciousness. That would be a sufficient explanation. Yet Cuba experienced a severe objective export decline, but did not strive for independence. The value of Cuban exports dropped from the 1790s to the following decade. Therefore, this hypothesis is not a sufficient explanation. Similar causes (export declines) have opposite consequences: loyalty in Cuba, insurrection in Venezuela.

There is a fourth alternative explanation. International economic and political events led to economic growth; economic growth exacerbated group conflict. Economic growth was stimulated by an imperial government that was eager to meet its defense needs and was engaged in political modernization. This resulted in more group conflict and further group consciousness. In some colonies, especially New Spain, political modernization was correlated with hispanization, and the denial of political access to Creoles.

The colonies that revolted shared a political wish. They sought to nationalize decisionmaking to deal with a variety of issues, among which economic issues were very important but not uniquely so. Venezuela's political wishes focused on its politico-economic problem of marketing cocoa; on the unresponsiveness of the colonial government in Caracas to the ethnic status demands of the Creole elite; and on the twin problems of shortage of plantation labor and keener competition for upper- and middle-income jobs.

Chile's political wishes had an international dimension: seeking to redress the balance of economic power with Peru. The colonial government in Santiago had been very responsive to the demands of the Creole elites, but Madrid had backed Lima in Chile's confrontations with Peru. Chile sought a new and different political relationship with Spain to improve its economic bargaining position on foreign trade vis-à-vis Peru. Only when Santiago's colonial government ceased to be responsive to the Creoles did they revolt.

Politics in New Spain had been focused on elite ethnic competition. Economic conflicts were woven into this fabric of competition, but by themselves they did not lead to independence. Economic competitors sought positional adjustments within existing economic structures, as did the Chilean elite. Mexican Creoles moved toward independence as a result also of successive political defeats. They wanted to nationalize decisionmaking power, where ethnic and economic issues were equally important. Foreign trade issues were less important than in Venezuela and Chile.

In sharp contrast, the Cuban Creole elite was able to nationalize decisionmaking without breaking with the empire. The governments in both Madrid and Havana were responsive to the Creole demands. Merchants and planters, in spite of group competition, cooperated at crucial times.

The colonial government in Havana was responsive to economic demands. The Cuban Creoles, engaged in decisionmaking, were among the prime formulators of the new policies. Conflicts over foreign trade policy between metropolis and colony were systematically and repeatedly settled in favor of the colony by extensive use of institutionalized procedures. This was the essence of nationalized political decisionmaking.

Cuba was an example of modernization within institutionalization. In Venezuela modernization and institutional breakdown took place. In Chile and in New Spain political breakdown occurred in a more traditional context, as the groups formed claimed new and distinctive legitimacy within a very traditional context. Politics were decisive in shaping the probability of revolt as well as in propelling or restraining the impact of economic and social change accounting for both insurrection and loyalty. Where political decisionmaking of economic and other issues was successfully nationalized (Cuba), there was no revolt; where it was not, revolts broke out.

## The Political Consequences of Capital Infusion

Capital resources were made available in Spanish America as a result of the boom in foreign trade. New efforts were made to mobilize capital; part of this mobilization was connected with Spain's own trade and financial links with the rest of more economically prosperous Europe. When capital resources are newly infused into a society, its sociopolitical effects depend on three preexisting conditions: the level of social mobilization; the degree of centralization of government power; and the character of the capital infusion. An infusion of new investment will build on the level of social mobilization so that the degree of pluralism increases most rapidly where capital infusion appears under relatively high levels of social mobilization, planting the seeds for a later challenge to the existing political conditions. The centralization of authority was similar throughout the empire. Despite a formally centralized structure, and despite efforts toward increased centralization in the late colonial period, there were a number of autonomous, quasi- or nongovernmental bodies with significant authority (the Church, guilds of merchants and miners, universities, the military). Capital infusion, it is argued, will increase pluralism in direct proportion to preexisting decentralization. However, in areas where slavery was extensive, there was a high degree of centralization of power over the slaves; where this preexisting degree of centralization of power was high, capital infusion accelerated this trend too.

Possible outcomes ranged from a society at low levels of social mobilization and moderate decentralization (such as Chile in 1810) where capital infusion had little effect, to a society with higher levels of social mobilization and higher centralization of power over slaves (such as Cuba in 1810) where the pluralism of the free society and the oppression of black slaves increased simultaneously with the coming of new capital.

The character of the capital infusion is important. If the infusion requires the diffusion of agricultural and manufacturing units throughout the society, as in sugar cane production, the pluralizing effect will be high. The processing of sugar cane required considerable investment in buildings, livestock, and machinery. The yearly harvest period was limited to a few weeks; large armies of labor were required to harvest the cane quickly and take it to the mill. After cutting, the cane had to be ground within forty-eight hours, lest it ferment. Because sugar is bulky, mills had to be built in the countryside because speedy transport to the mills was unfeasible under conditions of low technology. A part of the manufacturing process thus penetrated the country beyond the cities. The diffusion of modernization was not geographically limited. On the other hand, if the capital infusion is geographically concentrated and highly capital-intensive, as in mining production, then central government power may increase because more resources are supplied to the government than to its potential challengers. Production with a high level of vertical integration between all its stages, as in mining, has less of a pluralizing effect than production with a lower level of integration, where cultivation, milling, or refining may be done separately. The less integrated the production structures, the more autonomous groups there will be involved in such production.

What was the impact of capital infusion on internal changes? In Mexico, capital infusion into cochineal production in Oaxaca had virtually no pluralizing effects. Although the producers were Indians, the capital went to merchants and the local public officials, increasing the capabilities of traditional elites and local government officials. Little was passed on to the Indians whose level of social mobilization was exceedingly low. The wars of independence were eventually brought to Oaxaca from outside the region by Morelos, who was able to mobilize the small farmers for war. Only centralized rebel military power was able to challenge centralized colonial power; but this challenge was made possible in part by the preservation of small Indian farms that supported the rebel effort.

The infusion of capital into the mining areas had a more complex effect. Levels of social mobilization in the Bajío were higher than they were in Oaxaca. Preexisting government centralization was strong. The infusion itself was geographically concentrated and highly capital intensive relative to other investments at the time. The result was a fiscal revenue boom that strengthened the local, colonial, and imperial governments. However, the somewhat higher level of social mobilization inherent in any mining enterprise qualified this result in two ways. In the short term, the effort to exploit the miners more thoroughly led to geographically concentrated and intensive protests -- perhaps among the most severe in the colony's history. In the long term, the increasing modernization of the area made it a likely center of sedition in 1810. The 1810 revolt was traditional in many ways, but it would have been more difficult to carry out if the level of social mobilization, low as it was, had not brought forth some limited disruption of the social structure. In conclusion, government centralization advanced in the short term; but the seeds of long-term disruption were sown when a capital infusion took place where there was already incipient modernization.

A critical issue about these transformative effects is whether the outputs of primary production will serve as inputs to manufacturing production, or whether primary products will simply be exported unprocessed. Similarly, when the final products are not important for internal consumption (for example, wheat vs. minerals, sugar, or cocoa), the chances of further changes are low. The higher technological impact of some investments (mining) may be limited because the domain of persons affected is small.[18]

In contrast to sugar, coffee does not have to be processed where it is cultivated. The capital requirements for coffee production, especially under low levels of technology, are much less than for sugar cane production; the dry method of coffee processing does not need pulping machines and fermentation tanks compared to the more modern wet methods of coffee processing. Cocoa processing, too, requires far less capital invested in machinery than sugar cane (and, under modern conditions, it requires less capital in machinery and equipment than coffee).[19] Coffee and cocoa production are less capital intensive and thus have fewer forward economic linkages than sugar production under low technological conditions. Sugar requires a minimum level of manufacturing investment under virtually any technological conditions; mills and refineries are necessary. The range of technologies that can be used in coffee and cocoa production is broader than for sugar production, where the minimum manufacturing threshold is higher and mills must be spread throughout the countryside.

Sugar cane makes greater demands on government to transform society in the short term. It may also have greater short-term rewards for government. Its countryside may be opened up more quickly by economic forces. Short-haul transportation for bulky cargo is likely to develop more quickly. Financial institutions and credit to finance the heavy capital investment must become available more quickly. Investment in the construction of sugar factories in the countryside has secondary effects in the construction industry and in the training of semiskilled labor. And a manufacturing sector, however primitive, may have secondary effects for the development of skills in maintenance of machinery, chemical processes, and the like. The short and medium term backward and forward linkages are relatively more effective.

As a result, the transformative effects of sugar in Cuba were probably greater than the transformative effects of cocoa in Venezuela. Coffee production in both countries made no comparative difference. The agricultural, milling, and refining aspects of sugar led to greater internal differentiation, broadening the scope and domain of the modern economy throughout rural areas of the country. A processing industry developed in Cuba, not in Venezuela. This pluralizing effect of sugar was limited to the free society — the owners, merchants, foremen, and skilled workers.

Production that requires a close integration of the primary and manufacturing elements of production (such as mining or sugar cane) can afford less disruption than those that do not need as much integration. The links between extraction and refining of mining products often afford economies of scale which are inducements to vertical integration, requiring labor discipline. The need to keep sugar cane flowing into the sugar mill incessantly during the harvest means that law and order among slaves must be strictly maintained and that the supply of slaves must be adequate so the harvest will not lag. Life on a sugar cane plantation was harsher for a slave than it was on a cocoa or coffee plantation. Government cooperation with planters was more necessary where production requirements were more integrated and hierarchical; so the worsening of slave conditions in nineteenth-century Cuba is linked to the changes in the sugar economy. Perhaps the best summary of the scholarly consensus is that of Herbert Klein:

> Of all forms of slave labor, the contemporary chroniclers of Cuba qualified sugar plantation labor as the worst. Since it required more time for production and harvesting than other crops — the cutting and harvesting of the cane being one of the most toilsome of occupations — sugar work was exacting and grueling. Hours were

long, work harsh, *mayorales* or overseers extremely cruel, and mortality quite high by the island's standards.[20]

Sugar production was more likely to diffuse authority in the modernizing upper strata and centralize it in the lower strata of society than coffee or cocoa production. For the free population there was pluralism in the internal differentiation and broad scope and domain of production; for the slave population it meant greatly increased oppression. Unlike the geographically concentrated and slightly more socially mobilized traditional miners, large-scale slave protests were unlikely because communications across wider geographic areas were more difficult. Venezuela, in contrast, was less pluralized at the top and less centralized at the bottom. It stood between centralizing Mexico and pluralizing free Cuba.

## Chilean Colonial Stability

Chile was different. At least half of its wheat -- a popular food there -- was consumed locally. Coffee, cocoa, and sugar are less essential, and, where produced, domestic consumption accounted for only a small part of production. Subsistence agriculture is more likely to be disrupted by a capital infusion into less essential crops than into essential ones. The subsistence farmer must either be persuaded to grow less essential, commercial, export crops, or be displaced by commercialized, export-oriented farmers producing less essential crops for the market and purchasing their own food if necessary. On the other hand, when the capital infusion is in essential crops, the subsistence farmer (who may be a smallholder or a traditionally oriented large landowner) can gradually increase production without a sharp, sudden change in method and technology. Less essential crops require a change to new crops for a subsistence farmer; the essential crops require doing more of the same.[21]

Wheat production can expand and continue in a fairly traditional social structure, as in czarist Russia; it can also have long-term transformative effects, as in North America where free immigrant labor became involved. Annual crops require a great deal of care, and their production can benefit from social transformation. The effect of wheat in Russia may have developed from political constraints; the more "normal" long-term effect of an annual crop such as wheat may be modernization. The expansion of wheat production in North America entered new areas, not in subsistence farming; it was commercialized from the outset. An expansion of essential annual crop production (wheat) from a subsistence level brought about only gradual change in Chile or czarist Russia. The expansion of such crops into new areas, commercialized at the outset, would maximize both short- and long-term transformative effects as in the United States or Canada. The shift in a subsistence area to less essential perennial crops would yield maximum short-term single-step modernization, followed by a subsequent leveling off or stagnation, as in Cuba and Venezuela. A cheap labor policy, or slavery, reinforces these trends. For the period under study, modernization was proceeding faster in the Caribbean than in Chile.

One indicator of disruption of traditional agriculture is the fragmentation of semi-feudal landholdings. If agrarian capitalism is to prosper, land must become a commodity. A land market must develop, and land in this market must be subject to sale in parcels. Change in Chile was gradual and limited. Land tenure remained stable because increased wheat production did not require drastic change, and the increased income could be used to strengthen property stability.

Research in the valley of Puangue (near Santiago) by Jean Borde and Mario Góngora[22] shows that between 1690 and 1775 property ownership remained stable, despite the growth of both wheat production and population. Property was not seriously fragmented in Chile as a result of the first burst of agricultural economic growth in the formerly subsistence sector of large, previously unproductive estates. They began to produce wheat for export by doing a little more work than before, so there was not much social change, but an increase in income-strengthening property stability. There was more income for the elite, and few pressures on traditional patterns of ownership. Some localized property fragmentation in the valley of Puangue between 1750 and 1800 was secondary to the main theme of property stability. It appeared among less well-off families and was the the result of the decay of some family fortunes. When family income increased as a result of economic growth, property stability was strengthened.

Economic growth not only strengthened property relations but renovated traditional forms of property ownership. A *mayorazgo*, entailed estate, prevented the fragmentation of the land covered by each royal grant. The absence of significant fragmentation in Chile cannot be explained by the rise of mayorazgos because there were too few of them. Nevertheless, this semi-feudal, government-guaranteed approach to stable land ownership increased and flourished. While only one mayorazgo was established in Chile before 1700, six were established between 1700 and 1760, and ten between 1761 and 1800.[23]

## The Emergence and Development
## of Slavery and Serfdom

Slavery did not evolve in the same way in every Spanish American colony. Chile had far fewer slaves than Cuba or Venezuela because it had never relied extensively on the slave trade. The general hypothesis about the incidence of slavery or serfdom in primary producing countries is that free land, free peasants, and nonworking owners are not found together; only two of the three can coexist. If the marginal productivity of labor is high, and if there are to be nonworking owners, the government will impose serfdom or slavery, notwithstanding land availability.[24] Aristocratic or elitist values in the Spanish American empire combined with some small need for continued military availability on the part of the white descendants of the conquerors to lead to the nonworking owner. The practice of entrusting Indians to leading Spaniards shortly after the conquest reinforced the view that it was the role of the Spaniard to rule, administer, christianize, and enjoy the benefits of conquest. Various forms of Indian servitude prevailed on the continent, but along the Caribbean coastline and islands the Indian population had disappeared. The diffusion of capitalism in the Caribbean and the rise in demand for tropical crops made efficient production feasible and profitable once slaves were imported from Africa.[25] The Caribbean's comparative advantage did not include labor but rather political and economic structures guaranteeing a steady supply of labor through the slave trade. Mining production in Mexico and Peru had the comparative advantage of Indian serf labor.

Economic change differed in Chile. Increased wheat production required more labor. The new commercial orientation of large wheat producers in eighteenth-century Chile made them try to lure and keep new workers. The tenant farmer, *inquilino,* appeared in the central Chilean valleys as a result of the wheat-based economic growth. It was the response of large farmers to the need for more labor.[26] Given the military and aristocratic orientations in the elite, landowners preferred not to work the land. But they resorted to a form of serfdom far milder than that found in the other colonies. They did not import many slaves; and they did not have enough subdued Indians for the job.

Why was Chilean serfdom so mild? The tenant farmers were not Indians who had lived on the large farms. Rather, they had to be drawn to the farms first, and then gradually entrapped. There was a demographic increase of the Chilean labor force in the eighteenth century, but these people were born free. Many chose banditry; others worked for very low wages, and were eventually tied to the land. The need to attract them, the "rootlessness" of so many Chileans, and the absence of slave imports accounted for at least a modestly competitive labor-management relationship that required a relatively mild form of serfdom.[27]

Why did they not import slaves? Wheat may not be a slave crop, but a serf or free-farmer crop. Wheat presents an annual challenge to improve productivity, through irrigation, crop rotation, and seed selection. A certain required virtuosity can come either from the long-term experience of a serf producing for subsistence or perhaps for a market or from a free farmer who may quickly move to more modern capital intensive technology, especially in immigrant societies with scarce labor. Wheat production was too complex to be engaged in by those without training, and it was expensive to train them.

A slave crop is one that can be cultivated at the lowest levels of technology, where no prior experience or acquired skills are required; technical demands on the field hands are simple. Perennial tree crops, for example, require slight attention after the crop starts producing; sugar cane uses labor as a near-military gang.

The owning of slaves in Chile would have meant housing and feeding them during the winter, without economic returns. (In contrast, in tropical climates slaves could be exploited throughout the year.) Annual planting also would have required a large labor force, so reliance on slaves would have multiplied costs. It was probably cheaper and more efficient to do without slaves.

An alternative hypothesis must be rejected: that Chile was too distant. There were slaves in Chile, most of them in domestic service. But they did not make sense technologically or economically as agricultural labor, so they remained an urban luxury.

Rural Chile showed a diverse social structure with no more than limited serfdom. Although tenants were the largest single category (41 percent) in a work force of 46,744 people in rural Chile in 1813, the free farm owners (22 percent), many of whom were small owners, and the free salaried workers (37 percent) accounted for a clear majority of rural Chile's work force.[28]

The international economic infusion into Chile affected the internal political and social structure only gradually. The level of social mobilization was the lowest in the colonies under discussion. Chile changed gradually within a stable property structure. Serfdom was mild in comparison to that of other colonies. The result was a slowly evolving social and political structure, with a strong social bond between lord and tenant. The tenant was not hopelessly enslaved and oppressed as elsewhere. The wheat tenant was not a sugar or cocoa slave or an Indian compelled to produce cochineal.

The international economic effects pluralized authority at the top but centralized it at the bottom in Cuba. In Venezuela, pluralization at the top was less, but centralization at the bottom was also less. In New Spain, the central government was enormously strengthened, although the seeds for longer-term discord were sown. Thus, centralization may have gone farthest in New Spain and at the lower strata of Cuban society, with Venezuela in the middle. Pluralization proceeded in inverse relation to centralization. Apart from these, Chile was little affected by either centralization or pluralization.

## Government Modernization and the Balance Between Modernity and Tradition

Government modernization in Spanish America, and especially in New Spain, tended to exclude Creoles from government administration. Because Spaniards were but a tiny minority of the population in America, the net effect was political demobilization. The intendancy reform in New Spain accelerated the denial of access to elite public office to Creoles. All but one of the twelve intendants appointed in New Spain in 1786 were Spaniards. Each intendant had a legal adviser; all but three were Spaniards.[29]

The elites complained of these hispanizing effects of reform. The Crown was identifying loyalty to the empire with birth in Spain. There was thus a strong traditional, ascriptive element in the midst of aggressive government modernization. The Crown was, in fact, challenging the overarching legitimacy of the multinational empire. In claiming special political legitimacy for those born in Spain it was appropriating legitimacy for a particular ethnic group. Madrid sought to stimulate modernization with one hand and tradition with the other. It proclaimed free imperial trade, but was reluctant to grant freer trade with other countries. Though trade modernization went furthest in Cuba, the Crown was reluctant to permit many other changes in agrarian structures there to accelerate modernization. Though Spain ended the monopoly of the Caracas Company, it opposed freer trade for Venezuela. The Venezuelan colonial government curtailed and then suspended the slave trade, following closely the balancing principles of the empire. These mixed policies pitted the government against elite participants because they were either too modern or too traditional. And they prevented the growth of participation based on community consensus. All participation was conflict-oriented, and all of it necessarily antigovernment at some point.

Mexican mining shows the effect of modernization on political participation and how it forced the government to become a primary agent of change in conditions of considerable economic backwardness. The government went into business directly, establishing tobacco monopolies in the colonies or royal textile factories in Spain.[30] It pursued activist fiscal and other policies to promote economic change; engaged in mass political demobilization and promoted increased oppression; increased elite benefits and, at first, elite political participation, to further the goal of change. At the same time the government limited and circumscribed modernization, especially mass and elite political participation.

The Spanish Crown, through its bullionist trade policy, taxation, and direct business engagement, had a great stake in silver mining.[31] It levied a 10 percent tax on all silver extracted, required that all silver be sent to Mexico City for coinage at the royal mint, and monopolized the sale of mercury and gunpowder, both of which were essential for mining.

With its insatiable bullionist demands, the modernizing Crown under Charles III and his minister Gálvez stimulated supply. Beginning in 1769 they granted tax exemptions to new mines or to renovated old ones. By the 1790s procedures at the royal mint were streamlined. The government's monopoly of gunpowder, formerly leased to the private sector, was renationalized and turned over to bureaucrats. Cost reductions were achieved and passed on to the miners. By 1785 miners and refiners were exempt of all sales taxes on all their materials. These benefits were justified because production rose with each tax or monopoly price reduction to such an extent that the real tax and profit yield increased.

The effective level of oppression on the mass of the population increased. Mining wages in Mexico were typically four reales per day; miners also received the *partido*, a share of the ore. Once a miner filled his daily quota of ore, he divided the rest with the mine owner; shares ranged from a low of one-twelfth to a high of one-half. Under the impact of modernization, mine owners, supported by the state, moved to do away with the shares. From the 1760s to the first decade of the nineteenth century, one by one, all the big mines eliminated the partido. When miners revolted, the government crushed them. The oppression suffered by Mexican miners, consequently, was more severe when the war of independence broke out. They were the victims of Spain's brand of modernization from backwardness. On the other hand, the government increased political access and economic gains for mine owners.

However, the government limited and circumscribed modernization. The labor system of Guanajuato required considerable modernization and mobility. Yet, at the time of the revolts in the late 1760s, the otherwise modernizing Minister Gálvez, then *visitador* (government auditor), ordered the reactivation of traditional sumptuary laws. All those in the tributary class, even though they might have forgotten the Indian languages of their ancestors, were again required to wear Indian clothing and were prohibited from using horses.

This traditionalizing response was opposed by the modernizing elites to no avail. In 1782 one of the leading mine owners, the Count of Valenciana, argued that the laws prescribing special clothing for the Guanajuato Indians reduced demand for store-bought clothes. They prevented the more rapid expansion of the textile industry. The entrepreneurs also wanted to dispense with the laws prohibiting giving credit to the Indians to stimulate demand, and they opposed the continuation of the tribute as a burden on the mining salary structure and a limit on mining labor mobility. Spain did not budge.[32] It would sacrifice some modernization for the sake of preserving the traditional framework. It would alienate elite and mass and seek to curtail their participation.

The government also promoted the formation of economic societies throughout the empire and authorized the establishment of new consulados for the first time in two centuries. It was promoting an exchange between political and economic participation. Through centralization and rationalization of authority, and hispanization of the bureaucracy, political participation by Americans declined. They were encouraged instead to turn to economic, educational, scientific, and other pursuits.

The economic societies, formally chartered by the Crown, appeared in America in the last two decades of imperial rule; by 1810 there were nineteen of them. Their impact varied considerably from colony to colony. In Cuba, economic societies appeared in Havana and in Santiago. They were extraordinarily vigorous, promoting newspapers, education, immigration, research, and development. In Chile, on the other hand, such a society was never established.[33]

In the early 1790s, the Crown authorized the break-up of the monopoly that the Consulado of Mexico City had exercised over New Spain. New consulados were established in Veracruz and Guadalajara. They were also authorized and established in Havana, Caracas, and Santiago (and in Buenos Aires, Cartagena, and Guatemala; one had existed in Lima since the late sixteenth century). All consulados included a mercantile court, a commercial monopoly, and a responsibility for economic development. A special tax supported its activities. The responsibility for economic development, in tune with the theme of the age, was far more pronounced in the charters of the new consulados than in the original charters of the consulados of Mexico and Lima.[34]

Opportunities for capitalistic development exist in neopatrimonial cultures, but would-be capitalists often seek them in politics. In the late eighteenth century the Crown sought to redirect potential entrepreneurs toward the economy and away from politics. This apparent decentralization of authority promoted economic growth and increased effective centralization. Ten consulados penetrated the economy, promoted it, and regulated it, far better than two had done in the vast expanse of the American colonies. Monopolies were not eliminated, but were shared more widely.

The hybrid characteristic of the new economic institutions thwarted the purpose of political demobilization. The consulados became strong lobbies articulating and aggregating the views of merchants and producers on matters of economic policy. Although Spaniards had often a preponderant position in the consulados, Creoles were able to participate. Though Creoles were denied direct access to jobs in the bureaucracy more than before, they renewed their political access by lobbying. Although Spain may have sought political demobilization, elite differentiation and political pluralization resulted.

In conclusion, government modernization led to the relative political demobilization of the Creoles with regard to the bureaucracy. It led to mass political demobilization whenever it interfered with modernization. Modernization, however, was restrained by the government at both elite and mass levels when it seemed to get out of hand. Efforts to rechannel entrepreneurial energies into the economy and away from the polity failed; instead, the new economic organizations were politicized by their members and turned into lobbying agencies. The result — except in Cuba — was repeated conflict between them and various levels of Spanish government.

## The Napoleonic Invasion of Spain

The Napoleonic invasion of Spain decapitated the empire but failed to achieve a complete military conquest. French armies entered Spain in 1808, forcing the abdication of the monarch and placing Spain in Napoleon's hands. The imperial government was disorganized, but America was not conquered.

Spain had had a similar experience previously. Charles II, last Hapsburg King of Spain, died childless in November 1700. He named to succeed him his nephew: Philip, Duke of Anjou, grandson of Louis XIV of France. France's opponents, however, held that Charles, Archduke of Austria, was the legitimate successor, and Austria, England, the Netherlands, Denmark, Portugal, Savoy, and many German princes recognized him as king of Spain. The eastern part of the Spanish kingdom (Aragón, Cataluña, and Valencia) joined the Austrian party, the rest the Bourbons. Although initially the Bourbons controlled most of Spain, Cataluña revolted in 1704 and the Archduke was proclaimed King Charles III in Barcelona, adding Aragón and Valencia. From the west, the anti-Bourbon armies entered Salamanca and Madrid in 1706. Philip had to withdraw. The war swung back and forth. It was not until 1710 that Charles was definitively expelled from Madrid; Barcelona did not fall to Philip until 1714.

International war challenged legitimacy. It was, after all, the "war of the Spanish succession." But the American colonies, for the most part, recognized the will of Charles II. Despite international and civil war, despite the revolt of half of Spain against the French-originated monarch, despite the loss of Madrid to the Austrian party in two occasions, despite conflicting claims to legitimacy, the colonies remained loyal to Philip.[35] There was no American war of independence at the beginning of the eighteenth century, even though, as J. H. Parry has noted, "foreigners, especially Englishmen, . . . predicted the imminent break-up of the empire." Spanish ties with America were very weak during the first quarter of the eighteenth century, and much of the trade was taken by Spain's allies and enemies.[36]

When the answers to a question such as "Who will succeed the ruler?" cease to be predictable, significant procedures have been challenged. This challenge occurs because the overarching legitimacy of the system comes under doubt for reasons external to the political system. It need not take place because internal participants are interested in seizing power, although it may include such cases. The disruption precedes political participation; even the most traditionally oriented political struggle under these conditions could increase disruption. Political behavior that might have been accommodable under other circumstances occurs under fundamentally changed conditions.

And yet, even an international war challenging imperial legitimacy — the War of the Spanish Succession, for example — is neither a necessary nor a sufficient condition for political insurrection. It is a permissive condition that may accelerate underlying changes set in motion by other causes. There were dramatic differences in the degree of political and economic modernization between the beginning of the eighteenth and the

nineteenth centuries in Spanish America. Much more had changed when
the French, under Napoleon, entered Spain than when the French and the
Austrians fought over it. Spanish America in 1700 was about to emerge
from a century of stagnation and decay. Changes loomed ahead. The
challenge of international war could be absorbed because other conditions that might have triggered off insurrection were missing. Even in the
early nineteenth century independence did not follow automatically if
some processes of containment operated successfully.

The collapse of the Spanish American empire after 1808 differed from
other imperial breakdowns. Other historical centralized bureaucratic
empires were typically conquered. Their overall legitimacy was not fundamentally challenged; one empire replaced another. If French troops
had crossed the Atlantic, if the British fleet had not stood in their way, if
peninsular Spaniards had been more pliant, if Russia had not forced
Napoleon to divert his attention, if Napoleon's colonial experience in
Haiti had not been so bitter, if — perhaps the French empire might have
replaced the Spanish empire. Legitimacy would not have been externally
challenged, merely shifted to benefit the French. Yet the level of social,
economic, and political differentiation in Spanish America may have
gone too far to accept such a simple colonial replacement.

The closest twentieth-century analogy is the effect of World War II
upon Asian colonial empires. The Japanese occupation promoted nationalism and self-reliance in Southeast Asia. The ideology of self-
determination, as well as the ravages of war, contributed to the overthrow of colonialism. The fragile legitimacy of colonial systems was
questioned. Military resistance on the part of Southeast Asian peoples
was often quite independent of colonial command and legitimation. Not
colonialism, but self-determination, became the new basis of legitimacy
in the Indonesian Republic and the Democratic Republic of Vietnam,
among others. The procedures broke down, preexisting legitimacy broke
down, colonialism broke down.[37] There are, however, some important
differences between the impact of World War II on Asia and the impact
of the French Revolution and Napoleonic wars on Spanish America. The
general questioning of the legitimacy of the colonial system had advanced in Asia to a degree without parallel in 1810 Spanish America. The
external challenge was the accelerator, not the instigator. And modernization had probably gone farther at the end of World War II in Asia
than even relatively generous estimates for Spanish America in 1810.[38]

This externally originated disruption does not end the issue. The
colonialist response to the challenge can be creative, allowing some
modification of preexisting legitimacy whereby the colonial power

transfers some of its authority and source of legitimacy to institutions in the colony itself. Thus a degree of autonomy for at least some colonial groups appears necessary. (The British responded to the Malayan Emergency, from the very beginning, by granting some self-rule to the Malayan Sultans and, through them, to the Malayan community.)[39] In these cases, legitimacy must be shared.

Creative colonialism occurred in early nineteenth-century Cuba when war interrupted the imperial channels of foreign trade. The local government elite and the local planter elite cooperated to destroy the commercial monopoly of imperial channels permanently. The pace of modernization had advanced more rapidly than in other places, leading to the rise of a more modern-oriented elite. Because of the need for internal order, the government supported the shift in orientation. Relatively free trade came, breaking out of the more traditional neopatrimonial norm. Access to the local government remained basic to the private planting sector for internal purposes, but the internal economic dynamism propelled this elite to open the windows to freer trade. The imperial government acquiesced because the trade dealt with agricultural products, not minerals of far greater perceived strategic and economic value, and because the fiscal advantages of freer trade outweighed the costs of losing the monopoly. Modernizing forward-looking change occurred, imposed from above, through public and private collaboration. Remnants of neopatrimonial orientations existed, but the private-public partnership sought to open up new areas rather than preserve the old. The benefits accrued mostly to the elite and to government, without upsetting the social hierarchy much.

Most colonialism in early nineteenth-century Spanish America was not creative. International war led to political disruption even though much of the political behavior would have been accommodable in earlier times. War's new external challenge to systemic legitimacy was especially powerful in colonies or among individuals undergoing significant changes in status, politics, or economics. Elite groups were formed to seize the opportunity to pose new internal challenges to government. The key element is that other factors had intervened from the War of the Spanish Succession to the Napoleonic wars before these internal colonial group challenges occurred and independence came.

## The State of the Empire

As the Napoleonic invasion of Spain in 1808 neared, a message on the "state of the empire" might have mentioned these points. There had been a great many changes in the preceding decades, of which the political modernization of the government and economic growth were most important. Group and ethnic status conflict had intensified. The imperial and colonial governments had pursued so many varied policies that coherence had been lost.

Modernization had gone farthest in Cuba, as a result of both local initiative and long-term stimulus by Spain. The free population had been pluralized; the Church and traditional landowners had been joined by sugar and coffee planters and sugar mill operators. Traditional merchants remained, but new, aggressive, internationally oriented merchants had appeared. Whereas before only tobacco farmers had formed a middle-income group, now many black freedmen were improving their position in small industries or in the military. Slavery had become more oppressive on the slave. Modernization seemed to be getting out of hand in Venezuela. The colonial government and the local elite disagreed over trade and labor policies. Ethnic status conflict between elite and mass was more acute there than in any other colony. The government of New Spain had been centralized, and fiscal revenues had increased enormously. Elite ethnic status conflict was more serious. There were economic conflicts, but participants stressed changes in position rather than changes in structure. Miners and small farmers in the Bajío had been repressed, but social tensions continued. Chile lagged behind the other colonies, although it had experienced economic growth and some social mobilization. Its society had been transformed the least. The social bonds within it remained strong. Centralization had not been advanced, nor had society been pluralized. Traditional elites remained strong, and traditional orientations prevailed.

Throughout these colonies there were many challenges to government. Creoles pressed for a share in decisionmaking in government. In Cuba they succeeded. Their colonial government was very autonomous. Because the fiscal return to the Crown was so substantial, Madrid consented, even if unwillingly. In Chile the government and the elite got along nicely, but they were locked in conflict with Peru. A sense of Chilean community had been forged by these conflicts. Chileans challenged not the colonial government, but the imperial relationships.

The colonial governments placed selective brakes on modernization in Venezuela and in Mexico. This led to greater differentiation between the Americans and their colonial governments. In Mexico the government still ruled with strength. In Venezuela it was shaky. At the same time, centralization and rationalization of authority continued apace, especially in Mexico, deamericanizing elite posts in the bureaucracy:

The impact of the international wars on exports varied. New Spain did better, Cuba and Venezuela worse. Only the Venezuelans made a political issue out of it. The Cubans had so much control over their government that they knew they could not improve the situation. The Mexicans exploited their monopoly position.

Except for Venezuela, and social tensions in the Bajío, the empire might have seemed in good shape. The traditional elite competition, the slave revolts and other defensive collective violence, the social bandits, and even the often troublesome ethnic conflict remained accommodable. It was managed in the past, and the future did not seem that different. The transformation of Cuba might have provoked some concern, but only for the long term; strong adaptable and autonomous colonial government institutions coped well with the problems there. Were it not for those troublesome Mexican miners and would-be industrialists in the Bajío, and for rotting cocoa on the docks of La Guaira, it could have been said with confidence, as in the time of Emperor Charles V, that the sun never set in these four colonies of the Spanish empire.

# PART TWO

# The Coming of Independence

# 9

# Destroying Political Order

In April 1808 Charles IV and his son Ferdinand abdicated the Spanish Crown in favor of Napoleon. On May 2, learning that the remaining children of King Charles were about to be removed to France, the people of Madrid rioted. French troops, already in Spain, fired on the crowd, and the Spanish war of independence against the French began.

A Council of Regency was replaced by the Supreme Central Junta in the fall of 1808. A new Council of Regency, established at the beginning of 1810, issued a call for the Cortes, or parliament, to meet. The Cortes would be responsible for the formulation and approval of the liberal Constitution of 1812. All of these institutions recognized the Prince of Asturias, Ferdinand, who was in French custody, as the legitimate King of Spain, and governed in his behalf.[1] Their actual authority was extremely limited. The victorious French troops occupied virtually all of the Spanish peninsula, except for the city of Cádiz in the southwest. What remained of the Spanish empire was in America. The loyalty of the Americans preserved the continuity of the empire and continued to supply the resources that allowed Spanish forces to fight against the French.

With Spain occupied by French troops, and Charles and Ferdinand abdicated, the Spanish empire was plunged into a first-class internal and international crisis. However, all the colonies swore allegiance to the new provisional councils or juntas in Spain. The Cabildo (municipal council) of Santiago swore its loyalty to King Ferdinand VII on September 25, 1808; the Cabildo, the Governor, and the justices of the Audiencia recognized the sovereignty of the Supreme Junta shortly thereafter. To demonstrate its great loyalty, the Cabildo proposed to raise and arm 16,000 militiamen to be paid out of surcharges on existing taxes and the expropriation of certain property.[2] The Cabildo of Caracas swore loyalty to Ferdinand on July 26, 1808. The Cabildo of Havana swore loyalty in 1808 — in July to the King and the Junta of Sevilla, and in October to the King and the Supreme Central Junta.

However, since the beginning of the eighteenth century, when the war of the Spanish succession broke out, the Spanish American colonies had become more complex and internally differentiated. The consciousness of certain elite groups had increased as the result of conflicts over economic growth and government modernization. The time had come for these new groups to prove how powerful they were. It was easy to swear allegiance to the King; it was more difficult to establish who or what body should govern in the King's name.

## Disruptive Traditional Political Participation

Most traditional political participation was accommodated within Spain's centralized bureaucratic political system through regulation by the rulers. Even potentially disruptive resistance to change was defeated or coopted. Nevertheless, certain types of traditional political participation are likely to disrupt the system and, if sufficiently widespread, can lead to its breakdown. Such participation is still traditional because it does not depend on social mobilization or on the internal, autonomous capacity of the individual to participate. Rather, it depends on political mobilization by leaders or organizations external to the individual. Yet, in contrast to the accommodable varieties, disruptive traditional political participation questions the authority of the incumbent ruler, his right to rule, or the basic legitimacy of an important aspect of that system. Accommodable elite competition took advantage of the system; accommodable ethnic mobility was a change within the system — not of the system; even resistance to change protests did not involve basic challenges to political legitimacy.

Disruptive political participation challenges systemic legitimacy, but traditionally oriented participants try to circumscribe it so the rest of the political, social, or economic order can be frozen or minimally changed. The scope of participation is narrowed to a single issue: which individual or group will rule? Disruptive elites do not typically promise socio-economic change beyond the restoration of their perquisites. Disruptive elites seeking independence promote a change in the source of authority from the metropolis to the newly independent state, but the structure of political, social, and economic authority of the new state differs little from that of the colony. There may be a good deal of otherwise accommodable political participation within the course of a disruptive political movement, giving it a broader social base.

Coalitions of traditional political participants remain poorly integrated in their goals, structures, and policies. Many lower-class political participants are reluctant (or may refuse outright) to broaden the scope of their claims. Traditional participants engaged in military combat often refuse to go beyond certain territorial or issue limits of what they perceive is their world. The struggle remains highly fragmented, with each set of participants pursuing its own goals, with its own organizations (whose complexity varies by level of social structure), and following its own strategies. Coordination among members of this conglomerate is low. Although one critical goal looks forward, the others remain backward-looking or adjustive. The perspective of nonelite participants continues to be short range; once the rebellion subsides, the lower-class participants probably will withdraw from politics.

In short, this type of political participation is remarkably similar to those already discussed — with one important exception: there is a new, though sharply circumscribed, claim, seeking personnel replacement and very limited adjustments in the structure of authority that may lead to formal independence from a colonial power. There are two types of disruptive, traditional political participation: one results from political mobilization by a charismatic leader who claims to be the new legitimate ruler; another is the appropriation of systemic legitimacy by a single key group that had not made such a claim before. The whole system's legitimacy is identified with the legitimacy of one group, and its ability to make that claim stick. The political system breaks down if these phenomena spread.

Group appropriation of legitimacy typically evolves from one of the types of accommodable political participation after other factors have intervened. The main difference is its challenge to legitimacy. The group seeking to appropriate legitimacy in a new and distinct way may be an old established elite group that has undergone change; or it may be an ethnic group seeking power; or it may be an elite offshoot trying to establish itself as a counterelite. Group appropriation is often a disruptive manifestation of elite competition.

Group appropriation of political legitimacy occurs in many contexts. For example, efforts by leaders of the generally well-off Arab minority in Zanzibar (18.2 percent of the population in 1948) were perceived by competing African groups as an Arab appropriation of political legitimacy from the British to themselves. In late 1963 the British were replaced by an Arab-dominated independent government. Within one month of independence a revolt by the opposition Afro-Shirazi party succeeded, and the Arab attempt to appropriate political legitimacy came to an end.[3] Group appropriation of legitimacy had disrupted the preexisting political system fundamentally and irreversibly. Once accommodable elite and ethnic competition under the British system had turned disruptive of both the British system and also of rules of mutual toleration between the two major communities in Zanzibar. Political participation increased through the mutual competitive mobilization of existing communities, transforming the political system. Military coups and the rise of a Leninist revolutionary party are other examples of group appropriation of legitimacy. This variant of political participation is an early stage of what S. P. Huntington has called "praetorianism": the general politicization of social forces and institutions (including, but not limited to, the military). There may be praetorian armies, churches, business groups, universities, or unions.[4]

In centralized bureaucratic empires disruptive elite groups are socially differentiated to some extent, even if they have traditional orientations. Their seizure of power breaks the harmony of the political system because it enhances the special legitimacy of one political component to the detriment of others. When a group seizure of legitimacy takes place in such a traditional context, the dominant characteristics of the political participation remain otherwise traditional. In contrast to the seizure of power by a revolutionary group, or even the Afro-Shirazi rise in Zanzibar, very little else changes. Scope and goals are narrow; system-wide transformation is shunned. The group acts upon its members. When the external stimulus ceases, individual participation can be expected to cease. Because elite groups are often involved, group and individual participation may continue even if the group fails in its effort to seize power. This continued politicization of the elite group, even in defeat, enhances the chances for praetorianism. Mass political participation, however, ceases.

## Toward Disruption

A challenge to the overarching legitimacy of the empire, it was argued in Chapter 8, could make even otherwise traditional behavior have disruptive effects. Elite jockeying for power in the traditional setting would push farther toward disruption, leading to group appropriation of legitimacy.

News of the Napoleonic invasion of Spain and the double Bourbon abdication were known in New Spain in July 1808. The Ayuntamiento promptly swore allegiance to the King and the Viceroy, but argued that, in the temporary absence of the King, sovereignty resided in "the tribunals and corporations." This argument was simultaneously traditional and disruptive. Sovereignty did not reside in the people, not even rhetorically. Society was conceived in medieval, not liberal fashion. It was corporate, not individual. The Ayuntamiento's manifesto of August 5, 1808, addressed sovereignty as the rights of the corporate towns (los pueblos), not of the rights of the people (el pueblo). The Creole lawyer Francisco Primo de Verdad argued: "We recognize two legitimate authorities: the first is our Sovereign's, the second is our municipal corporation's."[5]

The Creole elite in Mexico was moving toward a new, but traditionally based claim of legitimacy. It stemmed in part from a patrimonial theory of legitimacy: the colonies were the personal possession of the monarch. In his absence, sovereignty resided in the organized elite corporations, not in the people at large. In the king's absence, all his kingdoms were coequal. New Spain could not be subordinate to any junta in Spain, because Spain did not have any rights to exercise over America in the absence of the king. It was, therefore, proper to swear continuing allegiance to the absent monarch, and also proper to establish autonomous governments in the colonies in anticipation of the king's return. The Viceroy, José de Iturrigaray, had been appointed by Manuel Godoy, the discredited Minister of King Charles IV. To gain support for his legitimacy, Iturrigaray sided with the Creoles. He called public juntas to discuss the locus of sovereignty. Though the basis of the argument was thoroughly traditional, it had never been discussed politically and openly; in this sense it was new. Moreover, one corporation -- the Creole-controlled municipality -- had put forth the special claim to supremacy noted above.

The Spanish-controlled corporations struck back. They adopted the view that gained ascendancy during the process of government modernization: that the special bearers of legitimacy were Spain and the Spaniards. On August 27, 1808, the Inquisition ruled that any theory that sovereignty resided in the corporations or in the people at large was heretical. The entire basis of government legitimacy in New Spain was uprooted on September 15, 1808. A wealthy Spaniard, Gabriel de Yermo, staged a coup overthrowing the Viceroy. The Archbishop of Mexico, the merchants of the Consulado, the Inquisition, and the justices of the Audiencia, all overwhelmingly Spaniards, supported the coup. The leading Creoles in the municipal corporation were arrested and taken to the Archbishop's prison. The aged Marshal Pedro de Garibay became Viceroy, to be replaced in August 1809 by the Archbishop of Mexico, Francisco Lizana, upon orders of the Supreme Central Junta of Spain.[6]

Competition between Creoles and Spaniards had been accommodable within the empire. Once the international shock hit the empire, fundamental procedures were questioned, and normally traditional behavior became disruptive. What had been jockeying for position turned into efforts to seize legitimacy by the Creoles and by the Spaniards. Yermo's coup preserved Spaniard power, at the cost of undermining the empire's legitimacy. It revealed the fact that New Spain was a Spanish colony for the benefit of Spaniards; not a kingdom coequal with Spain, but under the Crown for the benefit of whites. The issues split leading institutions and families, especially aristocratic Creole families, weakening their bonds to each other and to the empire.[7]

The same thing occurred in Chile, the colony least disturbed by changes up to then. On February 11, 1808, the Governor of Chile died. The international war had caused the Crown to change the rules of succession to the governorship in case of death, and in 1806 the Crown had stipulated that the governorship would pass on to the military man of highest rank. The Audiencia of Chile ignored this new rule and followed the old one, electing its most senior member to the governorship. A military junta of the frontier garrison army elected the most senior military man, the commandant of the corps of military engineers, Francisco García Carrasco, to the governorship. Faced with military revolt backed by the rule of law, the Audiencia retreated.[8]

The traditional elite jockeying for position could no longer be contained and turned disruptive. Despite the latent praetorianism of the Spanish military establishment, "political rebellion or insubordination was unheard of" in it.[9] The coup in Chile, although carried out in the name of the law, was staged mostly by the military. It (and the Audiencia's provocative step) shook the foundations of legitimacy. In New Spain the military supported the coup, though the civilian sector initiated it. The new viceroy, Pedro de Garibay, was a marshal in the Army.

In Venezuela, too, the externally originated challenge had important consequences that impelled the political system toward disruptive political participation. Creoles began feverish discussions concerning the future government of the colony almost immediately, even though the municipal corporation had sworn its loyalty. One proposal was that a Creole junta be established to take control of the government, even if the governor of the colony retained formal authority. The Governor of Venezuela, unlike his Mexican counterpart, was not involved in the Creole plan. In November 1808, the Audiencia ordered the arrest of several leading Creoles planning the seizure of power. Arrested were the

Marquis of Toro, the Count of San Javier, the Marquis of Casa León, two sons of the Count of Tovar, and many others. The legitimate foundations of rule in Venezuela had been shaken. In the absence of the monarch government had come to be based on arbitrary naked force.[10]

These were intraelite conflicts; subelites were involved in none of them. Blacks, Indians, and poor whites remained distant from the elites, and vice versa.

## Disloyal Americans

Although the result was disruptive, loyalty and traditionalism dominated early elite responses to external challenges. Yet not all participation was loyal. Disloyalty was apparent in some segments of some colonies. One important demand in the modernizing revolt of a coalition of black freedmen and slaves in Coro in 1795 was the establishment of an egalitarian republic. The Coro revolt had coalesced different kinds of people.

Another revolt, planned in Caracas in 1797, was headed by Manuel Gual and José María España, retired captains of the Spanish regular army in Caracas. Although the revolt did not take place, the conspiracy and its goals had strong modernizing elements. The conspirators sought independence; the removal of administrative, judicial, tax, and military authorities; abolition of the tobacco monopoly; the reduction or elimination of a wide range of taxes; free foreign trade; civil equality for blacks, whites, and Indians; and the abolition of black slavery and the Indian tribute, with compensation to slaveowners.

The social bases of this conspiracy indicate that there was an effort to build a broad coalition. The conspiracy included twenty-five Spaniards, fourteen Creoles, and thirty-three black freedmen. American-born whites tended not to join; the Creole elite preferred not to mingle with free blacks. This ethnic split between Creoles, on the one hand, and Spaniards and blacks, on the other, was a portent of what was to come. The Gual-España conspiracy had many of the characteristics of a military coup. Forty-one of the seventy-two conspirators came from the regular army or militia; many of the black conspirators were militiamen.[11] The military had provided mobility for blacks, as well as a channel for blacks and Europeans to perceive common interests and act jointly. The impetus for a military coup in Venezuela, breaking down the restraints upon the military, came from lower-class elements pushing for a modernizing breakthrough coup. Two later moves toward independence in 1806, led by Francisco de Miranda and supported financially and morally by the British, failed because the elite did not support them.

There was a lower-class conspiracy in New Spain in 1799 whose goals were to kill the Spaniards and proclaim independence. All the conspirators were Creoles: of the thirteen arrested, two were unemployed; the others were silversmiths, watchmakers, policemen, nightwatchmen, and shopkeepers. Only three were older than thirty.[12]

## Toward Revolt

Revolt struck first in Caracas. The basis of legitimate rule had been questioned. Creoles and Spaniards openly claimed exclusive legitimacy for themselves. The Spanish Supreme Central Junta ordered the suppression of Venezuelan commerce with neutrals in late June 1809. In April 1810 news reached Caracas that the French had conquered virtually all of southern Spain but Cádiz and that a new Council of Regency had been established in January. On April 18, 1810, two Spanish commissioners from the Council arrived, asking that Venezuela swear loyalty.

The Cabildo of Caracas called an open meeting on April 19, 1810, to discuss the new issues. The Governor was deposed. A Supreme Junta was established in Caracas. The Governor, the Intendant, several of the Audiencia justices, and leading military officers were deported. The Supreme Junta of Caracas swore allegiance again to King Ferdinand VII, but chose to rule the colony on its own — independent of any existing Spanish authority or council or junta — pending the king's return. This Supreme Junta was composed of the members of the municipal council and others from the colonial elite, including leading planters, merchants, and lawyers. The Spanish-controlled Audiencia was replaced by a Creole-controlled tribunal. On April 25, 1810, following the proposal of the Consulado of Caracas, the new government proclaimed resumption of free trade with all countries but Spain's active enemies.[13] Throughout the remainder of the year, all the principal cities and towns of the Captaincy General of Venezuela joined Caracas — except for Coro and Maracaibo in western Venezuela, which remained loyal to Spain.[14]

The reasons for the Creole elite seizure of power in Chile were almost exclusively political. The colony's economic disputes had been mostly with Peru; the Chilean colonial government had been responsive to its local elite. This broke down. Governor García Carrasco had come to power through a military coup, subsequently recognized and given a semblance of legitimacy by the Supreme Central Junta of Spain. The Audiencia (against which his coup had been directed) continued to oppose him. Governor García Carrasco may also have established a record for poor government. He alienated the University faculty in 1808 by his effort to dictate who the next rector should be. The Governor was also publicly, and perhaps accurately, implicated in mid-1808 in a spectacular scandal: a conspiracy to smuggle British goods into Chile and to murder the captain and eight sailors of the smuggling ship *Scorpion*. He interfered with the Cabildo of Valparaiso's selection of mayors for that city in 1809 and fought the Cabildo of Santiago. This erosion of the already questionable legitimacy of the government was compounded by increasing doubt about the future survival of the Spanish empire.

On May 25, 1810, Governor García Carrasco ordered the arrest of three leading members of Santiago's Creole elite suspected of conspiring against his authority. These wealthy elderly patriarchs were imprisoned until July, when the Governor ordered them deported to Lima. Riots protesting their deportation broke out in Santiago. On July 16, 1810, the Audiencia, supported by the Cabildo of Santiago and the military, deposed the Governor, electing eighty-three-year-old Mateo de Toro Zambrano, Count of the Conquest, as Governor of Chile. Toro was one of the wealthiest of the leading members of the Creole elite.

International events again forced the issue in Santiago. The Council of Regency in Spain had appointed a new governor to take García Carrasco's place. An open meeting of the Cabildo of Santiago voted on September 18, 1810, not to recognize the new governor but to establish a junta in Santiago to govern Chile. The President of the Junta would be interim Governor Toro; the vice-president would be another Creole, the Bishop of Santiago. The other five members of the Junta included two Spaniards, one the Regent of the Audiencia and the other the commander of the regular army; and three Creoles, a wealthy militia colonel, the Mayor of Santiago, and the leading member of the elite of Concepción, Juan Martínez de Rozas.[15]

Dramatic as these events were, they were not utterly unprecedented. The Cabildo of Concepción, Chile, had deposed Governor Antonio de Acuña y Cabrera in 1655, electing a new governor from among the town's citizens. The new governor and the Cabildo accepted the authority of the Crown, the Audiencia, and the Viceroy of Lima, without further disrupting the political system.[16] But the issue in 1810 was not just the deposition of one governor but also the refusal to accept another who had been sent from Spain. Santiago's Creoles appropriated enough legitimacy for themselves, and denied it to Spain, to shake the traditional relationship between Chile and Spain. They also established a junta on their own, modifying the ordinary channels of authority at a time when no Spanish King ruled Spain.

The open meeting of the Cabildo of Santiago also was not without precedent. There had been six such meetings during the first forty years after the conquest in the sixteenth century; there had been at least forty-one open meetings of the Cabildo of Santiago in the seventeenth century, and many more called that never met. There had been three such meetings in 1753-1754 to deal with the commercial crisis of that time. However, open meetings of the Cabildo of Santiago had become rare in the eighteenth century: only five had been called, and only the three at mid-century had met. None had been called since 1776, and none had met since 1754.[17] Thus, although Cabildo open meetings were not unprecedented in theory, they were in fact a new experience for most of the agitated Chileans who gathered in September 1810.

A parallel dispute developed in Santiago's Church circles. There was a struggle between two factions within the ecclesiastical Cabildo of Santiago over Church appointments. One was led by the Vicar of Santiago, and eventual royalist Bishop, José Rodríguez Zorrilla, and the other was led by Vicente Larraín, a member of a huge family clan. The justices of the Audiencia had to intervene to support the Vicar's authority against the demands of the ecclesiastical Cabildo. Although this dispute was at first unrelated to other political issues in the colony, it eventually merged with them. The Vicar became an ally of the Audiencia, jointly opposing the Junta of Santiago in late 1810 and in 1811. Most of the members of the ecclesiastical Cabildo found it easier to slip from rebellion against their Vicar to rebellion against the Governor, the Audiencia, and eventually Spain.[18]

The new government of Venezuela explicitly repudiated the authority of the Council of Regency in Spain, though it pledged its loyalty to King Ferdinand VII. The new Chilean government, in contrast, pledged its loyalty both to the King and to the Council of Regency during his absence. Venezuela's government could hardly wait to establish free trade, and did so upon the enthusiastic recommendation of the Consulado. That of Chile had to override the objections of its own Consulado; it did not proclaim free trade with Spain's allies and with neutrals (behind fairly high tariffs) to raise revenues until five months after the establishment of the junta. Creoles seized power in Venezuela and Chile for different reasons. They shared the need to nationalize decisionmaking under conditions of international uncertainty, but there was a much stronger economic basis for this decision in Venezuela. Political factors were paramount in Chile's first and moderate break with imperial authority.

International economic effects had pluralized the Venezuelan political system, weakening the central authority of the government and giving rise to groups with alternative and autonomous bases of power. Chile, on the other hand, had undergone relatively little transformation; its revolt was almost purely political. Although the Chilean economy had reached a level of maturity where moves toward greater autonomy might have been forthcoming in a few decades, such was not yet the case. The traditionally inspired corporations quelled the abusive exercise of executive authority. Their break with Spain was as limited as possible: they wanted to ensure that the García Carrasco episode would not be repeated and that they would participate in the selection of the Governor. They accepted the Council of Regency in Spain. In Venezuela, where pluralization had proceeded further, the Cabildo acted as an alternative and autonomous source of power, coordinating the efforts of the Creole elite and rejecting the legitimacy of Spain's Council of Regency. Economic factors were important in the decision.

In Mexico, where government centralization had prevailed, the Cabildo of Mexico and other Creole organs vied for power within the existing system, but were far more reluctant to break with Spain than similar groups in the other two colonies were. The Chilean elite could act from its traditional resources; the Venezuelans from their more modern pluralized resources. The Mexican Creole elite in the capital of New Spain failed to act in the absence of either a traditional or modern dispersed power. Revolt in New Spain came not from the center but from the periphery. There was a conspiracy in Valladolid (in western Mexico) in 1809. The conspirators were mostly Creole militia officers, with some lawyers and clergymen. And conspirators in Querétaro in 1810 were neither members of the central elites of the kingdom nor poor. The leader was a parish priest, Miguel Hidalgo. The second in command was the wealthy captain of the Queen's cavalry regiment. Others included militia officers, a regular army officer, a grocer, a farm administrator, a postal officer, a lawyer, and a priest. There was no Count or Marquis or Bishop; its social composition was closest to that of the Gual-España conspiracy. The Hidalgo revolt, which broke out in September 1810, was loyal to King Ferdinand, but its salient characteristics differed drastically from those of Creole seizures of power in Chile and Venezuela.[19]

## Ethnic Cross-Pressures and Elite Political Withdrawal

Individuals often belong to more than one group or stratum. Such multiple memberships may impel individuals politically in convergent or divergent directions. If the pressures are convergent, individuals may move in that direction with little difficulty. If there are cross-pressures, that is, if affiliations pull in opposite directions, individual choices are shaped by the intensity of the cross-pressures. If the intensity is low, choice between two directions may not be difficult. But individuals are apt to withdraw politically, at least for the duration of the cross-pressures, if the pulls in opposite directions are intense. They will avoid making a choice because it is too difficult or too painful.[20]

The cross-pressures hypothesis applies most often to specific, short-range events (an election, a rebellion) where the salience of the pressures is comparable. Over a longer period of time, otherwise cross-pressured persons may be able to engage in sequential behavior, responding to one pressure for a period of time, and then to another. Social roles may be fractured and compartmentalized so that seemingly incompatible identities may coexist within the same person. This can happen either if the time frame is long, or if the pressures have widely divergent salience (that is, one may be a union member and a member of an ethnic group, but one of these pressures may be far more salient than the other).[21]

There are three types of cross-pressures. Individuals may identify with two groups that make incompatible claims on them; or they may both identify with and be repelled by different aspects of different groups pulling in opposing directions; or they may fail to identify with two groups that make incompatible demands on them. Incompatible disidentifications are more likely to reduce participation than incompatible identification.[22] Cross-pressures can affect any of the variants of political participation.

In Spanish America, where there had been a major race war (directly or indirectly experienced) between whites and nonwhites within the memory of the ruling elites in a hierarchical ethnic system, the white Creole elite remained unified, withdrew politically in 1810, and failed to revolt. The hypothesis also applies, although less clearly, in the frontier regions of the empire, where whites and Indians engaged in intermittent warfare. There, too, the whites tended to remain unified and failed to revolt. This hypothesis applies only to the elite at the beginning of a period of possible revolt. This hypothesis of elite political withdrawal need not apply if a revolt had begun in a country's periphery and if it continued for a long time. There would also probably be an erosion of central elite solidarity during a revolt in the periphery, even if the central elite failed to revolt at the outset. Thus, members of the central elite may revolt in the long run, even if their country had experienced an ethnic war.

Many Creoles failed to revolt not because of cross-pressures but because they chose to side with Spain. However, many Creoles abstained politically more from fear of a socioethnic revolution than from love of

Spain. Theirs was a case of incompatible disidentification: repelled by Spain and by the lower ethnic strata, they withdrew politically. The consequence, though not the intention, of such withdrawal was support of Spain.

Creoles were different from Spaniards because they were born in America; they were different from other Americans because they were legally white. Legal, political, social, and economic measures tended to turn categoric strata into actual groups. Creole struggles with Spaniards over who should govern, like those with nonwhites over purity of blood, were salient political issues. The wars of independence were specific focused events. Those cross-pressured may not have liked Spain; but faced with a choice between potential gains by revolt and probable loss from socioethnic revolution, they opted for the status quo. The cleavage within the elite based on place of birth was obscured by the greater salience of the cleavage based on purity of blood. Some had been reminded, recently and devastatingly, that the conflict between the descendants of the conquerors and the descendants of the conquered could explode with ravaging effects.

But not all elites were so cross-pressured. If no major race conflict had been experienced, directly or indirectly, within the memory of the elites of 1810, the salience of the socioethnic cleavage was less, the elite would split, and revolt would occur. Then ethnic cross-pressures would be latent only. There would be much less behavioral inhibition, and political withdrawal would be less likely. This hypothesis applies principally to Cuba and to Coro and Maracaibo in Venezuela. It also applies, though less clearly, in the parallel systems of intermittent ethnic warfare in southern Chile and northern New Spain.

## The Hierarchical Ethnic Systems of Venezuela and Cuba

Three plausible alternative hypotheses need to be considered. One, that these areas failed to revolt because they were very traditional and relatively unaffected by economic or social changes. Two, that they failed to revolt because their Creoles had a special love for Spain or for Spaniards. And three, that the socioethnic issue was no more salient in these areas than anywhere else. There had been considerable mass violence in Venezuela, particularly in Caracas province, but most of it was traditional and accommodable. The social bandits, slave revolts, and other defensive collective violence were dangerous, but the political system had coped with them through repression or compromise. That was not enough to raise the importance of the socioethnic issue enough to inhibit the Creole elite revolt. Tense though ethnic relations may have been in Caracas, there had been no major race war before 1810. The hierarchical ethnic system had been maintained. Not many French planters from Haiti came to Caracas, although some authorities had expressed fear of a second Haiti. There was, in short, no overriding ethnic war fear in Caracas. The Gual-España attempted coup was perceived as a military movement, led by Spaniards themselves, even if black soldiers were in it. The Creole elite remained aloof from it; and it did not arouse ethnic fears.

The Coro revolt of black freedmen and slaves differed from other mass violence because it entailed a modernizing coalition -- the first of its kind. Coro was one of the most modernized areas of Venezuela. The pressures of economic growth had gone far toward transforming its social structure, and modernization pressures were acute. The Cabildo of Coro had aggressively tried to assert Creole superiority over Spaniards in the governing of the city and showed little love for them. But socially turbulent Coro, though modernizing and anti-Spanish, failed to revolt in 1810. The elites there, once bitterly divided, were unified by the black revolt. Family rivalries and rivalries among competing corporations (Cabildo, Church, civil-military authorities) were put aside when confronted by the major socioethnic challenge.

Coro was one of the last bastions of the Spanish empire in Venezuela. It defeated on its own an army of 4,000 militiamen sent by Caracas to "liberate" it, became one of the chief staging areas of royalist armies in their fight against the Creoles, and was one of the last cities in Venezuela to give up the fight for the colonial order and surrender to independence. Socioethnic issues remained paramount within the Coro elite. As late as 1817, while the tide was turning in favor of the patriot armies and their final victories might be in sight, a public manifesto of the attorney general (*síndico procurador*) of Coro's municipal council expressed his alarm over

> the shocks that create anxiety among the noble white families of this City and district, about the ease with which marriages among notoriously unequal persons are formalized these days . . . these facts [are] a public evil that has befallen the people and threaten them with the confusion of classes, subverting the ordered civil hierarchies, that are the essential base of our political system. These people cry out for an end to these abuses. The families of long-standing nobility and known purity of blood live amazed, awaiting the time when one of their own marries a mulatto or mestizo . . . at this rate, the households of time-honored nobility will come to

an end, and the qualities that were obtained by their ancestors in the battlefields, and that their descendants have preserved with so much toil and effort, will be erased forever.[23]

Coro's modernizing and anti-Spanish Creole elite suspended its struggle against the Spaniards when faced with racial war. Because of direct experience it was reluctant to change the political order. It would not allow disruption from Caracas and permitted Spain to launch a counterrevolution from its territory. All the while socioethnic issues remained in the fore of the Coro Creole elite consciousness.

A similar phenomenon seems to have occurred in Maracaibo, although the evidence is less impressive. There were many conspiracies in Venezuela, and most of them had little effect in making the socioethnic issues salient, for they could be easily repressed. The Maracaibo conspiracy in 1799 was different because it was directly connected with Haiti and with Franco-Haitian revolutionary ideas. The assassination of whites and the abolition of slavery seemed to be part of the plan. Thus, the local conspiracy acquired salience for the Maracaibo Creoles. The Maracaibo plot was uncovered in May 1799, and many arrests were made. The black militia sublieutenant Francisco Pirela was the local leader in association with the black and mulatto crews of two ships from Haiti that were stationed off the Maracaibo coastline. Considerable publicity about the event led to fear of a Haitian-sponsored black uprising in Maracaibo.

Maracaibo had exhibited modernizing tendencies somewhat in advance of Caracas and unease under the Spanish colonial system. The city fought the Caracas Company's trade monopoly with zeal and persistence, seeking to limit both the monopoly over the colony's trade and the Spanish monopoly over the monopoly. Maracaibo, too, though modernizing and anti-Spanish, failed to revolt in 1810; and, like Coro, it became a staging area for Spanish counterrevolutionary activity. It was not until January 1821, when the Spanish cause in Venezuela was hopeless, and a mere five months before Bolívar's total victory, that Maracaibo joined the independent republic.[24]

The Coro revolt was distinguished by its modernizing characteristic and setting; the Maracaibo conspiracy was distinguished by the direct Haitian connection. These features were different from the other traditional and accommodable Venezuelan black revolts and conspiracies. An objection may be raised that the black uprisings of Coro and Maracaibo should have deterred and warned Caracas. That would assume a much higher degree of national integration than was present in early-nineteenth-century Venezuela. Caracas had heard about Haiti, Coro, and

Maracaibo, but had not learned from them. The Captaincy General of Venezuela had not been established until 1777. Until that time, western Venezuela (where these cities were located) formed the separate Province of Maracaibo, independent of Caracas and directly dependent on Bogotá. The regional loyalty and a rivalry with Caracas that had developed shaped the response in 1810. The ethnic experiences of western Venezuela and Caracas were also very different. Caracas had not been host to modernizing black revolts or plots as Coro and Maracaibo had. These two regions of the Captaincy General did not share experiences, and communications between Maracaibo and Caracas contributed to this: it took three weeks for mail to travel between the cities. Therefore, given the low level of national integration and shared experiences in Venezuela, Caracas proceeded without learning from the other regions in the Captaincy General, even though it knew about them.[25]

Cuba was a modernizing Spanish colony, probably more so than any other. Ethnic issues among Creoles, Spaniards, and blacks were critically important. From the late 1780s on, the Cuban Creole elite argued strongly and successfully for an acceleration of the slave trade. They began to call for the encouragement of white immigration into Cuba shortly after the Haitian slave revolt to offset the increased numbers of slaves. The latter could not be decreased, so the former had to be increased. As early as January 1792 Francisco de Arango y Parreño, Havana's leading Creole, linked white immigration to the fear of a second Haiti. The Economic Society called for white colonization in November 1794, referring to the Haitian uprising as "the horrible destruction and unheard-of crimes committed there by the Negroes." The Consulado urged white colonization in 1796 to balance the "necessary" increase of slaves.[26]

There were isolated local slave uprisings in plantations throughout most of the island in 1792 and 1793 (near Havana, Trinidad, and Puerto Príncipe). Nicolás Morales, a black freedman, led an uprising in Bayamo in 1795, and another uprising took place in Boca Niguia in 1796.[27] All of these differed very little from those that had taken place sporadically before 1790, but they came to have a new ominous ring. As a result, the debates in the Consulado of Havana turned to safety measures in addition to white immigration in 1796. Nicolás Calvo argued that the Haitian revolt had succeeded because of "discord sowed by traitors." Arango y Parreño proposed that severe police regulations be adopted to prevent slave uprisings, but he concurred with Calvo that a second Haiti was unlikely in Cuba because Spain's slave policies were more humane than the French, and because the whites in Cuba (unlike those in Haiti) were united and loyal to Spain.[28] What started as a mere analysis of the situation soon became a political program for Cuban Creole elites. They would argue, cajole, and lobby, but they stopped short of taking steps or advocating measures that might provoke a second Haiti. The basic legitimacy of the imperial system, including slavery, could not be questioned.

Fear of a Haiti-like situation increased for two reasons. The economic structures of the two islands were similar enough to make comparisons plausible. Both depended on the production of sugar and coffee for export and on slave labor. However, the slaves of Haiti made up an overwhelming majority of the population, in contrast to Cuba where they were a minority. About 30,000 Frenchmen emigrated from Haiti to Cuba between 1790 and 1808, bringing tales of revolt, horror, death, or flight. Although most left when France invaded Spain, their effect on Cuba's white population — about 150,000 in the 1790s — was extraordinary.[29] Philip Foner has argued that "Many Creoles . . . were so frightened by the possibility of Negro revolts that they hardly dared to predicate political liberties for the whites . . . not a single tract in defense of the status quo in Cuba overlooked this slogan." Reviewing the causes for Cuban nonindependence, he concludes: "Most important was the fact that the vast majority of the Creole landowners hesitated to support a movement that might lead to emancipation of the slaves. They were frightened of the consequences that separation and independence might bring in their wake."[30]

Cuba, like Venezuela and Mexico, had a hierarchical ethnic system that had never had a major racial confrontation. But it experienced a race war in surrogate form, brought by migrating French planters from Haiti and fanned by a frightened sugar planter group in Cuba. The Creole elite clung to the status quo: no divided elite, no revolt, no independence.

Insignificant revolts kept the Creole elite and the Spanish government alert, although the basic political system remained remarkably stable throughout the 1820s, that is, through the entire period of the wars of independence on the continent. Two small Masonic conspiracies in Havana and Bayamo in 1809 and 1810 were crushed, and fifteen persons, a majority of whom were freedmen, were arrested. José Aponte, a free black carpenter, organized a conspiracy and established a Central Revolutionary Junta in Havana in late 1811. He also made connections with Haitian General Jean François. This conspiracy had national scope, with support in the cities of Puerto Príncipe, Bayamo, Holguín, and Baracoa, besides Havana and the surrounding areas. Aponte and eight others were seized in 1812, when revolts broke out in various parts of the island and sugar and coffee plantations were destroyed. The revolt was suppressed, but the whites remained fearful.[31]

On November 19, 1822, the *Diario Noticioso* of Havana commented on an expedition from the United States to free Puerto Rico that included among its goals the abolition of slavery and civil equality for blacks. The *Diario's* statement summarized much of the Creole elite attitude:

> The main feature of the conspiracy in Puerto Rico was to promote a rebellion of the blacks against the whites and to transform the island into a new Santo Domingo. This is not surprising for this is the objective of all the incendiaries who seek to promote separatism from the mother country. We know that this is their goal in our own fair island, and that they think nothing of provoking the most dreadful disorders which will destroy the country. Fortunately, the loyal members of our community have too much at stake to countenance such subversive activities.[32]

The Cuban Creoles were not just afraid of the blacks; they had little love for Spaniards. Many Spanish merchants in Cuba had opposed the planters' modernizing demands. When trade modernization eventually resulted from a broad coalition of Cubans and Spaniards, planters and merchants, the Cuban-Spaniard conflict simply shifted to other issues. It became public upon the promulgation of a decree permitting freedom of the press, approved by the Cortes in November 1810 and implemented in Cuba in February 1811. The Spanish party, headed by the Reverend Tomas Gutiérrez de Piñeres (thus called the Piñerista party), and by the Superintendent of the tobacco monopoly, Gómez Rumbau, used the newly freed press to attack the decisionmaking ascendancy of the Cuban Creoles. It claimed that government was too responsive to the Creoles; the Creoles responded in kind. Each side claimed that it represented the best and truest subjects of Spain.

The public disagreement between Creoles and Spaniards erupted again during the brief liberal ascendancy in the early 1820s, as Spain's other colonies became independent. The Creoles and the Piñeristas fought bitterly in the elections of deputies to Cortes in 1822 (which the Creoles won), and over the fate of the Intendant of Havana, whom the Piñeristas succeeded in ousting because he was too responsive to Creole demands. In short, Creole-Spaniard hostility was at least as great in Cuba as in most other colonies in America, perhaps excluding New Spain, throughout the period of the wars of independence.[33]

The Cuban Creoles systematically opposed efforts to upset the social structure anywhere in the empire. They became alienated from liberal Spaniards or Spanish Americans who wanted reform. Leaders of the newly independent American republics had few friendships and contacts with the Cuban elite, and interamerican support for Cuban independence in the 1820s came to naught. Florencio Pérez Comoto, of the Royal Patriotic Society of Havana, denounced Hidalgo's 1810 revolt in New Spain, extending to Mexico the argument about the need for Creole elite unity to preserve the social order.[34]

The Cuban elite fought the empire's liberals in the Spanish Cortes. On May 26, 1811, Miguel Guridi y Alcócer, liberal Mexican deputy to the Cortes, proposed the abolition of the slave trade. He was supported by Spanish liberals. The Cortes debated such proposals in public and at length over the vehement opposition of the deputy from Havana, Andrés de Jáuregui. Upon hearing this, Cuba's Governor Someruelos, the municipal council of Havana, its Consulado and Patriotic Society, protested vigorously that the abolition of the slave trade would cause irreparable harm to the Cuban economy. All Cuban corporations and public authorities were united and commissioned Arango y Parreño to write a long brief, *Representaciones a las Cortes,* to explain the Cuban elite case for the preservation of the slave trade.[35]

The Creoles did not disrupt the internal order. They failed to rebel, not because they loved Spaniards, but for other reasons, including ethnic fear and the responsiveness of the colonial and imperial governments. Ethnic cross-pressures, though not the only cause for the failure to revolt, were an important part of the explanation. The Creoles suffered from incompatible disidentifications with Spaniards and blacks; they withdrew politically. They engaged in the politics of economic lobbying instead, but not in the politics of direct independent government. A consequence, but not a cause, of such withdrawal was preservation of the status quo, hence imperial rule.

## The Parallel Ethnic Systems of Southern Chile and Northern New Spain

Most of the white elites in the parallel ethnic systems in the frontier regions of southern Chile and northern New Spain remained unified and failed to revolt. But the hypothesis applies somewhat less clearly to their cases. Some of the whites in these frontier regions revolted after 1810, albeit often only for a short period of time; they of course joined other regions in the final coming of independence. Alternative hypotheses concerning these areas cannot be rejected; many of the frontier regions were traditional, barely touched by modernization, and they also had special ties to Spain and its key institutions.

The island of Chiloé and the town-fortress of Valdivia, in Chile's southern frontier, were among Spain's final bastions in the Americas. The reconquest of Chile was launched from them under Peruvian leadership early in 1813. Valdivia was briefly allied with Santiago for a few months in late 1811 and early 1812, but it broke with that government in 1812 and sided with the Viceroy of Lima. Although central Chile's independence was secure after the battle of Maipú in April 1818, Valdivia was not conquered until January 1820. And although the battle of Ayacucho in December 1824 is often cited as the final defeat of Spain in continental South America, when even the Viceroyalty of Peru became independent, the island of Chiloé was not forcibly freed until invaded by Chilean troops in January 1826.[36]

Why were they so loyal? These frontier regions in southern Chile were the empire's southernmost military outposts facing hostile Arauco Indians. At the end of the eighteenth century Chiloé had a population of about 22,455, of whom 46.6 percent were Indians. About 18.2 percent of the total white population of Chiloé was in the militia; that proportion may have been as high as 73 percent of the adult white male population. Because they were crucial for imperial defense, the militarized whites of Chiloé received a situado (transfer of funds) from the Viceroyalty of Peru that averaged 40,000 pesos per year throughout the eighteenth century, rising to twice that in the war years at the close of the century.[37] Valdivia also received a situado from Peru averaging 100,000 pesos per year at the beginning of the nineteenth century; it received 36 million pesos from Peru between 1645 and 1810. It had depended on Peru also for food shipments until the beginning of the nineteenth century.[38]

Fear of the Indians, however important it may have been in explaining the prolonged loyalty of these regions, cannot be easily distinguished from alternative explanations. The situado had created a strong fiscal link to the Viceroyalty of Peru, which served as Spain's surrogate in Chile, to be used as leverage to obtain loyalty in the war against Santiago. Although Chile was to assume the responsibility for Valdivia's situado in 1790, Peru continued to contribute the bulk of the funds until the end of colonial rule. Chiloé had actually become a Peruvian, rather than a Chilean, dependency in 1767, to guarantee Chiloé's fiscal and military strength.

These regions were barely touched by modernization. Chiloé's eighteenth-century economy remained stagnant; its foreign trade was monopolized by Peru. It exported wood and fish and had a subsistence cattle production, but it had to import agricultural products. Valdivia experienced a more substantial agricultural, commercial, industrial, and construction development, financed by Peru, in the closing decades of the colony; it had a flourishing shipbuilding industry.[39] But it was well below the modernization levels of Cuba and western Venezuela.

Thus, southern frontier Chile remained loyal to Spain, through its Peruvian surrogate, because of ethnic fears, special ties to Peru, and relatively little modernization. Chiloé and Valdivia responded to the monarchical crisis of the early nineteenth century as central Chile had responded to the War of the Spanish Succession at the beginning of the eighteenth. No matter what the international events may have been, traditional areas remained loyal to Spain. They had to be conquered before they became independent.

The wars of independence had virtually no impact on northwestern Mexico. Troops from central Mexico penetrated southern Sinaloa in December 1810 and January 1811, but were quickly repelled. There was no autonomous movement toward insurrection in Sinaloa, Sonora, and Baja California until the early 1820s, when a conservative military independence movement swept all the provinces.[40] Farther north, the principal effect of the wars of independence on New Mexico was to disrupt alliances between the Spanish forces and Indian tribes; Arizona remained peaceful for a longer time.[41]

Northeast Mexico—the Provincias Internas—was more influenced by its own movement toward independence. Nuevo Santander (Tamaulipas), Nuevo León, Coahuila, and Texas had a strong military force because Indian pacification had not been completed and colonization had been slow. Towns in Tamaulipas joined the rebellion beginning in January 1811. Coahuila, more vulnerable to less pacified Indians, joined the rebellion only after it had been invaded by patriot forces. At Monterrey the Governor of Nuevo León joined the rebellion, but most of the province was lukewarm. Some of these provincial troops, however, refused to execute Spaniards and had second thoughts about the wisdom of insurrection. There was only one major battle in the entire Provincias Internas. Many of the small insurgent bands that roamed about the area in early 1811 were unable to recruit supporters. By the spring of that year northeast Mexico was pacified by the royalists in a three-month campaign, not to be disturbed again until the early 1820s.[42] The war of independence had more support in Tamaulipas than in the other northeast provinces. This may have been because there was less fear of Indians in this province than there was in Coahuila or in northwest Mexico. Indians accounted for only 23.2 percent of the population of the Tamaulipas region in 1810, whereas they are estimated to have accounted for 85 percent of the population of New Spain at that time. Indians even accounted for 24 percent of the population of Mexico City in 1810.[43]

Fear of Indians apparently ensured the unity and loyalty of northwest Mexico and of that part of northeast Mexico most affected by unpacified Indians. Only where Indians had become less of a problem did the war of independence prosper. But these frontier areas were among the empire's least modernized. And high military presence tied many to Spain. As in southern Chile, ethnic fears, special ties, and limited modernization accounted for regional unity and loyalty.

## Loyalty in Cuba

Because the Cuban elite failed to revolt, the shell of the political system did not crack there. Its traditional mass politics did not overflow to disrupt the empire. But why did the Cuban slaves fail to revolt, and what was the attitude of black freedmen toward Spain? Freedmen played a critical role in Cuban conspiracies, especially after 1810. Rapid economic change during the first third of the nineteenth century partly altered their role, reducing their social incorporation in comparison to what it had been in the late eighteenth century. Some freedmen may have suffered from sporadic efforts to reenslave them after 1790. Four reasons suggest that this hypothesis is plausible.

First is the nearly insatiable demand for slave labor on the part of the Cuban economy (see Table 3.2). The Anglo-Spanish treaty of 1817, imposed by England, planned the gradual abolition of the slave trade by 1820. The treaty triggered an acceleration of the trade; 67,059 slaves were brought to Cuba between 1817 and 1820.[44] The desperate search for labor may have led to the reenslavement of freedmen.

Second, there was a net decline of over 7,000 free blacks between 1817 and 1827. Assuming that the freedman population of 1817 grew at the same rate as the population as a whole, and assuming zero slave manumission, then the freedman population of 1827 should have been at least 144,000, instead of a mere 106,494, with an estimated deficit of about 38,000 persons, over one-quarter. Indeed, the freedman population should have grown faster than the population as a whole as a result of population growth and slave manumission. If the freedman population had grown between 1817 and 1827 at the same average annual rate that it grew between 1792 and 1817, then there should have been at least 175,000 freedmen in 1827, with a deficit of about 69,000 persons, or about 40 percent of the likely freedman population in 1827. If there was reenslavement, manumission could have been close to zero. Because many slaves were imported and there was some white immigration during these years, then the growth rate of the freedman population may have been slower than the growth rate of the population as a whole. Therefore, assuming the freedman population growth rate was only one-half the growth rate of the entire population between 1817 and 1827 (an annual average of 1.38 percent), and manumission was zero, this would yield a freedman population of about 130,000 in 1827, with a deficit of 24,000 missing freedmen. Several thousand freedmen may have been subject to reenslavement under this third most conservative estimate.[45]

Third, Havana had a large floating and only partially employed population composed heavily of freedmen. The Cuban elite spent a great deal of time and energy studying ways to suppress vagrancy and under-employment. All their recommendations amounted to the same thing: send them off to the fields and mills. The way was thus open for extensive reenslavement. The Crown stimulated a campaign to capture fugitive slaves. The royal order of 1796, written by Arango, was originally proposed by the Cuban elite. Many hunted down escaped slaves. Many freedmen were probably reenslaved in this way because of the great support for such activities and the profits to be made in recapturing fugitive slaves.[46]

Finally, the reenslavement hypothesis has cross-national support. Something similar happened in Puerto Rico. Sidney Mintz has argued that "the lack of sufficient slaves [in Puerto Rico] meant that some other source of labor supply had to be found. It was in the form of the coercion of free but landless citizens to work on the plantations." Laws were passed to exact more labor from the landless freedmen between 1815 and 1850.[47] This may have been a general practice in the Spanish Caribbean.

The increase in freedmen involvement in conspiracies and revolts can be easily explained if some were reenslaved. Nevertheless, the persistence of relatively favorable conditions prevented a mass uprising of freedmen. They continued serving in the militias throughout this first quarter of the nineteenth century; moreover, the evidence about wealthy freedmen reviewed earlier dates from this period. Enough freedmen may have been reenslaved to arouse a part of Cuba's free black community, but enough blacks remained free and loyal, defending the empire militarily and prospering.

Cuban slaves benefited from widespread manumission. Urban slaves had many opportunities for purchasing their freedom and engaging in a variety of jobs. But the dependence of sugar production on slavery resulted in especially brutal oppression. The expansion of the sugar industry after 1790 must have brought about a worsening of conditions for slaves who were shifted from "easy" to "tough" commercial plantations. Why did not more revolt?

The proportion of slaves in the brutal jobs of sugar production never reached a majority of the slaves in Cuba. Humboldt estimated that 25.4 percent lived on sugar plantations in 1825. Estimates from 1827-1830 put the number at 17.4 percent. The 1846 census estimates that they were 18 percent of the total black population. The peak was apparently reached in 1860, when sugar workers accounted for 38 percent of all the slaves and 24 percent of the black population.[48] In short, the majority of slaves worked on other kinds of plantations where the oppression and discipline were less severe, or in producing nonplantation crops, or in urban settings.

Second, the condition of slaves on the sugar plantations may not have worsened. The tendency between the 1790s and 1820s was to buy only African males just off the boat. They accounted for 81.8 percent of all the slaves in sugar mills from 1791 to 1822, a higher proportion than during preceding or subsequent periods. Women (African or Cuban-born) made up only 16 percent of the slaves.[49] If the *bozales* (African males) from the slave trade worked the sugar plantations, very few Cuban slaves who had been engaged in easy jobs were shifted to sugar production, so the condition of the slaves already in Cuba did not worsen much as a result of sugar production.

Third, slaveowners made sure that the bozales were so oppressed that they had little time to think about or do anything else. They were confined to barracks, and locked up at night. They worked six days a week during the harvest, with no more than five hours' sleep a day. Many slaveowners deliberately purchased fewer slaves than needed and overworked their gangs. The scarcity of women and children saved extra overhead expenses. Life expectancy in those early plantations may have been no more than seven years from the time of arrival -- although conditions may have improved somewhat after 1830.[50] In short, sugar production may not have worsened the conditions of "raw" slaves because they expected nothing better.

Finally, gambling may have diverted the poor in Cuba, more than in other countries, from politics. The government established a lottery in 1812 and systematically supported gambling and related entertainment. Most popular vices flowered on the island in the 1820s. While continental Spanish America was striking the final blows for independence, the Cubans relaxed social discipline. José Saco, one of the most perceptive analysts of Cuban society in the middle nineteenth century, described the central role of gambling in Cuban life. "There is no city, town, or corner of the island of Cuba," he wrote in 1831, "which has not been reached by this devouring cancer." He noted that "the lottery houses are open from dawn until ten or eleven o'clock at night."[51]

Although the first reaction to the collapse of imperial legitimacy in the four colonies was loyalty, too much had changed in Spanish America to allow a repetition of the mild response of the war of the Spanish succession a century earlier. Varieties of traditional but disruptive political participation began to appear in three of the four colonies; these led eventually to the revolts under the pressures of internal and international events. Spaniards as well as Creoles contributed to the destruction of political order. Ethnic cross-pressures were able to contain, in a few colonies or areas, the pressures that resulted in the dissolution of the empire elsewhere. Continued accommodation of traditional mass politics was also successful in Cuba, where the elite did not divide and fundamental legitimacy was not challenged. The choice between loyalty or insurrection in 1810 had little to do with metropolitan Spain's policies. Civil war broke out over much of Spanish America as a result of local events, constraints, and opportunities. In these early years of struggle, the metropolis was too weak to provide order or to generate hatred.

# 10

# War and Political Mobilization: First Phase

As the local colonial Creole and Spanish elites battled each other with words or with guns, trying to appropriate legitimacy, the dam that had contained mass politics broke, and the flood ensued. Otherwise defensive reactionary collective violence, slave revolts, social banditry, and ethnic conflict turned furiously disruptive. The elite lit the fuse; the mass dynamite exploded.

## New Spain

The Hidalgo revolt began in the Bajío, the complex modernizing area northwest of Mexico City. The underlying social and economic tensions there worsened in 1809 and 1810 to accelerate real and perceived suffering. The number of working looms in Querétaro, the principal textile city, dropped by 18 percent, from an average of 217 between 1802 and 1804 to one of 178 during the next three years. Although there was a recovery in 1809, the wars of independence devastated the city's textile economy. There were only 124 working looms in Querétaro in 1816, the lowest number since 1787.[1]

An agricultural crisis in 1809-1810 was the result of prolonged drought and premature freezing. The price of good maize, between 18 and 22 reales per fanega in 1807, rose to between 23 and 26 during the first half of 1809. In the Fall of 1809, thirty of forty-one districts in the central Mexican intendancy reported bad harvests. The price of good maize rose to 34 reales per fanega by the end of 1809; from June to August 1810 it rose to 36, almost double the 1807 level.[2] Hidalgo revolted in September 1810.

Food was also needed to feed the mules that kept the mining industry's mills running. The number of mills actively grinding in 1810 had fallen by about 30 percent; unemployment followed. The Cabildo of Guanajuato, on September 22, 1810 (one week after Hidalgo's revolt), said that the mine workers "have suffered all the effects of the hunger and sickness of this calamitous year. They . . . were the first to find their efforts rendered fruitless by the extreme decadence at which the mines have arrived."[3]

Nevertheless, economic hardship alone cannot explain the Bajío's insurrection in 1810. There had been ten agricultural crises in Mexico from 1724 to 1810. Food crises were thus not unprecedented. Moreover, the price rise in 1809-10, bad as it was, was much milder than that of the "year of hunger," 1785-86. The price of good maize had risen from 13 reales per fanega in 1784 to a high of 48 in 1786 -- more than three and a half times. Yet no war broke out in 1786 -- although social banditry increased -- but one did in 1810.[4] The critical role of political leadership in 1810 thus needs to be examined.

## Charismatic Political Participation

Charismatic authority, according to Max Weber, rests on "devotion to the specific and exceptional sanctity, heroism or exemplary character of an individual person, and on the normative patterns of persons revealed or ordained by him." Charismatically induced political participation disrupts the established political order because its bases of legitimation are challenged. As Weber puts it, "pure charisma does not know any 'legitimacy' other than that flowing from personal strength."[5] Charismatic authority is also disruptive because it is inherently unstable. The charismatic leader must prove himself continuously to his people. He may have internal doubts. He may be forsaken by his followers for yet another supercharismatic leader.[6]

David Apter has argued with respect to Ghana that "charisma and its functions has been the central motivating feature by which men have responded in the Gold Coast, so far as authority shifts are concerned . . . [especially] in the changing social life of rural Gold Coast." Yet the importance of charisma began to fade shortly after Ghana's independence, when traditional bases of legitimation sought to reassert themselves. The postindependence government often responded through coercion. The routinization of charisma was not successfully achieved, and sustaining it in a complex sociopolitical situation proved impossible.[7] Charismatic legitimation appeared and declined in several West African states in the 1960s; it was replaced by a wave of military coups.[8]

Charismatic legitimation has two disruptive effects on political participation. In early stages, charismatically induced participation weakens, erodes, or destroys whatever legal-rational legitimation there may have been in the colonial-bureaucratic structures. Men and women respond to the charismatic hero, and are externally mobilized by him to serve his own interests. In later stages, especially in societies past a primitive level of social differentiation, charismatic legitimation is difficult to sustain. It may exhaust itself. It may turn to coercion. Charismatically induced participation may then decline, and the bases of government may shift merely to those who can coerce most effectively. Because charismatically induced political participation responds to an external stimulus, it may cease when the stimulus ceases. Thus, the early political activists may be nowhere to be found when the praetorian guard is about to dismiss the erstwhile hero from political power. Except for the charismatic-based claim to legitimacy, other aspects of this sort of political participation are traditional, including those limitations typical of lower-class movements already mentioned.

Hidalgo was a charismatic political leader. The parish priest, he spoke Indian languages and dialects and was popular among Indians and the poor. Though nominally loyal to King Ferdinand, he called on all Americans, regardless of color and social position, to revolt against the Spaniards. He promised the abolition of the Indian tribute — a mainstay of the treasury — as well as the abolition of slavery, reduction of taxes, elimination of restrictions on industrial and agricultural production, a stimulus to wine production, and an end to taxes on rum or pulque. Part of Hidalgo's economic program was a clear appeal to the modernizing and entrepreneurial forces of the Bajío. His proposals concerning slavery, the tribute, and "sin taxes" on liquor appealed to the poor.

Hidalgo's appeal to the poor, however, relied less on programs and more on symbols, slogans, and banners, as befitted charismatic leadership and political participation. Religious orthodoxy was rigorously maintained. The rebels adopted the image of the Virgin of Guadalupe as their symbol. Indeed, the revolt had the appearance of a religious crusade, with a priest and his people doing battle against evil on behalf of the monarchy and religion.[9]

The preexisting social forces of the Bajío area, contained and accommodated up to this point, entered Hidalgo's revolt. The social bandits of the marginal areas could work easily under his leadership. Their guerrilla expertise could be put to good use. The Bajío's rural population was not enslaved. They were mobile and free enough to become the shock forces of insurrection. And the miners, whose social history in the preceding quarter-century was one of impoverishment and protest, joined Hidalgo too. The miners of Valenciana mine, the wealthiest and most productive of the area, were organized into a military regiment.[10]

A revolt of provincial elite leaders, led by a charismatic political leader, mobilized the Indians, the miners, and the social bandits into a large conglomerate. The revolt did not come from these masses; they were mobilized by external agents: the elite and a charismatic leader. The rebel army was a poorly coordinated and loosely integrated horde. The stated goals of the leadership reflected the modernizing characteristics of the area where the rebellion began. They were forward-looking; they put forth new claims. But the political participation of the masses was characterized by plunder and murder, by desire for personal gain, and by lack of discipline. This is characteristic of traditional political participation. When traditional political participants unite, they do so as a conglomerate, not a coalition. Their goals are poorly integrated. Each participant may have a limited scope of issues to affect — from stimulating wine production, to robbing a leading citizen, to rape. The elite may have a program; the conglomerate does not. The struggle for advantage may be uncoordinated, but it exists. The conglomerate is held together by a volatile charismatic leader.

Another issue was ethnic hatred of Spaniards. One way of distinguishing ethnic from other sources of conflict in the midst of violence is to examine the characteristics of the target population. In New Spain the rebel conglomerate's target was the Spaniards in particular and whites in general — rich, middle-income, or poor. Hidalgo's forces moved on the city of Guanajuato. He led some 9,000 Indians with bows and arrows, slings and clubs; 4,000 Indians with lances and machetes; 12,000 Indians, mestizos, and blacks on horseback; and only 100 veteran troops from the regiment of the Queen of San Miguel `el Grande. Guanajuato was defended by some 300 Spaniards and Creoles. They were all massacred. The city was open to two days of plundering. Hidalgo was reluctant to discipline his troops, using the fruits of pillage as rewards for combat duty. Shortly therafter, 60 Spaniards were killed at Valladolid, and hundreds more would die. Many of these were noncombatants.[11]

The rebellion had three general characteristics. Its claim to legitimacy derived from charismatic political leadership inducing lower-class participation. Second, the general appeals of the provincial elite had a broad politico-economic character that reflected its interests. This was the only modernizing element in the revolt. And third, the encompassing principle identifying the target of the mass political participants was ethnicity. The mass political participation was a mixture of defensive violence and social banditry, with but a loose political cover. This traditional political participation had become thoroughly disruptive, as the social and political mold which held it together had broken down. A hierarchical system of ethnicity, normally more peaceful than a parallel system, is likely to lead to a major social war once the social cement cracks.

## Venezuela

The Venezuelan rebels' approach to the social question was just the opposite. They were members of the central elite in Caracas and, unlike the provincial elite in the Mexican Bajío, stood to lose heavily if the socioeconomic order were overturned. Consequently, the key characteristic of the early Venezuelan rebellion was the effort to bring about political independence while "freezing" the rest of the social system. This was a Creole elite seizure of political power. Though these Creoles immediately took some modernizing steps to free foreign trade, they were keenly concerned with preventing further modernization of the society, the polity, or the economy. Their goal was to transfer legitimacy from the Crown to themselves, while otherwise preserving a traditional political system, with controlled structural change such as free trade -- and no more.

Venezuela, dropping the fiction of loyalty to King Ferdinand VII, proclaimed complete independence from Spain in July 1811. It was the first Spanish colony to do so; this is in accord with the view that the Venezuelan situation was the most extreme and least accommodable in the late empire. Immediately thereafter, the city of Valencia rose against Caracas and pledged its loyalty to the king. The contrast between the social policies adopted in Caracas and Valencia is striking.

On July 13, 1811, the Supreme Junta of Caracas called upon the citizenry to defend the republic. But it insisted on going into battle with its army preserving strict ethnic segregation. Articles VII and XVI of the decree said that citizens would gather "in Trinidad Plaza . . . The whites would enlist before the Church; the blacks to the east, and the mulattoes to the south . . . The slaves would remain at home at their masters' commands, without leaving them except under government orders."[12] The decree of the Supreme Junta of Caracas of June 25, 1811, had stipulated that militia battalions of whites and blacks would remain segregated, except that the top two officers of the black militia battalions were to be white. It also preserved the preexisting racial salary differential whereby white militia officers would get higher salaries than black militia officers of the same rank.[13] Caracas abolished the slave trade formally; in fact, it had been suspended informally for many years.

The royalist forces at Valencia, on the other hand, proclaimed the abolition of slavery and the civil equality of all citizens. The actions of republican Creoles and royalist Spaniards were consistent with the

Venezuelan tradition of race relations. But their consequences may have been unexpected. When the patriot, republican armies of General Miranda attacked Valencia, that city's black militiamen were among its main counterrevolutionary defenders.

The Caracas Creoles responded by repressing blacks. The following was published in *La Gaceta* on July 26, 1811: "The Supreme Executive Power has ordered the establishment . . . of Patrols or National Guards for the capture of fugitive slaves." The Guards "will make sure that necessary order is maintained in this part of our population dedicated to land cultivation." It generously concluded that "honest and hard-working slaves need not be afraid of these measures of economics and security with which the government seeks the well-being of the people of the country."[14] This decree also reflected the plantation labor shortage that Venezuela experienced in the late colonial period. The Creole elite tried to ensure the preservation of law and order and to increase its labor supply by capturing fugitive slaves, even in the middle of the war of independence. They were willing to alienate blacks and even risk losing the war for the sake of narrower political and economic interests.

## Counterinsurgency

One variety of incumbent response is counterinsurgency. The incumbent provokes or supports an insurgency against its challengers, against the government that the rebels seek to establish. There are two necessary preconditions for this incumbent response. The society must be highly fragmented or segmented, often in ethnic terms. And the incumbent government must have failed to establish full control over a given ethnic, cultural, or other social group prior to the revolt. This group could have had some autonomy subject to challenge by the rebellious countergovernment; or it may have been highly antagonistic to those who had rebelled to challenge the incumbent. In short, the social and political situation resembled simultaneous but different games. The relation between incumbent and rebels was zero-sum, where one's gains were another's losses, while the relation between the third group and either one of the other two was variable-sum, where there could be joint gains or losses.

When incumbents are challenged, they may risk a possible increased marginal long-term loss of control over the third group in order to decrease the probability of complete defeat by the rebels. Incumbents in desperate straits may promote counterinsurgency even in a largely subjugated group if the probability of immediate defeat at the hands of the rebels is quite high.

Counterinsurgency has been a time-honored incumbent response. For example, French commando warfare behind Viet Minh lines in Indochina (*Groupement de Commandos Mixtes Aéroportés* or *Groupement Mixte d'Intervention*) began in 1951; by 1954 some 15,000 fighters were involved. The fighting force was composed of a handful of French officers leading tribesmen who were ethnically and culturally different from the fighters in the Viet Minh forces. The nature of French-tribesmen relations was akin to a military alliance in international politics. The Meo, T'ai, and Moi tribesmen remained loyal to the French, for the French had treated them more fairly than they had been treated by the majority population. Since 1960 a special relationship developed in Laos between the Meo tribesmen and United States agents and forces carrying on the same technique in the next phase of the Indochina war. This technique was also illustrated in Indochina by relations among the religious sects, the Viet Minh, and the Saigon government. Cultural, religious, and military differentiation was important. The Cao Dai and the Hoa Hao sects pursued their own policies and interests in variable-sum games, alternatively fighting against or cooperating with incumbents and challengers.[15]

### Venezuela

The colonial governments and the imperial government responded to the early revolts and to the explosive social issue with a mixture of creativity and desperation. The Spanish response in Venezuela, characterized by desperation, led to a strategy of counterinsurgency. Crown officials mobilized the blacks against the white Creole elite risking more than marginal long-term loss of control. Venezuelan blacks were partly autonomous (freedmen, escaped slaves) and partly subjugated (slaves). Crown officials risked a social transformation with the abolition of slavery and the introduction of civil equality, but they were willing to pay this price in 1811. The royalist forces took the initiative in the political mobilization of blacks against Caracas to prevent a near-certain defeat by the rebels. In an ethnically fragmented Venezuelan society, neither the Crown nor the rebels had established complete control over the blacks. The government's appeal to the blacks in the short term against the rebels was a feasible strategy because the social and political distance between Creole elite rebels and the blacks they had long oppressed was greater than the distance between the blacks and the Crown, which had often supported black mobility over Creole elite objections. Black militia First Captains from Caracas, Aragua, and Valencia, for example, had supported the Captain General of Venezuela against the

Caracas Creole conspiracy of 1808. They pledged to fight ruthlessly if necessary to uphold the empire, expressing in writing their hatred of the Creoles.[16]

The first Venezuelan republic was defeated militarily in the summer of 1812, but the fight had been resumed by April 1813. The strategy of counterinsurgency, begun in 1812, took hold by 1813. General Simón Bolívar and the patriot forces had reentered Caracas by August 1813. The empire was fading in northern South America. The Creole elite, however, had not given much ground in its desire to "freeze" the social order. Military salaries had been equalized for all ranks in December 1811, so that equal work and equal risk would get equal pay. But the National Guard was introduced once again in 1813, as in 1811, to keep blacks in their place and recapture fugitive slaves.[17] Although the Creole Constitution of 1811 abolished legal ethnic discrimination and the slave trade (in fact, long interrupted), it preserved slavery and limited suffrage to property owners. These policies were implemented, even though Bolívar, among others, had perceived that the Spaniards had been mobilizing the blacks against the Creoles since 1812. He wrote in 1813 about the royalist campaign of the first half of 1812, which had ended in the defeat of the patriot armies: "a revolution of blacks, free and slave, broke out in the eastern coastal valleys, provoked, supplied, and supported by agents of [Spanish General] Monteverde. These inhuman and vile people, feeding upon the blood and property of the patriots . . . committed the most horrible assassinations, thefts, assaults, and devastation."[18] The would-be Creole elite Liberator of Venezuela had not yet acquired a sensitive understanding of the social condition of those black slaves and freedmen, nor had he come to realize that the balance of political forces rested on the ability to mobilize the black population to one side or another.

Slave revolts had erupted in the eastern coastal valleys by 1812. Whites, regardless of political persuasion, were the target, because ethnicity was the encompassing principle between 1812 and 1813. A coalition between blacks and the forces loyal to Spain was built up. The slave landlords of Caracas had revolted. They had upset the legitimate and stable normative system. They had spoken of freedom and self-determination. Yet they still oppressed the blacks, while freedmen perceived the Crown as a protector. The turning point was reached by 1813 when the commander of the republican forces, Bolívar, proclaimed "war to the death." The slaves, the fugitive slaves, and the freedmen from the plains joined those from the coast and rose up against the white lords of Caracas. Social banditry and defensive collective violence were politically and militarily mobilized, with little regard for ideology, by the royalist officer José Tomás Boves.

Boves had as many as ten or twelve thousand troops, but no more than a hundred and sixty were Spaniards. Although he was conscious of being an officer of the king, his target was the white population, combatant or noncombatant. He ordered the execution of the eighty-seven whites found in the town of Calabozo after the town had been taken over. Total white extermination continued in Santa Rosa. Between four and five hundred whites were killed in the Aragua town church. Estimates of the whites killed in Barcelona reached one thousand. A black lieutenant of Boves, Rosete, was responsible for the deaths of three hundred whites killed in the town of Ocumare.[19]

Black plainsmen were mobilized through a combination of charisma and economic interest. The Venezuelan historian Juan Uslar Pietri has written some very suggestive passages about the nature of Boves' legitimate authority:

> the plainsmen feared Boves; they knew that he was a tough man, capable of any action. He set the example in battle by being at the head of his soldiers . . . Courage was the only grounds on which respect could be gained from those guerrillas. All the men had blind faith in him . . . He led the life of a simple soldier, he spoke to them in their own dialects, he ate with them, he slept with them, and they were all his joy and entertainment . . . Boves, without manners or uniform, half-naked, spear in hand . . . preaching hatred of the whites and the wealthy, distributing their riches and permitting unrestrained pillage . . . an undisciplined and bloody guerrilla, led by terrible people who knew little of military tradition, and who were mostly slaves, smugglers, assassins, foremen, and convicts.[20]

The personal qualities of leadership were striking. The men followed him in full faith. Courage was the source of legitimacy. Political and military participation depended on mobilization by this striking leader. Charismatic political participation had drawn from social banditry and defensive collective violence, accommodable up to then. The intrusion of charismatic mobilization as a government strategy turned otherwise accommodable into disruptive participation. There were also economic incentives, for Boves permitted pillage by his troops, sometimes supervising it in order to supply his troops. Pillage served as an incentive to recruit troops and as a method of continuous payment.[21]

The Creole elite persisted in its efforts to "freeze" the social order, capture escaped slaves to ensure the labor supply, and defend landed property from invasions by freedmen or escaped slaves. This policy had the full support of Bolívar. The chief executive officer (*prior*) of the Consulado of Caracas wrote on April 29, 1814: "By order of His Excellency the Liberator, an assembly of landowners from the plains, Valencia, and the valleys of Aragua, Tuy, and Barlovento is hereby called so that they should exchange views about the establishment of regular patrols, which had existed before to trap bandits, capture fugitives, and preserve all landed property free from invasion."[22]

The power and the glory of Boves and his black plainsmen culminated in July 1814. Bolívar's armies were defeated. The Republic collapsed. The army of Boves entered Caracas and proclaimed the restoration of the empire. Bolívar summarized the issue well when, addressing himself to the Creole elite, he wrote: "Your brothers, not the Spaniards, have torn the country apart."[23]

Yet charismatic political participation is inherently unstable. As an officer of the Crown, Boves was supposed to restore royal authority; but he had unleashed a racial war which shook the foundations of Venezuelan society. The formal bureaucratic authority of the Crown was not upheld by Boves, who undermined military hierarchy and organization by substituting himself as the only source of authority and legitimacy. Whenever his soldiers disliked an intermediate officer, they asked Boves to remove him, and Boves repeatedly consented.[24] Promotion and demotion depended on his own personal authority. If he saved Venezuela for the Crown in the short run, he also destroyed the basis of political reconstruction by identifying authority with himself.

## Politicization of Socioethnic Cleavages

A second variety of incumbent response is the simultaneous politicization of significant social and ethnic cleavages by incumbent and challenger. The first precondition necessary for counterinsurgency must also be present for this strategy. A key difference is that the ruler's ideology, norms, and goals stress a type of government "above" those social cleavages. Even if the incumbent's authority over culturally or ethnically differentiated groups is not very strong, the government seeks political stability. This is characteristic of multinational empires as well as many states of Africa and Asia, independent since World War II, that have sought to stress the illegitimacy of those within-state differences. It is costly for the ruler to politicize the social cleavages perceived to be illegitimate because of the ruler's ideology, norms, and goals. Thus, the rebel challengers must typically take the initiative; under counterinsurgency, in contrast, the incumbent takes the initiative. The fragility of multinational political systems is seriously strained by the simultaneous politicization of significant social cleavages, but that cost must be paid if the incumbent is to survive.

There is often a significant change of the political system, even if the rebellion is defeated, when this strategy is adopted. For example, the Communist Party of Malaya after World War II sought to punish those who had collaborated with Japan. The encompassing principle of the conflict became ethnicity, overriding either communism or collaboration. The rebels' challenge came to be perceived as one of Chinese versus Malays and Indians. In order to win Malay support the British government futher politicized the ethnic cleavages. As a result, the civil service, regular police, special constables, and home guards were mostly Malays.[25] A similar sequence of events took place in Kenya during the Mau Mau "emergency". Those Kikuyu who had revolted felt a deep need for unity, which led them to an increased use of tribal as opposed to African national symbols; they inhibited participation by other tribes in their revolt. The British then isolated the Kikuyu and closely related tribes; up to fifty thousand persons of the Kikuyu, Embu, and Meru tribes may have been detained. The Kikuyu-non-Kikuyu cleavage was politicized simultaneously by government and opposition.[26] In the medium term, the simultaneous politicization of social cleavages and the steps toward reform taken to defeat the "emergencies" resulted in significant changes within the political systems. The British won the battle, but lost the challenge. They had to share legitimacy. The empire could not be maintained, and independence would be forthcoming.

Lower-class political participants, when mobilized, respond to politics in similar ways, whether they are mobilized by government or opposition. Their scope, goals, and perspectives remain narrow; they are very loosely integrated in a larger political movement. They may refuse to fight in areas far from their villages. They may desert if their families are threatened. They may refuse to come to the aid of distant allies.[27]

In New Spain the government followed this second type of response. When ethnic mobilization was initiated by the rebels, the colonial government in Mexico City resorted to the politicization of ethnic cleavages up to the point where its ideology and norm as a multinational empire might be threatened. The government responded to the rebels in kind, mobilizing the white Spanish and Creole population, but making certain also of some Indian support to preserve multinational norms.

There were critical differences between the situation in Mexico and Venezuela. The Venezuelan elite rebels sought to freeze the social order.

The Mexican elite rebels sought to change it. A desperate colonial government took the initiative and seized on socioethnic issues in Venezuela. The government in Mexico did not engage in socioethnic politicization until forced to do so by rebel mobilization. The consequences were similar: severe ethnic conflict.

The royalist argument attempted to unite the two Spanish elements against Hidalgo. The colonial government stressed ethnic bonds: common ancestry, blood, religion, monarch, intermarriage, and socioeconomic interest within the white segment of the population. The proclamations of government and church called upon the Creoles to rally not only to Spain but also to their ethnic group. Bishop-elect Abad y Queipo of Michoacán proclaimed on October 8, 1810, that "the priest Hidalgo and his subordinates intend to persuade and are persuading the Indians that they are the owners and masters of the land, of which the Spaniards deprived them by conquest, and that by the same means they would restore them to the same Indians." Individual Creoles made their decisions out of fear of an ethnic war. The armies of Hidalgo reached the edge of Mexico City within six weeks after the beginning of the uprising. Somewhat to the surprise of the revolutionary leaders, the city's Creoles turned against them. Hidalgo had to retreat from Mexico City.

The Crown had used the printing press to mobilize the Creole elite. All printing presses were in government hands during the critical six weeks prior to Hidalgo's retreat from Mexico City on November 2. Given the low level of social mobilization, and the fact that it was limited to whites, it is clear that the white elite was the target of the publication campaign. The rate of items published per week was 3.6 in 1809, 4.5 in 1810, and 2.8 in 1811. Throughout 1810, however, there was an extraordinary increase of the rate of publication, from 1.9 items per week for the year's first thirty-seven weeks to 15.38 items per week during the critical six and a half weeks between Hidalgo's revolt and his retreat from Mexico City (September 15-November 2). The rate of publication for the balance of 1810 remained high (8.5 items per week). Almost as many titles were published between September and December 1810 as in all of 1809, and more were published than in 1811.[28]

The Viceroy completed the job of circumscribing the domain of the Hidalgo revolt by mobilizing those Indians who had not been affected by it. He abolished the Indian tribute in October 1810 and ordered the decree translated into the Nahuatl language. Indians in corporate villages in central Mexico supported the government. A part of the hierarchical ethnic system could withstand the challenge.

The overriding critical issue was the role of ethnicity in decisionmaking. Other arguments appealed to the Creole elite, but none had so strong an effect as the description of "Hidalgo's horde."[29] As in Venezuela, the movement for independence had been largely defeated by the middle of the decade.

## Cooptation

The third kind of incumbent response, cooptation, is less threatening to the government. The integrity and continuity of the political system had been risked by the incumbent in the long term for the sake of survival in the short term through the use of other strategies. No such long-term risk is perceived by the government in this variant, though there may be one. The incumbent makes relatively marginal adjustments within the existing political system in order to win groups and strata over to its side. Some may be won over by genuine reform, others by the illusion of it, and yet others by having been given an even greater access to privilege and the spoils of power. Yet all are coopted. Elections may be introduced where there had been none before. Policies toward agriculture or other sectors of the economy may be changed; land tenure and use may be modified, often to the benefit of elite groups, and usually highly publicized in order to maximize support.

Cooptation is often used with other methods (as in Malaya and Kenya). One of the more successful recent cases took place in the Ivory Coast. Felix Houphouet-Boigny and his political party (PDCI) were political radicals immediately following World War II, challenging French rule in the Ivory Coast. The French responded with repression, and some simultaneous politicization of rival ethnic groups, but during the 1950s gradually turned to cooptation. Houphouet-Boigny, a full minister in the French government under Guy Mollet in 1955, supported the early Gaullist position rejecting independence in the later 1950s and subsequently led the Ivory Coast to reluctant independence, while continuing deep political, economic, and cultural ties with France.[30] A much less successful example of cooptation took place in Guinea. The French government there appeared to determine electoral outcomes as late as 1954, even if it meant suppressing opposition victory. As in the rest of West Africa, the loi cadre of 1956 reformed the political system and permitted wider electoral participation. Sékou Touré rose to power, but he and Guinea were rewarded much less than the Ivory Coast. Guinea was the only French subSaharan African territory to reject the Gaullist Constitution in 1958 and to pursue thereafter a policy independent of France.[31]

The Ivory Coast's loyalty to France was lubricated by a dramatic economic growth in the 1950s and the 1960s. Guinea experienced nothing comparable.

The critical factors in the success of cooptation are time and performance. Such policies often require a number of years before they can succeed; dramatic crises, such as the 1958 referendum in Guinea, can easily deter them. Though cooptation entails marginal adjustments in comparison with the two previous variants, there must be some rewards that can be perceived by the elite groups subject to cooptation.

## Cortes Elections in America after 1810

The colonial and imperial governments tried elite cooptation in New Spain by the electoral and parliamentary policies of Spanish liberals implementing the Spanish Constitution of 1812. The Council of Regency announced the convocation of the Cortes in 1810. Participation in the Cortes as a method of cooptation may have been fairly successful in 1810. The opening of the Cortes in Cádiz, the departure of the Mexican delegates to join it, and the Hidalgo revolt occurred at the same time. The colonial and imperial governments could claim that Creoles would have a greater say in the running of the empire and the colony. The Mexican deputies addressed their countrymen: "together with [the deputations] of the other provinces in the Cortes, [we] will make sure that the rights of all the parts which compose the monarchy with just equality are seen triumphant: so that all are left without a motive for complaint."[32]

Over the long term, however, the electoral or parliamentary method of cooptation was only moderately successful. The Cortes was in session from March 1, 1810, until May 11, 1814, when King Ferdinand declared the Constitution of 1812 null and void. The Cortes met again in 1820-21 during the brief period of liberal ascendancy in Spain. Five elections for deputies to the Cortes were held in 1810, 1812, 1813-14, 1820, and 1821.

The Constitution of 1812 stipulated that all male citizens over the age of twenty-one who were *vecinos* could vote. A citizen was one born in the Spanish dominions or naturalized, excluding those of African descent, even if they were not slaves. A vecino was a citizen who had a place of residence and an honest occupation; domestic servants, vagrants, and criminals could not vote. One had to be educated to be elected a deputy to the Cortes. Mexico City in 1812 had about 5,000 qualified electors. Therefore, a crude calculation would suggest that about one out of every six adult males in Mexico City was qualified to vote.

The voting regulations narrowed the electorate mostly to Creoles and Spaniards. Although one of the Cortes' political purposes was to gain the support of the Creoles, much good will was lost by the Viceroy's arbitrary rulings. In a clear Creole-Spaniard confrontation in the 1812 election in Mexico not a single Spaniard was elected to a post at any level of government. Claiming electoral fraud, the Viceroy and the Archbishop nullified the election, although the evidence available suggests that fraud was minimal. Despite much pressure from the Viceroy and the Archbishop, again no Spaniard was elected in the elections of 1813-14. This time, as in 1810 and later in 1820, the public authorities respected the electoral results.[33] Thus, the appeal to the Creoles through elections was somewhat marred by arbitrary actions of the Viceroy.

One weakness of the Cortes was that the parliamentary electoral system failed to become institutionalized. The Spanish members of the Cortes made ad hoc modifications of the Constitution of 1812 to guarantee Mexican representation, but the elected Mexican deputies had not yet arrived when it opened in 1810. Pending their arrival, seven Americans resident in Spain were appointed to the Cortes in March; one was subsequently elected (see Table 10.1). When most of the elected Mexican deputies arrived in Cádiz, these appointees were allowed to continue as members in order to bolster the Mexican representation. Only a few elected Mexican deputies arrived in time for the Cortes' meetings of 1813-14. Twelve deputies who had served between 1810 and 1813 were allowed to remain as members of Cortes for 1813-14, even though they had not been elected nor especially appointed for these sessions. This continued to strengthen the Mexican representation. When the Cortes met in 1820, the elected Mexican deputies had not yet arrived. Once again seven Americans resident in Spain were appointed; three were subsequently

Table 10.1  Source of legitimacy of Mexican deputies to the Cortes

| Deputies | 1810-1813 | 1813-1814 | 1821 |
| --- | --- | --- | --- |
| Number elected | 20 | 41 | 61 |
| Number elected who attended sessions | 15 | 8 | 45 |
| Number of nonelected (appointed or allowed to stay) | 6 | 12 | 4 |
| Total number attending | 21 | 20 | 49 |

Source: Charles R. Berry, "The Election of the Mexican Deputies to the Spanish Cortes, 1810-1822," in Nettie Lee Benson, ed., Mexico and the Spanish Cortes, 1810-1822 (Austin: University of Texas Press, 1966).

elected; the other four were allowed to remain members of Cortes for a part of the 1821 sessions, even after the elected delegates had arrived.

The difficulty was not the willingness of the liberal Cortes and imperial government to coopt the Mexican elite, but the failure to institutionalize successfully Mexico's structural access to the Cortes. The Atlantic Ocean was a formidable barrier to cross to get to Spain at a time of international war. Many elected deputies lacked incentives to make the trip in the absence of an electoral tradition. About one-quarter of the Mexican deputies elected in 1810 for the 1810-1813 period of sessions, and in 1820 for the 1821 period, failed to attend any sessions of the Cortes (Table 10.2, top row). Absenteeism rose to a staggering four-fifths for the

*Table 10.2* Institutionalization of Mexican access to the Cortes

| Deputies | 1810-1813 | 1813-1814 | 1821 | 1822-1823 |
|---|---|---|---|---|
| Percent elected who failed to attend the sessions | 25.0 N=20 | 80.5 N=41 | 26.2 N=61 | — |
| Percent attending this period of sessions who had attended a previous period | — | 60.0 N=20 | 12.3 N=49 | — |
| Percent who had been elected to and attended a previous period of sessions, and who were re-elected to and attended this period | — | 0.0 N=20 | 8.2 N=49 | — |
| Percent elected to this session who had been elected once before | — | 0.0 N=41 | 14.8 N=61 | 11.1 N=45 |
| Percent attending who were elected to Cortes office | 42.9 N=21 | 20.0 N=20 | 6.1 N=49 | — |

*Source:* Charles R. Berry, "The Election of the Mexican Deputies to the Spanish Cortes, 1810-1822," in Nettie Lee Benson, ed., *Mexico and the Spanish Cortes, 1810-1822* (Austin: University of Texas Press, 1966). Berry's data have been reorganized for this table.

1813-14 elections and sessions. Therefore, the first structural weakness was that so many elected deputies failed to assume their posts.

A parliament's institutionalization requires both the continuing access of its members to their constituencies and the establishment of boundaries between the organization and its environment. The first is necessary to insure that the organization will be adaptable, coping with new problems and challenges. The second is necessary to insure autonomy; the membership stabilizes and acquires expertise and professionalization.[34] The cumulative expertise of the Mexican deputies attending the 1813-14 session was considerable, but it had virtually vanished by the 1821 period.

The high degree of autonomy and expertise in 1813-14 was purchased at a high price. None of the delegates elected in 1810-1813 was reelected, regardless of their attendance records at either the 1810-1813 or the 1813-14 sessions. There were two kinds of Mexican delegates at the 1813-14 sessions of the Cortes: recently elected freshmen deputies without prior parliamentary experience, or experienced deputies who had not gone before the electorate since their first election or appointment. The vital role of an experienced legislator, whose mandate is refreshed and legitimated by the voters frequently, and who incorporates the electorate's demands into his work, was not being filled. Expertise dropped dramatically for the 1821 sessions. And only 8.2 percent of the Mexican deputies at this period were experienced legislators with a refreshed electoral mandate. (For the third period of sessions of the United States House of Representatives, the comparable statistic was 43.5 percent.)[35]

If all those elected had attended sessions, the rate of reelected, experienced legislators would have risen to almost 15 percent in 1821. In fact, some of the deputies elected in 1810 or in 1813-14 and in 1820 failed to attend the 1821 period of sessions, even though they had attended a previous period of sessions. And some of the deputies elected in 1810 or in 1813-14 and in 1821 who attended the 1821 sessions had failed to attend a previous period. The 1822-23 sessions of the Cortes never met because the King nullified the Constitution. Nevertheless, Mexican deputies had been elected for those sessions in 1821. If all had attended, the rate of experienced, reelected legislators would have dropped to 11.1 percent. And the proportion of expert Mexican deputies would decline further from 1813-14 to 1821 to 1822-23.

Institutionalization also requires that some of the deputies be rewarded within the organization by their peers. The ratio of membership to reward -- the percent of Mexican deputies elected to parliamentary office (president, vice-president, and secretary)--was quite high for the first period of sessions, but it dropped sharply and steadily for the next two.

Mexican access to the Cortes was never institutionalized. Absenteeism was high, sometimes the norm rather than the exception; there were few reelected experienced legislators at any time. Expertise was at a premium during the 1813-14 period of sessions, but at the high cost of separating the experienced legislators from any electoral renewal of their legitimacy and their information. Expertise dropped steadily and sharply after this; it would have reached a probable low in the 1822-23 sessions, had they met. Reward of deputies within the organization, high during the first period of sessions, dropped sharply and steadily thereafter.

At the time of Mexican independence only a handful of deputies could be thought to have a stake in the preservation of a liberal parliamentary empire through the Cortes. Reelection, expertise, and reward within it to individual Mexican deputies were low and declining. The link to Spain through the parliament, never strong, was measurably weaker in the early 1820s than during the previous decade. Cooptation through parliamentary institutions may have played a moderate role in the first five years after Hidalgo's revolt, but it had probably failed by the time of Iturbide's revolt.[36]

Cooptation through the Cortes did not prove terribly successful through legislation. The American deputies presented an eleven-point reform plan on December 16, 1810. There were five political demands: equality of representation in the Cortes between Spain and America in proportion to population; equal access to public offices for Americans; at least one-half of the public offices in each kingdom should be given to its natives; the establishment of a nominating board for all public offices; and the restoration of the Society of Jesus. None were approved.

There were six economic demands: among them, the lifting of all prohibitions on agricultural or industrial activities in America; free trade between America and Spain, between America and Spain's allies, and with all neutral countries; the extension of free trade to all of Spain's possessions in Asia, including the Philippines; the suppression of all government monopolies except that over mercury (the exploitation of mercury mines would not be a monopoly, but the administration of their production would still be so). Prohibitions on agricultural and industrial activities in America were lifted by the Cortes on February 9, 1811. Although the Cortes was moving cautiously toward the abolition of monopolies by 1813, it delayed implementation. The free-trade provisions were approved just before the King dissolved parliament, so they did not go into effect. The consulados of Mexico City and Veracruz opposed freer trade. Cortes granted freer trade when it reconvened in 1820; however, the trade issue in New Spain was problematic because of merchant elite opposition to it. And much liberal legislation approved by the Cortes, freedom of publication, for example, was never implemented by the viceroys in New Spain because they considered it an obstacle to suppressing the rebellion.[37]

Thus, Cortes legislation at best had but a mild success in cooptation. Crucial political demands were not granted or not implemented. Economic demands, especially those concerning free trade, suggested by many Mexican deputies were far more modernizing than their constituents would support. They were unrepresentative. The Cortes' policies in these issue areas were indecisive. In short, the performance of the liberal system did not win the Mexicans over. There were shortcomings in elections and in policy performance. The success of electoral and parliamentary cooptation between 1810 and 1814 was modest. New policies adopted in the early 1820s, however, would have a diametrically opposite effect: they seriously destabilized an already unstable political system bringing it closer to independence.

In Cuba the Cortes proved more a liability than an asset in retaining the loyalty of the Creole elite who, though economic liberals, were political conservatives. The Spaniards in Cuba had been politically mobilized during the liberal period and had challenged the Creole predominance in the island's government. Cuban Creoles and their organizations were shocked and angered by efforts to abolish the slave trade through Cortes action. Cuba sent one deputy to the Cortes in 1810; by 1812 and 1820 the number had increased to three (including the ever-present Arango y Parreño). One of these deputies in the early 1820s, the Reverend Félix Varela, supported the abolition of slavery, for which he was roundly condemned by his Cuban colleagues and by the Cuban planters. The Cortes, however, asked Varela to propose how it could be done.[38] During this same period the Spanish Piñerista party forced the dismissal of the Intendant of Havana who was closely associated with the Creole planters. The planter Creole elite breathed a sigh of relief when Ferdinand VII again suppressed the Constitution and dismissed the Cortes.[39] The Cuban Creole elite would be coopted for reasons other than access to the Cortes.

The Spanish government had no control over the Creole elites which had revolted in Venezuela and in Chile; therefore, there could be no elections for the Cortes. Two Venezuelans were appointed deputies by the Cortes in February 1810, but they were explicitly repudiated by the Supreme Junta of Caracas as soon as the break with Spain took place in the following weeks. The two remained as members of the Cortes and signed the Spanish Constitution of 1812, but they did not act on behalf of the Venezuelan elites or even keep in touch with them. Some Venezuelan delegates were also appointed when the liberal Constitution was restored in 1820, but it was too late.[40] Independence was a reality. The Cortes had also appointed two Chilean deputies in 1810; they, too, remained members. Although they were not explicitly repudiated by the Chilean authorities, these deputies had been living in Spain for some time and had lost touch with the course of events in Chile. The Chilean Creoles had no say in the selection of the deputies and did not send any delegates.[41] By the time the liberal Constitution was restored, in 1820, Chile had been independent for three years. In sum, cooptation through the Cortes did not succeed in Venezuela or Chile. It was probably harmful in Cuba. And it had a modest success in New Spain.

## The Revolutionary Elite in Mexico

The revolts against Spain in Venezuela and Chile originated in the Cabildo, the chief organization of the Creole elite. In both countries the rebels included members of the colonial nobility and other leading untitled members of the colonial elites. Only in New Spain did the revolt begin in the country's periphery. The Mexican revolutionary leaders were the least likely to have been a socioeconomic colonial elite. This case study, therefore, sets the minimum threshold of elite participation in the revolts. Information was coded from the biographies of 144 top Mexican revolutionary leaders from 1810 to 1822, although not all biographies included all variables.[42]

Although many of the rebels were Indians, only 3.5 percent of the leadership was composed of Indians. Only 7.6 percent ($N=92$) were illiterate; another 23 percent had fairly rudimentary education; most had secondary or higher education. Moreover, 27.5 percent of the revolutionary leadership was composed of priests, the largest single occupational group; 11.5 percent were lawyers, 13.0 percent were military officers in the militia or regular army, 16.0 percent belonged to other urban middle- and upper-class occupations (including merchants, painters, bureaucrats, surgeons, mining technicians, professors, and scientists), 11.5 percent were landowners or mine owners, and less than 1 percent were military cadets. Lower-middle and low-class occupations (military men from soldier to sergeant, artisans, and outlaws) and housewives accounted for 9.9 percent. Poor farmers, small farm owners, and laborers accounted for another 9.9 percent ($N=131$).

The leadership included few very high ranking or very low ranking people: most of the clergy were parish priests; no military officer held rank higher than captain; most of the lawyers and bureaucrats were not yet distinguished. In the main, the upper class of colonial Mexico was not represented. However, slightly less than one-fifth of the leaders could be considered lower middle or lower class in either city or countryside. The revolutionary leadership was an elite offshoot by ethnic classification, education, and occupation. Parish priests, junior officers, lawyers, and mining technicians and owners accounted for over two-thirds of the revolutionary leadership.

Two-fifths of the rebel leaders had access to public appointment because they were either clergymen or military officers. And one-third of the forty-nine leaders in urban occupations (law, other urban upper class, and urban lower class) had access to public appointment. But virtually no one employed in rural jobs (other than the military or the clergy) had access to public appointment, regardless of social class. Spatial proximity to the centers of appointment mattered. There are no further clear differences in general access to public office, but a class pattern emerges in the access to specific offices. One-fifth of the twenty-six urban and rural poor joined or were drafted into the military. Two-fifths of the lawyers and urban upper class had access to the civil and ecclesiastical bureaucracies.

If the military and clergy are added to those with access to public appointment, 53 percent of the rebel leaders had such access. It is, therefore, necessary to reject the view that the rebel leaders did not depend on public appointments. As members of a neo-patrimonial elite, they, too, sought and had had access to public appointment, though not to the good jobs. They had worked for the colonial government and may have resented the ascriptive promotion practices preferring Spaniards to Creoles for top positions in the civil, military, and ecclesiastical bureaucracies. The rebel leadership exhibits a high level of bureaucratization and low bureaucratic rank. They were not born into antagonism and disloyalty to the empire. They became disloyal as a result of their work experience and of their inability to rise according to their high educational achievement. Consistent with this hypothesis, all but one of the 115 leaders whose place of birth is known were born in New Spain. Only 36.2 percent of the rebel leaders were under the age of thirty; 51.7 percent were between thirty and forty-nine; the remaining 12.1 percent were over the age of fifty (N=58).[43] The decision to rebel was made by mature Creole men who broke with their own past in midcareer.

Clear objective criteria on the social mobility of the rebel leadership were difficult to set where family status or income or the income of the rebel leaders were concerned; only their level of education was known with some confidence. The following data thus require special caution. There appeared to be a fairly strong relationship between family socio-economic background and the rebel leader's income prior to rebellion.[44] Matching the general family level of well-being to the leader's income, the degree of vertical mobility is 20.5 percent (N=44). Thus, about one-fifth of the rebel leaders were worse off or better off than their family socioeconomic background may predict. There was a weak relationship between family background and education.[45] Over one-half had a level of education differing from what might be expected from the family's economic background; however, coding difficulties and inconsistencies could account for disparities. The relation between income and education was surprisingly weak.[46] There was certainly some social mobility among the Mexican revolutionary leadership, but it is difficult to say how much.

Fortunately, there is an alternative: spatial mobility, which often correlates quite well with social mobility. The spatially mobile are defined as those who were living and working in a place other than where they were born at the time immediately prior to their involvement in the war of independence. The nonmobile are those who were living and working in the place of their birth. Spatially mobile persons often seek more education or more income than their families have had.

Guanajuato was at the forefront of New Spain's modernization in the late eighteenth century. It was the main town in the Bajío, where the rebellion began. Creoles there were more apt to be spatially mobile than nonwhite Americans, though not by much. More striking is the relatively low level of spatial mobility in Guanajuato. In contrast, the revolutionary elite was very spatially mobile. These leaders were born and lived in seventy-one different places. Over one-half of them were spatially mobile, two and one-third times more mobile than Guanajuato's Creoles, and almost three times more mobile than nonwhite Americans in the town (Table 10.3).

This high level of spatial mobility meant that the revolutionary leaders were acquainted with the general condition of New Spain. They had traveled widely and had been exposed to parochial grievances throughout the viceroyalty. Because of their high level of education, they may have been able to aggregate and articulate these dispersed grievances into a somewhat coherent program. They may have had a national perspective well in advance of other Mexicans. The revolutionary leadership called for a broad program of reform with a strong economic plank. But the rank and file pursued individual or parochial goals, devoid of wider political content, through murder, theft, looting, and

*Table 10.3*  Spatial mobility in New Spain (percentages)

| | New Spain's revolutionary elite | Guanajuato's adult male work force (1792)[a] | |
| --- | --- | --- | --- |
| | | Creoles | Nonwhite Americans |
| Mobile | 52 | 22.5 | 18.3 |
| Nonmobile | 48 | 77.5 | 81.7 |
| N | | 4,098 | 6,267 |

*Source:* Alejandro Villaseñor, *Biografías de los héroes y caudillos de la independencia* (Mexico: Editorial Jus, 1962), 2 vols.; D. A. Brading, *Miners and Merchants in Bourbon Mexico, 1763-1810* (Cambridge: Cambridge University Press, 1971), p. 249, table 28.

a. The adult American-born male work force is used because there were few minors, only four women, and one Spaniard in the revolutionary elite. All Spaniards are spatially mobile by definition.

rape. The leaders of the war of independence may well have been Mexico's first nation-conscious leaders in a country that was not nationally conscious.

Spatial mobility was statistically independent of family socioeconomic background, sex, or age. Those born in Mexico City were no more likely to be spatially mobile than were those born elsewhere. Those who lived and worked in Mexico City were slightly more apt to be spatially mobile than those who lived elsewhere.[47] Spatial mobility, however, was significantly related to income and education.[48] The sharpest differences in the spatial mobility of leaders were between urban nonmanual employees and all others. Urban nonmanual employees were very likely to be spatially mobile; all others were not (Table 10.4).

Occupations were important in shaping spatial mobility. Clergymen were most likely to have had to leave their place of birth for education and subsequent assignment. Church leaders may have had a national perspective sooner than other elites. Although the military might be expected to provide for considerable spatial mobility, many were in the militia and served in their own communities. There is a sharp difference between town and country but no variation in spatial mobility by social class in the rural areas (Table 10.5).

The typical Mexican rebel leader was a white, middle-aged male, born in America, with a fairly substantial education. He was likely to have access to junior appointment in the civil, military, or ecclesiastical bureau-

*Table 10.4*  Spatial mobility of the Mexican revolutionary elite by social class (percentages)[a]

|  | Nonmanual | | Manual | |
|  | Urban | Rural | Rural | Urban |
|---|---|---|---|---|
| Mobile | 72.6 | 6.7 | — | — |
| Nonmobile | 27.4 | 93.3 | 100 | 100 |
| N | 62 | 15 | 15 | 1 |

*Source:* Alejandro Villaseñor, *Biografías de los héroes y caudillos de la independencia* (Mexico: Editorial Jus, 1962), 2 vols.
a. Chi square = 39.906; 3 degrees of freedom; $p < 0.001$; phi square = 0.43.

*Table 10.5*  Spatial mobility of the Mexican revolutionary elite by occupation (percentages)[a]

|  | Clergy | Other urban upper class | Lawyer | Military | Urban lower | Rural upper | Rural lower |
|---|---|---|---|---|---|---|---|
| Mobile | 86.4 | 71.4 | 58.3 | 57.1 | 42.9 | — | — |
| Non-Mobile | 13.6 | 28.6 | 41.7 | 42.9 | 57.1 | 100 | 100 |
| N | 22 | 14 | 12 | 14 | 7 | 13 | 13 |

*Source:* Alejandro Villaseñor, *Biografías de los héroes y caudillos de la independencia* (Mexico: Editorial Jus, 1962), 2 vols.
a. Chi square = 40.964; 6 degrees of freedom; $p < 0.001$; phi square = 0.43.

cracies. Access to public appointment was more frequent in the urban areas. Many, though not most, of the leaders were socially mobile; they were far more spatially mobile than even the citizens of Guanajuato. These well-educated Creoles had found themselves in mid-career with little prospect of significant advancement. Thus, the evidence supports the argument that the hispanization of top bureaucratic jobs in the last decades of the empire blocked the life chances of individuals who eventually turned to war.

The revolutionary elite's program was far bolder and more modernizing than would seem warranted from earlier analyses of both mass and elite politics in New Spain because of the national perspective acquired through their spatial mobility. These leaders could aggregate and articulate parochial grievances. They were alienated from more traditional elites, who lacked such perspective and clung to Spain, as well as from the more traditional mass that sought parochial, fragmented, backward-looking, depoliticized goals. The Mexican revolutionary elite, therefore, could not channel mass protest into a focused political purpose, nor could it easily win over the central elites. Its quandary was that it was too different from everyone else.

The rebellious elites in Chile and in Venezuela were also mature men of substance. In addition, they were closer to the center of the political system than the Mexican rebel leaders were. Because the central elites led the rebellion in these two countries, the national-parochial gap between rebel elite and colonial elite failed to develop there, although it continued between elite and mass.

Political participation and government response have been studied in the two colonies experiencing significant social disturbance during their wars of independence, as a result of the actions of the rebels, the government, or both. Socioethnic mass issues were very important in the wars in Venezuela and Mexico. On the other hand, economic issues seemed more important at the elite level. The Mexican rebel coalition was a conglomerate with disparate goals and issues. In Venezuela the government's coalition was the conglomerate with disparate goals and issues. The Venezuelan rebel elites sought a traditional group seizure of legitimacy -- except that they also wanted controlled structural change to free foreign trade. They resisted further modernization of the social and economic systems. The Mexican rebel elite, though its goals were much more modernizing, and thereby unrepresentative of both the Mexican central elite and the rebel mass following, behaved traditionally by basing its claim to legitimacy on charismatic leadership and engaging in charismatic inducement to political participation. At the mass level, social banditry and defensive collective violence merged with the wars of independence in both countries, but mass traditional participation did not become any more modern as a result.

The Venezuelan colonial government responded by dropping all restraints. It followed a strategy of counterinsurgency and stimulated charismatic political participation. It thus undermined its own legitimacy and long-term prospects for political stability. The colonial government of Mexico engaged in more cautious politicization of social cleavages only in response to rebel action. It sought to preserve multinational ideology and legitimacy by seeking some Indian support. And it followed a strategy of electoral and parliamentary cooptation which, though only modestly successful, was an indication of political creativity under duress. Study of the Mexican rebel elite suggests that these were mature Creoles who had had work experience and access to public appointment in neopatrimonial fashion, but whose promotion had been blocked. They were very spatially mobile and, consequently, had a more national perspective than most other Mexicans.

The first phase of the war showed the empire's resiliency thanks mostly to the fears, hopes, loyalty, and imagination of its American subjects. Imperial rule was successfully defended, in part by exploiting the political weaknesses of the insurrection. But the methods used by government officials -- while effective in the short run -- sowed the seeds of the later and more decisive phase of the insurrection.

# 11

# War and Political Mobilization:
# Second Phase

The first efforts to gain independence failed in Chile, Mexico, and Venezuela. Loyal Americans defeated those who sought to break with Spain. And yet, many of the issues of the first phase were still unsettled and some of the leaders of the insurrection remained alive. The second phase of the wars of independence was characterized by two features. One was the redesign of insurgent strategies to mobilize and control political participation during war. The other was the reassertion of metropolitan Spain's direction of the war efforts; this resulted in a greater reliance on repression carried out by Spaniards. The greater skill displayed by the insurgent elites and the unsubtle repression of a newly nationalistic Spain finally broke the bonds of interest and loyalty that had kept these colonies in the empire for three centuries.

## Political Participation

Venezuela's initial efforts to proclaim and win independence were destroyed by the social question. The Creoles had sought to move toward independence with a rigid social system. The blacks rallied to the Crown, which had been their protector during the last decades of the colony. To achieve independence in Venezuela, top Creole leadership strategy had to change. That came about only when nothing else seemed to work, although the motivation of the Creole leadership may well have been sincere. And much of the change would be undone as soon as possible.

José Tomás Rodríguez Boves died in combat in December 1814. The renewed war of independence is a fascinating example of the structural continuity of sources of conflict. It also makes it clear that the political participation of the illiterate rural plainsmen was not grounded in social mobilization or political partisan organization but depended on external

196

mobilization by charismatic leaders. After the death of Boves the black plainsmen found another leader: General José Antonio Páez. Both Páez and Boves behaved similarly. They adopted the mode of life of the plainsmen, including their lusts and their pleasures, and promised them well-being. Courage and boldness were essential for their leadership. They used same symbols. The armies of Boves in 1814 wore a black feather and displayed black flags; Páez's flag was also black. Páez and his plainsmen were doing the same thing that Boves and his plainsmen had done: fighting white elitist Caracas.[1] However, Caracas was republican in 1814, and royalist in 1817. The results of the first struggle restored the empire, those of the second overthrew it.

Bolívar himself had to make some changes to win over Páez and the plainsmen. Upon his return to Venezuela, he decreed the abolition of slavery, contingent upon all newly freed male slaves' joining his army. His style, described by José Gil Fortoul, also changed. Bolívar had to

appear folksy, strong, bold, capable of anything; eat like the plainsmen . . . ; run on horseback like them, chasing cattle and deer; swim across the rivers like them; sleep like them . . . out in the open air if necessary; dress like them in rough clothes . . . indulge in vulgar language; dance with young mulatto women outdoors, while guitars played . . . live like the toughest soldiers, without fear of beast, heat, cold, wind, or the enemy; and be at the head of his troops fighting with the same courage.[2]

The transformation of the aristocratic white Creole leader was the transformation of the Venezuelan war of independence. In June 1821 Bolívar entered Caracas.

The bases of the cleavage had begun to shift during the earlier stage of the war. Bolívar had declared "war to the death" in 1813, to which Boves responded in kind. Bolívar's version raised the specter of an ethnic war against those born in Spain and the Canary Islands. These persons, and Spain, had come to appear "foreign." The Spanish empire had been multinational. But the Bourbon reforms and the policies of the liberal Cortes had appropriated imperial legitimacy for Spain and Spaniards to the exclusion of Americans. They had disrupted imperial legitimacy. The multinational empire had come to be seen as a colonial empire. American rebels found it easier to shoot foreign Spanish lords. The encompassing principle of the target population was ethnicity. In February 1814 Bolívar ordered the execution of all the Spaniards who had been taken prisoner. Between eight hundred and twelve hundred were killed.[3] These were not combatants, but people in the custody of the republican army.

Traditional mass political participants, when they seem to join a broad national coalition, have local rather than system-wide perspectives. Their own goals remain narrow. These coalitions are poorly integrated conglomerates. Disruptive but traditional political participants—including those mobilized by charismatic leaders—often refuse to fight too far from their villages, families, and peasant locale, eventually fragmenting authority in the independent countries.

The Venezuelan war of independence was not integrated militarily. It was a conglomerate of local armies, headed by Arismendi in Margarita Island, Páez in the plains, and Santiago Mariño in the east. The Spaniards controlled the center (Caracas) and the west (Coro, Maracaibo). In February 1818 Bolívar ordered Páez to bring his plainsmen into the valley of Aragua, toward the center of the country. Páez refused, claiming that it was bad for the cavalry. Since the plainsmen obeyed no one but him directly, they turned south, instead of north. While Bolívar was preparing to cross the Andes to invade New Granada (later Colombia), he ordered Páez to occupy Cúcuta. Páez again refused and returned to the plains. In March 1819 Bolívar ordered Arismendi to transfer some of his troops from Margarita Island to the mainland. Arismendi refused. When the central command insisted, Arismendi mutinied in May 1819. None of his soldiers would leave the island. The Venezuelan patriot army was a conglomerate of parochial armies, each willing to fight primarily in its own region only.[4]

Bolívar's economic incentive for parochial participants and their charismatic leaders was confiscation of the property of royalist Spaniards and Americans, decreed in the fall of 1817. That property would be used to pay for the cost of the war; the surplus would be redistributed among officers and soldiers. The rebel government's documents could be redeemed for land. The program of redistribution of wealth was highly skewed in favor of the officers. Large landholdings were transferred from Spaniards to rebel military leaders, above all, General Páez. The following list[5] shows the thousands of pesos assigned to officers and troops:

| | |
|---|---|
| Commander-in-chief | 25 |
| General, division | 20 |
| General, brigade | 15 |
| Colonel | 10 |
| Lieutenant colonel | 9 |
| Major | 8 |
| Captain | 6 |

| Lieutenant | 4 |
| Sub-lieutenant | 3 |
| Sergeant | 1 |
| Corporal | 0.7 |
| Soldier | 0.5. |

This program had two traditional features: the new rebel government was used in traditional neopatrimonial fashion to provide political access for individual private gain; and the chief beneficiaries of such a neopatrimonial structure and policy were members of the emerging elite.

In Mexico the political consequences of the social question were not so drastic. The revolt continued along similar paths, reinforcing some of the more radical social programs. Hidalgo had decreed in Guadalajara, in December 1810, that land confiscated from enemies of the rebellion should be turned over to the tillers of the soil. This decree, primarily a politico-military measure, already had produced social consequences.[6]

Upon Hidalgo's defeat the Reverend José Maria Morelos became the principal leader of the Mexican rebellion. As a priest and a heroic military leader, he continued the style of charismatic political leadership Hidalgo had initiated. Morelos confirmed the essential features of Hidalgo's program: abolition of slavery and the tribute. He also emphasized more strongly the distinction between those born in America and those born in Spain through repeated use of the term "American" in his appeals for support. Because Morelos was more committed to military discipline, his forces looked less like a horde than Hidalgo's had.[7] Morelos also led a congress of political leaders in 1813 to declare Mexican independence.

More military discipline and more American appeals permitted the formation of a coalition among rebellious provincial elites, headed by Morelos, and an organized radical offshoot of the elite in Mexico City. The Guadalupes, a secret society of pro-independence sympathizers in Mexico City, served as an informal political party in the elections to the 1813-1814 Cortes. They also helped establish an insurgent press to counterbalance the royal government's press, sheltered refugees, stimulated morale, spied, and provided information. This group, organized after Hidalgo's revolt failed to enlist the support of the Mexico city elite,[8] drafted the Medidas políticas, a political program, for Morelos in 1812; they were issued in 1813. Although Morelos has come to be known as a radical social reformer, and although the Medidas were issued under his command, the initiative and the writing appear to have come from the Guadalupes. The revolutionary features of the Mexican rural uprising appeared mainly when the rural force became allied with this part of the central elite. The Medidas emphasized the destruction of the property of those who collaborated with the Spanish government; its main purpose was politico-military. But the social policies were drastic, giving the rebels a new aura of radical social coherence. All the rich, the nobles, and the high officials, whether Creoles or Spaniards, were to be considered enemies of the nation. Their properties, goods, and money were to be subject to confiscation. Half would go to the poor and half to the military treasury. All tobacco and sugar plantations and all mines would be destroyed. All the large farms (those more than two leagues) would be ravaged, as well as all dams, aqueducts, houses, and shops belonging to the large landowners. The gold, silver, and other precious possessions of the churches would be seized. The tillers of the soil would become free proprietors of a limited amount of land in uncultivated farms.[9]

One element of the Medidas was not enforced stringently: the confiscation of church property. Morelos' campaigns, like those of Hidalgo, made much use of religious symbolism to recruit support against the impious enemies. The seizure of church income from tithe yields was also kept to a minimum. In the bishopric of Oaxaca, where Morelos was operating, only 7.2 percent of such yields were taken by the rebels in 1812 and only 2.4 percent in 1814. The rebels may have turned over to the bishopric as much as 46.4 percent of its tithe income in 1815. The war, not rebel actions, cut the absolute level of the tithe yields in Oaxaca to half of its normal level.[10]

The extension of the war to Oaxaca supports the view that middle peasants — those who retain some real independence — are prime candidates for insurrection. Many Indians in the valley of Oaxaca had retained the ownership of land, defending it successfully through litigation and by force. Spanish-owned estates there were relatively small and changed often from family to family. The Indian landholdings were among the most stable in the valley in the late colonial period. Thus, Morelos brought the war to an area which had many small Indian and white landholders autonomous enough to rule themselves. Although in the north the Bajío's rural population was far more mobile than that of Oaxaca, both areas had relatively large rural middle sectors which could be mobilized for war. Peasants were not so enserfed that they could not envision a different world.[11]

Morelos was defeated and captured in the fall of 1815, and rebellion subsided. The Bajío, where the struggle had begun, was the scene of the most violent repression. The city of Morelia was destroyed, in part because most of its proprietors had supported the insurgency.[12] But guerrilla war, led by Vicente Guerrero, an uneducated Indian peasant in his middle thirties, continued uninterrupted until Mexican independence was achieved.

Cross-pressures in Mexico led to the political withdrawal of the clergy, and most of the Mexican nobility viewed both sides with enough skepticism to withdraw politically, although they compromised pragmatically with them.[13] Both sides used religious symbols extensively. The armies of independence fought under the banner of the Virgin of Guadalupe, the royalist under the banner of the Virgin of Remedios. In the battle of the Virgins, clergymen were caught in between. The clergy accounted for a large share of the revolutionary elite. On the other hand, the viceroyalty's united episcopal hierarchy supported the government through 1820. Some of the priests were Creoles, others were Spaniards. Ethnic political and religious cross-pressures were considerable, and the result seems to have been the political withdrawal of the vast majority of clergymen. Karl Schmitt claims that of a maximum of 10,000 priests in New Spain in 1810, no more than 1,000 were "known by name to have participated actively on one side or the other."[14] Of 7,341 counted clergymen in 1810 Nancy Farriss has identified 401 (excluding mere spies, chaplains, or conspirators) who fought in the wars of independence (5.5 percent of the count); 54 percent of these were insurgents, the remainder royalists.[15] In short, not more than one-tenth of the clergy were active politically. About a twentieth, almost evenly divided, may have fought in a struggle where religious symbolism was crucial and where the stakes of the Church were high.

The politics of Chile were significantly different from those of Mexico, Venezuela, and Cuba. There was little social turmoil even during war, in part because Chilean economic growth had occurred under conditions that reduced its possible transformative effects. It had the least oppressive labor system of the countries under study and one of the least modernizing elites. Ethnic factors were also limited. The Indians inhabited a "foreign" territory, outside the social relations of the colony, in a parallel ethnic system. The elite ethnic conflict was probably far less severe in Chile than in the other colonies, and certainly far less so than in New Spain. These factors helped mute the social transformations of the Chilean wars of independence. The cross-pressures experienced by Chileans were incompatible identifications. They were attracted both to Spain and Spaniards and to Creole power and Chilean autonomy. Chilean Creoles, therefore, gave extensive support to the royalist forces, while some Spaniards supported the patriot cause.

Noncombatants fared better in Chile than they did in New Spain and Venezuela. The triumphant royalist forces imprisoned the Creole independence leaders in November 1814; but only two were killed while in custody.[16] During the wars, pro-independence forces under General José Miguel Carrera confiscated property, harassed royalist citizens, and executed some royalist prisoners. The extent, however, did not match the violence in Venezuela and Mexico. In contrast to those two countries, violence against civilians was one reason civilian authorities removed General Carrera from army command.[17]

The royalist forces mobilized the Arauco Indians. Because the Araucos lived in a geographically separate territory and did not interact much with the rest of Chile the mobilization's main effect was to provide Spanish troops with open communications across the otherwise unsubdued territory to Spanish outposts in southern Chile, where the Indians also supported the activities of Spanish guerrilla forces. But these limited operations by the Arauco Indians essentially were outside the Spanish-Creole-mestizo social structure and a minor feature of the Chilean wars.[18]

The nonethnic character of the Chilean struggle for independence was manifested in Creole and Spaniard service on both sides. The royalist army of General Mariano Osorio had 5,000 troops in 1814, of which only 600 came directly from Spain. There were many royalist Creoles. The rich property owner Luis Urréjola and his brothers supported the reconquest led by General Osorio. The royalist Commander of Militias in Chillán in 1813, Clemente Lantaño, was a native of that city. Royalist guerrilla leaders such as Juan Antonio Olate or Vicente Benavides had been born in Chillán and Quirihue, respectively. Their charismatic qualities, as well as Benavides' reliance on banditry, increased lower-class support for the royalist forces even as late as the early 1820s.[19] When the Creole Bishop of Santiago died, in April 1811, the vicar named by standard ecclesiastical procedure was the royalist Creole José Rodríguez Zorrilla. The pro-independence government of General Carrera forced the ecclesiastical council to reverse itself in favor of Spanish-born Rafael Andreu Guerrero, who was sympathetic to independence. Another Spanish-born "patriot" was Fernando Márquez de la Plata who served on the first Chilean Junta in 1810. The pro-independence Spaniard Colonel Carlos Spano died defending the city of Talca against the royalist armies in the last days of Chile's first efforts toward independence.[20]

Many of the political struggles of late colonial Chile were the result of family struggles. The large Larraín Salas family, known as the "Eight

Hundred," lacked entails, large dowries, legacies, or connections to high officials. But, through their numbers and their marriages, they were able to manipulate colonial institutions and so advance family fortune and status. One result of their struggle for advantage was the exacerbation of political disputes with other families.[21] Whole families warred against each other, more often for gain than for ideological conviction.[22] Few rebels had close kinship ties to royalists, so brothers seldom fought each other and kinship rarely was responsible for changing from one side to another. Chile thus differed from Mexico where, as early as 1808, families divided.

Cross-pressures provoked some political withdrawal through incompatible identifications in a war where Creole and Spaniard served on both sides, and where the appeal of independence and the appeal of Spain were strong. Large groups within the elite and even larger proportions of the mass of the population failed to join either side unless they were in the middle of a battle area. Soldiers taken prisoner easily switched sides.[23] The issue of independence was not yet clear. Chile, however, was characterized more by ambivalence and mixed support than by political withdrawal. Some individuals supported Spain and the patriot cause at different times during the decade of the wars. This can be attributed to unbridled opportunism, as well as coercion, but many Chileans were sincerely attracted to both sides. They thought Spain had been good to them, except for an unfortunate recent misunderstanding.

### Chile's Ambivalent Elite

The Creole elite supported both patriot and royalist forces. The royalist authorities of Santiago called an open meeting of the municipal council on February 9, 1817; it was attended by sixty-one persons, twenty of whom were Spaniards, the rest Creoles. By the following week Santiago had fallen to the patriot armies and on February 16, 1817, the new government called another open meeting of the municipal council. Eleven of the same Creoles who had participated in the royalist meeting participated in the patriot meeting! And four of the nine councilmen in Santiago's patriot municipal council had been among the "royalist sixty-one."[24]

The sixty-one elite members who supported Spain in 1817, divided by place of birth, can be compared to a group of ninety-seven Chilean Creole revolutionary leaders who were arrested by the triumphant Spanish forces in 1814 and imprisoned on Juan Fernández Island (see Table 11.1). No less than one-third of the elite members, regardless of political attitude or place of birth, were public officials. The proportion of the elite with access to public appointment (public officials, military

*Table 11.1* Social bases and political attitudes of the Chilean elite, 1814-1817 (percent)

| Occupation | Creoles | | Spaniards |
| --- | --- | --- | --- |
| | Patriots | Royalists | |
| Public officials | 33 | 32 | 40 |
| Military officers | 32 | 22 | 15 |
| Unknowns, others | 18 | 22 | 5 |
| Clergymen | 10 | 0 | 0 |
| Merchants | 4 | 12 | 40 |
| Lawyers | 2 | 10 | 0 |
| Landowners | 1 | 2 | 0 |
| N | 97 | 41 | 20 |

*Source:* Computed from Jaime Eyzaguirre, "La conducta política del grupo dirigente chileno durante la guerra de la independencia," *Estudios de historia de las instituciones políticas y sociales* 2 (1967): 234-239, 253-269.

officers, and clergymen) was 75 percent of the Creole patriots, 54 percent of the Creole royalists, and 55 percent of the Spaniards. The Chilean rebel elite had more access to public appointment than the loyal royalists, and any one of the three Chilean elite groups had more political access than the Mexican revolutionary elite (53 percent). The Mexican elite rebels came from the provinces, the Chilean elite rebels from the capital city. In Mexico, as in Chile, those who had jobs in the city had more access to public appointment than those who had rural occupations. The Mexican rural elite had considerable access to government, but less than the urban elite in either Mexico or Chile.

Priests, prime contributors to the revolutionary leadership in Mexico, contributed less in Chile. However, all the highly politicized clergymen were rebels. Lawyers were also far more notable in Mexico's rebel elite than in Chile's; most lawyers in Chile were loyalist Creoles. Officers in the militia or army accounted for 13 percent of the Mexican rebel elite, for 32 percent of Chile's. The level of militarization was uniformly higher for the three groups of the Chilean elite than for the Mexican revolutionary elite, consistent with the hypothesis that Chile's rate of military participation was significantly higher than New Spain's. There were more military in Chile among Creoles than Spaniards, and among patriots than royalists. Four out of every ten elite Spaniards were merchants, but only 11.6 percent of the Creoles were; 93 percent of all merchants were royalists. The small number of merchants in the rebel elite was also evident in Mexico (2.3 percent).

The "unknowns" were a higher proportion among Creoles than Spaniards. Unknowns were those who had not been members of the colonial elite prior to 1810, nor top politico-military leaders afterward. Many had risen moderately since 1810 because of the turmoil. Their rise was a crude indicator of political mobility as a result of the Chilean war of independence. These politically upward mobile men, however, were just as important to the cause of rebellion as to the cause of loyalty to the empire. Assuming that many unknowns were poor, the urban and rural lower-class contribution to the rebel leadership may have been comparable in Chile (18 percent) and in Mexico (19.8 percent).

Charles Griffin has noted that "there do not seem to have been instances of high military commanders of recognized mixed blood" in Chile, in comparison to Mexico or Venezuela.[25] This is undoubtedly correct because there were fewer recognized "mixed bloods" in Chile than in the two other colonies. Griffin's statement, however, is not incompatible with these findings. Mexico's unknowns became known because of the wars of independence; Chile's unknowns remained so. Although it was not drastically shaken, Chile's social hierarchy was not unaltered, for some unknowns rose enough so that Spanish authorities rounded them up and sent them to prison!

## Government Response

Counterinsurgency had succeeded in Venezuela by 1814. Spain's simultaneous cooptation and politicization of cleavages had succeeded in Mexico by 1815. Napoleon had been defeated in Europe. Ferdinand VII had taken his rightful place as King of Spain, voiding the liberal Constitution of 1812 and dissolving the Cortes. That removed one possible avenue to coopt the colonials, should it be needed again. Counterinsurgency and the simultaneous politicization of socioethnic cleavages are political strategies governments prefer to avoid. When the politico-military balance improved, Spain retreated from them. The death of José Tomás Rodríguez Boves in Venezuela, following his military victory, as well as military victory in New Spain made strategy changes possible. Spain's absolute monarchy was less willing to compromise. The Crown thought that the remaining rebels needed to be eliminated and the best method, having ruled out other strategies, was repression.

### Repression

A fourth variant of government response is repression. It has been tried often, with a mixed record of success and failure. The effectiveness of incumbent control varies curvilinearly with the size and resources of its military and internal security forces and with the severity of incumbent repression.

Incumbent control is lowest when the size and resources of its military and internal security forces, and the severity of repression, are at an intermediate level. Incumbent control is high when challenges to it and its repression are low. As the challenge to government increases, incumbent repression may rise to a moderate level, where its control may decline because resistance to the incumbent rises faster than incumbent repression. If the government has the necessary military and police capability, increased repression may increase incumbent control. A government lacking such capabilities may remain at the point where it is likely to be defeated. Alternatively, government capabilities may weaken after maximum repression is applied; the actual level of repression may return to an intermediate level, while the rhetoric of repression remains high. The government then is likely to lose control and be defeated when there are memories of repression, high levels of repression rhetoric, and low enforcement. Military loyalty and ability and the consistency of the application of repression shape also the probability of incumbent success.[26] Repression may be exclusively military or may combine military and political techniques. Success is more likely when such government repression has political support. A government that goes beyond military techniques and wins political support for its policies (often through some cooptation) is more likely to succeed than one that relies on military policies alone.[27]

Repression was tried first in Chile in almost pure form, uncontaminated by the other methods used elsewhere. The colony was repressed even during the first phase of the rebellion and this continued into the second phase. The major difference between the two phases of Chile's wars of independence was a change within the strategy of repression from a reliance on combined politico-military methods to the reliance on military methods exclusively that began in 1814.

Chile had experienced relatively little social transformation and considerable political ambivalence during the wars of independence. This ambivalence made reconciliation possible. Chile and Venezuela differed at the outset of their break with Spain because the former recognized the authority of both the King and the Council of Regency while the latter recognized only the King, moving toward complete independence in slightly more than a year. In contrast, Chile did not proclaim formal independence at all between 1810 and 1814; its 1812 constitution still recognized the symbolic authority of King Ferdinand VII. Although the importance of this should not be exaggerated, it is one more indicator of a general pattern of political ambivalence. Chile was too attracted to Spain to be fully ready subjectively for independence.

At first, Spain was ambivalent toward Chile, too. The Council of Regency recognized, in reciprocity, the authority and legitimacy of the Chilean Junta established in September 1810. The Viceroy of Peru, José Fernando de Abascal, was more conditional: he recognized the legitimacy of the deposition of Governor Francisco García Carrasco by the Audiencia and the legitimacy of the appointment of Mateo de Toro Zambrano, Count of the Conquest, as governor. During late 1810 and early 1811, however, the pro-independence factions gathered strength. The alarmed royalist Spanish party moved to seize political legitimacy, and a Spanish lieutenant colonel, Tomás de Figueroa, with support from the Audiencia, attempted a military coup. The coup was defeated, and the Audiencia was dissolved by the Junta. Then, in 1811 and 1812 the attitude of the Viceroy of Peru began to change from suspicion to hostility.

The military bastion of Valdivia in southern Chile had sworn loyalty to the government of Santiago in November 1811. Stimulated by financial support from Lima, a few months later Valdivia broke with Santiago and sided with the Viceroy. The Viceroy organized a small expedition of fifty men against Chile, departing in December 1812, at the beginning of the southern hemisphere's summer. The expeditionary force landed in southern Chile. It organized the population of Chiloé and Valdivia and marched north toward Concepción, which fell in March 1813 (to be retaken by patriots in May).[28]

The Viceroy's response to the cautious Chilean secession was a masterful mix of political and military repression. Virtually the whole royalist army was recruited in Chile, although the original force had been organized in Lima. The strategy was to stimulate a civil war and to repress the rebellion. There was no cooptation nor much of a royalist effort to politicize social cleavages. The main danger was that the Peruvian origin of the strategy would become too visible, arousing Chilean subjective national consciousness forged in the conflicts with Peru. The royalists mobilized Chilean political support for repression on the grounds that the patriot armies were incapable of preserving law and order and were committing crimes and excesses. Royalist forces supported and sheltered many Chileans who fled from the patriot armies.

As the next southern summer began, the Viceroy sent a second expedition of two-hundred men from Peru, to organize the final drive against Santiago. The royalist forces had fought the patriots without decisive success, meanwhile building political support for the royalist military

response by exploiting the patriot excesses. The reorganized and reinforced royalist forces entered Talca in March 1814. They defeated the
patriot armies at Cancharrayada and entered Concepción in April 1814.

The underlying politico-military mix of the repressive policies and the
ambivalence of both royalist and patriot forces was then vividly illustrated. The aristocratic commander-in-chief of the royalist forces, the
Spanish Brigadier Gabino Gaínza, and Chile's rebellious Creole elite
signed the Treaty of Lircay on May 3, 1814. Under its terms, Chile would
recognize the sovereignty, legitimacy, and authority of King Ferdinand
VII, and, in the interim, of the Council of Regency. Chile would send
deputies to the Cortes to ratify the Spanish Constitution of 1812. The existing government of Santiago would continue to exercise full authority
within the territory of Chile on Spain's behalf, and it would be authorized to permit trade with Spain's allies or with neutral countries. The
royalist armies would withdraw from Chilean territory. Chile would
reestablish commercial relations with the rest of the empire. All property
confiscated by the government of Santiago since September 1810 would
be restored to the rightful owners. The government of Santiago would
also pay an indemnity of 30,000 pesos to the royalist armies for costs to
be incurred. Prisoners would be exchanged, military ranks would be
reciprocally respected, and amnesty would be reciprocally granted.[29]

The "Spirit of Lircay" did not last long. It was sabotaged by parts of
both sides. Yet there was enough good faith in signing it to make it a
significant event. It was the most far-reaching reciprocal effort at reconciliation between Spain and one of its rebellious colonies. It illustrated
the strong political component of the royalist strategy and the prevalence
of reciprocal ambivalence. Many rebellious elite Chileans could con-
template their reincorporation into the empire with pleasure.

The Treaty of Lircay was sabotaged by some patriot and royalist officers in the field. It was also rejected by the Viceroy. With absolutism
reemerging in the Spanish empire, the Viceroy was in no mood for
political compromise. This may have been his most serious mistake, for
it changed his strategy from politico-military to purely military repression. The Viceroy relieved Gaínza of his command and sent a third expedition, led by Colonel Mariano Osorio with six-hundred Spanish
troops fresh from Spain. The patriot armies were decisively defeated at
Rancagua in October 1814; Santiago fell to Osorio within days. Patriot
leaders and their families by the thousands crossed the Andes into Argentina. The first Chilean drive toward autonomy had failed.[30]

The Viceroy's flat rejection of Lircay was the rejection of politics. During the course of thirty months, moreover, he had gradually escalated
the non-Chilean component of the repression by means of three expedi-

tions: from fifty to two-hundred to six-hundred. This third group was made up of the first troops from Spain that had arrived in Chile since the beginning of the fighting. At last Spain had been able to divert forces from Europe to America.

Although the Viceroy's early strategy fomented civil war in Chile, his later actions Peruvianized and hispanicized the royalist side. By 1814 Chilean patriots were no longer fighting Chilean royalists; they were confronting the long hated viceroyalty of Peru in its efforts to subdue Chile, and a newly intransigent and arbitrary Spain. Subsequent events reinforced this emerging perception. The royalist regime pursued a militarily repressive policy—no cooptation, no political mobilization: the leaders of the rebel elite were arrested and sent to prison. Santiago's corporate bodies petitioned the Crown in March 1815 for amnesty for all political prisoners. Though the Crown granted their petition, the Governor of Chile refused to implement it. The same institutionalized procedure that saved Cuba for Spain contributed to the loss of Chile. Political imprisonment continued. The royalist government hispanicized elite jobs in the military because many Creole military officers had joined the rebellion. The government established a tribunal to enforce careful vigilance and prohibited civilians to go out after sunset.

Chilean exiles in Argentina aided Argentine plans to invade Chile and march northward toward Peru. Buenos Aires believed its security would be threatened so long as Spain controlled the viceroyalty of Peru and could reconquer its colonies from there. The Chileans hoped to return to power with newly gained popular acclaim. Chile was invaded in February 1817. Quick victory brought the patriot armies into Santiago the same month.[31] Within a year, however, the same General Osorio, setting out from Peru, landed in southern Chile once again and moved northward. The battle of Maipú, in April 1818, confirmed the independence of Chile. The fourth Peruvian expedition to prevent Chilean independence met a more united and secessionist Chile.

The Peruvianization and hispanicization of the war—by expeditions or by the making of critical decisions—had heightened the Chilean elite's consciousness of separateness. Their old Peruvian antagonist tried to impose its will on them. Spain had devolved authority in South America onto Peru, so confidence in Spain declined. The shift within the strategy of repression emphasized an almost purely military component after 1814. The royalist government remained in power by force alone. When that force proved insufficient, it fell. Venezuela and Chile had a similar experience. Spain and Spaniards had appropriated legitimacy. A multinational empire came to be seen as a colonial one. Americans could come to think of Spaniards as ruling foreigners.

The military character of the wars of independence in Chile had a subtler effect. Other than random devastation, there was relatively little transformation of the socioeconomic structure. The socioethnic upheaval that characterized the wars in Venezuela and Mexico was missing in Chile, which in 1818, though ravaged by war, had fairly stable social, economic, and political structures.[32] Political reconstruction though not easy, would be less difficult and more successful than in other countries.

Despite the military character of much of the wars, certain features typical of traditional political participation were apparent. At the outset, the Chilean elite as a group seized legitimacy; but that was virtually the only significant change. Some elites, such as the Audiencia, were thoroughly traditional, applying medieval rules to depose Governor García Carrasco for arbitrariness and corruption. But traditional behavior proved disruptive in a transformed context where overarching legitimacy had been challenged internationally. Mass traditional political participants, locally or parochially oriented, refused to go far from their villages. The royalist army in Chile, like the Venezuelan patriot armies, faced this problem. When it tried to smash through the patriot lines toward Santiago in April 1813, troops from the southern island of Chiloé refused to cross the Maule River.[33] It was too far from home.

The policy of reconciliation, which flourished briefly in Chile at Lircay in 1814, was not attempted to any comparable degree in the other colonies under study. At Lircay the Spanish commander-in-chief recognized that the Chilean government in Santiago was legitimate to some degree. The most that would be done up to 1820 in Venezuela or Mexico was the granting of amnesty to rebels who surrendered. British efforts to mediate between Spain and her colonies (1811-1813) never materialized because of Spanish restrictions on the scope and domain of the mediation, and Spain's unwillingness to grant enough trade incentives. The domain was restricted to South America, for Spain was confident that it had control of the situation in Mexico.[34] Spain, instead, pursued a military strategy exclusively in all its colonies, as soon as it safely could. This happened in Venezuela and Mexico after 1814. It was easier in Mexico after Morelos was defeated and captured in the fall of 1815. Subsequently, only the elimination of guerrillas remained.

Field Marshall Pablo Morillo was appointed Captain General of Venezuela in August 1814 to complete the job Boves had begun, but without reliance on the political mobilization of blacks. He sailed from Spain with 10,000 troops, thus hispanicizing the civil war in Venezuela to an unparalleled degree. Yet elements of civil war persisted, for in November

1818 Morillo's army still had a majority of Venezuelan-born troops; almost all his cavalrymen were Venezuelans.[35]

As Spain shifted toward almost pure military repression, Bolívar had turned gradually into a charismatic leader, politically mobilizing blacks. His job was made easier by a change in Crown policies. Blacks had been mobilized by Boves through a combination of charisma and pillage incentives. King Ferdinand VII, however, wanted to pacify Venezuela, not transform it. Boves was dead; Ferdinand ordered his forces to cease pillaging. Royal officials in Venezuela recommended a massive program of gracias al sacar to end the legally inferior condition of blacks, but the King apparently rejected that alternative as too drastic.[36]

Initially, Morillo's repression resembled Chile's first phase in that it combined political and military methods. For example, in 1816 thirty-one of Venezuela's top forty-three officials were Creoles, including the new Archbishop of Caracas and members of the Audiencia. His policy of conciliation, however, was never too generous. Even in 1815, when he was presumably being conciliatory, he ordered the confiscation and public sale of property belonging to supporters of independence.[37] But late in the year Morillo shifted to military methods almost exclusively. Areas he thought he had pacified rose up again.

Morillo's eventual failure in Venezuela (like the eventual independence of New Spain) cannot be explained by internal factors alone. Independence came to Venezuela and Mexico in part because the Spanish army collapsed. International war not only undermined political legitimacy but it also disrupted military commands. The regular army dissolved when Napoleon invaded Spain. Spain's independence from Napoleon was won by irregular guerrilla forces; when the war ended, they were incorporated into the new army. Most of these new army officers had headed peasant bands. Their parochial perspective was compounded by a lack of socialization into military procedures and chains of command, and they were opposed to pursuing colonial wars. The liberal Cortes, fearing that the senior army officers would impose a military dictatorship during the war of independence, had accelerated the promotion of these younger guerrilla leaders. The professionals came to scorn the Cortes and the Constitution of 1812, the lower-class irregulars to support them. On his resumption of the throne in 1814, King Ferdinand restored also the authority of the senior officers. The senior generals did not want to promote the nonprofessional irregular force officers. In fact, they demoted some of the most prominent guerrilla leaders of the war of independence. Pablo Morillo was an exception; he had begun as a noncommissioned officer. The liberal revolts from 1814 to 1819 were often instigated by military officers in the middle to junior ranks who had fought in the irregular forces and whose promotion had been subsequently blocked. Thus, one key effect of the international wars was the disruption of standard procedures regarding promotions and chain of command in the Spanish military.[38]

Morillo's troops were plagued by desertions, quarrels, and insubordination as early as 1816, when the royalist forces were still winning. Also, the Field Marshall depended on the guerrilla leaders who headed the remnants of Boves' troops. When, by 1819, the tides of war had turned, whole battalions deserted. Morillo wrote to the Crown in January 1818, requesting a transfer, because of the "cowardly manner" in which Spanish officers fled from the rebels. By July 1820 he was describing the dissolution of his army: the rate of desertions rose to 336 in August, and to 1,800 in December.[39] Although the American experience worsened morale and discipline, demoralization affected Spanish troops everywhere. Lord Wellington charged that in the Spanish army "there is no general capable of commanding a corps or even of administering it; there is no general staff nor supply and, worst of all, there is not even anyone ashamed of such things and capable of making the slightest effort to remedy them."[40]

An expeditionary force for America began to assemble in Cádiz in the fall of 1819. There was no proper shelter, supply, or sanitary facilities. Disease spread — including the disease of not wanting to fight distant Venezuelans. Major Rafael de Riego led a mutiny of this army against the military and political establishment. The Constitution of 1812 was restored, and Cortes was called.[41]

Field Marshall Morillo proclaimed the Constitution of 1812 in Venezuela in June 1820 as his army was dissolving. He also entered into negotiations with Bolívar. An armistice was signed at Trujillo in November 1820. Troops would remain quartered where they were. Economic interchange between Spanish and patriot zones would be possible. The conduct of the war was regularized by a separate protocol on noncombatants, the wounded, and prisoners of war.

Spain offered Venezuela the same terms Brigadier Gaínza had offered Chile at Lircay: rejoin the empire, send deputies to the Cortes, and take an oath to uphold the Spanish Constitution. Preferential commercial relations within the empire would be reestablished. Trade would be permitted with allies and neutrals. Rebel military commanders would keep their posts under a Spanish commander-in-chief. To relieve pressure on other land, royal and unsettled lands would be given to Indians, mulattoes, and mestizos. Reconciliation on those terms was not possible.

Bolívar demanded recognition of the independence of the Republic of Colombia (Venezuela plus New Granada). He was willing to yield Quito and Panama to Spain. He was opposed to both reincorporation into the empire and to confederation with Spain. He was willing to accept an offensive and defensive alliance, and offered reciprocity in low trade tariffs. He was also opposed to a European prince for Colombia.[42]

The Lircay formula might have reinstated Chile in the empire as an autonomous colony. That formula was similar to Cuba's de facto condition. Bolívar's terms, however, were recognition of the independence of northern South America by Spain — or else. He was willing to permit generous relations between sovereign partners, but no less. Unlike the Chileans, Bolívar was not ambivalent. It was too late for cooptation. With the collapse of Morillo's army, and the defection of Maracaibo, total victory was assured. It came in June 1821, at Carabobo.

The demoralization of the Spanish army continued in New Spain and in the rest of South America. The final defeat of the royalist forces in Peru and Upper Peru (Bolivia) followed a succession of coups that undermined the legitimacy of the empire and the colonial authorities there.

The shift to pure military repression by a self-confident absolute monarch in 1814 proved disastrous for Spain. It was based on overestimating military morale and capabilities, and on underestimating the alienation engendered in Americans by a policy of repression based on ever weakening military strength. Given military weakness and the rhetoric, memories, and policies of repression, the empire collapsed, as it surrendered some support (Venezuelan blacks) or alienated more (Chilean and Mexican elites). As military strength weakened and support was lost, military defeat ensued in Venezuela and Chile.

The character of the second phase of the wars of independence was set by Spain: military repression and hispanicization of politics. Spain was defeated on its own terms. It had turned a civil war into a colonial war. It claimed legitimacy for itself and for Spaniards, excluding those born in America. Spaniards thus became foreigners to Americans. America might have been saved for a liberal Spain that might have coopted the Creole elite in the Cortes, but not for Ferdinand's narrow Spanish nationalism that stressed military colonialist absolutism and was unwilling to share decisionmaking.

# 12

# Toward Political Reconstruction

The wars of independence underscored the problems of political order. With the defeat of Spain in Chile, Mexico, and Venezuela, a new order had to be rebuilt on the ashes of the old. Successful insurrections had to establish new bases of enduring loyalty. But the reconstruction of politics was not just a concern of the newly independent countries. To retain its loyalty, Spain had to reorganize Cuban politics, economics, and society. The crisis of the empire had been so profound that the need to reorder was a task that the ever faithful Cuba had to undertake under Spain's sovereignty. Political reconstruction became a common endeavor for both former insurrectionists and persistent loyalists.

## Preserving Political Order in Cuba

Spain's policies in Cuba after 1808 illustrate cooptation as a government strategy to anticipate and prevent rebellion. The changes there were so far-reaching that they reconstructed the political, social, and economic systems. This was no mere response to threat. Cuba was transformed by events unlike those in other parts of the Spanish empire and even in Cuba itself.

The imperial and colonial governments had stimulated modernization in Cuba. Government institutions had adapted to it. Before 1810, however, Cuban modernizers had been defeated in some significant areas, especially land policy. Spain decided to accelerate its earlier policies of accommodating modernization in Cuba. Between 1814 and 1819 it undertook a full-scale program of land reform to meet the needs of the modernizing Cuban planters. It coopted them and severed the old agrarian structures of the colony. The new order in Cuba appeared at the same time that Spain turned to military repression elsewhere in America.

To understand the land reform, preexisting land policies must be analyzed. Spain authorized municipal governments to grant *mercedes* of land in the sixteenth century. These were grants of rights to land use, not to land ownership (as befitted a neopatrimonial political system, where land belonged to the Crown). The grantees had to supply beef and other food to the towns. The mercedes, which had to be inherited in common, could not be divided. Many boundary disputes incurred because the grants were circular and often overlapped. In 1729 the Crown removed the land-granting authority of the municipal councils, gradually centralizing it in the executive of each colony. The decree of 1729 further stipulated that those who had held undisputed possession of the land before 1700 would be granted formal ownership. Otherwise, title to the land could be challenged before the government to settle ownership. This gave rise to many lawsuits and contributed to property instability.

The first land reform decree was issued by a restored King Ferdinand VII in June 1814. Land grantees were released from the obligation to supply towns with food and could devote the land to any purpose. Titles to land ownership could be established by prescription, whereby ownership would be recognized if a grantee could prove occupation of uncultivated land for a century or its exploitation for forty years. The second land reform decree, August 1814, revoked what remained of the Navy's privileged access to Cuban forests. The third change was an April 1819 judicial decision of the Audiencia ruling that the division of communal landholdings was legal. Anyone with a stake of 20 pesos could force a division of communal property, provided the boundaries of the entire tract could be ascertained. The fourth change was the royal decree of July 1819 confirming the ownership rights of land grantees of the 1814 decree and extending the right to establish legal title by prescription to squatters on royal land.[1] The decisions, which overrode the objections of the Navy and traditional landowners, opened up Cuba's lands to commercial agriculture, specifically to sugar and coffee. Land became a commodity to be divided and sold in parcels. Property ownership was secure by title.

In July 1817, responding to the demands of tobacco farmers, the government abolished the tobacco monopoly.[2] Tobacco cultivation was freed and stimulated so that white immigrants could be attracted to Cuba to produce it. Cuban tobacco was produced by white farmers who were small property owners in contrast to plantation crops produced by slaves. Whites made up about 30-36 percent of the population, freedmen 3-6 percent, and slaves 58-67 percent, in areas producing plantation crops (sugar and coffee). In tobacco-producing areas whites were about 62 percent of the population, freedmen 24 percent, and slaves only 14 percent.[3]

A council on white immigration (Junta de Población Blanca) was established by the colonial government in September 1815 to promote white immigration. Royal support for white colonization was reinforced in decrees of 1817 and 1818. Free passage, some land, and title and sales tax exemptions were granted. New white immigrants founded towns in Cienfuegos, Guantánamo, Mariel, and Nuevitas during the 1820s.[4] Between 1816 and 1836 the school enrollment of whites in Havana province jumped 279 percent and that of blacks 204 percent. This was about four times the rate of population growth during the same period.

In September 1814 the Council of Indies forbade the entry of non-Spanish ships to the colonies. In time-honored fashion, Governor Apodaca refused to implement the order in Cuba. At last, in February 1818, King Ferdinand formally authorized unimpeded free trade for Cuba, although in fact the colony had been enjoying free trade for many years. The liberal Cortes of 1820 decreed the reestablishment of the restricted system of trade. The Cuban elite protested, and, as usual, the public authorities refused to enforce it. The Cortes modified their decree in January 1822, exempting Cuba, and formally authorizing the colonial authorities to modify import taxes. The elite's experience with the liberal political regime was unsatisfactory, and they welcomed the restoration of absolutism. King Ferdinand confirmed his free trade decree of 1818 in 1824.[5]

The Crown had systematically exempted Cuban internal production from certain taxes, including Church tithing, to transform the island's fiscal base. The government eliminated many internal taxes and relied on external tariffs. The tariffs themselves were often lowered. The volume and value of production for export (and the goods imported) increased, paid these lower tariffs, and, consequently, increased fiscal revenues. Fiscal receipts thus increased while the rate of taxation fell as a result of economic growth. The *almojarifazgo* (tax on imports and exports) accounted for 14 percent of all revenues in 1794, rising to 50.1 percent by 1817, and to 58.9 percent by 1821. Maritime rents accounted for 67.6 percent of revenues in 1828.[6]

The imperial and colonial governments (more under the absolute monarchy than under the liberal Cortes) had responded systematically and comprehensively to the needs of the Cuban elite. They had coopted them and had reconstructed the Cuban political system. The Spaniards in Cuba seized upon the new freedoms of the two brief liberal periods to attack the close relations between the Creole elite and the government. It was the Spaniards, not the Creoles, who felt slighted. The Cuban elite was not repressed into submission. It was a partner in a wide transformation of the country. The municipal council of Havana, the Consulado, the Economic Society, and other institutions initiated many of the proposals that the government turned into law. They were lobbies, research units, and coparticipants in implementation.

The Spanish government also appointed Creoles to the Intendancy. Next to the Governor, the Intendant was the chief civilian authority in the island and in charge of the critically important economic and fiscal policies. Spanish-born intendants had worked closely with the Creoles since the 1790s, so closely that one of them (Ramírez) became the special target of the Spanish party's attempt to reduce Creole power during the liberal period in the early 1820s.[7] King Ferdinand appointed the patriarch and leader of the Cuban elite, Francisco de Arango y Parreño, Intendant of Cuba in 1824. He was replaced in 1825 by Claudio Martínez de Pinillos, who served as Intendant until 1851. Pinillos, born in Havana in 1782, had been named Treasurer General of the Army in 1814, and acting Intendant twice between 1814 and 1825. He replaced the aging Arango as leader of the Cuban elite during the second quarter of the nineteenth century.[8]

All was not well politically, however. Several conspiracies had failed, but they indicated that a number of black freedmen and subelite whites were dissatisfied with the prevailing politics of the colony. The Haitian conquest of the Spanish part of the island of Santo Domingo frightened Cuban Creoles. Cuban subelite dissatisfaction, however, became more serious during the 1820s. The most important conspiracy to bring about independence, Soles y Rayos de Bolívar, was organized in 1821. As its name suggests, the original source was external to Cuba. Led by the Creole José Francisco Lemus, who had been a colonel under Bolívar, it appealed to students, subelite whites, and black freedmen. It was crushed in 1823-24, before there had been any rebellion, with the support of Cuban Creole slaveholding planters. Although it is claimed that as many as six hundred persons were involved, only two dozen were arrested.

The actual extent of the conspiracy is difficult to establish. The Governor of Cuba, Francisco Vives, exaggerated its magnitude as a bureaucratic excuse to gain more authority. Vives wrote to Madrid about his successful repression of the conspiracy: "perhaps I will not be able to do it again without the necessary means to save the country." It is difficult to see how two dozen arrestees, or even six-hundred conspirators, could have posed such a threat. Virtually unlimited powers to govern by martial law were granted to Governor Vives in 1825, but they were used sparingly. His governorship was more noted for corruption, easy living, vice, and gambling than for effective law enforcement.

A liberal constitutionalist conspiracy of 1824, led by Ensign Gaspar Rodríguez, was duly suppressed. The freedmen Francisco Agüero and Manuel Sánchez landed in a small boat in east-central Cuba in 1826, but were easily defeated. A secret society of Cuban exiles in Mexico, the Gran Legión del Águila Negra, was first organized around 1827. Although supposedly widespread, it was crushed after six arrests in 1830.[9] In short, Cuba's movement for independence, led by intellectuals and students, and influenced by the newly independent Spanish American republics, was very limited.

The most important difference in most of these conspiracies was the reported role of freedmen. Spanish governmental institutions, and especially the military, continued to be responsive to many freedmen. Although the loyalty of black soldiers would be questioned in later decades, this was not yet so. Spain expressed its confidence in their loyalty and military competence by sending an expedition of three-hundred of them to defend Florida against the United States in 1812, even as José Antonio Aponte plotted a black uprising.[10]

In order to save its last important colony, the Spanish government transformed the basic structures of the island. It responded to specific demands not only from the Creole elite but also from small tobacco farmers and black military officers. Cooptation, transformation, and reconstruction were the dominant reasons why Cuba remained Spanish. The extreme powers of the governor, granted in 1825, were not exercised systematically until the 1830s under Governor Tacón. Corruption and indolence dominated the prosperous 1820s. Movements toward independence were not very serious.[11]

Some have hypothesized that the laws preventing Cuban-born persons from serving in the army or the civil service were rigidly observed. This is patently wrong. It has also been hypothesized that Cuba was an armed camp and that martial law was in effect for fifty years. This is misleading. Beginning in the 1830s, Spain turned more and more to a policy of martial law — a possible explanation for Cuba's continued failure to become independent. But this did not take place until after the first quarter of the nineteenth century. Large numbers of Spanish troops did not arrive in Cuba until they were defeated in the mainland. Even during the 1820s the government remained primarily in the hands of the Creole elite under Arango and Pinillos, and it was still benefiting the free middle-income, middle-status segment of the population. The size of the

army was irrelevant to the suppression of conspiracies in the 1820s. That
was a police matter.

Another hypothesis is that Cuba was an island isolated by the Spanish
fleet. But at that time there was no Spanish fleet capable of cutting it off.
And there was, on the other hand, some knowledge of how to mount a
seaborne invasion to impose independence from outside. The Argentine
and Chilean armies were transported by sea to Peru under the leadership
of General San Martín and Lord Cochrane, although the liberation of
Peru was not achieved until the land armies of Bolívar could invade from
the north. A full seaborne invasion of Cuba would undoubtedly be difficult. Cochrane's Navy in 1820 depended heavily on foreigners. All the
captains of his eight warships were from England or from the United
States, and 39 percent of his 1,600 seamen were Europeans or North
Americans. Although this indicates the limited capabilities of the new
South American republics, it also suggests how a naval expedition
against Cuba might have been mounted. Bolívar's Gran Colombia had a
total of ten warships in the Caribbean and the Pacific Ocean, with two
more on order (in addition to others patrolling rivers), but it could equip
only three frigates on its own — hardly enough for an invasion of Cuba in
the early 1820s. However, an Argentine fleet, sent to the Caribbean to
disrupt trade, blockaded the city of Santiago de Cuba for a month in
1817. But it behaved more like pirates taking booty than as a regular
navy.[12] Geographic obstacles, then, were severe but only because there
was no will to repeat in the Caribbean what had succeeded so well in the
Pacific Ocean: the recruitment of foreigners to build up a disciplined
navy able to defeat the Spanish Navy.

Others argue that the infusion of Spaniards, fleeing from the mainland, kept Cuba attached to Spain. And yet it was the Spaniards who
protested that government was too responsive to the Creoles. The
Spaniards added disruption, not stability.[13] Another hypothesis seeks to
explain the conspiratorial spirit of the age. The smaller planters found it
difficult to keep abreast of the rising cost of sugar production. The rift
between the two classes of planters that emerged during this period was
unlike the traditional regional one between the cattle-producing east and
the sugar-producing west.[14] But this rift did not mature until the 1830s
and 1840s.[15]

The view that repression played a role in keeping Cuba Spanish cannot
be discounted, but it seems that Cuba remained loyal because most of the
goals of the elite and the free white and black subelites could be or had
been achieved under colonial rule. There was mobility for free blacks
and some wealth for all free people. Independence, on the other hand,

raised the prospects of a second Haiti or of the civil and international wars that had taken place on the mainland. Unlike the newly independent republics, Cuba could play two metropolitan countries against each other to increase its margin of autonomy: politically dominant Spain was pitted against economically dominant United States. Imperialism was divided, increasing local autonomy.

The prevailing ideology in Cuba emphasized economics rather than politics. Even Félix Varela, former deputy to the Cortes, who was politically aware and had been implicated in the Soles y Rayos conspiracy, noted in 1824 that "in the Island of Cuba there is no love for Spain, nor for Colombia nor for Mexico, nor for anything other than boxes of sugar and bags of coffee." The leading intellectual, politico-literary journal, *El revisor político literario*, published the following in 1823:

> A book by a traveling charlatan who visited this city [Havana] for a few days in 1817 . . . has just been published in France. He and many like him call us to task for our ignorance. They would want to find here astronomers, chemists, botanists, in short, all kinds as in London and Paris, and they do not remember that scientists are born where they are needed; here we accord more esteem to a skilled sugar technician than to an ideologue. When our pockets are full, when our wealth matches that of countries which are one thousand years old, then (I do not doubt it) we will be scientists because we will have to . . . We now need those who sell industry, not ideology.[16]

And Baron von Humboldt observed: "Notwithstanding the efforts of the patriotic society of the island of Cuba, which encourages the sciences with most generous zeal, they prosper very slowly in a country where cultivation and the price of colonial produce engross the whole attention of its inhabitants."[17]

Bourgeois ideology leads to revolution when politics stands in the way of its fullfillment. Such was not the case in Cuba where politics and economics correlated nicely. Cuba had no revolution—not because it was too traditional, not because it was prevented from having it, but because everything that its bourgeoisie wanted was accomplished without it—and at less cost!

## Varieties of Political Reconstruction

Five variants of political reconstruction should be considered. Two assume relatively high levels of social mobilization: in one, political participation may expand gradually, with relatively little opposition, as in nineteenth-century Britain or the United States;[18] in the other, political participation expansion may be resisted somewhat, as in continental Europe before the twentieth century.[19] The other three variants assume relatively low levels of social mobilization. The third features continued political mobilization through the Leninist-type building of a party and new instruments of government; political participation, though controlled, expands.[20] In the fourth an attempt may be made to reduce the concentration of power in the executive — as happened in post independence United States — and there is mass political demobilization. The fifth variant reconstructs a relatively strong and centralized executive, while demobilizing politically.

Early nineteenth-century Spanish America had low levels of mass social mobilization. A major source of its traditional political participation was the activating of the masses by political leaders and organizations. People otherwise unlikely to participate in politics were mobilized by agents such as charismatic political leaders and elite organizations; but once the mobilization ceased, the mass political participation ceased, too.

After independence, governmental structures had been changed because the insurgents had won. Temporary political participants could not return or be returned to old molds, which had been broken. The reestablishment of political order required that the old molds be repaired or new ones established. The Leninist path obviously could not be followed in the Spanish America of the 1820s because Lenin had not yet been born.

Available political theories were the two main political traditions of the Spanish monarchy: the medievalists and the Bourbons. Both emphasized low levels of political participation and political demobilization, but the Bourbons emphasized a strong government. The Bourbons resisted intermediate bodies and intermediate authority more than the Hapsburgs, who in turn resisted it more than their predecessors in Castille and Aragón. The Bourbons sought greater centralization of authority and expansion of central power. Local elites could flourish in the pre-Hapsburg period, less so under the Hapsburgs, but least so under the Bourbons. Thus, the choice in Spanish American reconstruction in the early nineteenth century was between deconcentration of executive power from preexisting levels, or a build-up of centralization, both associated with political demobilization.

The way in which these options work depends in part on the options chosen by the defeated incumbent. For example, if the incumbent had chosen cooptation and the opposition had chosen the deconcentration of executive power, a violent confrontation could be avoided, mutual claims adjusted, and new elite groups could enter a reconstructed and more broadly based government. If the incumbent had chosen relatively pure military repression, then the traditional fabric of society, though torn, may not have been fundamentally changed. Revulsion against repression could also have increased the probability that the deconcentration of executive power would be chosen for political reconstruction.

If the incumbent had chosen counterinsurgency or the politicization of social cleavages, then deconcentration of executive power was not likely to be chosen. Loyalty to the previous government and the intensity of the struggle would work against accommodation. Autonomous politicized lower-class segments that supported the previous incumbent would present fundamental challenges to the authority of any new government, which, accordingly, would prefer a centralized executive strategy. If a charismatic leader won, he probably would establish a strong central executive. If elite groups played an important role and held potential charismatic leaders in check, then they would most likely favor the deconcentration of executive power.

All these new incumbents aim at political demobilization. However, political demobilization may not be successful. If the incumbent had relied on counterinsurgency or politicization of fundamental social cleavages, the resulting wounds may be too deep and raw to heal easily. Groups that are relatively autonomous may resist centralization. The temporary collapse of central authority under prolonged civil war in countries with poor communications and transportation may have resulted in increased regionalism. These are obstacles in the centralizing path to demobilization.

Where charismatic political mobilization prevails or where social bandits are active, there are often several such leaders. They, too, will resist centralization in the executive. Charismatically induced political participation works toward nation-building only when the leader comes out of the more modern political center. Charismatic political leaders who were former social bandits are a force for regionalism and national fragmentation. These are the leaders and followers who during wars sometimes refuse to fight beyond the perceived borders of their peasant neighborhood. If elite groups coexisted with charismatic political leaders and social bandits during the struggle, the result may be a severe clash to decide between the two demobilization strategies whose outcome depends on the relations of power established during the struggle.

Stalemate and low but continuing levels of warfare prevail where there is no clear candidate (individual or group) to lead toward political reconstruction. Demobilization becomes intermittent and incomplete. Local leaders or groups may attack the government from time to time. Large groups of people are not enabled to participate on their own, but are activated militarily each time by leaders or primitive organizations in traditional ways. Warfare had become recurrent. Violence becomes a permanent feature of these political systems. Society is politicized; politics are militarized.

No new government is established. No new order appears. The failure of government and the efforts toward political demobilization amid low social mobilization lead to little modernization. It is a political system with a high level of noise and disturbance, but with little change. Despite many claims and demands, there is little modernization of politics, the economy, or society. Violence and stalemate overcome reconstruction.

Reconstruction is also affected by the institutionalization of insurgent organizations and procedures. Insurgents that develop complex, coherent, adaptable, and autonomous organizations and procedures are more likely to overcome decaying governmental institutions. They are also more likely to establish successful countergovernments more quickly. One indicator of incipient insurgent institutionalization is the degree of differentiation between military and nonmilitary tasks in the struggle against the government. Another is whether the civilian arm of the insurgency can establish successful procedures for the removal of military leaders. The restoration of a minimum level of institutionalization, in a society where it had broken down, is most probable where the internal and external effects that led to the breakdown of institutionalization had had the least effect.

When does independence come? In countries where no group can achieve it by force, independence requires that the primary cleavage in the society become a political one vis-à-vis the colonial power. The socioethnic cleavage had to be restricted to an anti-colonial and anti-Spanish attitude. Ethnicity already had frustrated independence in Venezuela, Mexico, and Cuba. So a traditional Creole elite committed to seize power would make enough socioethnic concessions to woo mass participation and to build a pro-independence multiethnic coalition. But with victory achieved, the elite would try to freeze the social order and avoid significant structural concessions. The attack shifts to the foreigner in one's midst, especially the foreign colonial power. Few in societies at low levels of social mobilization had to be persuaded to shift from an internal socioethnic to a politico-international cleavage. The masses lacked the autonomous capacity to participate. Could their leaders be attracted to independence with the promise of an enhancement of power, wealth, or status?

After independence, a broad multiethnic coalition stressing a cleavage only above and outside the social hierarchy may find it difficult to remain united as old issues reappear and new ones develop. Politically effective divisiveness arises out of social bifurcation, that is, out of either the cumulation of cleavages leading to sharply differentiated groups within the society or the primacy of one cleavage over all others.[21] Political independence rarely meets the test of a deep social bifurcation because typically only the colonial country and a few of its colonists are involved. Internal social differentiation is put aside. Independence, once achieved, is a self-liquidating issue. Aristide Zolberg has described how a multiethnic, multiparty situation had been transformed into a dominant party coalition in Africa, adding:

> Paradoxically, it is the very success of the dominant parties in achieving political unanimity which has contributed most to growing insecurity in recent years. The co-optation of various elements into the ruling organization has not necessarily erased the differentiations that sustained opposing groups in the first place. Furthermore, the rewards of power have become so great that there is increasing competition among even the most faithful of lieutenants for the uppermost positions.[22]

In sum, when political independence becomes the dominant cleavage and political unanimity is established to achieve it, then the social question and earlier political conflicts are temporarily frozen. Former enemies unite in seeking independence. Once independence is achieved, that temporary union is removed, and fragmentation of politics may resume. Then the elite will attempt to continue to freeze the social system, perhaps even withdrawing some of the concessions it had made.

## Dissident Political Reconstruction in Spanish America

Political order had collapsed in Spanish America after 1810. The task of the rebels was not just to achieve independence but also to lay down the bases for a new political order. What efforts were made toward political reconstruction during the wars of independence? What was the outcome of the social issues raised in two of three colonies that rebelled?

### Venezuela

Insurgent strategy changed radically during the second phase of the war. Charismatically induced political mobilization of blacks was undertaken and fundamental cleavages were shifted from the internal social system to colonial anti-Spanish international issues. The only significant social concession was the abolition of slavery, conditional on the slaves' joining the rebel forces. Although rebel propaganda often conveyed the impression that slavery would be abolished altogether, the Creole elite would move toward independence only with a relatively frozen social order. The abolition of slavery would destabilize the labor supply — one of the elite's chief concerns in instigating rebellion.

The Congress of Angostura of 1819, called to prepare political reconstruction, was dominated by the Venezuelan Creole elite. The Congress rejected Bolívar's plea for abolition, limiting it to those who had served in the republican armed forces. It confirmed the long-standing abolition of the slave trade, but it postponed the freedom of existing slaves. The 1821 Congress of Cúcuta demonstrated the creativity of slaveowners. Those who were slaves would remain so. But the Congress proclaimed that all children born in Venezuela of slaves would henceforth be free. The trick was that this freedom could not be claimed until age eighteen. A child would have to serve its mother's master until then, postponing effective abolition until 1839. In effect, the slavery system was reconstructed. As 1839 arrived, slaveowners put further pressure on the government to save the labor supply. A decree of 1840 confirmed that the slaves were free; however, in another burst of oppressive creativity, the decree obliged these presumably free people to remain as apprentices under their masters until age twenty-five. Given the relatively low life expectancy of slaves, by then most of their life was thus used up.[23]

The second source of comfort to the Creole elite was the effective suppression of black political leadership. Although blacks had to be allowed access to political power if the independence coalition was to succeed, the amount of control they could exercise was circumscribed. Bolívar learned of the efforts by General Manuel Piar to mobilize blacks and mulattoes in Guayana in 1817 to seize power. Piar, though a mulatto, had referred to himself as white until the heat of the ethnic conflict of the wars of independence, when he identified himself as black. Piar was executed in October 1817; the main charge against him was that he had "planned a conspiracy to destroy the present government and to assassinate the whites who serve the Republic," and had "convoked black men, tried to blind them with the false idea that they were reduced to utter misery, tried to arm them, and passed himself as a black man."[24] The view that blacks were in "utter misery" would not appeal to the Creole elite who were responsible for that condition.

The execution of General Piar and the reconstruction of an effective slave system reassured the elite that the symbolic politics of charismatic participation would not seriously affect social policy. Venezuela became independent with a relatively unchanged social order.

The Creole elite itself took care of the third important measure: to block the access of black freedmen to the University and, hence, to elite jobs. This turned the clock back, undoing the policies of social mobility of the Spanish Crown. The University continued to require "purity of blood" as late as 1822 — previous royal orders to the contrary and liberal rebel rhetoric about civil equality notwithstanding. After 1822 the University required only that there should be proof of adherence to Roman Catholicism and of legitimate birth. This second requirement, which effectively excluded many poor whites and blacks, preserved a white and aristocratic University. When these formal requirements were not sufficient to keep blacks out, the University resorted to harassment and humiliation. One lonely black student withdrew from the University in 1826 for these reasons.[25]

The reconstruction of slavery fixed the bottom of the social system at 1810 level. The University restricted access to the elite. And the repression of black leadership prevented the rise of an alternative elite with roots in the lower class. By limiting external agents of political mobilization, given low levels of social mobilization, and resisting the possible social transformations of the wars and of modernization, elite political control was assured and mass political demobilization set in.

The source of political legitimacy, however, was unclear. The revolt of 1810 was a collective movement led by the elite corporate organizations. The elite's concern for legality caused them to draft the Constitution of 1811. With the defeat of the first efforts toward independence, each politico-military leader became his own source of authority. This shift from elite group to charismatic legitimacy was compounded by preexisting regionalist forces. The Caracas proclamation of autonomy from Spain in 1810 was followed by similar actions in Cumaná, Barcelona, Margarita Island, Guayana, Barinas, Mérida, and Trujillo. But only the first three sent delegates to Caracas to organize a national government. The others claimed autonomy from both Spain and Caracas.

Civilian government lasted only two months of active war. The Congress then named General Francisco de Miranda, Dictator of Venezuela; he was subsequently defeated. Bolívar entered Venezuela in 1813 under the authority of the rebel government of New Granada. Once there, he acted on his own. His basis of legitimacy was himself and his military power; there was no Junta and no Congress. A popular assembly in Caracas, called in January 1814, merely confirmed his dictatorship. An assembly of generals and some civilians sought unsuccessfully in Curiacó in 1817 to curb his authority. That same year Bolívar named a Council of State to administer the government and a Council of Government to rule in his absence. But his own authority, relying increasingly on charismatic appeals, remained unchallenged and unrestrained.

Venezuela's regionalism reproduced the basic pattern of legitimacy throughout the country. Regional elite group legitimacy was replaced by regional charismatic legitimacy, in which the leader controlled his area and ruled on his own authority.[26] But charismatic legitimacy is fundamentally unstable: the leader has to improve the conditions of his people. This source of legitimacy lends itself to fragmentation. With as many sources of legitimacy as charismatic leaders the establishment of a unified central government is very difficult.[27]

The 1819 Congress of Angostura, the first of its kind, confirmed Bolívar's dictatorship. The Congress of Cúcuta, taking the first steps to routinize charismatic legitimacy, proclaimed the Constitution of 1821 for northern South America, which would become the Republic of Colombia (including today's Venezuela, Colombia, Panama, and Ecuador). Actually the new constitution was suspended because Bolívar would have full dictatorial powers whenever he was in military campaign—which was all the time.

The first effort to establish constitutional civilian supremacy was in July 1824. The Congress (in Bogotá) voted that Bolívar's new powers as Dictator of Peru were incompatible with his presidency of Colombia. Bolívar postponed resigning until December 1824, but his final victories against Spain destroyed Bogotá's opposition. In February 1825 the Congress unanimously voted to reject his resignation. Whatever constitutional basis of legitimacy may have existed in Colombia ended in June 1828 when Bolívar suspended the Constitution on his own "higher" authority and ruled by decree. Only a dictatorial executive power was permissible for a charismatic leader.

Venezuela faced a similar problem. Conflicts had arisen among the various politico-military leaders. By far the most disruptive was General José Antonio Páez who ruled in the plains with the full authority that might be expected of a charismatic leader who recognized no constitutional authority in Bogotá. In March 1826 the Bogotá Congress deposed Páez from the post of military commandant of Venezuela. Páez revolted immediately, and, that June, began to govern Caracas and Valencia without any legal limits on his authority. Bolívar entered Venezuela in December 1826. Páez acknowledged his authority, but no other. A hierarchy of personal leadership was recognized temporarily, but constitutional government was not. Bolívar governed in Venezuela, too, on his own authority, suspending Bogotá's. In effect, the Republic of Colombia had been dissolved. The formal dissolution, however, did not come until the fall of 1829, when "popular assemblies" in Valencia and Caracas seceded from Colombia and granted General Páez dictatorial powers. Regional leaders, however, continued to exercise considerable local authority, barely recognizing Páez's central government in Caracas.[28]

The elite came to support Páez as the last best hope of a reconstructed political order. He ruled Venezuela for a decade and a half under the nominal authority of the Constitution of 1830, basing his political legitimacy on charisma to attract the plainsmen, and on military force and economic incentives. The social and economic systems were reconstructed conservatively; slavery was preserved. Social and political turmoil were rampant, but social and political mobility were limited to a few leaders who benefited from their military power and from the redistribution of wealth begun by Bolívar to assist his military officers. Independence came with a relatively frozen social order and inherently unstable charismatic political leadership.

The story of nineteenth-century Venezuela after the fall of Páez reenacts these circumstances. As one political leader was unable to deliver the symbolic, political, and economic goods, another arose. Thus, considerable political upheaval took place even though the social structure endured, lasting with but few changes throughout most of the century. But during the first years of independence, charismatic legitimacy did provide a modicum of political and social stability that permitted economic recovery.

## Mexico

In 1820, when the liberal Spanish Constitution was restored, New Spain, except for Guerrero's persistent guerrillas, was loyal and largely pacified though confronted by a metropolitan political system that its conservative elite found offensive. Dislike turned into a serious political crisis as a result of a shift in the policies of the Cortes. These policies, mostly ineffective in the first liberal constitutional period, in the second period were able to drive New Spain's conservatives to secession.

On Auguest 14, 1820, the Cortes voted to expel the Society of Jesus from the empire and to confiscate its property. The Cortes moved to repeal ecclesiastical privilege or fueros on September 25, 1820, although Article 249 of the Constitution of 1812 had guaranteed them. The clergy was deprived of its separate privileged judicial system and would be subject to civil jurisdiction in criminal cases. That same month the Cortes voted a sweeping reform of the religious orders. All monasteries of monastic orders and all convents — except those of the mendicant orders (Franciscans and Dominicans) — and colleges of military orders were suppressed; their benefices would accrue to the bishops and the Crown. Religious orders were prohibited from establishing new convents, accepting novices, or ordaining new members. The real estate of the suppressed convents was confiscated. Entailments on real estate were abolished and future restrictions on the free exchange of real estate prohibited. Churches, monasteries, convents, hospitals, brotherhoods, and other religious organizations were prohibited from acquiring entailed real estate.[29]

The repeal of ecclesiastical immunity affected the lower clergy the most. Because they had little property, these privileges were important sources of the poorer clergy's power and prestige. The government's attack severed the bonds of loyalty of many clergymen to Spain. Many clergymen had already fought in 1812, and thereafter, against similar provisions by the earlier liberal Cortes. The decrees of 1820 surpassed those of the 1812 Constitution by far. Many of the 1812 decrees and laws were aimed only at insurgent clergymen who lost their acclesiastical immunities thereby, whereas the provisions of 1820 had universal application.[30]

The attack on Church property raised different issues. In 1813 the Church owned 47.1 percent of the value of all real estate in the city of Mexico, and an earlier attack on it had wreaked havoc on New Spain's economy.[31] The Royal Law of Consolidation, issued on December 26, 1804, fourteen days after Spain declared war on England, provided for the confiscation and forced sale of much of the Church's real estate owned by "pious works." The Church had been the principal capital lender in New Spain, and the law called in all of its debts: urban and rural properties morgaged to the Church had to pay some cash immediately; if they could not, they were sold at auction. Proceeds from the sale were deposited in a Royal Amortization Fund. This was, in effect, a forced loan from the Church to the Crown, where the latter paid only 3 percent annual interest. The resulting financial crisis alienated the Church and the elites. The Council of Regency rescinded it in January 1809 in a attempt to win over New Spain's disaffected elites. But the government held onto the funds collected before that date, and in 1812 it stopped repaying principal or interest. The government collected somewhat over 12 million pesos from the Church as a result of the law.[32] Church and elites in New Spain in 1820 did not want to repeat that experience.

On September 29, 1820, the Cortes extended an earlier law to the colonies; this deprived the colonial militiamen of their privilege of trial by military courts for nonmilitary offenses. The military fuero of the militia was eliminated. A proposed law to deny military jurisdiction in all civil and criminal cases (except those of a strictly military nature) in the regular army was published in Spain on October 25, 1820. It was enacted for Spain in May 1821 and given a first reading to extend it to the colonies in June 1821.[33]

In May 1821 the Cortes established a committee to look into ways of pacifying America. The committee praised Spain and made no recommendation except to urge the government to bring proposals concerning America before the Cortes. It laid the blame for America's troubles on bad governors, not on Spanish laws and interests. An American minority filed a dissent and proposed reforms in the organization of the empire moving toward a multinational commonwealth with autonomous members. The government responded that these proposals were contrary to the Constitution and that neither the executive nor the Cortes could implement them. The new government may have been liberal for some purposes, but it viewed America as a colonial empire and Americans as subjects of Spaniards.[34]

News of the ecclesiastical reforms had reached New Spain by October 1820. The decrees were formally published there in January 1821. News of the proposed changes in military privileges arrived as early as July 1820. The clergy of the city of Puebla, with the support of the Bishop, petitioned the Viceroy to suspend anticlerical laws. There were riots in Puebla for two days. The Bishop of Guadalajara denounced the reforms in a pastoral letter. The deacon of the Cathedral of Valladolid, Michoacán, called openly for independence.[35]

In February 1821 the Creole General Agustín de Iturbide, commander of the royalist forces in southern Mexico, together with the illiterate Indian General Vicente Guerrero, chief of the guerrillas, signed the Plan de Iguala. Independence for New Spain required that the earlier internal socioethnic division be blurred and transformed into a politico-international division vis-à-vis Spain. This was Iguala's task. Article 1 proclaimed the continued union of the Roman Catholic Church and the State; no other religious practices were to be tolerated. Article 2 proclaimed independence. Articles 3 and 4 proclaimed the monarchy. Thus, Iguala brought about minimum change consistent with independence in order not to frighten away the economic, political, and religious elites except insofar as they bore upon the direct tie with Spain. The most radical proposal, needed to win over Guerrero's supporters, was civil equality of all ethnic groups with regard to employment.

Guarantees for the established order were impressive. Article 13 guaranteed the stability of property relations. Article 14 guaranteed the privileges and property of the clergy and religious orders, specifically nullifying many of the Cortes' ecclesiastical reforms. Article 15 guaranteed job security to the civil bureaucracy. Article 17 confirmed all military officers in their posts and reestablished privileged military jurisdiction in civil and criminal matters for soldiers and militiamen.

Thus, independence was achieved by setting aside the socioethnic issue and stressing a single limited cleavage: the break with Spain.[36]

The Creole bishop of Puebla, a personal friend of Iturbide, encouraged him. The Bishop of Guadalajara gave Iturbide 25,000 pesos in December 1820 and announced his official support in spring 1821. The Bishop of Puebla openly pledged support in early August 1821. By fall 1821 the entire hierarchy was supporting independence publicly — except for the Archbishop of Mexico City, who remained loyal to Spain to the end.[37]

The Army of the Three Guarantees — independence, Roman Catholic religion, and civil equality — headed by Iturbide and Guerrero, gathered widespread support throughout the old viceroyalty. By the Treaty of Córdoba, August 1821, the Spanish authorities in Mexico recognized Iguala, hence Mexican independence. Mexican independence, although subsequently disavowed by an outraged government in Spain, was sealed. After a halfhearted, fruitless search for a Spanish prince, Iturbide was proclaimed Emperor of Mexico in May 1822. Unlike Bolívar, he could not be called a charismatic leader.

The Junta of Guatemala adhered to Iguala with the following statement: "Independence has been proclaimed and sworn on the fifteenth of the month only in order not to depend on the government of the Peninsula, and to be able to do in our country everything that we had been able to do before. All the laws, ordinances, and orders which were in effect before remain duly in effect."[38]

Some liberal anticlerical legislation remained on the books. The Inquisition, the Jesuit Order, and the Hospitaler Orders were disbanded, their lands and funds seized, and their functions turned over to the city government or the secular clergy. Independence necessitated certain changes. Civil equality among whites and nonwhites was essential to build mass support and to win over Guerrero's guerrillas. And economic decisionmaking, including freedom of trade, was nationalized as a necessary consequence of the appropriation of sovereignty.[39]

One symbol of unity among the whites was the distribution of titles of nobility. There were sixty-three titled noblemen in New Spain in 1810; when the titles were granted, 68 percent went to Spaniards, the rest to Creoles. (However, because titles were inherited, 81 percent of the titleholders in 1810 were Mexican-born.) King Ferdinand VII created a new noble order in 1815, the Caballeros de Isabel la Católica, to reward service in America. Although all but one of the original title grants went to Spaniards, subsequent grants had decreased their share to half of the thirty-eight knights in 1822. Emperor Iturbide made thirty-four grants of titled nobility, one-third of which went to Spaniards.[40] Thus, the Spanish share declined from two-thirds to one-half to one-third — though it was not Iturbide's intention to rule out Spaniard participation in the running of independent Mexico.

Independence had come to New Spain with a relatively static social order. Very little had changed, although the changes effected were important ones. The Creole elite, supported by the military and Church hierarchies, had seized legitimate authority from Spain. Liberal anticlericalism in Spain provided a basis for pious mass support in New Spain. And the refusal of Spain's liberal government to share power with the Creole elite finally propelled a conservative revolution in New Spain. Top Spanish elite officeholders turned their offices over to Creoles. The Spanish expeditionary army was repatriated, leaving the Creole military in power. Commercial restrictions were abolished. Otherwise, as far as the subelites were concerned, very little in the social or economic system changed.

The destruction of imperial legitimacy failed to establish the bases for new legitimate authority. Fathers Hidalgo and Morelos were charismatic leaders deriving their authority from religion and military courage — a striking and effective combination of the divine and the heroic. Hidalgo was a rebel leader for a few months only: from September 1810 until his capture in March 1811. He had little time to think about political reconstruction, and there is scant evidence that he did.

Morelos was a rebel leader for a number of years, and he promoted the political reconstruction of Mexico. From October 1810, when he began his career as a rebel leader, until late spring 1813, Morelos stressed only his charismatic legitimacy. In June 1813, however, he issued a call for a Congress at Chilpancingo.

His proposed Reglamento of September 1813 called for an executive: a Generalissimo to serve for life, elected by army officers with the rank of colonel or above. Morelos, who appointed six of the eight delegates to Congress, was elected Generalissimo. As in Venezuela, this charismatic political leader envisioned a strong executive authority. However, by late 1813 Morelos had been seriously defeated in military combat. He resigned as Generalissimo in January 1814 and was stripped of most of his troops by Congress. The Congress (expanded nominally to sixteen members) assumed political authority and gave military authority to other commanders. But it was more worried about survival than about legislation. Six of its members drafted the Constitution of Apatzingán, proclaimed in October 1814 when the war was virtually lost, which established a weak three-man executive (with Morelos one of the three). By the beginning of 1815 Morelos was clearly once again the chief, if not exclusive leader, of what remained of a much weakened rebellion. He and most of the officers of the rebel government were captured in the fall of 1815.[41]

The decline of Morelos in 1814, unlike similar situations that occurred in Venezuela in the mid-1820s and Chile in 1813-14, followed decisive military defeat. When Morelos was succeeding on the battlefield, there was no serious civilian effort to curb his authority. This indicates that there was less of an attempt to rely on something other than charismatic legitimacy in Mexico than in the other two colonies. On the other hand, in 1814, in reaction to the eclipse of the top military leader, an attempt was made to deconcentrate executive authority. Power, however, remained in the hands of the military. And there is no evidence that the Constitution of Apatzingán greatly altered the course of events. The civilian ascendancy to be witnessed in Chile was still missing. Mexico ranked higher than Venezuela in the effort to deconcentrate authority but lower than Chile.

The chief problem with deconcentrating authority in Mexico was that the new power holders did not have traditional bases of legitimacy. They were not members of the central colonial elites as in Venezuela or Chile. Thus, in fact, deconcentration meant the fragmentation of authority which devolved onto military commanders. Collective government in Mexico during 1814 was aggregated praetorianism, not a drive toward political reconstruction under congressional civilian control. The defeat of its military leaders left the country with no possibility of effective political reconstruction because no alternative bases of legitimacy had been developed.

Routinization of charisma was difficult by 1820 because no generally recognized leader remained, except Vicente Guerrero, whom the elite did not want in control. The central Mexican Creole elite, moreover, unlike those in Venezuela and Chile, had failed to revolt until the very end. It entered the period of independence without any real "rebellious" legitimacy acquired during years of struggle to govern the country. On the other hand, certain military chieftains, including Vicente Guerrero, had fought for independence continuously. In the absence of elite political legitimacy to govern, and in the presence of a possible challenge to their rule from Guerrero and other rebel military, the elite concentrated on preserving the social order.

Much of the executive power would be left in the hands of military men. Mexico lacked a distinguished member of the elite with charismatic political appeal among the lowest strata, such as Bolívar in Venezuela, and a competent elite with a tradition of rebellion against Spain, as in Chile, to build a new legitimacy. The size of the military, moreover, made political demobilization more difficult. Each petty chieftain had a stake in keeping in touch with people who could be politically mobilized for booty and power. With the elite politically crippled, there would be opportunities for political chaos. Only naked force could bring someone to power and keep him there. On this fragile ground, Mexican political reconstruction began.

There were many coups, countercoups, conspiracies, rebellions, and proclamations during the first quarter-century of Mexican independence.[42] They far out numbered those in Venezuela, which relied on the charisma of Bolívar and Páez in the early years of independence. Venezuelan instability came after the fall of Páez in the mid-1840s. Mexican political instability and rampant praetorianism started with the coming of independence.

Despite considerable political activity in Mexico, there was little political change. Even liberals recoiled from significant social change which might affect the subelites. They wanted a republic of free property owners or an "aristocracy of talent." Whenever the Indian or mestizo masses stirred, the liberals retreated from political change. Their main proposal was secularism: curbing the power of the Church, and even in this respect they were singularly unsuccessful during the first quarter-century of independence. The brief regimes of this period never held power more than a few months. Charles Hale summarizes the early years of the Mexican republic in his study of the leading Mexican liberal of the time, Dr. José María Luis Mora:

> The clash of political ideas of the pre-*Reforma* [pre-mid-1850's] was carried on within Mexico's social elite. Creole Mexico, whether liberal or conservative, stiffened at the prospect of "democracy" — active participation in politics by a Vicente Guerrero, by the Maya Indians of Yucatán . . . Creole social conservatism had great resilience during the nineteenth century . . . liberalism during the age of Mora remained an elite concept.[43]

In sum, Mexico became independent with a relatively unchanged social order and continuing efforts maintain it. There was greater political instability than in Venezuela because the bases of government were even shakier. Intermittent internal and international warfare injured the Mexican economy, which failed to recover. By the 1840s the rate of economic recovery was fastest in Chile, next so in Venezuela, and slowest in Mexico. The failure of political reconstruction in Mexico led to political praetorianism and stalemate, selective but incomplete social demobilization, and economic stagnation.

### Chile

In Chile social issues did not play a prominent role in the war of independence, unlike Venezuela and Mexico which achieved independence only by obscuring them. The failure of Chile's first move toward independence resulted from a combination of military defeat and cross-pressured political withdrawal. Independence finally was imposed from the outside through military conquest which required little political mobilization. Political mobilization had been very high in Venezuela and Mexico, but very low in Chile, where the central elites played key roles.[44] Chile's externally imposed independence was part of Buenos Aires' grand military design for the expulsion of Spain from South America. Chilean leaders participated as officers fighting a military battle, not as political leaders mobilizing a people.

In his study of the wars of independence in Latin America, Charles Griffin has noted that "the relatively stable agrarian economy of Chile with its strong personal ties between landowner and inquilino provided fewer opportunities for social change than the more elaborately stratified population of Peru, Colombia and Mexico."[45] Demobilization was far easier in Chile because there had been so little mobilization in the first instance.

Counterinsurgency had been tried in Venezuela, and the politicization of social cleavages was tried in Mexico. Political authority was weakened in both countries during the nineteenth century because these new social forces had not been completely demobilized — the imperial framework, once shattered, was not reconstructed in the same way. Charismatic political legitimacy had been unstable in Venezuela and became even more so after the fall of Páez. In Chile, however, these two incumbent strategies, so destabilizing in the long run, were not used. And the role of charismatic political leadership was limited and contained. Incumbent strategy in Chile relied on repression, which battered the country but did not alter its social structure. Legitimacy rested with the elite group that seized power and that would successfully prevent its reconcentration.

The Chilean elite moved to establish civilian collective supremacy during the wars of independence, foreshadowing the oligarchic political system that flourished in the 1830s and thereafter. These efforts were not totally successful, but there was more civilian ascendancy in Chile during the wars of independence than there had been in Mexico and Venezuela.

Elections for a Congress, held on a restricted franchise in early 1811, were won of course by the Creole elite. This congressional government was overthrown in September 1811 by a coalition of General José Miguel Carrera, a segment of the Santiago elite led by the Larraín family, and the Concepción regional elite. Another coup, two months later, established Carrera as the sole leader; subsequently he dissolved Congress.

Carrera was a striking leader with considerable political support. Although he does not seem to have had the appeal of Bolívar, Páez, Hidalgo, and Morelos, he was the closest Chilean version of a charismatic political leader. Like other such leaders, his Constitution of 1812 vested executive power in himself. A three-man Junta ruled in his absence, and there was also a seven-man Senate. Carrera named members of the Junta and the Senate.

Chile differed from the other colonies because its civilian elite had a greater consciousness of its interests. Despite his bravado, Carrera was unable to win militarily in 1813; a stalemate resulted. The ambivalence of the elite, horror at some of the devastation perpetrated by Carrera's armies, and a desire for peace combined to bring about a decision by the Junta in Santiago to relieve Carrera and his brothers of their military commands. After a few weeks of hesitation the Junta's decree was accepted by Carrera and Bernardo O'Higgins became commander-in-chief. In the (southern hemisphere) fall 1814, as the Spanish forces threatened autonomous Chile, the Junta resigned, after electing Francisco de la Lastra, one of the leading members of Santiago's Creole elite, Dictator of Chile. A military coup by General Carrera overthrew the Lastra dictatorship in July 1814. A civil war developed between Carrera and O'Higgins during July and August that was interrupted by the landing of the third Spanish expedition under General Osorio.[46]

This brief recounting of Chilean politics underlines several differences between Chile, Venezuela, and Mexico. Unlike Venezuela and Mexico, where political legitimacy rested for years on the power and authority of particular leaders, the establishment of a legal base for rule was far more common in Chile, whose elite stressed continuity with the colony and new elections in early 1811. Even Carrera, after two coups in late 1811, established a constitution within a year. The Venezuelan Constitution of 1811 also reflects the legal concern of its Creole elite. But legal government collapsed in Venezuela as soon as the war began and legitimacy had to depend on the authority of military leaders. This did not happen in Chile. The Chilean elite was strong enough to maintain some commitment to legal forms throughout the wars with but brief interruption. In Mexico, where the central elites did not begin a revolt, even a weak legal constitutional basis had to wait three years.

Civilians lost in Mexico and Venezuela, but won in Chile where their supremacy prevailed over Carrera's command. Venezuelan civilians were singularly unsuccessful, and in Mexico, Morelos, too, was replaced, but by other military officers after serious military defeat. Carrera was replaced only because he could not break out of military stalemate. Chileans turned power over to a leading elite civilian when they concentrated executive authority in the face of danger; they kept civilian and military authority separate. The Venezuelan Congress of 1811 turned the dictatorship over to Miranda, the military commander; a similar thing occurred with Morelos in Mexico in 1815. Power in Chile was divided between civilian and military organs, even while Carrera was the chief executive of Chile from 1811 to 1813.

It would be wrong to overemphasize the role of a collective civilian elite in Chile. Carrera's three military coups clearly undermined legal civilian continuity. Nevertheless, Chile had a vigorous organized elite which did not surrender its claim to be the source of legitimate authority before charisma or praetorianism.

When the first Chilean movement toward independence collapsed, it was probably an open question as to whether legitimacy in independent Chile would be based on charismatic political legitimacy or on the political legitimacy of the traditional elite. This was far more than could be said for Venezuela, where charismatic legitimacy prevailed, or Mexico, where the reliance on sheer military force was increasingly prevalent. The possibility of an alternative to praetorianism and charismatic legitimation made Chile different.

Independence in Chile eventually was imposed from the outside. General O'Higgins then "became Supreme Director because of a military feat, not because he had garnered the support of a reasonably large portion of the active citizenry."[47] O'Higgins could not be considered charismatic; he was not flashy or personalist, nor was he generally perceived as having special religious sanction. Although his personal courage was respected, his claim to heroic qualities was questionable for he had been decisively defeated in some of the most important battles of the Chile's wars of independence: Cancharrayada (1814), Rancagua (1814), and again at Cancharrayada (1818).

So independence was won without the aid of a charismatic leader, leaving open the road to legitimate government based on collective civilian elite rule. There was no guarantee, no inevitability, that this outcome would take place, but the very existence of the possibility was enough to distinguish politics in Chile. The elites of Mexico and Venezuela had been socially but not politically resilient. The elites of Chile were both.

## Prevailing Ideologies

Skepticism has been expressed about the usefulness of explanations that stress the importance of the intellectual ideas of the French Enlightenment and revolution, or of the revolution in the United States, as causes of the wars of independence. These ideas, widespread in Spanish America, were used to justify some revolts. Precisely because they were found in virtually every colony, including Cuba, the problem arises that a similar cause (these ideas) cannot be used to explain opposite consequences (insurrection and loyalty). These ideas were contradictory; many thinkers disagreed about them. Two features of the liberal intellectual ideas of the late eighteenth century were typically absent in the Latin American wars of independence: there were few new curbs on the power of the Church to disestablish it politically and to create a secular state; and there was limited expansion of the suffrage.

The Venezuelan Constitution of 1811 proclaimed the union of Church and State and maintained religious intolerance. Religious disestablishment came only from the struggles of the 1830s. A free male over the age of twenty-one, who was a property owner, could vote in a first-echelon election if he had property worth between 200 and 600 pesos (depending on whether he was single or married). To be an elector in the higher-echelon election, single men in Caracas had to have property worth 6,000 pesos, married men 4,000 pesos; outside Caracas, the rates were 4,000 and 3,000 pesos respectively. These high property qualifications disenfranchised all but landowners, professionals, and high bureaucrats. Given prevailing salaries, no unmarried black or mulatto military officer could be a first-echelon elector and none could be a second-echelon elector. The Constitution established the sanctity of property and freedom of industry and trade. While formally guaranteeing freedom of the press, it permitted political and religious censorship. Its most radical provision was the civil equality of all Venezuelan citizens. However, since slavery was not abolished, and most free blacks were politically disenfranchished, this was a weak provision.

The Venezuelan Constitution of 1830 gave voting rights to those with property yielding an income worth 50 pesos or income from a profession or trade worth 100, or a salary of 150 pesos, but only for first-echelon elections. Property requirements for second-echelon electors, who had more power, were set at 200, 300, and 400 pesos respectively.[48] Venezuela's most modernizing thinkers were willing to do away with monarchy and nobility and to reform education and the economy; but even they thought of the "people" as property owners only, and they were reluctant to accept the full implications of equality as conceived in the French revolution. They also barely limited the Church's secular prerogatives.[49]

The wars of independence in Mexico, under Hidalgo and Morelos, were characterized by religious fanaticism. The Constitution of Apatzingán of 1814 established the Catholic Church and maintained religious intolerance. Following Iguala, the Constitution of 1824 and those thereafter until 1857 maintained an established Church, religious intolerance, and separate ecclesiastical jurisdiction in civil and criminal affairs. By act of Congress, August 1823, the decrees of the Cortes of 1820 were nullified. The Church was free to acquire entailed property. The liberal Congress of Chilpancingo, called by Morelos in 1813, proclaimed the sanctity of property. It did not take up the more radical agrarian program with which Morelos had come to be associated. There were property requirements to vote in independent Mexico — though they were meaningless without elections. Most liberals believed in property qualifications for voting, and all delegates to the liberal national constituent Congress of 1856 were landowners.[50]

The Chilean Constitutions of 1812, 1818, 1822, 1828, and 1833 established Roman Catholicism as the state religion. Religious toleration was included only in the Constitution of 1828. It was absent in all others, and some proclaimed intolerance explicitly. Simon Collier, who believes that these liberal external ideas played an important role, summarized the Chilean position on voting rights: "If popular elections were a cardinal element in the new philosophy of representative government, universal suffrage was not. The 'people,' on the whole, did not in practice mean much more than the creole aristocracy and intelligentsia. There were many sections of the population, it was held, which were incapable of voting properly." All of Chile's electoral laws (1810, 1813, 1823-1828, 1831, and 1833) included literacy and property ownership as voting requirements. Chile's leading elite liberals were as convinced about the need for such qualifications as its conservatives were. Literacy alone effectively limited voting to the elite.[51]

In sum, the prevailing ideologies in these three rebellious colonies and some key characteristics of eighteenth-century liberalism differed. The revolts in the three Spanish American countries were not secularizing. Religious fanaticism was at a high pitch in Mexico; it was least so in Venezuela. But the role of the Church was not fundamentally questioned anywhere. Property qualifications remained high and prevalent enough so that only landowners, upper-class professionals, public officers, merchants, and industrialists were enfranchised. Participation in the political system was restricted to the elite, as it had always been. Such restrictions even disenfranchised small businessmen and professionals of modest means who would be incorporated in the French and North American revolutions. In contrast, little expansion of political enfranchisement beyond the elite took place in Chile, or was comtemplated in Mexico or Venezuela.

If some key modern ideas were rejected, this does not mean that all prevalent ideas were traditional; but there was no ideological replacement. Instead, there was a very selective and limited merger of traditional ideas with one new and necessary idea: political independence. This led to rule by the native elites alone or in alliance with military leaders. The impact of Enlightenment ideas on politics in Spanish America may have been more substantial after independence than before. Independence threw these colonies into disarray and may have facilitated the spread of the Enlightenment's more liberal political ideas. The Enlightment may have been more a consequence than a cause of independence.[52]

Although Cuba did not revolt, the strategy pursued by Spain in holding onto it was so profound that, in fact, a reconstruction took place. The Cuban Creole elite shared legitimacy. Bases for political authority were seriously challenged in the newly independent countries. Because of the low levels of social mobilization they moved successfully toward political and social demobilization. The Chileans were the only ones with the option of civilian, constitutional government, based on elite rule, at the time of independence; elsewhere, traditional elites collapsed. The Venezuelans relied exclusively on charismatic political legitimacy; Mexico was quickly overcome by praetorianism. The prevailing ideologies that guided the early constitutional efforts adopted the bright idea of independence but couched the political system very conservatively, rejecting secularization and mass political participation.

# 13

# The Problem Revisited

The central theme of this book is the relation between political participation and government response and the ability of political institutions to adapt beyond transient crises. These issues have been analyzed in four Spanish American countries at a critical point in their histories. Three became independent; the political, social, and economic structures of the fourth were transformed within a continuing colonial setting.

## Plausible Hypotheses Rejected

One basic process of social science undertaken in this book is the elimination of plausible alternative hypotheses. The social mobilization hypothesis does not explain the surge of political participation. Levels of social mobilization were far too low for it to apply on a mass basis. The "precursor" hypothesis holds that the wars of independence were an extension of mass political explosions that took place before 1810. But traditional, even violent, mass political participation had been accommodated in the empire through compromise or repression. Traditional procedures of positional social mobility operated also as a safety valve. The military establishment was responsive to its soldiers, even to black freedmen. Other factors had to intervene before mass political explosions could disrupt the political system.

The subjective foreign-trade hypothesis holds that independence came because Spain's restrictions on foreign trade had become intolerable. However, significant sectors in the elites of Chile and Mexico were opposed to freer trade, while a desire for it was accommodated in Cuba. The hypothesis is not a necessary explanation of the coming of independence because independence came even in the absence of demands for freer trade in Chile and Mexico. Nor is it sufficient to explain independence, because it failed to come in Cuba in the presence of subjective demands for freer trade. Two versions of the objective foreign-trade hypotheses were considered. One holds that an objective decline in exports, regardless of the level of elite consciousness, is necessary to explain independence. But Mexico went to war in 1810, after a period of increased export values. The second holds that, though not all wars of independence can be explained by loss of foreign trade or elite consciousness, a war of independence resulted whenever foreign trade losses appeared. But Cuba experienced declines in the value of foreign trade prior to 1810 and failed to revolt. Thus, hypotheses about foreign trade losses or, generally, about objective economic relative deprivation do not explain patterns of both insurrection and loyalty.

The hypothesis that economic growth is inherently disruptive of the political and social systems was not supported. The economic growth of Chile was not very disrupting, where economic issues were less important than in other countries. On the other hand, perhaps the most spectacular economic growth took place in Cuba, which failed to revolt. Accordingly, the same cause had opposite consequences.

Modern intellectual ideas were present in all four colonies before 1810, so this factor does not discriminate between insurrection and loyalty. In addition, the presence of these ideas does not account for the differing attitudes on freer foreign trade: two colonies were for it and two against it. Mexico's intellectual modernization does not parallel its preference for restrictive trade, while a less intellectually modernized colony, Venezuela, preferred freer trade. Modern intellectual ideas such as religious secularization and the expansion of political participation were rare in pro-independence intellectual thought and the early constitutions. Modern ideas were part of a world environment, but their causal effect was unclear.

The hypothesis that the collapse of imperial legitimacy in 1808 explains the wars of independence was insufficient. A comparable collapse of imperial legitimacy a century earlier failed to produce similar consequences. Cuba remained loyal between 1808 and 1815, while the Napoleonic Wars raged, and not all parts of the rebellious colonies revolted. Other factors had to be present. Moreover, the initial response in Chile, Mexico, and Venezuela was not rebellion, but increased traditional jockeying for position. Several conspiracies or revolts seeking independence had appeared prior to the imperial collapse; they could not have been caused by it.

The hypothesis that fondness for Spain explains the failure to revolt is not accurate enough. Cuba, Coro, and Maracaibo failed to revolt, but their dislike for Spaniards was probably as keen as that in the rebellious colonies. Intraelite ethnic competition is not a sufficient explanation of a turn toward independence, because it was very strong in otherwise loyal Cuba, Coro, and Maracaibo; the hypothesis that the loyal areas were less modernizing also did not fit, for these were rather modernized areas, but within a hierarchical ethnic system. However, southern Chile and northern New Spain, characterized by parallel ethnic systems, were less modernized and more tied to Spain.

Although not all modernizing elites revolted, not all central elites failed to revolt. Central elites revolted in Venezuela and in Chile in 1810, in Mexico in 1821. The hypothesis that the Creole elites revolted because they lacked access to public office is also weak. They had continuing high access in Cuba and Chile; and between a majority and three-quarters of the rebel leadership in Mexico and Chile had had access to appointment in the civil, military, or ecclesiastical bureaucracies. Nor does a simple decline in the proportion of American-born members of high offices explain revolt, for substantial declines had occurred earlier in the eighteenth century without leading to insurrection. The wars of independence were not youthful explosions; they were begun and conducted by mature men. The titled nobility headed the Venezuelan and Chilean movements for autonomy and independence. Even in Mexico, the income, education, occupation, public access, and spatial mobility of those most responsible for independence suggest that they were an elite offshoot.

Government did not collapse because it was traditional and rigid. Considerable efforts toward its modernization had been made, and even radical or liberal ideas were used at times. Spain mobilized whites or blacks and promoted elections and parliamentary opportunities as needed for imperial preservation. It usually had been responsive to traditional elites — but not only to them. The Crown promoted social mobility for blacks within the traditional and accommodable system. Black freedmen were welcomed into the military, and the Crown relied heavily on black political mobilization in Venezuela to retain power.

Four special hypotheses about Cuba's nonrevolt were rejected: that the colony's political leaders were all Spanish so that Creoles had no experience of leadership; that Cuba was repressed militarily; that the influx of Spaniards fleeing from the mainland kept the colony loyal to Spain; and that geographic obstacles prevented outside liberation. The colony's political leadership included Creoles in some of the most distinguished positions. The supression of conspiracies in the 1820s was a police, not a military matter. Spaniards were the disruptive element in Cuba; Creoles were far less so. Though Cuba's insularity was undeniably an obstacle, the South American insurgents had demonstrated some ability to mount seaborne operations, to impose liberation from the outside, while Spain had no fleet capable of stopping it. The will to overcome those surmountable obstacles, however, was missing. The flurry of conspiracies in Cuba during the first quarter of the nineteenth century cannot be traced to a rift between big and small planters; this did not occur until the 1830s and 1840s.

Not all newly independent countries were immediately plunged into praetorianism, nor do the bases for political reconstruction date exclusively from the post-independence period. On the contrary, post-independence stability was related to the conduct of the wars themselves and to government and insurgent strategies.

Certain specific events which contributed to political disruption between 1808 and 1810 had occurred in the empire's past without producing such drastic consequences. The agricultural crisis of 1809-10, for example, created conditions for insurrection in New Spain, but such crises had been commonplace in the eighteenth century. The deposition of a Governor in Chile or the calling of an open meeting of Santiago's Cabildo or municipal corporation had occurred in the past, but the empire was not overturned. These events later became disruptive because other social, economic, and political changes had taken place, but by themselves they do not to explain the insurrections.

The insurrections, John Lynch has argued, were "the culmination of a long process of alienation in which Spanish Americans became aware of their own identity, conscious of their own culture, jealous of their own resources."[1] Although these processes indisputably were crucial to the coming of the insurrections, they, too, prove insufficient. The Cuban Creole elite developed a national consciousness as much as any other studied in this book. Why did they not revolt? The Chileans, on the other hand, according to Nestor Meza Villalobos, had acquired "consciousness of a common destiny, a feeling of fatherland," by the end of the first quarter of the eighteenth century, clamoring for satisfaction of grievances.[2] Why did they not revolt sooner? In New Spain, however, José Valero Silva explains, "there was not a prior notion in the colony about Mexico as a nation in 1810." That formation of national consciousness would have to await the period of the Reform, the Júarez presidency, and international wars in the middle nineteenth century.[3] Why, then, did Mexico revolt at all in 1810? National self-consciousness was indeed critical as it built up through the eighteenth century. But the political relations between elites and government would be more decisive in explaining the coming of insurrection or the preservation of loyalty in 1810: could nationally self-conscious elites remain in the empire, as Cubans or Chileans long did, because governments accommodated them? Would divided, conservative, and not nationally conscious elites, such as the Mexicans, be driven from the empire by governmental action?

## Participation and Government Response Explained

A centralized bureaucratic empire, such as Spain's in America, required a balance of internal social, economic, political, religious, and intellectual forces. Modern resources must be adequate but limited. The traditional basis of legitimation must be harmonized with the ruler's need to acquire modern resources to expand the scope and domain of his power. The Spanish American empire broke down when its internal balance and harmony collapsed in all four colonies. Cuba's transformation between 1790 and 1825 was so vast and irreversible that there were serious political, economic, and social discontinuities with the pre-1790 period.

The empire broke down because it was both too traditional and too modern. With regard to Venezuelan planters or Mexican mine workers, the rulers proved too intolerant of modernization. In 1820 Mexican elite groups with organizational capability and traditional orientations ended imperial rule. Post-independence Mexico was more economically backward than pre-independence Mexico, and less politically and socially stable. It was a case of demodernization. The relatively high level of economic differentiation and productively contributed to many changes in Cuba and Venezuela, but the absence of widespread universalistic values in ethnic relations blocked further modernization in Venezuela, Mexico, and Cuba.

Breakdown was long in coming. International war and political and economic changes affected the Spanish American empire. The threat to the empire led to accelerated government modernization throughout the colonies, especially in Cuba where the threat was most acute. International economic growth in northwest Europe increased the demand for primary products produced in these colonies, with the result that internal economic growth occurred in all — but with different consequences. Chile experienced the least social and political transformation. There was an accelerated centralization of government power in Mexico and of its control over and cooptation of central elites. Accordingly, the central Mexican elites failed to revolt until they were effectively expelled from the empire by the liberal Cortes in 1820.

Cuban politics and society were centralized at the bottom (slavery), but pluralized at the middle and top. Repression of slaves would become more effective, while cooptation of elites and black freedmen proceeded apace. The levels of centralization and pluralization were mixed in Venezuela. These effects of economic growth depended on three conditions: the preexisting level of social mobilization; the preexisting level of government centralization; and the ecological and economic characteristics of the capital infusion itself.

The international political threat and the need to induce economic modernization led to the expansion of the military and the modernization of government, although mass and elite traditional participants resisted it. Government modernization was also associated with the hispanization of elite positions, especially in New Spain. The result was a severe relative deprivation of jobs, power, and status for the Creole elite. But this led to a crisis only because the greater efficacy of the imperial government had increased the stakes for Creole elite membership in the top councils. Earlier in the eighteenth century before the modernization of government, a mere decline in the Creole elite share of top posts was insufficient to provoke revolt. The imperial government itself initiated the challenge to the overarching multinational legitimacy of the empire by claiming special rights and deference for those born in Spain. Instead of equal kingdoms under a patrimonial ruler, there would be a Spanish kingdom with American colonies. Spain and Spaniards thus subverted the empire. The government also sought unsuccessfully to channel Creole energies away from politics and toward economics.

Government modernization continued to exhibit the ambivalent policies of a centralized bureaucratic empire. Many changes were made in an attempt to increase production, but systematic efforts were also undertaken to demobilize and suppress mass political participants, especially mine workers, in areas undergoing modernization. Government modernization was still bound by the norms of the empire seeking adequate but limited modernization.

Mass traditional political participation had been accommodated within the empire. There were institutionalized procedures for positional upward social mobility for blacks and Indians. Resistance to change had been repressed or coopted throughout centuries of imperial rule. Social bandits, slave revolts, urban food or religious riots, and peasant uprisings had scarred the history of Spanish America. The empire was often frightened, but it knew how to contain them within the existing framework.

Traditional elite political participation, which was neopatrimonial, had also been accommodated within the empire. The elite sought access to government jobs, military privilege, or economic advantage; it opposed government efforts to set it free. Even under conditions of economic growth, traditional elites sought to increase access to government in traditional ways. Elite and mass shared certain characteristics of traditional political participation. Goals were typically adjustive or backward-looking. Many sought to restore lost rights or circumstances. Others resisted change or sought to adjust their position within the system. But there were only very few claims to rights that had never been enjoyed and few efforts to bring about fundamental structural change.

These traditional peoples, lacking the psychological capacity to participate on their own in politics, were mobilized by external agents, such as organizations or political leaders. Some of these were transient, such as urban mobs, where individuals united to do jointly what they would not do alone; others were of long standing, such as the merchants' guilds (consulados). Even social bandits typically acted in groups. The scope of traditional political participation was narrow for each level of social stratification. Coalitions were conglomerates, where each participating group had its own narrow goals and perspectives, often refusing to provide aid beyond their own region. Mass political participants also had a primitive low level of organization. Their behavior was parochial and fragmented, not system-wide. Their time perspectives were short. Their participation was recurrent, but not continuous or regular.

Economic growth had been largely accommodated within the existing systems in Chile and in Mexico. The elites vied for position, often assuming backward-looking stances, but did not argue for fundamental changes in structure. The Chilean colonial government was especially responsive to the demands of the Chilean landowning elite. Chilean and Mexican elites opposed freer foreign trade and sought to maintain or improve their political position in an attempt to maximize private gain. These neopatrimonial traditional and accommodable elites fought over the division of existing monopolies into two new monopolies, or over the establishment of a new monopoly, or over an improvement of their bargaining position within an existing politically determined relationship. At times they struggled over a politically induced opening into a secured market or over a share in the control of monopoly. These neopatrimonial petitions wanted only to adjust their position in the existing system.

Certain kinds of economic growth accelerated changes in elite norms. The elites whose countries produced primarily for export because domestic consumption was limited, or whose products had an inelastic supply, making production adaptation difficult, were more likely to demand structural changes in foreign trade. Some elites began to demand more far-reaching modernizing changes. Thus, normative and structural modernization entered the political, social, and economic system because of changes at the top, not because of mass social mobilization. Severe conflicts developed between traditional and modern elites and between modern elites and the government, especially in Venezuela.

Socioethnic status played a paramount role in social stratification. Social mobility was often conceived in terms of status, relatively independent of economic considerations. Enemy targets were often defined in terms of ethnicity or status. Elite obstacles to black advancement were aimed at blacks, not at poor whites; fear of black mobility focused on the deprivation of relative status so valued in a hierarchichal society. The government's sponsorship of ethnic mobility for the lower strata was resisted by an elite that feared for its status, its power, and its job monopoly. Increased socioethnic demands and counterdemands shook the political system at the same time that economic pressures accelerated.

Status struggles also appeared within the elite, with the ascriptive line drawn at place of birth. The conflict for status and power between Creoles and Spaniards existed in all four colonies, though it was probably most pronounced in New Spain. The status values at the core of this conflict were often perceived in zero-sum terms where one's gains was another's loss and where relative gains and losses were critically important. Nevertheless, Creole-Spaniard disputes alone do not explain loyalty or insurrection — otherwise Chile might have been loyal, Cuba might have revolted, and New Spain might have revolted earlier. The key factor was government policy toward the elites concerning such disputes. Insurrection was most likely where the colonial governments in America alienated local elites. Loyalty was most likely where these were accommodated even at the risk of alienating some Spaniards (as in Cuba). Thus, political bargaining between government and elites was decisive.

The inflation of political demands is an especially serious problem for regimes attempting political modernization. These regimes try to centralize, rationalize, and accumulate political power. They try to stimulate demand for the use of such power and they try to use it effectively. Problems arise when political demands for the exercise of government authority increase faster than the government's ability to respond. Rival ethnic group status claims are susceptible to political inflation. Governments can rarely favor only one among several relatively equal ethnic groups. An inflationary spiral increases the probability of a shift from nonviolent and legal political competition to more violent and illegal or extralegal political competition. Ruthless coercion by the government and insurrection by its opponents may replace the politics of bargaining, bribes, and bluffs.[4]

Economic growth oriented toward export often increased the cohesion of certain elite groups developing a "national" elite consciousness. This led eventually to the formation of coalitions of merchants and planters in Venezuela and Cuba, seeking modernization and overcoming previous and remaining differences. Traditional Chilean elites and government united in reaction to Peruvian domination of their trade relations. Though Chile sought no more than an adjustment of its bargaining position, the sense of Chilean identity of interests grew through intercolonial conflict with Peru.

By the beginning of the nineteenth century the Creole elite in all four colonies wanted to nationalize decisionmaking, appropriating authority for themselves. The critical factor was the political bargaining relationship between local elites and the government of the empire and of each colony. This goal existed for different reasons. The Mexican Creoles sought power and status for themselves. They were opposed to the hispanization of their government. Some also wanted it for economic modernization, especially in the Bajío area. The Venezuelan elite wanted to free its foreign trade, prevent social mobility for blacks into elite roles, and establish a steady and more stable labor supply for the plantations. Foreign trade disasters, the loss of relative status, competition for elite jobs, and the shortage of plantation labor could all be traced to Spanish policies.

The Chileans wanted more autonomy so that they might improve their bargaining position vis-à-vis Peru. During the final years of the colony, they also wanted to control the selection of the colonial executive to prevent the repetition of arbitrary rule. The Cubans wanted freer foreign trade, a more ample and steady slave labor supply, transformation of land structures, the abolition of monopolies, the elimination of religious encumbrances on production, the promotion of white immigration, expansion of the educational system, a share in goverment policymaking, and fiscal reform.

The imperial crisis of legitimacy occurred in 1808 after important changes had taken place following the last imperial succession crisis. Economic growth and government modernization had altered social, economic, and political relationships. The empire was far more internally differentiated. There was a greater elite "national" consciousness within each colony. There was greater group consciousness in each of the competing elites. Conflicts over the allocation of status, power, and wealth in the colonies and the empire remained unresolved when the international crisis struck. International or intercolonial conflicts had fostered the first change; intracolonial status, power, or economic conflict the second.

When legitimacy was in question many groups, both elite Spaniards and Creoles, moved simultaneously to appropriate political legitimacy. The grounds may have been socioethnic, as in Mexico, or more economic, as in Caracas. Coups and countercoups undermined the legitimacy of each of three colonial governments at the time that the legitimacy of the entire imperial system was in question. Group formation and consciousness, resulting from increased status and economic conflict, broke the political shell that provided a consensual framework for the empire after imperial and colonial legitimacy cracked.

The international challenge to overarching legitimacy altered the context of politics. Even very traditional behavior, such as the deposition of the Governor of Chile on medieval grounds for arbitrary exercise of his authority, had dramatic disruptive consequences, even though past governors of Chile had been deposed without further disruption. Certain mass and subelite political movements of the late colonial period, especially in Caracas, Coro, and Mexico, exhibited modernizing characteristics far beyond what their elites were prepared for. These movements failed.

The elite break with Spain came first in Caracas, where severe economic pressures combined with the undermining of the legitimacy of both imperial and colonial governments to impel the Creole elite to seize power. The break in Chile took place in a more traditional and political context. Because the centralization of authority had been so severe, the break in New Spain occurred not at the center of the viceroyalty, but in the more modernizing of all Mexican peripheries, the Bajío.

Cuba and some areas of Venezuela failed to revolt because ethnic cross-pressures restrained their elites. Ethnic issues were very salient in these modernizing areas. Incompatible disidentifications with Spain and with blacks led the Creole elite to defend the status quo. Its consequence was to preserve political order for Spain.

In addition, Cuba failed to revolt because the nationalization of decisionmaking had effectively taken place within the colonial context. The Creole elite had achieved its political and economic goals at little cost. The black slave population was severely repressed in the sugar sector, where international economic changes had centralized authority, although native black slaves did not suffer more because most sugar sector slaves were new imports. Cuba's freedmen, unlike those in Venezuela, had been extensively coopted into the military. During the last quarter of the eighteenth century the military absorbed every third free black man, thus relieving job market pressure and allowing free blacks status and power. The reenslavement of some freedmen after 1817 was not widespread enough to alienate the entire black community, but it increased freedman participation in revolts and conspiracies. Many black freedmen, however, increased their wealth significantly during this period.

Cuba was coopted, transformed, and modernized within a changed imperial structure. The colonial government used institutionalized procedures to suspend the application of imperial decrees that might have alienated the Cubans. Cuba's colonial government was adaptable and autonomous. In cooperation with leading Creoles, it formulated a coherent strategy of national transformation. Decisionmaking was nationalized. Institutionalization and modernization went hand in hand.

Once institutionalization broke down in other colonies, mass political participation could engulf the political system. The peripheral rebel elite in Mexico chose this course, with emphasis on charismatic political authority. The rebel elite of Venezuela, on the other hand, chose to freeze the social system to achieve its goals. In Chile mass politics were better contained by the elites during the wars of independence, even though institutionalized government had broken down. Social change had been limited in this parallel ethnic system, and Chile's stable and valued social organizations and procedures preserved much of the social order until political disputes had been resolved.

In an attempt to shore up its position in the short term, a desperate colonial government in Venezuela risked long-term prospects for order. Following a strategy of counterinsurgency, it mobilized the blacks and incorporated slave revolts and social bandits in a struggle to save the colony. In Mexico the colonial government responded in kind to the rebel initiative that politicized socioethnic cleavages. As befitted a multinational ruler, it also sought to maintain Indian support.

The empire sought to coopt the Creoles through elections and parliaments. The early secession of the central elites in Chile and Venezuela, however, nullified the impact of such a strategy there. Parliament's liberalism was a liability in Cuba, where the proposed suppression of the slave trade and the abolition of slavery were resisted by the Creole elite. Cooptation through elections and parliament was more successful in Mexico as a means of containing the Hidalgo revolt; but in the long run there was failure to institutionalize Mexican participation in the Cortes. Problems included the Mexican deputies' absenteeism, limited experience, failure to be reelected, and limited rewards — all of which became worse with time. The first period of the Cortes could not coopt through legislation; the laws of the second led to Mexico's secession. In Chile and Venezuela the revolts were not simple explosions of rage by poor, ill-educated, or marginal people; they were led by the most influential men of those colonies. Even in Mexico, the rebel provincial elite was composed of well-educated and mature men, men who had had much access to public appointment, but whose promotion had been blocked.

With the return of absolutism in Spain, aristocratic and military values again prevailed. The empire shunned socioethnic mobilization as soon as it could, and after 1814 the imperial strategy turned toward repression. Where repression had already been in force, as in Chile, purely military methods of repression replaced a politico-military mix. Military force was met with counterforce in Chile, where the early ambivalence of the elite and mass, incompatibly identified with autonomy and empire, turned gradually but decisively away from Spain.

At the same time, Venezuela's Creole leaders made some minimal concessions to win black support and stressed charismatic political authority. The rebels were favored by structural continuity: black plainsmen consistently fought against white Caracas, except that in the first period Caracas was patriot and in the second it was royalist.

At the end of the Napoleonic Wars expeditionary troops from Europe were sent to all the colonies. The wars, heretofore internal, were thus hispanized and internationalized. It was easier for the pro-independence forces to shift from an internal socioethnic to an international-political cleavage. Spain's problem was compounded in Chile, where the war was not only internationalized and hispanized but also Peruvianized. The sense of Chilean national identity within the elite had been forged in conflict with Peru, and independence from Peru was sought at least as much as from Spain. The Creoles' military victories and political mobilization were helped by the eventual dissolution of the Spanish armies in America. The international crisis had destroyed the military's internal chains of command and meritocratic promotions.

The return of the liberal Cortes in 1820 led to the passage of legislation aimed directly at the central Mexican ecclesiastical, bureaucratic, and military elites that had held the colony loyal to Spain, and that were effectively expelled from the empire. The drive toward independence by Mexico's peripheral elites had divided the central elites enough already so that the ethnic cross-pressures were not strong enough to prevent a final break with Spain.

Elite concessions to mass politics in Venezuela and in Mexico were sharply limited: in the former, there was limited abolition of slavery; in the latter, formal civil equality. In both, military officers shared the booty of a fallen empire. More important, both moved toward independence with a relatively unchanged social order. Venezuelan independence was accompanied by the reconstruction of a slavery system (less extensive than the previous one) that ensured the continuity of the labor supply. Black political leadership was suppressed. The elite continued to block black access to the University, hence to elite jobs and the professions. In Mexico independence brought with it many guarantees for the Church, the military, the bureaucracy, and property owners. The key change was independence itself, and even that under a native monarchy.

Social changes and disruptions had been less significant in Chile, so demobilization was less severe there. Only the Chilean elite had managed to retain a significant measure of autonomy, authority, and legitimacy throughout the wars of independence. This helped provide legitimacy for the new political order based on both tradition and participation in the rebellion. The Venezuelan Creole elite collapsed early. Political authority came to be based on charismatic authority, and, though unstable in many ways, its moderate routinization served to launch the Venezuelan state. Mexico's traditional elite had not been engaged in the struggle for independence. On the other hand, some of the rebel charismatic political leaders had been defeated and killed; others were unacceptable to the elite. Civilian supremacy was not established during the wars. Mexico, which entered upon independence without a basis for a reconstructed political order, slipped gradually into praetorianism.

Long-term social, political, and economic changes had differentiated the Spanish American empire internally and had led to the formation of consciously competing groups. When imperial legitimacy broke down, these preexisting groups turned from competition over status and wealth to competition for power. Their unrestrained conflict in the political arena led to a collapse of colonial legitimacy. Subsequent internal pressures and the strategies followed by the colonial governments shaped the outcomes of the struggles. The first phase was won by the government because it mobilized and defeated the insurgents on their own grounds. Governments prevented the insurgents from shifting the internal cleavage — the drive to gain more social, economic and political power — into an international cleavage fighting against Spain for independence. Government strategy changed between the two phases. Indiscriminate repression in Chile, the abandonment of black political mobilization in Venezuela, and the political rebuff to the Mexican central elites alienated support for Spain. Spain came to rely on a single instrument, the military, which subsequently crumbled.

The explanation of the proximate beginnings of the wars of independence in 1810, therefore, hinges on the political behavior of elites: do they revolt or not, and how. An answer to that question requires the analyzing of the political bargaining relations of elite, mass, and government. The key variable during the second phase, however, was government behavior, although the central elites somewhat modified their behavior in Venezuela and in Mexico. Politics is at the heart of the explanation in both phases. The nature of elite participation and government response were the constant factors, shaping insurrection or loyalty. Economics, society, the Napoleonic invasion, or Enlightenment ideas, although they contribute to explanations in particular cases, do not explain systematically variations in insurrection and loyalty within and among colonies during the period of the wars of independence.

The explanation of political reconstruction relies on analysis of the elite. Where the elites had effectively nationalized decisionmaking, as in Cuba, there would be widespread and not very costly reconstruction. Where the elites were able to maintain a critical minimum legitimacy, as in Chile, they would control the reconstruction. Otherwise, the choice was an unsatisfactory one — between unstable charismatic legitimation or praetorianism.

Political bargaining between government and elites shaped elite decisions to revolt or to remain loyal. By 1820 Spain had lost interest in bargaining, apart from the special case of Cuba. It had virtually ceased being responsive, and most elites, even New Spain's conservative leaders, were ready to sever the ties of three centuries. But political bargaining had been an important factor in shaping the specific form of loyalty and insurrection. Political order was preserved in Cuba because of a large political coalition that included the colonial government in Havana, the Creole elite, planters and merchants, and even some black freedmen. The losers in Cuba were the newly imported African slaves as well as, at times, the more traditionalizing policies of the imperial government and the more liberalizing policies of the Cortes. At the other end of the spectrum, Mexican politics became so praetorian because it had become virtually impossible to form and to sustain political coalitions. Conflicts among ethnic, economic, and political groups were very severe. Iturbide's temporary coalition achieved independence but it brought neither political order nor structural change. Mexico would have no orderly civic life.

Chilean independence was the result of a coalition between some Chilean elites, alienated by Spain's and Peru's repressive policies, and the Buenos Aires government, desirous of expelling the Spanish threat from southern South America. Within Chile the relative unimportance of social and ethnic conflicts—when compared to Venezuela or Mexico— permitted the maintenance of enough social cohesion to enable a new ruling political coalition to establish political order after independence sooner than in any other new Spanish American state. Venezuelan independence was embittered by the development of two large opposing coalitions. The first included the various wings of the elites, including planters and merchants in Caracas and surrounding areas. The other included the royalist forces in the military and the Church, the black freedmen from the plains opposing the lords of Caracas, and two key areas in western Venezuela. Venezuelan independence was accomplished only when Bolívar was able to break apart the loyalist coalition wooing the black plainsmen.

In conclusion, political bargaining and the formation of political coalitions are the principal explanations for both loyalty and insurrection during the breakdown of the Spanish American empire. The specific issues varied from colony to colony, among the regions of each colony, and between time periods. But the constant factors were the relationship between elite political participation and local government response and the development of political coalitions among them and within them. Outcomes ranged from a successful elite political coalition and high local government responsiveness in loyal Cuba to the declining government responsiveness and the inability of the elite to sustain coalitions in insurrectionist Mexico. Bargaining was the norm in Cuba, but not in Venezuela. Comparatively stable elite coalitions prevailed in Chile as bargaining with imperial officials became impossible. These factors account systematically for both loyalty and insurrection and, in the longer run, for order or praetorianism.

## Implications for the Study of Other Colonies

This book has examined four Spanish American colonies within a larger comparative social science framework. How do its principal findings bear on other Spanish and Portuguese colonies in the Americas during the early years of the nineteenth century? Although a detailed analysis is beyond the scope of this work, certain elements of comparison and contrast should be highlighted.

### Brazil

The political bargaining relationship between elites and government was the critical factor in other colonies. The major events leading to Brazilian independence began when the Portuguese court, fleeing the Napoleonic invasion of Portugal in 1807, was transferred to Brazil. The Portuguese monarch redefined Brazil's status, making a mere colony the heartland of his empire. Unified Brazilian independence eventually would become possible in part because Brazil became the center of a united centralized bureaucratic empire. It was no longer a Portuguese dependence. The Crown initiated major policy changes resembling Spain's accommodation of Cuban modernization. Education was promoted; the sciences were allowed a more prominent role in higher education; theater and the arts were supported. In January 1808, Brazilian ports were open to foreign trade in all but a few products; trade was further liberalized in July 1814. Freedom of manufacturing was granted in April 1808. The Bank of Brazil was founded. Countless bureaucratic jobs were created to run the monarchical bureaucracy. Honors and titles of nobility were awarded to the local Brazilian elite, which was incorporated thereby into the transplanted empire. Brazil became a cokingdom with Portugal in December 1815.[5]

Loyalty was stimulated in Brazil, as in Cuba and western Venezuela, by fear of a black uprising. John Norman Kennedy has written that "the specter of social upheaval haunted the Bahian elite in the late eighteenth and early nineteenth century." This northeastern Brazilian elite, well informed about events in France and Haiti, had been reminded of black restlessness by mulatto and slave rebellions in the Bahia region. These intensified after 1790, especially in 1798 and in 1807. Bahia's frightened white elite, divided before 1750, closed ranks to minimize conflicts and strengthen intraelite ties. Bahia and other areas of the northeast were Portugal's last bastions in Brazil in 1822 (though also because of a concentration of Portuguese troops there). Bahia was a modernizing area whose sugar production had recovered at the end of the eighteenth century when Haitian production collapsed after its slave revolution. Concern about a racial revolution was widespread among Brazilian elites beyond Bahia. Fears of threats to the social fabric of a slave society gave the elites incentives to compromise with Portugal, which accommodated them in return.[6]

Loyalty in Brazil was also possible because, as in Chile and Cuba, there was extensive American-born access to government jobs. Stuart Schwartz has noted that the "colonial-born control most of the nonprofessional offices of justice and treasury, but they had also penetrated into the ranks of the superior magistracy . . . Clerks, notaries, tax collectors, customs officials, judges and even governors were drawn from the colonial elite or joined to it by blood or interest." The modernization of government under the Portuguese Minister Pombal did not make the American-born officeholders the target of reform — as many in the Spanish colonies had been. On the contrary, the American-born were welcomed into the expanding bureaucracy.[7] Although mining production declined in late colonial Brazil, international trade expanded, as did credit, cash transactions, agriculture, and livestock production.

Why, then, did Brazil become independent? Relations between Portugal and Brazil changed by the end of the second decade of the nineteenth century, in ways not unlike some of those in Spain's relations with Mexico. The monarchy had been concerned with the protection of Portuguese interests, even as Brazil's autonomy had been increasing. Yet the clash between Portuguese and Brazilian interests worsened only after the liberal revolt broke out in Portugal in August 1820. The Portuguese Côrtes, like their Spanish counterparts, considered America more as a colony than as a cokingdom separately owned by the Crown and wanted to curtail Brazilian autonomy, abrogating in 1821 many of the changes introduced after 1807. Foreign merchants trading in Brazil were harassed. Provincial governors were ordered to respond to Lisbon rather than to Rio de Janeiro. The Côrtes ordered Prince Dom Pedro to return to Portugal; on January 9, 1822, he disobeyed. The Côrtes sent troops to Pernambuco and Rio de Janeiro, but Pedro blocked their landing. In June 1822 Pedro summoned a Congress to discuss guidelines for an independent Brazil. In September he formally proclaimed Brazilian independence, and himself Emperor.[8]

The Brazilians accomplished what the Mexicans could not: a transfer from colony to independence without social upheaval and as a monarchy. The difference was that Brazil never experienced a war of independence. It was spared dealing with leaders such as Hidalgo, Morelos, or Guerrero. The relationship between the government in Rio and Brazilian elites was more comparable to that in Cuba. While even liberal Spain continued to accommodate Cuba in the 1820s, liberal Portugal no longer accommodated Brazil. That decision of the Lisdon government to "recolonize" Brazil was comparable to decisions made by the Spanish Cortes alienating the Mexican elites. But Brazilian loyalty through 1820 had not disrupted the bases for legitimacy. Mexican insurrection since 1810 had made the reconstruction of political order extremely difficult. Brazil had a monarch in place and a monarchical bureaucracy at work since 1808. Mexico had to start anew.

Brazilian elites sought a social transformation no more than the Cuban, Mexican, or Venezuelan elites did. There had been conspiracies but they rarely became revolts. They had limited support and their impact remained local. The only elite revolt in late colonial Brazil occurred in Pernambuco in 1817, led by planters, the clergy, and administrators. The Catholic clergy had opposed some secularizing trends in government modernization, and the backward-looking Pernambuco revolt sought the restoration of Catholic privileges. It guaranteed the right to own slaves and did not challenge economic or social structures. Its chief goal was to free the country from remaining colonial restrictions.[9] As Emilia Viotti da Costa put it: "Upper class fears of a mass rebellion explain why the idea of achieving independence with the support of the prince was so attractive: the nation would be freed from the yoke of Portugal without having to resort to mass mobilization."[10] A Mexican solution with a Cuban experience!

## Buenos Aires

Brazilian insistence on order was matched by Buenos Aires' sustained insurrection. From the time a Junta assumed power, wresting it from Spain on May 25, 1810, Buenos Aires never again came under Spanish rule. Spain pacified Chile, Venezuela, Mexico, and other rebellious colonies by 1815, but never the city and the region ruled by Buenos Aires. In fact, these areas became the base for the patriot reconquest of Chile and for the subsequent expedition to overthrow the viceregal government in Lima. Why was Buenos Aires a focus of insurrection?

Buenos Aires' experiences had weakened its ties to the empire. When the British occupied the city in 1806, the Spanish viceroy fled. The British were defeated by a Creole force led by Santiago Liniers, a French officer in the Spanish service. The Audiencia deposed and imprisoned the viceroy when he returned; it proclaimed Liniers acting captain-general. The close relationship between Liniers and the Creoles alienated the wealthy Spaniards who dominated the Cabildo; in January 1809 they staged an unsuccessful coup. Buenos Aires, the premier trading center of southern South America, chafed under Spanish restrictions on foreign trade. Its merchants thrived on imports servicing the continent's southern half. Its ranchers prospered by exporting their products. Although the interior provinces preferred protection from European competition, they were weakly represented in Buenos Aires. The last viceroy of the River Plate area arrived to replace Liniers with orders not to admit foreign ships in the river. When news arrived in mid-May 1810 that the French had conquered Seville and that a Council of Regency had been established in Cádiz, Creole patricians moved to appropriate legitimacy for themselves. The new Junta of Buenos Aires was presided by Cornelio de Saavedra, the Creole military officer responsible for suppressing the Spanish coup of 1809.[11]

Unlike Cuba, which depended on Spanish military protection for its defense, Buenos Aires Creoles proved more competent than the Spanish government in defeating the British. As in Chile, where a governor was deposed by the Audiencia, so the viceroy in Buenos Aires was deposed —

except that this was unprecedented in Buenos Aires. The Viceroy of New Spain sought to align himself with the Creoles; he was deposed by a successful Spanish military coup. The acting captain-general of Buenos Aires was put in office by Creole troops and kept there by them upon the failure of the attempted coup by Spaniards. Unlike in Santiago, Mexico City, or Havana, where Creoles addressed the Crown, the viceroy, or the governor through the Cabildo, Spaniards controlled the Cabildo of Buenos Aires and prevented its effective use as a Creole voice. As in Cuba and in Venezuela, foreign trade was critical for the Creole elites. Spain responded restrictively to Buenos Aires' need for unfettered foreign trade, as it had done in Venezuela, but not in Cuba. Therefore, on every issue affecting political bargaining between Buenos Aires and the Spanish government, the outcome led away from loyalty and toward insurrection.

Although the black population of the River Plate provinces was a substantial minority, whites predominated. As in Chile, there were many Indians beyond the colony's frontier in a parallel and warlike competitive relationship with Buenos Aires that strengthened the bonds of social cohesion within the colony. Insurrection in the River Plate region would not be plagued by the kind of ethnic struggles that took place in Venezuela and Mexico. Given the impetus toward independence and the absence of an ethnic deterrent, the Buenos Aires elite broke with Spain, overcoming a royalist minority composed mostly of Spaniards in high civil and ecclesiastical bureaucracies. Spain was never again able to mount a military reconquest.

## Peru

The experiences in Portuguese America and in Buenos Aires confirm this book's general thesis. The experiences of upper and lower Peru are more difficult to explain, albeit for different reasons. Why did Peru remain so loyal for so long, and why did upper Peru (called Charcas, and eventually Bolivia) experience one of the first instances of political disruption after the Napoleonic invasion of Spain?

From the time of the conquest to the eighteenth century Lima had been the "city of viceroys," the imperial political and symbolic center of Spanish South America. It had also been the empire's economic center because trade with Spain from many regions had been channeled through it. Lima's decay began with the Bourbon reforms of the eighteenth century that established a new viceroyalty based in Bogotá and another in Buenos Aires. By the end of the eighteenth century Lima had lost its empire and was left with only the territory of today's Peru. Lima had housed the shell of an imperial bureaucratic structure which had lost much of its function. The persistence of the bureaucracy ruling over a shrunken territory, as well as Spain's new demands of funds for war, required an increase in taxes. Capitation taxes were extended to non-Indians. The alcabalá was increased by one-third. Excise taxes and export-import taxes were imposed. Protests broke out in many places against these new taxes in the late 1770s.[12]

The heaviest burden of these new measures fell on the Indians, who revolted in November 1780, led by José Gabriel Túpac Amaru. This was the most serious challenge to Spanish rule in America before independence. Although many of the demands of the Túpac Amaru revolt were typical of peasant protests — against taxes, tax collectors, purchasing systems, and so forth — an ethnic element was also prominent. Túpac Amaru claimed title as an hereditary Inca and signed proclamations as the new ruler of an Inca empire. The revolt of tens of thousands of Indians spread throughout southern Peru. Túpac Amaru was killed in May 1781. Pacification was achieved by the beginning of 1782.[13]

In the early nineteenth century, therefore, the elite of Peru, especially in Lima, was committed to Spain because it was still the symbolic center representing Spain in a part of America, because it depended on Spain for bureaucratic employment, and because Peru had experienced a major ethnic war in the core of a hierarchical ethnic system. The fear of ethnic war solidified Creole support for the Crown once again in August 1814, when Brigadier Mateo Pumacahua, an Indian by birth, led an uprising in the city of Cuzco. By March 1815 Pumacahua and his associates had been defeated. J. R. Fisher has noted that "the threat of social revolution led to a rapid withdrawal of Creole support for the rebellion" of Pumacahua.[14] This revolt revived the memories of ethnic fear that kept the Peruvian elite loyal to Spain. Some Creole support for insurrections in 1780 and in 1814 in Cuzco took the form of regional protest against Lima's rule. But Creoles quickly became loyalists as the Indian character of these revolts came to predominate.

And yet Peruvian loyalty remains an enigma because Peru suffered so much in the late colonial period. Its loss of an empire, resulting from the Bourbon reforms, triggered an economic depression because the privileges and monopolies on which earlier prosperity had been built were lost. Imperial free trade meant that Lima could no longer monopolize Spanish South American trade. Peruvian agriculture stagnated and Peruvian industry declined in the last quarter of the nineteenth century. Only silver mining production increased, doubling during these years and remaining at close to peaks levels until 1812 — after Creole opinion had been mobilized to support counterindependence movements.[15]

Creole access to public office was another key variable because so many elites depended on bureaucratic employment. Leon Campbell has argued that "by the eighteenth century at least, and probably earlier, the exclusion of Creoles operated only at the Viceregal level." By the middle of the eighteenth century native-born Peruvians had occupied at times bishoprics in Lima, Cuzco, and Arequipa. They had contributed four captains-general, five lieutenants-general, and seven field marshalls of the regular army. Native-born citizens of Lima had held the presidencies of eight of the ten Audiencias of Spanish America. Native-born Creoles dominated the Audiencia of Lima from the 1740s.[16] However, Creole participation in high government posts in Peru — as in New Spain but not Cuba — declined in the last quarter of the eighteenth century never to recover — unlike in Chile. Creoles were denied many high ranks in the Army after 1784 because they were deemed untrustworthy.[17] Creole control over the Audiencia of Lima was also ended. In 1774 only one of the twelve Audiencia justices was born in Spain; by 1792 the Spanish-born had a majority of the Audiencia of Lima which they never again relinquished. In 1797, as still in 1809, ten of the thirteen justices had been born in Spain. The number of Lima-born justices declined steadily from eight in 1774 to one in 1809. The Cabildo of Lima in 1793 had requested that one-third of the justices be Peruvian-born; in 1809 it demanded one-half. As Mark Burkholder has noted, "on the eve of independence, the prevailing Creole attitude toward obtaining high office was reactionary, focused on a reversal of recent policy, rather than revolutionary and directed toward providing Americans with unprecedented political and social status."[18] Peru, too, had a Creole-Spaniard conflict over officeholding, although the Creoles, even if they were much less likely to hold office, were never banned from the levers of power.

Economic decline was not enough to produce independence. Cuba remained loyal, in spite of a foreign trade crisis in the opening years of the nineteenth century, because its elite participated actively in government. Mere Creole exclusion from office could not produce independence. Mexico City's elites and other Mexican elites remained loyal partly because they participated in a dramatic economic expansion, even though their access to high public appointment had declined. The Peruvian elite, however, had lost a political empire, was plunged in an economic depression, and was denied access to public appointments which it had once enjoyed. Except for the fear of ethnic war, all factors point toward independence. And yet Lima and Peru remained loyal to the end.

Spanish government strategies after 1810 may have coopted some elites. Lima's bureaucracy found a new function: imperial preservation, including the reconquest of Chile, upper Peru, and Quito, none of which were any longer under Peru's strict jurisdiction. Viceroy Abascal coopted Creoles through appointments to the presidency of Cuzco and the intendancy of La Paz, among others, even in the face of Spaniard opposition. Elections to the Cortes were held in Peru, as in New Spain, and were hotly contested.[19] The Indian tribute was abolished in September 1811. Indian forced labor (*mita*) was abolished a year later. The tribute, however, was gradually reintroduced under a different name and had in fact been fully restored by 1815.[20] Although the viceroy implemented most of the changes mandated by the Cortes, he tried to limit their effectiveness because he opposed them. The Spanish and viceregal policies of cooptation, therefore, probably restored the political bargaining relationship somewhat with the Creole elites, though with the same limitations that existed in Mexico. Possibly the biggest single incentive for loyalty among Peruvian Creoles was their new mission as the militant restored center of royalist loyalty in America.

And loyal they were. Americans were the majority of Spain's Peruvian army throughout all phases of the wars. At least half of the troops sent to reconquer Chile under General Mariano Osorio in 1818 were Peruvian-born. Peruvians, including free blacks in the military, had subdued revolts in the early years of the war. Peru had to be conquered militarily before it would become independent. Small towns and rural areas in northern Peru revolted against San Martín's liberating conquest. This broadly based royalist resistance included all social clases. More than one-quarter of the members of the Peruvian Congress of 1823 had to be drawn from Colombia, Argentina, and Chile. Of the fourteen Peruvian congressmen who remained during the brief Spanish reoccupation of Lima in 1823, eight switched to become royalists. The Peruvian Congress had elected José de la Riva Agüero president in February 1823. Nine months later Riva Agüero proposed to the Viceroy that Peru become a monarchy under a Spanish Prince selected by the Spanish King; in the meantime, the Viceroy would govern Peru.[21] Bolívar arrested Peru's first traitor President. José Bernardo Tagle, Marquis of Torre Tagle, who had been a deputy to the Cortes from Lima and later Intendant of Trujillo, replaced Riva Agüero as President of Peru. Early in 1824 Peru's second head of government committed treason by defecting to the Spanish side during the second Spanish reconquest of Lima.[22]

The masses also remained loyal to Spain. Even as Peruvian independence approached, most of the fighting for Peru's independence was done by non-Peruvians. Peruvians accounted for only 42 percent of the fighting forces, and 48 percent of the casualties on the independence side at the battle of Junín in August 1824; the rest were from countries to the north and south. Twice-weekly statistics for the independence armies from May to September 1824 show that Peruvians accounted for no more than two-thirds of the recruits. Peruvian recruits were only equal to 83 percent of the losses of the independence army, that is, they were insufficient even to maintain the independence forces at a steady replacement level.[23] Non-Peruvian independence troops had to be imported to the very end.

Peru's outstanding loyalty to the Crown seems to go well beyond the bounds of the political bargaining relationship that prevailed in the closing days of the colony. Peruvians had suffered more than most colonies from imperial reform in politics, economics, and access to office. Their new imperial mission after 1810 may have reestablished a new political relationship with Spain which accounted for their extraordinary loyalty.[24]

## Bolivia

The puzzle in Bolivia (or Charcas or upper Peru) is different. The great Túpac Amaru revolt had encompassed parts of western Bolivia as well as southern Peru. The revolt had lasted longer in Bolivia. The city of La Paz was twice under Indian siege. The colonial authorities, led by the Audiencia of Charcas, based in the city of Chuquisaca (also called La Plata and eventually renamed Sucre), successfully mobilized American-born and Spanish-born whites to defend themselves and the colony. If fear of an ethnic war maintained a white elite loyal to Spain anywhere, it should have done so in Bolivia. And yet the all-Spaniard Audiencia of Charcas, with the support of the Creole Cabildo and the faculty and students of the University of Chuquisaca, deposed the President of Charcas on May 25, 1809, on the grounds that he had been collaborating with the claims of the Princess-Regent of Portugal, Carlota Joaquina of Bourbon, to assume the throne of Spain in place of both Ferdinand VII and Charles IV. The Audiencia refused also to recognize the authority of the Supreme Junta of Seville to rule in Charcas, claiming that the Crown owned all its kingdoms separately and that, in the King's absence, Charcas had as much a right to govern itself as Seville. In La Paz, the Cabildo deposed the intendant and the bishop on July 16, 1809. A ruling Junta, established in La Paz, made the first open demand for independence from Spain which recognized no other authority. The insurrection of La Paz was defeated brutally by an army sent from Lima by the Viceroy of Peru. The insurrection of Chuquisaca was put down more moderately by an army sent from Jujuy by the Viceroy of Buenos Aires. Many of the leaders in La Paz were killed; the Audiencia of Charcas was purged.[25]

Events in Bolivia after 1809 are more understandable. Bolivia became a battleground between the loyal armies of the Viceroy of Peru and the armies of insurrectionist Buenos Aires. The interests and loyalties of Bolivians during this period shifted depending on the prevalence of one army or another. Two groups, however, can be oulined. First, a number of the many guerilla armies that operated in Bolivia after 1809 were social bandits. Grievances against Spain were never clearly articulated; people deserted and shifted sides frequently. Indians fought on all sides as military fortunes swayed. Most guerillas wanted freedom for themselves and for their own soil. Like social bandits elsewhere, they rarely wanted to fight beyond their own region, nor did they have a larger vision of what a Charcas independent of Spain, Peru, or Buenos Aires might be.[26] Second, after 1809 most Bolivian Creole elites favored the royalists rather than the patriots. Their leadership was one reason why Charcas became the last major major bastion of Spanish rule in America, even after lower Peru had been invaded by the armies of San Martín and Bolívar. Independence came to Bolivia when these same royalist Creole elites changed sides to support independence as Bolívar's armies dealt the final blows to Spain at Junín and Ayacucho in 1824, and Sucre sealed Bolivia's independence in 1825.[27]

The Bolivian experience after 1809 conforms to much of this book's argument. The Creole elites, as might have been expected, remained loyal to Spain until the end. Independence came with a minimum of change in the social structure. Social banditry, charismatic appeals, and military force destroyed the old bases of legitimacy without establishing adequate bases for political reconstruction. Praetorianism prevailed in independent Bolivia. Yet the enigma of 1809 remains. Why did such vulnerable elites risk social upheaval by taking such radical steps in 1809?

The arguments of this book can explain insurrection and loyalty in colonies other than those studied here in some detail.[28] Other experiences raise different questions requiring further investigation. Although the search for additional explanations must continue, political bargaining and coalition formation, including government response, remain the more effective systematic explanations for loyalty and insurrection in early-nineteenth-century Iberian America.

# Notes

## 1. Introduction

1. Alexis de Tocqueville, *The Old Regime and the French Revolution*, trans. Stuart Gilbert (Garden City, N.Y.: Doubleday, Anchor, 1955), p. xii.

2. For an elegant narration of the historical events, colony by colony, see John Lynch, *The Spanish-American Revolutions, 1808–1826* (New York: W. W. Norton, 1973). See also the brief interpretative essays by Richard Graham, *Independence in Latin America* (New York: Alfred A. Knopf, 1972), and Jay Kinsbruner, *The Spanish-American Independence Movement* (Huntington, N.Y.: Robert E. Krieger, 1976). For other views on the origins of the wars of independence, see William H. Godson, III, "Views of the Causation of Spanish-American Independence: An Examination of Selected Nineteenth Century South American Historians," unpub. diss., American University, Washington, 1974.

3. For a discussion of the evolution of modernization theory, see Samuel P. Huntington, "The Change to Change: Modernization, Development and Politics," *Comparative Politics* 3, no. 3 (April 1971): 285-292.

4. Karl W. Deutsch and Richard L. Merritt, *Nationalism and National Development: An Interdisciplinary Bibliography* (Cambridge: MIT Press, 1970), introduction.

5. For a discussion of problems with a comparative approach, see Arend Lijphart, "Comparative Politics and the Comparative Method," *The American Political Science Review* 65, no. 3 (September 1961): 686-689; Dankwart A. Rustow, "Modernization and Comparative Politics: Prospects in Research and Theory," *Comparative Politics* 1, no. 1 (October 1968): 45-47. For a historian's argument on behalf of the comparative method in history, see C. E. Black, *The Dynamics of Modernization: A Study in Comparative History* (New York: Harper and Row, 1967), ch. 2.

6. Computed from Jacques Barbier, "The Culmination of the Bourbon Reforms, 1787-1792," *Hispanic American Historical Review* 57, no. 1 (February 1977): 61.

7. Giovanni Sartori, "Concept Misinformation in Comparative Politics," *The American Political Science Review* 64, no. 4 (December 1970): 1033; Hayward R. Alker, Jr., *Mathematics and Politics* (New York: Macmillan, 1965), pp. 18-28; Hubert M. Blalock, *Social Statistics* (New York: McGraw-Hill, 1960), pp. 11-16.

## 2. Imperial Legitimacy and Stability

1. S. N. Eisenstadt, *The Political Systems of Empires* (New York: Free Press, 1963), pp. 19-23.

2. These reflections on the Spanish empire have been heavily influenced by: Francisco José Moreno, *Legitimacy and Stability in Latin America: A Study of Chilean Political Culture* (New York: New York University Press, 1969), pp. 3-43; Richard M. Morse, "Political Theory and the Caudillo," in Hugh M. Hamill, Jr., ed., *Dictatorship in Spanish America* (New York: Borzoi, 1965), pp. 53-57; Richard M. Morse, "The Heritage of Latin America," in Louis Hartz, ed., *The Founding of New Societies* (New York: Harbinger, 1964), pp. 138-159; Stanley J. Stein and Barbara H. Stein, *The Colonial Heritage of Latin America: Essays in Economic Dependence in Perspective* (New York: Oxford University Press, 1970), pp. 68-81; and J. H. Parry, *The Spanish Seaborne Empire* (New York: Alfred A. Knopf, 1967), pp. 197-206; Mario Góngora, *Studies in the Colonial History of Spanish America* (Cambridge: Cambridge University Press, 1975), pp. 67-126, 159-205.

3. Eisenstadt, *Political Systems*, pp. 27, 301, 314, 316, 322, 354, 355.

4. Max Weber, *The Theory of Social and Economic Organization*, trans. A. M. Henderson and Talcott Parsons (New York: Free Press, 1965), pp. 347, 351-352, 355.

5. Eisenstadt, *Political Systems*, pp. 343, 354-355.

6. David Easton, "An Approach to the Analysis of Political Systems," *World Politics* 9 (1957): 383, 387-395.

7. Karl W. Deutsch, "Social Mobilization and Political Development," *American Political Science Review* 55, no. 3 (1961): 494; Daniel Lerner, *The Passing of Traditional Society* (New York: Free Press, 1964), p. 46; Seymour Martin Lipset, *Political Man: The Social Bases of Politics* (Garden City, N.Y.: Doubleday, Anchor, 1963), pp. 183-229; Robert Lane, *Political Life* (New York: Free Press, 1965), pp. 45-79; Gabriel Almond and Sidney Verba, *The Civic Culture* (Boston: Little, Brown, 1965), pp. 12-18, 315-336. José L. Reyna, *An Empirical Analysis of Political Mobilization: The Case of Mexico* (Ithaca, N.Y.: Latin American Studies Program, Ph.D dissertation Series, Cornell University, 1971), pp. 35-50, provides a broad summary of empirical findings on social mobilization as it relates to political participation; most of the findings support the hypothesis. For a propositional inventory on the hypothesis, see Lester W. Milbrath, *Political Participation: How and Why Do People Get Involved in Politics?* (Chicago: Rand McNally, 1965), pp. 16-17, 111-130.

8. Deutsch, "Social Mobilization," pp. 495-496, 498-500.

9. Lerner, *Traditional Society*, p. 50; Almond and Verba, *Civic Culture*, p. 206; Deutsch, "Social Mobilization," p. 494; Milbrath, *Political Participation*, pp. 51, 53-54, 56-57, 61, 63-64, 68, 77, 79-80.

10. Norman H. Nie, G. Bingham Powell, Jr., and Kenneth Prewitt, "Social Structure and Developmental Relationships, Part 1," *American Political Science Review* 63, no. 2 (1969): 365, 370, 374; Part 2, pp. 825-828; Alex Inkeles, "Participant Citizenship in Six Developing Countries," ibid., pp. 1122-1123, 1139-1141;

Joan M. Nelson, *Migrants, Urban Poverty, and Instability in Developing Nations,* Occasional Papers in International Affairs, no. 22 (Cambridge, Mass.: Center for International Affairs, Harvard University, 1969), pp. 25-26, 66-67. See also Joan Nelson, "The Urban Poor: Disruption or Political Integration in Third World Cities," *World Politics* 22, no. 3 (1970): 393-414; Wayne A. Cornelius, Jr., "Urbanization as an Agent in Latin American Political Instability: The Case of Mexico," *American Political Science Review* 63, no. 3 (1969): 854-857; Wayne A. Cornelius, Jr., "The Political Sociology of Cityward Migration in Latin America: Toward Empirical Theory," in Francine F. Rabinowitz and Felicity M. Trueblood, eds., *Latin American Urban Research* (Beverly Hills, Calif.: Sage Publications, 1971), I, 95, 147; Bradley M. Richardson, "Urbanization and Political Participation: The Case of Japan," *American Political Science Review* 67, no. 2 (1973): 433-452; Gerald W. Johnson, "Political Correlatives of Voter Participation: A Deviant Case Analysis," ibid. 65, no. 3 (1971): 768-776; Samuel P. Huntington and Jorge I. Domínguez, "Political Development," in Fred Greenstein and Nelson Polsby, eds., *The Handbook of Political Science* (Reading, Mass.: Addison-Wesley, 1975), III, pp. 33-47; Samuel P. Huntington and Joan Nelson, *No Easy Choice: Political Participation in Developing Countries* (Cambridge, Mass.: Harvard University Press, 1976); Sidney Verba and Norman H. Nie, *Participation in America* (New York: Harper and Row, 1972), part 2.

11. Deutsch, "Social Mobilization," pp. 497-498.

12. For sources, assumptions, and calculations and a full presentation of pertinent information, see Jorge I. Domínguez, "Political Participation and the Social Mobilization Hypothesis: Chile, Mexico, Venezuela and Cuba, 1800-1825," *The Journal of Interdisciplinary History* 5, no. 2 (Fall 1974): 243-260.

13. For evidence of the decline of school enrollments in Mexico City between 1803 and 1820, see Timothy E. Anna, *The Fall of the Royal Government in Mexico City* (Lincoln: University of Nebraska Press, 1978), pp. 176-198.

14. George A. Kubler, "Cities and Culture in the Colonial Period in Latin America," *Diogenes* 49 (1964): 59-60.

15. Kendall's *tau-b* corrects the ties in Table 2.1. For a discussion of rank order correlations, see Hubert M. Blalock, *Social Statistics* (New York: McGraw-Hill, 1960), pp. 317-324.

16. Richard M. Morse, "Latin American Cities: Aspects of Function and Structure," *Comparative Studies in Society and History* 4, no. 4 (1962): 474, 479-480, 493; Richard M. Morse, "Some Characteristics of Latin American Urban History," *American Historical Review* 67, no. 2 (1962): 322; Kubler, "Cities."

17. Deutsch, "Social Mobilization," p. 497.

18. Marius B. Jansen and Lawrence Stone, "Education and Modernization in Japan and England," *Comparative Studies in Society and History* 9, no. 2 (1967): 209, 216, 228; Seymour Martin Lipset, *The First New Nation: The United States in Historical and Comparative Perspective* (Garden City, N.Y.: Doubleday, Anchor, 1967), pp. 108-109.

## 3. Ethnicity

1. Donald L. Horowitz, "Three Dimensions of Ethnic Politics," *World Politics* 23, no. 2 (January 1971): 232-236.

2. H. H. Gerth and C. Wright Mills, eds., *From Max Weber: Essays in Sociology* (New York: Oxford University Press, 1958), p. 189.

3. José Terrero, *Historia de España* (Barcelona: Ramón Sopena, 1958), pp. 117-126, 145-192; J. H. Parry, *The Spanish Seaborne Empire* (New York: Alfred A. Knopf, 1967), pp. 27-37.

4. Parry, *Spanish Seaborne Empire*, p. 32.

5. For a general discussion of the differences and similarities between the Spanish American and other hierarchical or vertical ethnic systems, see Samuel P. Huntington and Jorge I. Domínguez, "Political Development," in Fred I. Greenstein and Nelson W. Polsby, eds., *The Handbook of Political Science* (Reading, Mass.: Addison-Wesley, 1975), III, 67-73; for discussions of the Spanish American case, see Magnus Mörner, *Race Mixture in the History of Latin America* (Boston: Little, Brown, 1967), pp. 1-8, 21-73; Mario Góngora, *Studies in the Colonial History of Spanish America*, trans. Richard Southern (Cambridge: Cambridge University Press, 1975), pp. 1-32, 127-158; and Leslie B. Rout, Jr., *The African Experience in Spanish America: 1502 to the Present Day* (Cambridge: Cambridge University Press, 1976), pp. 80-98. For reviews of literature about the colonial period, see Karen Spalding, "The Colonial Indian: Past and Future Research Perspectives," *Latin American Research Review* 7, no. 1 (Spring 1972): 47-76; and Frederick P. Bowser, "The African in Colonial Spanish America: Reflections in Research Achievements and Priorities," in ibid., pp. 47-94.

6. Victoria Lerner, "Consideraciones sobre la población de la Nueva España (1793-1810)," *Historia mexicana* 17, no. 67 (1968): 338.

7. Federico Brito Figueroa, *Historia social y económica de Venezuela* (Caracas: Universidad Central de Venezuela), I, 160. For a superb collection of data on the Bishopric of Caracas, see John V. Lombardi, *People and Places in Colonial Venezuela* (Bloomington: Indiana University Press, 1976).

8. Arnold J. Bauer, *Chilean Rural Society from the Spanish Conquest to 1930* (Cambridge: Cambridge University Press, 1975), p. 14; María Isabel González Pomes, "La encomienda indígena en Chile durante el siglo 18," *Historia* 5 (1966), p. 97; Jaime Eyzaguirre, *Historia de Chile* (Santiago: Zig Zag, 1965), pp. 254-258; Francisco Encina, *Historia de Chile* (Santiago: Nascimiento, 1946) V, 162-169; Guillermo Feliú Cruz, *La abolición de la esclavitud en Chile* (Santiago: Ediciones de la Universidad de Chile, 1942), pp. 39-40, 101-102; Gonzalo Vial Correa, *El africano en el reino de Chile* (Santiago: Universidad Católica de Chile, 1957), pp. 45, 48; and Marcello Carmagnani, "Colonial Latin American Demography: Growth of Chilean Population, 1700-1830," *Journal of Social History* 1, no. 2 (Winter 1967): 179-191.

9. Louis de Armand, "Frontier Warfare in Colonial Chile," *Pacific Historical Review* 23 (1954): 125-132; Eugene H. Korth, *Spanish Policy in Colonial Chile* (Stanford, Calif.: Stanford University Press, 1968), pp. 227, 292; Bauer, *Chilean Rural Society*, pp. 7, 15.

10. Data from Lyle N. McAllister, *The "Fuero Militar" in New Spain, 1764-1800* (Gainesville: University of Florida Press, 1957), pp. 93-99; Encina, *Historia de Chile*, V, 529-533; Eyzaguirre, *Historia de Chile*, pp. 242-246; Carmagnani, "Colonial Latin American Demography," pp. 183-185; Christon I. Archer, *The Army*

*in Bourbon Mexico, 1760-1810* (Albuquerque: University of New Mexico Press, 1977), pp. 22, 110-111, 228, 240; Isidro Vizcaya Canales, *En los albores de la independencia: Las provincias internas de Oriente durante la insurrección de don Miguel Hidalgo y Costilla, 1810-1811* (Monterrey: Instituto Tecnológico y de Estudios Superiores de Monterrey, 1976), pp. 41-42; and Timothy E. Anna, *The Fall of the Royal Government in Mexico City* (Lincoln: University of Nebraska Press, 1978), pp. 83-84.

11. C. H. Haring, *The Spanish Empire in America* (New York: Harbinger, 1963), pp. 197-198, 215, 263-264; Rout, *African Experience,* pp. 126-152; Góngora, *Studies in Colonial History,* pp. 159-162; Mörner, *Race Mixture,* pp. 41-48, 53-62.

12. M. N. Srinivas, *Social Change in Modern India* (Berkeley: University of California Press, 1966), pp. 6-7, 23.

13. The main sources for this section are Lloyd Rudolph and Susanne Hoeber Rudolph, *The Modernity of Tradition* (Chicago: University of Chicago Press, 1967), pp. 27-35, 115-116; Srinivas, *Social Change,* pp. 32-42; Robert L. Hardgrave, Jr., *The Nadars of Tamilnad* (Berkeley: University of California Press, 1969); and Huntington and Domínguez, "Political Development," pp. 25-26.

14. See also Eric A. Nordlinger, *Conflict Regulation in Divided Societies,* Occasional Papers in International Affairs, no. 29 (Cambridge, Mass.: Center for International Affairs, Harvard University, 1972). Although he discusses parallel communal systems, Nordlinger, too, stresses the importance of political leadership for the regulation of communal group conflict.

15. Brito Figueroa, *Historia social,* I, 165.

16. Translated from Valenilla Lanz, *Cesarismo democrático* (Caracas: Tipografía Garrido, 1961), pp. 48-49.

17. Brito Figueroa, *Historia Social,* I, 166.

18. James F. King, "The Case of José Ponciano de Ayarza: A Document on *Gracias al Sacar,*" *Hispanic American Historical Review* 31, no. 4 (November 1951): 642-644.

19. Eleázar Córdova Bello, "La revolución social en la emancipación de América," *Revista de historia* 4, nos. 19-20 (1964): 84.

20. Valenilla Lanz, *Cesarismo,* pp. 44-45, 62; Brito Figueroa, *Historia Social,* I, 168.

21. Caracciolo Parra Pérez, *El régimen español en Venezuela* (Madrid: Javier Morata, 1932), p. 133; Ildefonso Leal, "La universidad de Caracas y los pardos," *Revista de historia* 3, no. 15 (1963): 51-74; Rout, *African Experience,* pp. 156-159; Mörner, *Race Mixture,* pp. 45, 63-65.

22. Herbert S. Klein, *Slavery in the Americas: A Comparative Study of Virginia and Cuba* (Chicago: Quadrangle, 1971), pp. 128-147, 162; and Alexander von Humboldt, *The Island of Cuba,* ed. J. S. Thrasher (New York: Derby and Jackson, 1856), p. 275.

23. Klein, *Slavery,* pp. 78-85, for the 1789 Code, also pp. 202-204, on job opportunities; Humboldt, *Island of Cuba,* p. 190.

24. Pedro Deschamps Chapeaux, "El negro en la economía habanera del siglo 19: Agustín Ceballos, capataz de muelle," *Revista de la Biblioteca Nacional José Martí,* 3rd ser., 10, no. 1 (January–April 1968): 54-57.

25. Klein, *Slavery*, pp. 205-210; Pedro Deschamps Chapeaux, "El negro en la economía habanera del siglo 19: Flebotomianos y dentistas," *Revista de la Biblioteca Nacional José Martí*, 3rd ser., 13, no. 1 (January–April 1971): 75.

26. Magnus Mörner, "The History of Race Relations in Latin America: Some Comments on the State of Research," *Latin American Research Review* 1, no. 3 (Summer 1966): 24.

27. Charles Gibson, *The Aztecs Under Spanish Rule* (Stanford: Stanford University Press, 1964), pp. 153-156, 191-192, 194-196, 201-208; Lyle N. McAlister, "Social Structure and Social Change in New Spain," *Hispanic American Historical Review* 43, no. 3 (August 1963): 357-359; Eric R. Wolf, *Sons of the Shaking Earth* (Chicago: Phoenix, 1962), p. 212; Magnus Mörner and Charles Gibson, "Diego Muñoz Camargo and the Segregation Policy of the Spanish Crown," *Hispanic American Historical Review* 42, no. 4 (November 1962): 558-562.

28. Charles Gibson, "The Aztec Aristocracy in Colonial Mexico," *Comparative Studies in Society and History* 2, no. 2 (January 1960): 195-196; Gibson, *The Aztecs*, pp. 164-165.

29. Gibson, *The Aztecs*, p. 162.

30. Ibid., pp. 399-401; D. A. Brading, "Grupos étnicos, clases y estructura ocupacional en Guanajuato (1792)," *Historia mexicana* 83 (January–March 1972): 476-477; and John K. Chance, *Race and Class in Colonial Oaxaca* (Stanford: Stanford University Press, 1978), p. 165. For a discussion of black freedmen, see Frederick P. Bowser, "The Free Person of Color in Mexico City and Lima; Manumission and Opportunity, 1580-1650," in Stanley L. Engerman and Eugene D. Genovese, eds., *Race and Slavery in the Western Hemisphere: Quantitative Studies* (Princeton: Princeton University Press, 1975), pp. 331-368.

31. José L. Becerra López, *La organización de los estudios en la Nueva España* (Mexico: Cultura, 1963), pp. 124-126.

32. Wilbert H. Timmons, *Morelos: Priest, Soldier, Statesman of Mexico* (El Paso: Texas Western College Press, 1963), pp. 2, 3, 9.

33. Gerth and Mills, eds., *From Max Weber*, pp. 188-190; Horowitz, "Three Dimensions of Ethnic Politics," pp. 233-234.

34. Ted Robert Gurr, *Why Men Rebel* (Princeton: Princeton University Press, 1971), pp. 124-125, 146.

35. Two cases of ethnic conflict in traditional or only partially modernized systems that recently exploded into violent confrontations are Zanzibar and Rwanda. Although the normative support for the hierarchy was far greater in Rwanda, both countries were close to the hierarchical model of ethnic systems. Their experience supports the hypothesis that the breakdown of hierarchical systems often leads to a significant social transformation, that it may be accompanied by considerable violence, and that the failure of the political system to accommodate all relevant ethnic groups is critical. René Lemarchand, "Revolutionary Phenomena in Stratified Societies: Rwanda and Zanzibar," *Civilisations* 18, no. 1 (1968): 21, 25.

36. Leo Kuper, "Theories of Revolution and Race Relations," *Comparative Studies in Society and History* 13, no. 1 (January 1971): 99-100. See also Karl W. Deutsch, *Nationalism and Social Communication* (Cambridge, Mass.: MIT Press, 1966), pp. 123-130.

## 4. Resistance to Change

1. E. J. Hobsbawm, *Primitive Rebels* (New York: Frederick A. Praeger, 1959), pp. 15, 23, 24.

2. Eric R. Wolf, "The Mexican Bajío in the Eighteenth Century," *Synoptic Studies of Mexican Culture*, Middle American Research Institute Publications, no. 17 (New Orleans: Tulane University Press, 1957), pp. 183-185, 188-189.

3. Miguel Acosta Saignes, *Vida de los esclavos negros en Venezuela* (Caracas: Hespérides, 1967), pp. 249-251; Federico Brito Figueroa, *Historia Económica y social de Venezuela* (Caracas: Universidad Central de Venezuela, 1966), I, 160.

4. Acosta Saignes, *Vida*, pp. 256-257, 259-261.

5. Ibid., pp. 257, 272-274, 282-288.

6. Federico Brito Figueroa, *Las insurrecciones de los esclavos negros en la sociedad colonial venezolana* (Caracas: Cantaclaro, 1961), pp. 54-58.

7. Manuel Moreno Fraginals, *El ingenio: El complejo económico-social cubano del azúcar* (Havana: Comisión Nacional Cubana de la UNESCO, 1964), p. 151.

8. José Luciano Franco, "Maroons and Slave Rebellions in the Spanish Territories," in Richard Price, ed., *Maroon Societies: Rebel Slave Communities in the Americas* (Garden City, N.Y.: Doubleday, Anchor, 1973), pp. 42-43; Francisco Pérez de la Riva, "Cuban palenques," in ibid., pp. 49-57.

9. Richard Price, "Introduction: Maroons and Their Communities," in Price, ed., *Maroon Societies*, pp. 5, 13-15, 24.

10. R. K. Kent, "Palmares: An African State in Brazil," in Price, ed., *Maroon Societies*.

11. Diego Barros Arana, *Historia general de Chile* (2nd ed.; Santiago: Nascimiento, 1933), VII, 506-511; Arnold J. Bauer, *Chilean Rural Society from the Spanish Conquest to 1930* (Cambridge: Cambridge University Press, 1975), pp. 15-16.

12. Charles Tilly, "Revolutions and Collective Violence," in Fred Greenstein and Nelson Polsby, eds., *Handbook of Political Science* (Reading, Mass.: Addison-Wesley, 1975), III, 506-509. The term "defensive" in the text is analogous to Tilly's "reactive"; Tilly's "proactive" collective violence is included in the definition of modern collective violence; his "competitive" collective action has some parallels with what I have called "adjustive" goals. See also Charles Tilly, "Collective Violence in European Perspective," in Hugh Davis Graham and Ted Robert Gurr, eds., *Violence in America: Historical and Comparative Perspectives* (Washington: United States Government Printing Office, 1969), pp. 14, 15, 19; Hobsbawm, *Primitive Rebels*, p. 108; Samuel P. Huntington, *Political Order in Changing Societies* (New Haven: Yale University Press, 1968), pp. 264-274; Barrington Moore, Jr., *Social Origins of Dictatorship and Democracy* (Boston: Beacon, 1967), pp. 420-434, 459-460, 467-480.

13. Computed from Agustín Cué Cánovas, *Historia social y económica de México, 1521-1854* (Mexico: F. Trillas, 1960), pp. 183-187. The Pearson product-moment correlation between the frequency and the duration of revolts per decade is 0.74.

14. Cué Cánovas, *Historia social y económica de México*, pp. 183-187; D. A. Brading, *Miners and Merchants in Bourbon Mexico, 1763-1810* (Cambridge:

Cambridge University Press, 1971), pp. 27, 148, 233-235; and Luis Chávez Oroz-co, "Prólogo," in *Conflicto de trabajo: Con los mineros de Real del Monte: año de 1766*, ed. Instituto Nacional de Estudios Históricos de la Revolución (Mexico: Talleres Gráficos de la Nación, 1960), pp. 12-13, 20.

15. Seymour Martin Lipset, *Political Man: The Social Bases of Politics* (Garden City, N.Y.: Doubleday, Anchor, 1963), pp. 242-246; Glaucio Soares and Robert L. Hamblin, "Socio-economic Variables and Voting for the Radical Left: Chile, 1952," *The American Political Science Review* 61, no. 4 (December 1967): 1053-1065; and Gerald W. Johnson, "Political Correlatives of Voter Participation: A Deviant Case Analysis," *The American Political Science Review* 65, no. 3 (September 1971): 768-776.

16. Gaston V. Rimlinger, "The Legitimation of Protest: A Comparative Study in Labor History," *Comparative Studies in Society and History* 2, no. 3 (April 1960): 330-336, 343.

17. Bradley Benedict, "El Estado en México en la época de los Habsburgo," *Historia mexicana* 92 (April–June 1974): 593-596; Maria Teresa Huerta Preciado, *Rebeliones indígenas en el noreste de México en la época colonial* (Mexico: Instituto Nacional de Antropología e Historia, 1966), pp. 79-80, 104-105. See also María Elena Galaviz de Capdevielle, *Rebeliones indígenas en el norte del reino de la Nueva España* (Mexico: Campesina, 1967), and Maria del Carmen Velázquez, "La comandancia general de las provincias internas," *Historia mexicana* 27, no. 2 (October–December 1977): 163-176.

18. See also Sergio Villalobos, *Tradición y reforma en 1810* (Santiago: Universitaria, 1961), pp. 92-97; Barros Arana, *Historia*, VII, 511-521; Néstor Meza Villalobos, *La conciencia política chilena durante la monarquía* (Santiago: Universidad de Chile, 1958), pp. 186-206, 230-235.

19. Hugh Thomas, *Cuba: The Pursuit of Freedom* (New York: Harper and Row, 1971), p. 23.

20. Roland D. Hussey, *The Caracas Company, 1728-1784* (Cambridge, Mass.: Harvard University Press, 1934), pp. 60-61.

21. Ibid., pp. 66-69; and Leslie B. Rout, Jr., *The African Experience in Spanish America: 1502 to the Present Day* (Cambridge: Cambridge University Press, 1976), pp. 112-113.

22. Hussey, *Caracas Company*, pp. 115-117.

23. Brito Figueroa, *Insurrecciones*, pp. 49-53. For a different view about this conspiracy, see Rout, *African Experience*, pp. 119-123.

24. One's normative outrage can cry out against slavery; social science requires that specific tests be applied to the significance of slave revolts. Little is gained by stressing the "contribution" of slave revolts to this or that world historical trend. For a critique of "contributionism," see Orlando Patterson, "Rethinking Black History," *Harvard Educational Review* 41, no. 3 (August 1971): 297-315.

25. The principal sources are Pedro M. Arcaya, *Insurrección de los negros de la serranía de Coro*, publication no. 17 (Caracas: Instituto Panamericano de Geografía e Historia, 1949), pp. 16-19, 22-41; Pedro M. Arcaya, *Población de origen europeo de Coro en la época colonial* (Caracas: Biblioteca de la Academia Nacional de la Historia, 1972), p. xxix; Brito Figueroa, *Insurrecciones*, pp. 59-77; and Acosta Saignes, *Vida*, pp. 318-322.

26. Data computed from Arcaya, *Población,* p. xxix, and from Brito Figueroa, *Insurrecciones,* pp. 67-69.

27. For a somewhat different view of slave revolts, see Rout, *African Experience,* pp. 122-125; for a catalog of protest in Venezuela, all but the last of which the colonial government accommodated well, see Manuel Vicente Magallanes, *Luchas e insurrecciones en la Venezuela colonial* (Caracas: Tiempo Nuevo, 1972).

## 5. The Record of Economic Growth

1. Demetrio Ramos, "Trigo chileno, navieros del Callao, y hacendados limeños entre la crisis agrícola del siglo 17 y la comercial de la primera mitad del siglo 18," *Revista de Indias* 26, nos. 105-106 (July–December 1966): 227-233; Sergio Sepúlveda, *El trigo chileno en el mercado mundial* (Santiago: Editorial Universitaria, 1959), pp. 16-19, all seek to explain the Peruvian decline. Ruggiero Romano argued that "Chile did not experience a commercial increase during the second half of the eighteenth century," that "it is possible that there may have been a quantitative expansion of the export trade during the second half of the century," but "a decline in wholesale prices" canceled out this effect. Romano's conclusion is not supported by his data. His inferences were based on tax records of production between 1751 and 1787, which show that the tax yield had never been above 100,000 pesos before 1768, whereas they were never under that between 1773 and 1787. Tax yields between 1751 and 1760 had never risen above 75,000 pesos; tax yields were above 120,000 pesos in eleven of the fifteen years between 1773 and 1787. Romano's study of prices focused on sixteen consumer products, of which twelve remained at the same level and only three declined. These data do not support an argument about falling prices; on the contrary, his evidence suggests a very substantial expansion of production at relatively stable long-term prices. *Una economía colonial: Chile en el siglo XVIII* (Buenos Aires: Editorial Universitaria, 1965), pp. 29-31, 39-40.

2. Sepúlveda, *Trigo chileno,* pp. 22, 31; Ramos, "Trigo chileno," pp. 247-248. Data were converted from fanegas to metric quintals, where 1 fanega = 73 kilograms, and 1 metric quintal = 100 kilograms. The second statistic is an annual average.

3. Hernán Ramirez Necochea, *Antecedentes económicos de la independencia de Chile* (rev. ed.; Santiago: Editorial Universitaria, 1967), pp. 51-52.

4. Federico Brito Figueroa, *Historia económica y social de Venezuela* (Caracas: Universidad Central de Venezuela, 1966), I, 105.

5. "Representación del Consulado en favor del establecimiento del comercio con las naciones neutrales," in Eduardo Arcila Farías, ed., *El Real Consulado de Caracas* (Caracas: Universidad Central de Venezuela, 1957), pp. 174, 243-244.

6. Alejandro de Humboldt, *Viaje a las regiones equinocciales del nuevo continente,* trans. Lisandro Alvarado (Caracas: Biblioteca Venezolana de Cultura, 1941), pp. 169, 176.

7. Computed from data in Eduardo Arcila Farías, *Economia colonial de Venezuela* (Mexico: Fondo de Cultura Económica, 1946), p. 174.

8. Humboldt, *Viaje,* p. 89. The first figure is an annual average.

9. Brito Figueroa, *Historia,* I, 105.

10. Francisco Depons, *Viaje a la parte oriental de tierra firme* (Caracas: Tipografía Americana, 1930), p. 340.

11. From D. A. Brading, *Miners and Merchants in Bourbon Mexico, 1763-1810* (Cambridge: Cambridge University Press, 1971), p. 96.

12. See also ibid., p. 131.

13. Francisco López Cámara, *La estructura económica y social de México en la época de la reforma* (Mexico: Siglo XXI Editores, 1967), p. 77.

14. Annual price and production data from Brian R. Hamnett, *Politics and Trade in Southern Mexico, 1750-1821* (Cambridge: Cambridge University Press, 1971), pp. 169-170.

15. Enrique Florescano, *Precios del maíz y crisis agrícola en México (1708-1810)* (Mexico: El Colegio de México, 1969), pp. 181, 193-194.

16. From Jan Bazant, "Evolución de la industria textil poblana, 1544-1845," *Historia Mexicana* 13, no. 4 (1964): 482, 500-507.

17. Computed from Brading, *Miners and Merchants,* p. 229.

18. Brading, *Miners and Merchants,* p. 232; and Eric R. Wolf, "The Mexican Bajío in the Eighteenth Century," *Synoptic Studies of Mexican Culture,* Middle American Research Institute Publications, no. 17 (New Orleans: Tulane University Press, 1957), pp. 183-184.

19. Clark W. Reynolds, *The Mexican Economy: Twentieth Century Structure and Growth* (New Haven: Yale University Press, 1970), p. 312.

20. Jacobo de la Pezuela, *Diccionario geográfico, estadístico, histórico de la isla de Cuba* (Madrid: Mellado, 1863), I, 62. See also Manuel Moreno Fraginals, *El ingenio: Complejo económico social cubano del Azúcar* (Havana: Editorial de Ciencias Sociales, 1978), III, 43-44.

21. Ibid., p. 225.

22. Ramón de la Sagra, *Historia económico-política y estadística de la isla de Cuba* (Havana: Viudas de Arazoza y Soler, 1831), computed from pp. 103, 120, 126-127.

## 6. International War and Government Modernization

1. For a general discussion of political modernization, see Samuel P. Huntington, *Political Order in Changing Societies* (New Haven: Yale University Press, 1968), pp. 34, 94, 103, 106, 128-129. For a discussion of the role of government in accelerating growth, see Alexander Gerschenkron, *Economic Backwardness in Historical Perspective* (Cambridge, Mass.: Harvard University Press, 1962), pp. 7, 16-17.

2. Quoted in R. A. Humphreys, *Tradition and Revolt in Latin America and Other Essays* (New York: Columbia University Press, 1969), p. 78. For a general discussion of Bourbon policies in Spain, see Richard Herr, *The Eighteenth Century Revolution in Spain* (Princeton: Princeton University Press, 1958); for the importance of Bourbon policies for legitimacy in America, see Mario Góngora, *Studies in the Colonial History of Spanish America* (Cambridge: Cambridge University Press, 1975), pp. 159-187.

3. For a study of the spread of the system, see Gisela Morazzani de Pérez Enciso, "Organización de las intendencias," *Revista de historia* 4, no. 22 (1965): 11-35.

4. Ibid.; also Emeterio S. Santovenia, "Política colonial," in Ramiro Guerra y Sánchez, José M. Pérez Cabrera, Juan J. Remos, and Emeterio S. Santovenia, eds., *Historia de la nación cubana* (Havana: Editorial Historia de la Nación Cubana, 1952), II, 59.

5. Mario Briceño-Iragorry, *Tapices de historia patria* (Caracas: Tipografía Garrido, 1942); and José Gil Fortoul, *Historia constitucional de Venezuela* (4th ed.; Caracas: Dirección de Cultura y Bellas Artes, Ministerio de Educación, 1954), I, 117-121.

6. Morazzani, "Organización," pp. 21-25.

7. Francisco A. Encina, *Historia de Chile* (Santiago: Nascimiento, 1946), V, 394-395.

8. D. A. Brading, *Miners and Merchants in Bourbon Mexico, 1763-1810* (Cambridge: Cambridge University Press, 1971), pp. 45-48.

9. Andrés Lira González, "Aspecto fiscal de la Nueva España en la segunda mitad del siglo 18," *Historia mexicana* 17, no. 67 (1968): 390. Annual averages given for 1773-1776 and 1777-1779.

10. Brading, *Miners and Merchants*, pp. 51-54.

11. Lucas Alamán, *Historia de Méjico* (Mexico: Editorial Jus, 1968), I, 65-67; Diego López Rosado, *Historia económica de México* (Mexico: Universidad Nacional Autónoma de México, 1963), pp. 133-136.

12. Brading, *Miners and Merchants*, pp. 90-91.

13. Computed from Herbert S. Klein, *Slavery in the Americas: A Comparative Study of Virginia and Cuba* (Chicago: Quadrangle, 1971), pp. 218-219; Encina, *Historia*, V, 60-61, 73, 529-534; Lyle N. McAlister, *The "Fuero Militar" in New Spain, 1764-1800* (Gainesville: University of Florida Press, 1957), pp. 93-99; Christon I. Archer, *The Army in Bourbon Mexico, 1760-1810* (Albuquerque: University of New Mexico Press, 1977), pp. 22, 110-111, 240; Marcello Carmagnani, "Colonial Latin American Demography: Growth of Chilean Population, 1700-1830," *Journal of Social History* 1, no. 2 (Winter 1967): 183-185; and Timothy E. Anna, *The Fall of the Royal Government in Mexico City* (Lincoln: University of Nebraska Press, 1978), pp. 83-84.

14. Computed from Francisco Depons, *Viaje a la parte oriental de tierra firme* (Caracas: Tipografía Americana, 1930), pp. 179-182.

15. Bruce M. Russett et al., *World Handbook of Political and Social Indicators* (New Haven: Yale University Press, 1964), pp. 74-76.

16. Margaret L. Woodward, "The Spanish Army and the Loss of America, 1810-1824," *Hispanic American Historical Review* 43, no. 4 (1963): 587.

17. This discussion draws heavily from McAlister, "Fuero Militar," pp. 6-11.

18. Ibid., pp. 14, 33; Alamán, *Historia*, I, 58; and María del Carmen Velázquez, *El estado de guerra en Nueva España* (Mexico: Colegio de México, 1950), pp. 154-161, 164, 172-176.

19. McAlister, "Fuero Militar," pp. 11, 45-51; Christon I. Archer, "Pardos, Indians, and the Army of New Spain: Inter-Relationships and Conflicts,

1780-1810," *Journal of Latin American Studies* 6, no. 2 (November 1974): 231-255; and Archer, *Army in Bourbon Mexico*, pp. 224, 237.

20. Depons, *Viaje*, pp. 175-178.

21. Klein, *Slavery*, pp. 218-219; Depons, *Viaje*, pp. 175-178; Ramón de la Sagra, *Historia económico-política y estadística de la isla de Cuba* (Havana: Viudas de Arazoza y Soler, 1831), p. 3; José M. Pérez Cabrera, "Movimiento de población," in Guerra y Sánchez et al., eds., *Historia de la nación cubana*, III, 348. The following facts and assumptions were used in computations. The free black male population over age fifteen for Cuba in 1827 (60.8 percent) was computed directly from the census of that year. The same rate was applied to the same population stratum in the early 1770s, for which there is a military count for 1770 and a population count in 1774. The 1774 count gave the free black male population from which the adult share was calculated and the military ratio. This is consistent with Lombardi's finding that the Venezuelan population under age six accounted for 28 percent of the population. For Venezuela, the Cuban age structure and an even sex ratio were assumed to apply. Its free black population was taken from ch. 3; then the military ratio was computed. For a justification of the application of Cuban age structure data to Venezuela, see Jorge I. Domínguez, "Political Participation and the Social Mobilization Hypothesis: Chile, Mexico, Venezuela and Cuba, 1800–1825," *The Journal of Interdisciplinary History* 5, no. 2 (Fall 1974): 246-247. See also John V. Lombardi, *People and Places in Colonial Venezuela* (Bloomington: Indiana University Press, 1976), p. 137. For a discussion of Cuban slave demography, see also Jack Ericson Eblen, "On the Natural Increase of Slave Populations: The Example of the Cuban Black Population, 1775-1900," in Stanley L. Engerman and Eugene D. Genovese, eds., *Race and Slavery in the Western Hemisphere: Quantitative Studies* (Princeton: Princeton University Press, 1975); and Stanley L. Engerman, "Comments on the Study of Race and Slavery," in ibid., pp. 509-510.

22. Woodward, "The Spanish Army," p. 587; Encina, *Historia*, V, 531.

23. Brading, *Miners and Merchants*, pp. 325-326; Archer, *Army in Bourbon Mexico*, pp. 195-199, 212-213, 234.

## 7. Elite Competition

1. Max Weber, *The Theory of Social and Economic Organization*, trans. A. M. Henderson and Talcott Parsons (New York: Free Press, 1965), pp. 352-353.

2. William P. Glade, *The Latin American Economies* (New York: American Book, 1969), pp. 146-147.

3. Wilbert E. Moore, *Social Change* (Englewood Cliffs, N.J.: Prentice-Hall, 1963), p 1.

4. Eric R. Wolf, *Peasant Wars of the Twentieth Century* (New York: Harper and Row, 1969), pp. 276-286; Barrington Moore, Jr., *Social Origins of Dictatorship and Democracy* (Boston: Beacon, 1967), pp. 467-483.

5. Wolf, *Peasant Wars*, pp. 289-294; Moore, Jr., *Social Origins*, pp. 459-466.

6. Samuel P. Huntington, *Political Order in Changing Societies* (New Haven: Yale University Press, 1968), pp. 34, 94, 103, 106, 128-129.

7. Demetrio Ramos, "Trigo chileno, navieros del Callao y hacendados limeños entre la crisis agrícola del siglo 17 y la comercial de la primera mitad del siglo 18," *Revista de Indias* 26, nos. 105-106 (July–December 1966): 276, 282-285.

8. Ibid., pp. 286-294; and Carlos Ugarte, "El Cabildo de Santiago y el comercio exterior del reino de Chile durante el siglo 18," *Estudios de historia de las instituciones políticas y sociales* 1 (1966): 27-29.

9. Sergio Sepúlveda, *El trigo chileno en el mercado mundial* (Santiago: Universitaria, 1959), pp. 28-29.

10. Ramos, "Trigo chileno," pp. 300-320.

11. Fernando Silva Vargas, "Perú y Chile: notas sobre sus vinculaciones administrativas y fiscales (1785-1800)," *Historia* 7 (1968): 156-171, 176-179, 197, 200-201; and Demetrio Ramos, *Minería y comercio interprovincial en hispanoamérica (siglos XVI, XVII y XVIII)* (Valladolid: Universidad de Valladolid, 1970), pp. 310-311.

12. Sérgio Villalobos, *El comercio y la crisis colonial: Un mito de la independencia* (Santiago: Universitaria, 1968), pp. 222-235. For a discussion of Chilean desires of independence from Peru, not Spain, see Néstor Meza Villalobos, *La conciencia política chilena durante la monarquía* (Santiago: Universidad de Chile, 1958), pp. 244, 257-260; Hernán Ramírez Necochea, *Antecedentes económicos de la independencia de Chile* (rev. ed.; Santiago: Universitaria, 1967), pp. 80-84, for a catalog of these protests.

13. Sergio Villalobos, *Tradición y reforma en 1810* (Santiago: Universitaria, 1961), pp. 80-83, 87; Ramírez Necochea, *Antecedentes*, p. 125; Ugarte, "El Cabildo," p. 33; Villalobos, *El Comercio*, pp. 105-108, 178, 187-189, 238-244.

14. Villalobos, *Tradición*, pp. 87-89; Ramírez Necochea, *Antecedentes*, pp. 128-131.

15. Villalobos, *El Comercio*, pp. 254-255.

16. For evidence of traditional accommodable Chilean elite competition relying on the Cabildo, see Julio Alemparte, *El cabildo en Chile colonial* (2nd ed.; Santiago: Andrés Bello, 1966), e.g., pp. 201-202, 271-273; and Meza Villalobos, *La conciencia política chilena*, pp. 177-180, 184-206, 270-305.

17. Marvin D. Bernstein, *The Mexican Mining Industry, 1890-1950: A Study of the Interaction of Politics, Economics and Technology* (Yellow Springs, Ohio: Antioch Press, 1965), pp. 11-12.

18. D. A. Brading, *Miners and Merchants in Bourbon Mexico, 1763-1810* (Cambridge: Cambridge University Press, 1971), pp. 329-334.

19. Ibid., pp. 164-167.

20. Robert S. Smith, "The Institution of the Consulado in New Spain," *Hispanic American Historical Review* 24, no. 1 (February 1944): 61-83.

21. Robert S. Smith, "Shipping in the Port of Veracruz, 1790-1821," *Hispanic American Historical Review* 23, no. 1 (February 1943): 11-14; Brading, *Miners and Merchants*, pp. 116-119; Ramos, *Minería y comercio*, pp. 298-299.

22. Enrique Florescano, "El problema agrario en los últimos años del virreinato," *Historia mexicana* 80 (April–June 1971): 492-493, 495. For a general discussion of the trade objectives of competing Mexican elites, see Enrique Florescano, *Estructuras y problemas agrarios de México (1500-1821)* (Mexico: Sep-Setentas, 1971), pp. 214-216.

23. Romeo Flores Caballero, "Del libre cambio al proteccionismo," *Historia mexicana* 76 (April–July 1970): 493-495.

24. Brian R. Hamnett, *Politics and Trade in Southern Mexico, 1750-1821* (Cambridge: Cambridge University Press, 1971), pp. 3-6, 18-19, 37-40, 48-49, 55, 75-94.

25. Brian R. Hamnett, "Obstáculos a la política agraria del despotismo ilustrado," *Historia mexicana* 77 (July–September 1970): 72-73.

26. Roland D. Hussey, *The Caracas Company, 1728-1784* (Cambridge, Mass.: Harvard University Press, 1934), pp. 122-129, 152-153, 162-168; and Eduardo Arcila Farías, *Economía colonial de Venezuela* (Mexico: Fondo de Cultura Económica, 1946), pp. 225-230, 254-256.

27. Carlos E. Muñoz Oráa, *Los comuneros de Venezuela* (Merida: Universidad de los Andes, 1971), pp. 65, 73, 76-78, 82-83, 91-94, 133-134, 154; data on the elite's social origins were compiled from biographies on pp. 99-129. Muñoz Oráa argues that the revolt was basically a mass movement and that the elites were unwilling participants or had been carried away by enthusiasm. He provides evidence that two rich men were unwilling insurrectionists, but no others. On the contrary, Spanish officials thought that most of these elites had been quite willing to take the lead in a tax protest. The colonial government imprisoned eleven of the fourteen very rich men who had become *Capitanes de Pueblos*, as well as the four well-off men. Thus it seems that local elites willingly led a mass movement to protest against rising taxes.

28. Mercedes M. Álvarez F., *Comercio y comerciantes y sus proyecciones en la independencia venezolana* (Caracas: Tipografía Vargas, 1963), pp. 86, 92; and Arcila Farías, *Economía colonial*, pp. 355, 357.

29. "Representación del Consulado en favor del establecimiento del comercio con las naciones neutrales," in Eduardo Arcila Farías, ed., *El Real Consulado de Caracas* (Caracas: Universidad Central de Venezuela, 1957), pp. 237-241.

30. Arcila Farías, *Economía colonial*, pp. 363-370; Arcila Farías, ed., *El Real Consulado de Caracas*, pp. 28-29, 224-225, 242-243.

31. Álvarez, *Comercio y comerciantes*, pp. 88, 90-91.

32. For further discussions of coalition building among planters and merchants, see Arcila Farías, ed., *El Real Consulado de Caracas*, pp. 27-28.

33. For other studies of the Caracas Consulado, see Manuel Nunes Dias, *El Real Consulado de Caracas (1793-1810)* (Caracas: Academia Nacional de la Historia, 1971); and Mercedes M. Álvarez F., *El tribunal del Real Consulado de Caracas* (Caracas: Ediciones del Cuatricentenario de Caracas, 1962), 2 vols.

34. Álvarez, *Comercio y comerciantes,*p. 115; Arcila Farías, ed., *El Real Consulado;* and Arcila Farías, *Economía colonial*, pp. 370, 382.

35. James F. King, "Evolution of the Free Slave Trade Principle in Spanish Colonial Administration," *Hispanic American Historical Review* 22, no. 1 (February 1942): 50.

36. Arcila Farías, *Economía colonial*, pp. 409, 416.

37. Francisco Depons, *Viaje a la parte oriental de tierra firme* (Caracas: Tipografía Americana, 1930), p. 90; and Miguel Acosta Saignes, *Vida de los esclavos negros en Venezuela* (Caracas: Hespérides, 1967), pp. 118-120.

38. John Lynch, *The Spanish-American Revolutions, 1808-1826* (New York: W. W. Norton, 1973), pp. 190-192.

39. "Exposición del Prior del Real Consulado de Caracas, Don Vicente Linones, sobre el malestar de la agricultura debido a la escasez de mano de obra," in Germán Carrera Damas, ed., *Materiales para el estudio de la cuestión agraria en Venezuela, 1800-1830* (Caracas: Universidad Central de Venezuela, 1964), pp. 6-7.

40. Miguel Acosta Saignes, *Vida de los esclavos negros en Venezuela* (Caracas: Hespérides, 1967), pp. 313-314.

41. Arcila Farías, ed., *El Real Consulado*, pp. 193-194.

42. Ildefonso Leal, ed., *Documentos del Real Consulado de Caracas* (Caracas: Universidad Central de Venezuela, 1964), pp. 18-22.

43. The following discussion draws from work of Huntington, *Political Order*, pp. 12-24; see also Ted Robert Gurr, *Why Men Rebel* (Princeton: Princeton University Press, 1971), pp. 282-296.

44. For a long list of such reforms, see Emeterio S. Santovenia, "Política colonial," in Ramiro Guerra y Sánchez, José M. Pérez Cabrera, Juan J. Remos, and Emeterio S. Santovenia, eds., *Historia de la nación Cubana* (Havana: Editorial Historia de la Nación Cubana, 1952), II, 54-59, 65-68, 70-71.

45. Ramón de la Sagra, *Historia económico-política y estadística de la isla de Cuba* (Havana: Viudas de Arazoza y Soler, 1831), pp. 279-281; and Ramos, *Minería y comercio*, pp. 310-311.

46. Manuel Moreno Fraginals, *El ingenio: El complejo económico-social cubano del azúcar* (Havana: Comisión Nacional Cubana de la UNESCO, 1964), I, 16, 19.

47. Julio J. Le Riverend Brusone, "Desarrollo económico y social," in Guerra y Sánchez et al., eds., *Historia de la nación cubana*, II, 210-212.

48. Manuel Moreno Fraginals, "Iglesia e ingenio," *Revista de la Biblioteca Nacional José Martí*, 3rd ser., 5, nos. 1-4 (January–December 1963): 13-15, 20-22.

49. Ibid., pp. 24-27; and Sagra, *Historia*, pp. 237-239.

50. The sources for this information are: Sagra, *Historia*, pp. 134-144; Julio J. Le Riverend Brusone, "Historia económica," in Guerra y Sánchez et al., eds., *Historia de la nación cubana*, III, 215-216; Ramiro Guerra y Sánchez, "Cuba, centro de rivalidad internacional en el Caribe," in ibid., III, 7, 12, 14.

51. Le Riverend, "Historia económica," pp. 216, 269, 289.

52. Duvon C. Corbitt, "*Mercedes* and *Realengos*: A Survey of the Public Land System of Cuba," *Hispanic American Historical Review* 19, no. 3 (August 1939): 262-285; and Manuel Moreno Fraginals, *El ingenio: Complejo económico social cubano del azúcar* (Havana: Editorial de Ciencias Sociales, 1978), I, 159.

53. Diego Barros Arana, *Historia general de Chile* (2nd ed.; Santiago: Nascimiento, 1933), VII, 461; Le Riverend, "Historia económica," p. 188.

54. Lucas Alamán, *Historia de Méjico* (Mexico: Jus, 1968), I, 17-18, 22.

55. Luis Villoro, *La revolución de independencia* (Mexico: Universidad Nacional Autónoma de México, 1953), pp. 24-25.

56. Hugh M. Hamill, Jr., *The Hidalgo Revolt: Prelude to Mexican Independence* (Gainesville: University of Florida Press, 1966), pp. 22-24.

57. Ibid., pp. 25, 31.

58. Mark A. Burkholder and D. S. Chandler, *From Impotence to Authority: The Spanish Crown and the American Audiencias, 1687-1808* (Columbus:

University of Missouri Press, 1977), apps. V, VII; Brading, *Miners and Merchants*, pp. 35-37, 40, 42, 323.

59. Computed from Ernesto de la Torre Villar, "La iglesia en México, de la guerra de independencia a la reforma," *Estudios de historia moderna y contemporánea de México* 1 (1965): 17-18. For a suggestion that Creoles may have run more religious orders at the beginning of the eighteenth century, see Luis Navarro García, "La administración virreinal en Mexico en 1703," *Revista de Indias* 29, nos. 115-118 (January–December 1969): 361.

60. Computed from Christon I. Archer, "To Save the King: Military Recruitment in Late Colonial Mexico," *Hispanic American Historical Review* 55, no. 2 (May 1975): 228-229.

61. Jaime Eyzaguirre, *Historia de Chile* (Santiago: Zig Zag, 1965), p. 253; and Francisco A. Encina, *Historia de Chile* (Santiago: Nascimiento, 1946), V, 127-137.

62. Javier González Echenique, "Notas sobre la 'alternativa' en las provincias religiosas de Chile indiano," *Historia* 2 (1962–1963): 196.

63. Jacques Barbier, "Elite and Cadres in Bourbon Chile," *Hispanic American Historical Review* 52, no. 3 (August 1972): 417-418, 425-434; quotation on p. 434; Burkholder and Chandler, *From Impotence to Authority*, apps. V, VII.

64. For two historians who agree that the subjective perception of the desirability or need of independence was lacking up to 1808, but who otherwise disagree, see Ramírez Necochea, *Antecedentes*, p. 23, and Alberto Edwards Vives, *La fronda aristocrática* (Santiago: Editorial del Pacífico, 1959), p. 32.

65. Eyzaguirre, *Historia*, p. 254.

66. Simon Collier, *Ideas and Politics of Chilean Independence, 1808-1823* (Cambridge: Cambridge University Press, 1967), pp. 20-21.

67. Villalobos, *Tradición*, pp. 100-104; Encina, *Historia* (1947), VI, 7-18.

68. Ildefonso Leal, "La universidad de Caracas y la sociedad colonial venezolana," *Revista de Historia* 3, no. 13 (1962): 29-31; Burkholder and Chandler, *From Impotence to Authority*, apps. V, VII.

69. Gurr, *Why Men Rebel*, pp. 319-333.

70. James C. Davies, "The J-Curve of Rising and Declining Satisfactions as a Cause of Some Great Revolutions and a Contained Rebellion," in Hugh Davis Graham and Ted Robert Gurr, eds., *Violence in America* (Washington: U.S. Government Printing Office, 1969), p. 547; Huntington, *Political Order*, pp. 53-56; Chalmers Johnson, *Revolutionary Change* (Boston: Little, Brown, 1966), pp. 59-87; Crane Brinton, *Anatomy of Revolution* (Englewood Cliffs, N.J.: Prentice-Hall, 1938); Mancur Olson, Jr., "Rapid Growth as a Destabilizing Force," *The Journal of Economic History* 23, no. 4 (December 1963): 529-552.

71. The general source for this biographical material is Encina, *Historia*, V, 20-23.

72. Collier, *Ideas*, p. 40.

73. Villalobos, *Tradición*, p. 87.

74. Collier, *Ideas*, pp. 5, 60, 74, 83.

75. Ibid., pp. 5, 113-114.

76. The general sources are William W. Pierson, Jr., "Francisco de Arango y Parreño," *Hispanic American Historical Review* 16, no. 4 (November 1936): 451-478; and Guerra y Sánchez et al., eds., *Historia*.

## 8. The Impact of the International System

1. Stanley J. Stein and Barbara H. Stein, *The Colonial Heritage of Latin America: Essays in Economic Dependence in Perspective* (New York: Oxford University Press, 1970), pp. 45-53; C. H. Haring, *The Spanish Empire in America* (New York: Harbinger, 1963), pp. 293-313; Demetrio Ramos, *Minería y comercio interprovincial en hispanoamérica (siglos XVI, XVII y XVIII)* (Valladolid: Universidad de Valladolid, 1970), pp. 116-117, 157-159, 283.

2. See Gottfried Haberler, "International Trade and Economic Development," in Richard S. Weckstein, ed., *Expansion of World Trade and the Growth of National Economies* (New York: Harper and Row, 1968), pp. 102-110; Karl Marx, "The Future Results of British Rule in India," in Shlomo Avineri, ed., *Karl Marx on Colonialism and Modernization* (Garden City, N.Y.: Doubleday, Anchor, 1969).

3. There is no claim that the entire cultural or political system was shaped by these environmental conditions and biological-physical activities, nor that they set firm boundaries on the processes of change of those systems. The argument is simply that "ecological" variables were important at these low levels of technology.

4. Charles P. Kindleberger, *Foreign Trade and the National Economy* (New Haven: Yale University Press, 1962), pp. 26-29, 72-77. Certain characteristics of the specialization in the production of primary products for export under conditions of slavery and low technology may place a ceiling on this dynamism by providing for no more than single-step modernization. There is enough economic modernization to clear the land, invest in the necessary buildings and primitive machinery and equipment, and provide for the transportation of production to the harbors for export. The cost of slaves is so high that the slaveowner has an incentive to use this labor before making yet another investment in machines to substitute for slave work. The slaves have little education. If they are freed, the rest of a relatively backward economy cannot absorb them easily. Slaveowners may be reluctant to risk freedom for the slave after oppression. Unless new technology comes from abroad, such production under conditions of serfdom or slavery remains more labor-intensive in the long run in both mining and agriculture than would be the case if cheap, slave labor were less available. The methods used were more modern than before the expansion of production, but economic modernization under slavery proceeded only through a single step. Long-term transformative capacities were muted. The educative effect of foreign trade through slave plantation agriculture is very limited. Growth occurs through expansion only — by bringing more land and more labor to use the same methods on the same crop. Hla Myint, *Economic Theory and the Underdeveloped Countries* (London: Oxford University Press, 1971), pp. 108-114; Kindleberger, *Foreign Trade*, pp. 102-108, 196-205; for a more extreme view, see H. W. Singer, *International Development: Growth and Change* (New York: McGraw-Hill, 1964), pp. 164-167. For a discussion of backward and forward linkages necessary for economic growth, see Albert O. Hirschman, *The Strategy of Economic Development* (New Haven: Yale University Press, 1958), pp. 98-119.

5. For economic and botanical perspectives, see W. W. McPherson and Bruce F. Johnston, "Distinctive Features of Agricultural Development in the Tropics," in

Herman M. Southworth and Bruce F. Johnston, eds., *Agricultural Development and Economic Growth* (Ithaca, N.Y.: Cornell University Press, 1967), pp. 186, 193; Raj Krishna, "Agricultural Price Policy and Economic Development," in ibid., pp. 503-517.

6. P. P. Courtenay, *Plantation Agriculture* (New York: Frederick A. Praeger, 1965), pp. 56, 79, 98; Gordon Wrigley, *Tropical Agriculture: The Development of Production* (London: Faber and Faber, 1969), p. 81; Vernon D. Wickizer, *Coffee, Tea, and Cocoa: An Economic and Political Analysis* (Stanford: Stanford University Press, 1951), pp. 283-284, 305-306. For a methodological discussion, see Clifford Geertz, *Agricultural Involution: The Process of Ecological Change in Indonesia* (Berkeley: University of California Press, 1963), pp. 2-7; Hugh Thomas, *Cuba: The Pursuit of Freedom* (New York: Harper and Row, 1971), pp. 40-41; Manuel Moreno Fraginals, *El ingenio: Complejo económico social cubano del azúcar* (Havana: Editorial de Ciencias Sociales, 1978), I, 175-181.

7. Computed from Sergio Sepúlveda, *El trigo chileno en el mercado mundial* (Santiago: Universitaria, 1959), p. 22; and Eduardo Arcila Farías, *Economía colonial de Venezuela* (Mexico: Fondo de Cultura Económica, 1946), p. 174.

8. Computed from the following: Hira de Gortari and Guillermo Palacios, "El comercio novohispano a través de Veracruz, 1802-1810," *Historia mexicana* 17, no. 67 (1968): 447; Clark W. Reynolds, *The Mexican Economy: Twentieth Century Structure and Growth* (New Haven: Yale University Press, 1970), p. 312, table A.1, col. D; Jacobo de la Pezuela, *Diccionario geográfico, estadístico, histórico de la isla de Cuba* (Madrid: Mellado, 1863), I, 46; and Ramón de la Sagra, *Historia económico-política de la isla de Cuba* (Havana: Viudas de Arazoza y Soler, 1831), pp. 103, 120, 126-127.

9. Alejandro de Humboldt, *Viaje a las regiones equinocciales del nuevo continente*, trans. Lisandro Alvarado (Caracas: Biblioteca Venezolana de Cultura, 1941), pp. 172-173; and "Exposición del Prior del Real Consulado de Caracas, Don Vicente Linones, sobre el malestar de la agricultura debido a la escasez de mano de obra," in Germán Carrera Damas, ed., *Materiales para el estudio de la cuestión agraria en Venezuela, 1800-1830* (Caracas: Universidad Central de Venezuela, 1964), p. 6.

10. All quotations from documents in Eduardo Arcila Farías, ed., *El Real Consulado de Caracas* (Caracas: Universidad Central de Venezuela, 1957), pp. 239, 244, 246-247.

11. Hernán Ramírez Necochea, *Antecedentes económicos de la independencia de Chile* (rev. ed.; Santiago: Universitaria, 1967), pp. 80-84.

12. See Roland D. Hussey, "Traces of French Enlightenment in Colonial Hispanic America," and Harry Bernstein, "Some Inter-American Aspects of the Enlightenment," in Arthur P. Whitaker, ed., *Latin America and the Enlightenment* (2nd ed.; Ithaca, N.Y.: Cornell University Press, 1961).

13. Charles C. Griffin, "The Enlightenment and Latin American Independence," in ibid., p. 137.

14. James A. Field, Jr., "Transnationalism and the New Tribe," *International Organization* 25, no. 3 (1971): 355-363.

15. Carl L. Becker, *The Heavenly City of the Eighteenth-Century Philosophers* (New Haven: Yale University Press, 1965), discusses these issues in considerable detail.

16. Griffin, "The Enlightenment," pp. 138-140.

17. Hussey, "Traces of French Enlightenment," pp. 28-43; Alexander von Humboldt, "Problems and Progress in New Spain," in Lewis Hanke, ed., *History of Latin American Civilization* (Boston: Little, Brown, 1967), I, 465. Hussey (p. 48) says that Cuba "apparently felt little of any new [intellectual] stimulus before 1808"; the Humboldt text suggests that this is false.

18. In addition to the citations in Note 4 above, see R. E. Baldwin, "Export Technology and Development from a Subsistence Level," *The Economic Journal* 73, no. 289 (March 1963): 85-89.

19. Courtenay, *Plantation Agriculture*, pp. 16, 18, 46, 77-83, 87; Wickizer, *Coffee, Tea*, p. 276.

20. Herbert S. Klein, *Slavery in the Americas: A Comparative Study of Virginia and Cuba* (Chicago: Quadrangle, 1971), p. 150. Similarly, Gwendolyn Mildo Hall's study, concerned with fully developed, and oppressive, slave plantation societies, notes the differences between eighteenth- and nineteenth-century Cuban slavery; the full force of slavery was felt much more during the latter century; *Social Control in Slave Plantation Societies: A Comparison of St. Domingue and Cuba* (Baltimore: Johns Hopkins Press, 1971).

21. This is not to argue that perennial tree crops have more sustained, long-term transformative effects than annual crops. On the contrary, the long-term transformative effects of these crops, often emphasizing cheap or slave labor policies, is single-step. The range of outcomes in annual crop production, such as wheat, is more widespread. See above, Note 4.

22. This discussion is indebted to Jean Borde and Mario Góngora, *Evolución de la propiedad rural en el valle del Puangue* (Santiago: Universitaria, 1956), pp. 57-61, 72-76, 79-87.

23. Computed from Domingo Amunátegui Solar, *Estudios históricos* (Santiago: Imprenta y Litografía Leblanc, 1940), pp. 41-64.

24. Evsey D. Domar, "The Causes of Slavery or Serfdom: A Hypothesis," *The Journal of Economic History* 30, no. 1 (March 1970): 18-32.

25. Eric Williams, *Capitalism and Slavery* (New York: Capricorn, 1966), pp. 3-29.

26. Borde and Góngora, *Evolución*, pp. 57-61, 72-76, 79-87; and Jaime Eyzaguirre, *Historia de Chile* (Santiago: Zig Zag, 1965), pp. 264-266.

27. Arnold J. Bauer, *Chilean Rural Society from the Spanish Conquest to 1930* (Cambridge: Cambridge University Press, 1975), pp. 15-16; Ruggiero Romano, *Una economía colonial: Chile en el siglo XVIII* (Buenos Aires: Universitaria, 1965), pp. 44-45.

28. Computed from Horacio Aránguiz Donoso, "La situación de los trabajadores agrícolas en el siglo 19," *Estudios de historia de las instituciones políticas y sociales* 2 (1967): 6.

29. D. A. Brading, *Miners and Merchants in Bourbon Mexico, 1763-1810* (Cambridge: Cambridge University Press, 1971), p. 64.

30. J. Clayburn LaForce, "Royal Textile Factories in Spain, 1700-1800," *The Journal of Economic History* 24, no. 3 (September 1964): 337-363, explores many of these issues.

31. The general source is Brading, *Miners and Merchants*, pp. 140-149.

32. Eric R. Wolf, "The Mexican Bajío in the Eighteenth Century," *Synoptic*

*Studies of Mexican Culture,* Middle American Research Institute Publications, no. 17 (New Orleans: Tulane University Press, 1957), pp. 187, 190-192.

33. J. H. Parry, *The Spanish Seaborn Empire* (New York: Alfred A. Knopf, 1967), pp. 315, 331-333; Julio J. Le Riverend Brusone, "Historia económica," in Ramiro Guerra y Sánchez, José M. Pérez Cabrera, Juan J. Remos, and Emeterio S. Santovenia, eds., *Historia de la nación cubana* (Havana: Editorial Historia de la Nación Cubana, 1952), III, 264-271; and Francisco A. Encina, *Historia de Chile* (Santiago: Editorial Nascimiento, 1946), V, 32.

34. In addition to the sources in Note 31 above, see Ralph Lee Woodward, Jr., "The Merchants and Economic Development in the Americas, 1750-1850," *Journal of Inter-American Studies* 10, no. 1 (January 1968): 145-149; Robert S. Smith, "The Institution of the Consulado in New Spain," *Hispanic American Historical Review* 24, no. 1 (February 1944): 61-83.

35. José Terrero, *Historia de España* (Barcelona: Ramón Sopena, 1958), pp. 416, 463-467; for an example of the impact of the war on Venezuela, see E. B. Núñez, "El partido austriaco en Caracas," *Revista de historia* 3, no. 13 (1962): 11-14; Anabola Borges, "Fiesta en Caracas," *Revista de historia* 3, no. 11 (1962): 15-17. For the barely noticeable impact of the war on Chile, see Diego Barros Arana, *Historial jeneral de Chile* (Santiago: Rafael Jover, 1885), V, 457-463, 468-469, 533-537. For a brief discussion of Mexican loyalty during the war, see Bradley Benedict, "El estado en México en la época de los Habsburgo," *Historia mexicana* 92 (April–June 1974): 603, 605.

36. John H. Parry, *Trade and Dominion: The European Oversea Empires in the Eighteenth Century* (London: Weidenfeld and Nicolson, 1971), pp. 98-105; quotation p. 105; and Ramos, *Minería y comercio,* pp. 256-258.

37. Rupert Emerson, *From Empire to Nation: The Rise to Self-Assertion of Asian and African Peoples* (Boston: Beacon, 1962), pp. 30-32.

38. For a comparison of levels of social mobilization between Asia at the time of World War II and 1810 Spanish America, one may look at the data in Chapter 2 and at data for Asian countries in Bruce M. Russett et al., *World Handbook of Political and Social Indicators* (New Haven: Yale University Press, 1964), tables 9, 31, 44, 63, 64.

39. Edgar O'Ballance, *Malaya: The Communist Insurgent War, 1948-1960* (Hamden, Conn.: Archon, 1966), pp. 82-84.

## 9. Destroying Political Order

1. José Terrero, *Historia de España* (Barcelona: Ramón Sopena, 1958), pp. 521-531.

2. Sergio Villalobos, *Tradición y reforma en 1810* (Santiago: Universitaria, 1961), pp. 173-174; and Néstor Meza Villalobos, *La actividad política del Reino de Chile entre 1806 y 1810* (Santiago: Universitaria, 1956), pp. 52-55.

3. Michael F. Lofchie, "Zanzibar," in James S. Coleman and Carl G. Rosberg, Jr., eds., *Political Parties and National Integration in Tropical Africa* (Berkeley: University of California Press, 1964), pp. 482-484, 490, 494-495, 504, 507-509.

4. Samuel P. Huntington, *Political Order in Changing Societies* (New Haven: Yale University Press, 1968), pp. 192-197.

5. Frances M. Foland, "Pugnas políticas en el México de 1808," *Historia mexicana* 5, no. 1 (1955): 30-33, 37.

6. Ibid., p. 39; D. A. Brading, *Miners and Merchants in Bourbon Mexico, 1763-1810* (Cambridge: Cambridge University Press, 1971), pp. 341-342; and Timothy E. Anna, *The Fall of the Royal Government in Mexico City* (Lincoln: University of Nebraska Press, 1978), pp. 35-63.

7. Doris M. Ladd, *The Mexican Nobility at Independence, 1780-1826* (Austin: University of Texas Press, 1976), pp. 105-110.

8. Villalobos, *Tradición*, p. 158.

9. Stanley G. Payne, *Politics and the Military in Modern Spain* (Stanford: Stanford University Press, 1967), p. 6. See also Christon I. Archer, *The Army in Bourbon Mexico, 1760-1810* (Albuquerque: University of New Mexico Press, 1977), pp. 283-300.

10. José Gil Fortoul, *Historia constitucional de Venezuela* (4th ed.; Caracas: Dirección de Cultura y Bellas Artes, Ministerio de Educación, 1954), I, 189-192.

11. Ibid., pp. 158-164; and computed from data in Francisco Depons, *Viaje a la parte oriental de tierra firme* (Caracas: Tipografía Americana, 1930), p. 87.

12. Hugh M. Hamill, Jr., *The Hidalgo Revolt: Prelude to Mexican Independence* (Gainesville: University of Florida Press, 1966), p. 93.

13. Eduardo Arcila Farías, *Economía colonial de Venezuela* (Mexico: Fondo de Cultura Económica, 1946), p. 382; Gil Fortoul, *Historia*, I, 201-210.

14. Angel Grisanti, *Repercusión del 19 de abril de 1810 en las provincias, ciudades, villas y aldeas venezolanas* (Caracas: Tipografía Lux, 1959), pp. 25-27, 40-41; Mario Briceño Perozo, *Los infidentes del Táchira* (n.p.: Biblioteca de Autores y Temas Tachirenses, 1961), pp. 18-19, 21; and Stephen K. Sloan, *Pablo Marillo and Venezuela, 1815–1820* (Columbus: Ohio State University Press, 1974), p. 30.

15. Villalobos, *Tradición*, pp. 158-160, 191-235; Meza Villalobos, *La actividad*, pp. 62-63, 70-71, 106-151.

16. Julio Alemparte, *El cabildo en Chile colonial* (2nd ed.; Santiago: Andrés Bello, 1966), pp. 271-273.

17. Computed from Horacio Aránguiz Donoso, "Estudio institucional de los cabildos abiertos de Santiago de Chile (1541–1810)," *Revista de Indias* 32, nos. 127-130 (January–December 1972): 217-220.

18. Julio Retamal Favereau, "El cabildo eclesiástico de Santiago en los prolegómenos de la independencia de Chile," *Historia* 6 (1967): 294-305, 308-310, 312-313.

19. Hamill, *Hidalgo Revolt*, pp. 97-98, 104-107.

20. Lester W. Milbrath, *Political Participation: How and Why Do People Get Involved in Politics?* (Chicago: Rand McNally, 1965), p. 132; Seymour Martin Lipset, *Political Man: The Social Bases of Politics* (Garden City, N.Y.: Doubleday, Anchor, 1963), pp. 211-226.

21. For further discussion and data, see Robert Melson and Howard Wolpe, "Modernization and the Politics of Communalism: A Theoretical Perspective," *The American Political Science Review* 64, no. 4 (December 1970): 1126-1128.

22. Robert E. Lane, *Political Life* (New York: Free Press, 1965), pp. 197-203.

23. Federico Brito Figueroa, *Las insurrecciones de los esclavos negros en la*

sociedad colonial venezolana (Caracas: Cantaclaro, 1961), pp. 60-62, 71; see also Gil Fortoul, *Historia*, I, 213-214, 290-291, 418.

24. Brito Figueroa, *Las insurrecciones*, pp. 79-81; Gil Fortoul, *Historia*, I, 171, 213-214, 290-291, 441; Eleázar Córdova Bello, *La independencia de Haití y su influencia en hispanoamérica*, publication no. 13 (Instituto Panamericano de Geografía e Historia, 1967), pp. 131-142.

25. Mario Briceño-Iragorry, *Tapices de historia patria* (Caracas: Tipografía Garrido, 1942); and Depons, *Viaje a la parte oriental*, p. 409.

26. Duvon C. Corbitt, "Immigration in Cuba," *Hispanic American Historical Review* 22, no. 22 (May 1942): 282-284.

27. Philip S. Foner, *A History of Cuba and Its Relations with the United States* (New York: International Publishers, 1962), I, 63.

28. William W. Pierson, Jr., "Francisco de Arango y Parreño," *Hispanic American Historical Review* 16, no. 4 (November 1936): 468-469; Corbitt, "Immigration," pp. 285-286.

29. Julio J. Le Riverend Brusone, "Historia económica," in Ramiro Guerra y Sánchez, José M. Pérez Cabrera, Juan J. Remos and Emeterio S. Santovenia, eds., *Historia de la nación cubana* (Havana: Editorial Historia de la Nación Cubana, 1952), III, 187-188.

30. Foner, *History*, pp. 73, 83.

31. Emeterio Santovenia and José Rivero Muñiz, "Desavenencias entre colonia y metrópoli," in Guerra y Sánchez, eds., *Historia*, III, 128-129, 137-138; Foner, *History*, pp. 89-92. For a discussion of conspiracies in Cuba during the period of the Spanish American wars of independence, see Francisco Morales Padrón, "Conspiraciones y masonería en Cuba (1810–1826)," *Anuario de estudios americanos* 29 (1972): 343-377.

32. Foner, *History*, p. 106.

33. Ramiro Guerra y Sánchez, "Cuba: Centro de rivalidad internacional en el Caribe," in Guerra y Sánchez, eds., *Historia*, III, 38-40, 58-64; and Santovenia and Rivero Muñiz, "Desavenencias," pp. 140-142.

34. Hamill, *Hidalgo Revolt*, p. 10.

35. Guerra y Sánchez, "Cuba," pp. 30-32; Santovenia and Muñiz, "Desavenencias," p. 135.

36. David E. Worcester, *Sea Power and Chilean Independence*, University of Florida Monographs in the Social Sciences, no. 15 (Gainesville: University of Florida, 1962), pp. 57-58, 81.

37. Computed from Carlos Olguín Bahamonde, *Instituciones políticas y administrativas de Chiloé en el siglo 18* (Santiago: Jurídica de Chile, 1970), pp. 85, 95-97, 102. The possibly high computation of white adult male military participation was obtained by assuming that males were half of the white population and that half of the males were adults.

38. Gabriel Guarda, "La economía de Chile austral antes de la colonización alemana," *Historia* 10 (1971): 241, 292-293.

39. Olguín Bahamonde, *Instituciones*, pp. 48-53, 57, 64-66; Guarda, "La economía," pp. 250, 296-297, 302-303.

40. David Piñera, "La independencia en el noroeste de México: estudio

historiográfico," *Estudios de historia moderna y contemporánea de México* 5 (1976): 43-44.

41. Sidney B. Brinckerhoff and Odie B. Faulk, *Lancers for the King* (Phoenix: Arizona Historical Foundation, 1965), p. 92; Alicia V. Tjarks, "Demographic, Ethnic and Occupational Structure of New Mexico, 1790," *The Americas* 35, no. 1 (July 1978), p. 82.

42. Juan F. Zorrillas, *Tamaulipas en la guerra de independencia* (Mexico: Librería de Manuel Porrúa, 1972), pp. 78, 83, 85-89; Isidro Vizcaya Canales, *En los albores de la independencia: Las provincias internas de Oriente durante la insurrección de Don Miguel Hidalgo y Costilla, 1810-1811* (Monterrey: Instituto Tecnológico de Estudios Superiores de Monterrey, 1976), pp. 97, 126-127, 148, 193-195, 217.

43. Ibid., pp. 16-19; and Pedro Carrasco, "La transformación de la cultura indígena durante la colonia," *Historia mexicana* 98 (October–December 1975): 177.

44. Arthur F. Corwin, *Spain and the Abolition of Slavery in Cuba, 1817-1886* (Austin: University of Texas Press, 1967), pp. 28, 35.

45. Herbert Klein argues in *Slavery in the Americas: A Comparative Study of Virginia and Cuba* (Chicago: Quadrangle, 1971), p. 202, n. 14, that the number of freedmen for 1827 is wrong; he prefers Humboldt's estimate of 130,000. This is not convincing because the census data are more reliable than Humboldt's estimates. Humboldt himself preferred census data and accepted corrections based on them. Because Klein does not distinguish enough between eighteenth- and nineteenth-century conditions of slavery in Cuba, he appears reluctant to admit that slavery in Cuba was not consistently less oppressive than in Virginia.

46. Manuel Moreno Fraginals, *El ingenio: El complejo económico-social cubano del azúcar* (Havana: Comisión Nacional cubana de la UNESCO, 1964), I, 151-152.

47. Sidney Mintz, "Labor and Sugar in Puerto Rico and in Jamaica, 1800-1850," *Comparative Studies in Society and History* 1, no. 3 (March 1959): 277-278.

48. Alexander von Humboldt, *The Island of Cuba*, ed. J. S. Thrasher (New York: Derby and Jackson, 1856), p. 275; Klein, *Slavery*, pp. 150-152.

49. Manuel Moreno Fraginals, *El ingenio: Complejo económico-social cubano del azúcar* (Havana: Editorial de Ciencias Sociales, 1978), II, 86-87.

50. Klein, *Slavery*, pp. 152-153.

51. José A. Saco, "Memoria sobre la vagancia en la isla de Cuba," *Obras de Don José Antonio Saco* (New York: Librería Americana y Estrangera, n.d.), I, 7, 10.

## 10. War and Political Mobilization: First Phase

1. John Super, "Querétaro *Obrajes:* Industry and Society in Provincial Mexico, 1600-1810," *Hispanic American Historical Review* 56, no. 2 (May 1976): 212.

2. See the excellent study of maize prices by Enrique Florescano, *Precios del maíz y crisis agrícolas en México (1708-1810)* (Mexico: El Colegio de México, 1969), pp. 149, 181, 189, 221.

3. D. A. Brading, *Miners and Merchants in Bourbon Mexico, 1763-1810* (Cam-

bridge: Cambridge University Press, 1971), p. 342. For a general discussion of agricultural production in the Bajío, see also David A. Brading, "La estructura de la producción agrícola en el Bajío de 1700 a 1850," *Historia mexicana* 90 (October–December 1973): 197-237.

4. Florescano, *Precios,* pp. 146, 153, 168-169, 173, 174-176, 219; see also Enrique Florescano, *Estructuras y problemas agrarios de México (1500-1821)* (Mexico: Sep-Setentas, 1971), pp. 105, 192.

5. Max Weber, *The Theory of Economic and Social Organization,* trans. A. M. Henderson and Talcott Parsons (New York: Free Press, 1965), p. 328; and H. H. Gerth and C. Wright Mills, eds., *From Max Weber: Essays in Sociology* (New York: Galaxy, 1958), p. 248.

6. Gerth and Mills, *From Max Weber,* pp. 248-250; Seymour Martin Lipset, *The First New Nation: The United States in Historical and Comparative Perspectives* (Garden City, N.Y.: Doubleday, Anchor, 1967), pp. 19-26.

7. David E. Apter, *Ghana in Transition* (New York: Atheneum, 1963), pp. 323, 325-330.

8. Aristide R. Zolberg, *Creating Political Order: The Party-States of West Africa* (Chicago: Rand McNally, 1966), pp. 137-145.

9. Hugh M. Hamill, Jr., *The Hidalgo Revolt: Prelude to Mexican Independence* (Gainesville: University of Florida Press, 1966), pp. 111, 132-135, 195. For a somewhat different view of Hidalgo's program, see Enrique Florescano, "El problema agrario en los últimos años del virreinato," *Historia mexicana* 80 (April–June 1971): 504-507.

10. Eric R. Wolf, "The Mexican Bajío in the Eighteenth Century," *Synoptic Studies of Mexican Culture,* Middle American Research Institute Publications, no. 17 (New Orleans: Tulane University Press, 1957), pp. 189, 193.

11. Hamill, *Hidalgo Revolt,* pp. 91-92, 111, 135, 140-141, 183.

12. Document from Presidencia de la República, *Las fuerzas armadas de Venezuela en el siglo XIX: La independencia (1810-1830)* (Caracas: Arte, 1963), I, 101, 103.

13. Ibid., pp. 96-97.

14. Juan Uslar Pietri, *Historia de la rebelión popular de 1814* (Caracas: Edime, 1962), pp. 30-33.

15. For the data on Indochina, see Bernard B. Fall, *Street Without Joy* (Harrisburg, Pa.: Stackpole, 1963), pp. 263-272; Joseph Buttinger, *Vietnam: A Dragon Embattled* (New York: Frederick A. Praeger, 1967), I, 410-411, 784-786.

16. Angel F. Brice, "Estudio Preliminar," in *Conjuración de 1808 en Caracas,* publication no. 14 (Caracas: Instituto Panamericano de Geografía e Historia, 1968), I, xix-xxii; II, 1207-1208.

17. Germán Carrera Damas, *Tres temas de historia* (Caracas: Universidad Central de Venezuela, 1961), p. 98; and Presidencia de la República, *Las fuerzas armadas,* I, 122.

18. Presidencia de la República, *Las fuerzas armadas,* I, 305.

19. Uslar Pietri, *Historia,* pp. 96, 101, 118.

20. Ibid., pp. 94, 95, 96.

21. Germán Carrera Damas, ed., *Materiales para el estudio de la cuestión agraria en Venezuela, 1800-1830* (Caracas: Universidad Central de Venezuela,

1964), pp. xi-xii, xvii-xviii, xxiii-liv. See also Germán Carrera Damas, *Boves: Aspectos socioeconómicos de su acción histórica* (Caracas: Ministerio de Educación, 1968), esp. pp. 29-96, 167-244; and Germán Carrera Damas, *Temas de historia social y de las ideas* (Caracas: Universidad Central de Venezuela, 1969), pp. 126-133. Carrera Damas has emphasized Boves' tactical use of pillage to provide incentives for the troops and pay for expenses; Boves was not an agrarian reformer, nor is there evidence that he sought to change Venezuela's agrarian structure.

22. From Vicente Lecuna, "Documentos de carácter político, militar y administrativo, relativos al período de la guerra a muerte," *Boletín de la Academia Nacional de la Historia* 18, no. 70 (April–June 1935): 314.

23. Quoted in Laureano Valenilla Lanz, *Cesarismo democrático* (Caracas: Tipografía Garrido, 1961), p. 19.

24. Uslar Pietri, *Historia*, p. 93.

25. Lucian W. Pye, *Guerrilla Communism in Malaya* (Princeton: Princeton University Press, 1956), pp. 49-64, 71-79, 97, 109; Edgar O'Ballance, *Malaya: The Communist Insurgent War, 1948-1960* (Hamden, Conn.: Archon, 1966), pp. 82-84, 107, 120, 125.

26. Donald L. Barnett and Karaji Njama, *Mau Mau from Within* (London: MacGibbon and Kee, 1966), pp. 67, 114, 331-332. For an example of the same variant in South Vietnam, see W. Robert Warne, "Vinh Binh Province," in George K. Tanham, ed., *War Without Guns* (New York: Frederick A. Praeger, 1966), pp. 39-40, 51, 54-55.

27. For an example from Indochina, see Fall, *Street Without Joy*, p. 266.

28. Hugh M. Hamill, Jr., "Early Psychological Warfare in the Hidalgo Revolt," *Hispanic American Historical Review* 41, no. 2 (May 1961): 207, 215, 218, 220, 222, 230-231. See also Hugh M. Hamill, Jr., "Royalist Counterinsurgency in the Mexican War for Independence: The Lessons of 1811," *Hispanic American Historical Review* 53, no. 3 (August 1973): 470-489. For a general discussion of Mexico City's response to insurrection, see Timothy E. Anna, *The Fall of the Royal Government in Mexico City* (Lincoln: University of Nebraska Press, 1978), pp. 64-97.

29. Hamill, "Early Psychological Warfare," pp. 227, 232-234.

30. Aristide R. Zolberg, *One-Party Government in the Ivory Coast* (rev. ed.; Princeton: Princeton University Press, 1969), pp. 106-146, 149-154, 168-169, 220-221, 234-236.

31. Victor D. Dubois, "Guinea," in James S. Coleman and Carl G. Rosberg, Jr., eds., *Political Parties and National Integration in Tropical Africa* (Berkeley: University of California Press, 1964), pp. 186-195; Zolberg, *One-Party Government*, p. 363.

32. Hamill, "Early Psychological Warfare," p. 23.

33. Nettie Lee Benson, "The Contested Mexican Election of 1812," *Hispanic American Historical Review* 26, no. 3 (August 1946): 339-350; and Charles R. Berry, "The Election of the Mexican Deputies to the Spanish Cortes, 1810-1822," in Nettie Lee Benson, ed., *Mexico and the Spanish Cortes, 1810-1822* (Austin: University of Texas Press, 1966), pp. 11, 17-18, 23-25. The computation of the qualified electorate in Mexico City is obtained by dividing the population of the

city (see Chapter 4) into 4 to get a crude estimate of the adult males, to which the statistic in the text is then applied. See also Doris M. Ladd, *The Mexican Nobility at Independence, 1780-1826* (Austin: University of Texas Press, 1976), p. 119.

34. Nelson W. Polsby, "The Institutionalization of the U.S. House of Representatives," *The American Political Science Review* 62, no. 1 (March 1968): 145-146.

35. Ibid., p. 146.

36. For yet another effort to use electoral methods on a local scale with moderate success to win support for the empire, see Roger L. Cunniff, "Mexican Municipal Electoral Reform, 1810-1822," in Benson, ed., *Mexico*.

37. The sources are: W. Woodrow Anderson, "Reform as a Means to Quell Revolution," and John H. Hann, "The Role of the Mexican Deputies in the Proposal and Enactment of Measures of Economic Reform Applicable to Mexico," both in Benson, ed., *Mexico*. See also Anna, *Fall of the Royal Government*, pp. 98-139.

38. For a brief discussion of the political and social thought of Félix Varela, see Luis Leal, "Félix Varela and Liberal Thought," in A. Owen Aldridge, ed., *The Ibero-American Enlightenment* (Urbana: University of Illinois Press, 1971), pp. 238-242.

39. Emeterio Santovenia and José Rivero Muñiz, "Desavenencias entre colonia y metrópoli," in Ramiro Guerra y Sánchez, José M. Pérez Cabrera, Juan J. Remos, and Emeterio S. Santovenia, eds., *Historia de la nación cubana* (Havana: Historia de la Nación cubana, 1952), III, 135, 142; Ramiro Guerra y Sánchez, "Cuba: Centro de rivalidad internacional en el Caribe," in ibid., pp. 26-27, 30-31, 57-59, 63; and Hugh Thomas, *Cuba: The Pursuit of Freedom* (New York: Harper and Row, 1971), pp. 96-97.

40. José Gil Fortoul, *Historia constitucional de Venezuela* (4th ed.; Caracas: Dirección de Cultura y Bellas Artes, Ministerio de Educación, 1954), I, 194, 332.

41. Francisco A. Encina, *Historia de Chile* (Santiago: Nascimiento, 1947), VI, 125-126.

42. Alejandro Villaseñor, *Biografías de los héroes y caudillos de la independencia* (Mexico: Jus, 1962), 2 vols. The biographies have been coded for quantitative analysis.

43. Because age was computed as of the beginning of the rebellion in 1810, there is a youthful bias to the computation. Those who did not become rebel leaders until after 1810 were older at the time when they made their move.

44. $T^2 = 0.45$. Although the data are not a sample, some statistics are used to facilitate interpretation. The chi-square is a test for statistical independence or significance. Two measures of association are also used. Tschuprow's $T^2$ coefficient ranges from zero in the case of no relation between two variables, to unity in the case of a perfect association between two variables, when the numbers of rows and columns are equal. The phi-square coefficient has the same range, reaching unity as a maximum only in a 2 x k table. For further discussion, see Hubert M. Blalock, Jr., *Social Statistics* (New York: McGraw-Hill, 1960), pp. 212-221, 225-230.

45. $T^2 = 0.18$; chi-square is not significant at 0.10 for $N = 27$.

46. $T^2 = 0.27$; for comparative data, see Seymour M. Lipset and Reinhard Bendix, *Social Mobility in Industrial Society* (Berkeley: University of California Press, 1962), p. 25.

47. Chi-square significant at 0.004 for one degree of freedom; phi-square = 0.08.

48. In both cases, chi-square significant at 0.001 for 3 degrees of freedom. For income, phi-square = 0.20, N = 90; for education, phi-square = 0.32, N = 69.

## 11. War and Political Mobilization: Second Phase

1. Laureano Valenilla Lanz, *Cesarismo democrático* (Caracas: Tipografía Garrido, 1961), p. 27; Juan Uslar Pietri, *Historia de la rebelión popular de 1814* (Caracas: Edime, 1962), p. 192; José Gil Fortoul, *Historia constitucional de Venezuela* (4th ed.; Caracas: Dirección de Cultura y Bellas Artes, Ministerio de Educación, 1954), I, 400-401.

2. Gil Fortoul, *Historia*, I, 402-403.

3. Ibid., I, 348; Uslar Pietri, *Historia*, p. 113.

4. Gil Fortoul, *Historia*, I, 404-405, 422, 428.

5. Presidencia de la República, *La fuerzas armadas de Venezuela en el siglo 19: La independencia (1810-1830)* (Caracas: Editorial Arte, 1963), II, decree of Sept. 3, 1817. Germán Carrera Damas, ed., *Materiales para el estudio de la cuestión agraria en Venezuela, 1800-1830* (Caracas: Universidad Central de Venezuela, 1964), pp. 315-317, 323-325.

6. Jesús Silva Herzog, *El agrarismo mexicano y la reforma agraria* (Mexico: Fondo de Cultura Económica, 1959), p. 40.

7. Wilbert H. Timmons, *Morelos: Priest, Soldier, Statesman of Mexico* (El Paso: Texas Western College Press, 1963), pp. 51-53.

8. Wilbert H. Timmons, "*Los Guadalupes:* A Secret Society in the Mexican Revolutionary War for Independence," *Hispanic American Historical Review* 30, no. 4 (November 1950): 453, 454, 456-457, 461-463, 468, 478-479.

9. Wilbert H. Timmons, "José María Morelos — Agrarian Reformer?" *Hispanic American Historical Review* 45, no. 2 (May 1965): 184, 188, 193, 195.

10. Computed from Woodrow Borah, "Tithe Collection in the Bishopric of Oaxaca, 1601-1867," *Hispanic American Historical Review* 29, no . 4 (November 1949): 511-512; see also Timmons, *Morelos*, p. 55.

11. William B. Taylor, *Landlord and Peasant in Colonial Oaxaca* (Stanford: Stanford University Press, 1972), pp. 197, 200-201; and William B. Taylor, "Haciendas coloniales en el valle de Oaxaca," *Historia mexicana* 90 (October–December 1973): 306-307, 322-323.

12. Alejandra Moreno Toscano, "Cambios en los patrones de urbanización en México, 1810-1910," *Historia mexicana* 86 (October–December 1972): 160, 162.

13. Doris M. Ladd, *The Mexican Nobility at Independence, 1780-1826* (Austin: University of Texas Press, 1976), p. 114.

14. Karl M. Schmitt, "The Clergy and the Independence of New Spain," *Hispanic American Historical Review* 34, no. 3 (August 1954): 290, 292, 295, 297, 299-300, 304-305.

15. Computed from N. M. Farriss, *Crown and Clergy in Colonial Mexico* (London: Athlone Press, 1968), pp. 198, 254-265. A less complete count by Ernesto de la Torre Villar found 161 priests who fought in the wars of independence out of 7,000 priests in the country (2.3 percent of the total); 79.5 percent of them were insurgents.

16. Jaime Eyzaguirre, *Historia de Chile* (Santiago: Zig Zag, 1965), p. 373.

17. Francisco A. Encina, *Historia de Chile* (Santiago: Nascimiento, 1947), VI, 471-475, 512-520.

18. Ibid., VI, 480-481.

19. Fernando Campos Harriet, *Los defensores del rey* (Santiago: Andrés Bello, 1958), pp. 27-29, 39-40, 122-125.

20. Eyzaguirre, *Historia*, pp. 372, 355-356.

21. Mary Lowenthal Felstiner, "Kinship Politics in the Chilean Independence Movement," *Hispanic American Historical Review* 56, no. 1 (February 1976): 65-67, 72-73.

22. Ibid., pp. 73-75.

23. Encina, *Historia*, VI, 712-714.

24. Jaime Eyzaguirre, "La conducta política del grupo dirigente chileno durante la guerra de la independencia," *Estudios de historia de las instituciones políticas y sociales* 2 (1967): 250-251.

25. Charles C. Griffin, "Economic and Social Aspects of the Era of Spanish American Independence," *Hispanic American Historical Review* 29, no. 2 (May 1949): 179.

26. Ted Robert Gurr, *Why Men Rebel* (Princeton: Princeton University Press, 1971), pp. 239-251, discusses these issues. For another explanation of authority problems, see William Kornhauser, "Rebellion and Political Development," in Harry Eckstein, ed., *Internal War* (New York: Free Press, 1964), esp. pp. 146-149, on rebellion and insufficient authority.

27. For a comparative study of repression highly sensitive to these distinctions, see Edward W. Gude, "Batista and Betancourt: Alternative Responses to Violence," in Hugh Davis Graham and Ted Robert Gurr, eds., *Violence in America: Historical and Comparative Perspectives* (Washington: U.S. Government Printing Office, 1969).

28. Encina, *Historia*, VI, 214, 216-217, 225, 232-241, 248, 317-319, 398, 410-411, 415-416.

29. Ibid., VI, 459, 471-479, 547, 569, 607, 614-615, 620-626.

30. Ibid., VI, 627-632, 665-666, 712, 720-721.

31. Eyzaguirre, *Historia*, pp. 373-377.

32. See also Jaime Eyzaguirre, *Historia de las instituciones políticas y sociales de Chile* (Santiago: Universitaria, 1967), pp. 51, 58-59; Francisco José Moreno, *Legitimacy and Stability in Latin America: A Study of Chilean Political Culture* (New York: New York University Press, 1969), pp. 80-97; Griffin, "Economic and Social," p. 179.

33. Encina, *Historia*, VI, 438.

34. John Rydjard, "British Mediation Between Spain and Her Colonies, 1811-1813," *Hispanic American Historical Review* 21, no. 1 (February 1941): 29-50; John Lynch, "British Policy and Spanish America," *Journal of Latin American Studies* 1, no. 1 (May 1969): 1-30.

35. Sebastián González García, "El aniquilamiento del ejército expedicionario de Costa Firme (1815-1823)," *Revista de Indias* 22, nos. 87-88 (January–June 1962): 138-139.

36. Magnus Mörner, *Race Mixture in the History of Latin America* (Boston:

Little, Brown, 1967), p. 85; Leslie B. Rout, Jr., *The African Experience in Spanish America: 1502 to the Present Day* (Cambridge: Cambridge University Press, 1976), pp. 173-174.

37. Laura F. Ullrick, "Morillo's Attempt to Pacify Venezuela," *Hispanic American Historical Review* 3, no. 4 (November 1920): 539-544, 546; Stephen K. Sloan, *Pablo Morillo and Venezuela, 1815-1820* (Columbus: Ohio State University Press, 1974), pp. 78-79, 139, 153-163.

38. Stanley G. Payne, *Politics and the Military in Modern Spain* (Stanford: Stanford University Press, 1967), pp. 7-9, 16-18.

39. Margaret L. Woodward, "The Spanish Army and the Loss of America, 1810-1824," *Hispanic American Historical Review* 43, no. 4 (November 1963): 589-591; Ullrick, "Morillo's Attempt," pp. 535, 546; Payne, *Politics*, p. 8; Sloan, *Pablo Morillo*, pp. 203, 206-207.

40. Quoted in Payne, *Politics*, p. 8.

41. Ibid., p. 19.

42. William S. Robertson, "The Policy of Spain Toward Its Revolted Colonies, 1820-1823," *Hispanic American Historical Review* 6, nos. 1-3 (February–August 1926): 24-26, 29; Gil Fortoul, *Historia*, I, 430, 432-441.

## 12. Toward Political Reconstruction

1. Duvon C. Corbitt, "*Mercedes* and *Realengos:* A Survey of the Public Land System of Cuba," *Hispanic American Historical Review* 19, no. 3 (August 1939): 263-277.

2. H. E. Friedlaender, *Historia económica de Cuba* (Havana: Jesús Montero, 1944), p. 223.

3. Alexander von Humboldt, *The Island of Cuba*, ed. J. S. Trasher (New York: Derby and Jackson, 1856), pp. 238-239.

4. Duvon C. Corbitt, "Immigration in Cuba," *Hispanic American Historical Review* 22, no. 2 (May 1942): 289-292.

5. Ramón de la Sagra, *Historia económico-política y estadística de la isla de Cuba* (Havana: Viudas de Arazoza y Soler, 1831), pp. 147-151; Ramiro Guerra y Sánchez, "Cuba: Centro de revalidad internacional en el Caribe," in Ramiro Guerra y Sánchez, José M. Pérez Cabrera, Juan J. Remos, and Emeterio S. Santovenia, eds., *Historia de la nación cubana* (Havana: Editorial Historia de la Nación Cubana, 1952), III, 45.

6. Computed from Sagra, *Historia*, pp. 284-287, 304-305.

7. Guerra y Sánchez, "Cuba," pp. 24, 31-32, 38-39, 52-53, 58-59, 63, 68-69.

8. Fermín Peraza, *Diccionario biográfico cubano* (Havana: Anuario Bibliográfico Cubano, 1953), listed alphabetically.

9. Philip S. Foner, *A History of Cuba and Its Relations with the United States* (New York: International, 1962), I, 104, 113-122; Emeterio Santovenia and José Rivero Muñiz, "Desavenencias entre colonia y metrópoli," in Guerra y Sánchez et al., eds., *Historia*, III, 143-146; José Luciano Franco, *El gobierno colonial de Cuba y la independencia de Venezuela* (Havana: Casa de las Américas, 1970), pp. 96-101; José Luciano Franco, "Política continental americana de España en Cuba, 1812-1830," *Publicaciones del Archivo Nacional de Cuba* 15 (1947): 325-327.

10. Guerra y Sánchez, "Cuba," p. 44.

11. For comments on the 1820s, see ibid., p. 71; José A. Saco, "Memoria sobre la vagancia en la isla de Cuba," *Obras de Don José Antonio Saco* (New York: Librería Americana y Estrangera, n.d.), p. 1.

12. Donald E. Worcester, *Sea Power and Chilean Independence*, University of Florida Monographs in the Social Sciences, no. 15 (Gainesville: University of Florida, 1962), pp. 57-58; Franco, "Política continental," pp. 367, 369; René de la Pedraza, "Politics and the Economy in the Hispanic Antilles, 1789-1820" (Ph.D. diss., University of Chicago, 1977), p. 149.

13. These four hypotheses are taken from Hugh Thomas, *Cuba: The Pursuit of Freedom* (New York: Harper and Row, 1971), pp. 90, 103.

14. From Foner, *History*, pp. 108.

15. Arthur F. Corwin, *Spain and the Abolition of Slavery in Cuba, 1817-1886* (Austin: University of Texas Press, 1967), p. 50; Manuel Moreno Fraginals, *El ingenio: El complejo económico-social cubano del azúcar* (Havana: Comisión Nacional Cubana de la UNESCO, 1964), I, 68-69.

16. Both quotations from Julio J. Le Riverend Brusone, "Historia económica," in Guerra y Sánchez et al., eds., *Historia*, III, 289.

17. Alexander von Humboldt, "Problems and Progress in New Spain," in Lewis Hanke, ed., *History of Latin American Civilization* (Boston: Little, Brown, 1967), p. 465.

18. Allen Potter, "Great Britain: Opposition with a Capital 'O'," in Robert A. Dahl, ed., *Political Oppositions in Western Democracies* (New Haven: Yale University Press, 1966); Robert E. Lane, *Political Life* (New York: Free Press, 1965), pp. 8-26.

19. See, for example, Nils Stjernquist, "Sweden: Stability or Deadlock," in Dahl, ed., *Political Oppositions*, pp. 117-121; Hans Daalder, "The Netherlands: Opposition in a Segmented Society," in ibid., pp. 190-206, 417; and Otto Kirchheimer, "Germany: The Vanishing Opposition," in ibid., pp. 237-238.

20. Samuel P. Huntington, *Political Order in Changing Societies* (New Haven: Yale University Press, 1968), pp. 334-343.

21. Samuel P. Huntington, "Social and Institutional Dynamics of One-Party Systems," in Samuel P. Huntington and Clement H. Moore, eds., *Authoritarian Politics in Modern Society* (New York: Basic Books, 1970), pp. 10-12.

22. Aristide Zolberg, *Creating Political Order: The Party-States of West Africa* (Chicago: Rand McNally, 1969), p. 92.

23. John V. Lombardi, "Manumission, *Manumisos* and *Aprendizaje* in Republican Venezuela," *Hispanic American Historical Review* 49, no. 4 (November 1969): 656-658, 675.

24. Presidencia de la República, *La fuerzas armadas de Venezuela en el siglo 19: La independencia (1810-1830)* (Caracas: Arte, 1963), II, 300-301.

25. Ildefonso Leal, "La universidad de Caracas y la sociedad colonial venezolana," *Revista de historia* 3, no. 13 (1962): 39.

26. José Gil Fortoul, *Historia constitucional de Venezuela* (4th ed.; Caracas: Dirección de Cultura y Bellas Artes, Ministerio de Educación, 1954), I, 212-213, 293-295, 300, 335, 338-339, 341-343, 378, 399-400, 428-429, 450.

27. For a general argument, see Eric Wolf and Edward Hansen, "Caudillo Politics: A Structural Analysis," *Comparative Studies in Society and History* 9, no. 2 (January 1967): 168-179.

28. Gil Fortoul, *Historia*, I, 411, 461-462, 495, 498, 587-612, 631-632, 680-685.

29. James M. Breedlove, "Effect of the Cortes, 1810-1822, on Church Reform in Spain and Mexico," in Nettie Lee Benson, ed., *Mexico and the Spanish Cortes, 1810-1822* (Austin: University of Texas Press, 1966), pp. 125-129.

30. N. M. Farriss, *Crown and Clergy in Colonial Mexico, 1759-1821* (London: Athlone Press of the University of London, 1968), pp. 11-12, 230-231, 246-248.

31. Computed from María Dolores Morales, "Estructura urbana y distribución de la propiedad en la ciudad de México en 1813," *Historia mexicana* 99 (January–March 1976): 367.

32. Romeo Flores Caballero, *Counterrevolution: The Role of Spaniards in the Independence of Mexico, 1804-1838*, trans. Jaime E. Rodríguez O. (Lincoln: University of Nebraska Press, 1974), pp. 14-31, 38; Farriss, *Crown and Clergy*, pp. 243-244; Brian R. Hamnett, "The Appropriation of Mexican Church Wealth by the Spanish Bourbon Government — The 'Consolidación de Vales Reales,' 1805-1809," *Journal of Latin American Studies* 1, no. 2 (November 1969): 85-113. For the impact of the law on New Spain's nobility, see Doris M. Ladd, *The Mexican Nobility at Independence, 1780-1826* (Austin: University of Texas Press, 1976), pp. 96-104. See also Asunción Lavrín, "The Execution of the Law of Consolidación in New Spain: Economic Aims and Results," *Hispanic American Historical Review* 53, no. 1 (February 1973): 27, 43.

33. Neill Macaulay, "The Army of New Spain and the Mexican Delegation to the Spanish Cortes," in Benson, ed., *Mexico*, pp. 148-150.

34. W. Woodrow Anderson, "Reform as a Means to Quell Revolution," in ibid., pp. 198-201; Timothy E. Anna, *The Fall of the Royal Government in Mexico City* (Lincoln: University of Nebraska Press, 1978), pp. 187, 191-193, 202-209, 224-226.

35. Karl M. Schmitt, "The Clergy and the Independence of New Spain," *Hispanic American Historical Review* 34, no. 3 (August 1954): 307; Farriss, *Crown and Clergy*, pp. 247-250; Breedlove, "Effects of the Cortes," p. 130; Macaulay, "Army of New Spain," p. 149.

36. Agustín Cué Canovas, *Historia social y económica de México, 1521-1854* (Mexico: F. Trillas, 1960), pp. 235-238.

37. Schmitt, "The Clergy," pp. 307-310.

38. Quoted in Luis Villoro, *La revolución de independencia* (Mexico: Universidad Nacional Autónoma de México, 1953), p. 184.

39. Ladd, *Mexican Nobility*, pp. 126-127.

40. Ibid., pp. 3, 58-60. For a discussion of Iturbide's rule, see Flores Caballero, *Counterrevolution*, pp. 62-77.

41. Wilbert H. Timmons, *Morelos: Priest, Soldier, Statesman of Mexico* (El Paso: Texas Western College Press, 1963), pp. 112-119, 127-132, 136-137, 154-155; Anna Macías, *Génesis del gobierno constitucional en México, 1808-1820* (Mexico: Sep-Setentas, 1973), pp. 78, 81, 94-95, 98, 106, 116, 160, 170-171.

42. For a list, see Manuel López Gallo, *Economía y política en la historia de México* (Mexico: Solidaridad, 1965), pp. 80-82.

43. Charles A. Hale, *Mexican Liberalism in the Age of Mora, 1821-1853* (New Haven: Yale University Press, 1968), p. 298.

44. For a comparative assessment, see Tulio Halperín Donghi, *Historia contemporánea de América Latina* (Madrid: Alianza, 1969), p. 105.

45. Charles C. Griffin, "Economic and Social Aspects of the Era of Spanish American Independence," *Hispanic American Historical Review* 29, no. 2 (May 1949): 179.

46. The sources are Jay Kinsbruner, *Bernardo O'Higgins* (New York: Twayne, 1968), pp. 66-77; Jaime Eyzaguirre, *Historia de Chile* (Santiago: Zig Zag, 1965), pp. 357, 361-370; Francisco A. Encina, *Historia de Chile* (Santiago: Nascimiento, 1947), VI, 226-227, 252-257, 286-287, 350-354, 398-400, 511-526, 639-646.

47. Quotation from Kinsbruner, *Bernardo O'Higgins*, p. 91; see also Francisco José Moreno, *Legitimacy and Stability in Latin America: A Study of Chilean Political Culture* (New York: New York University Press, 1969), p. 87.

48. Luis Marinas Otero, ed., *Las constituciones de Venezuela* (Madrid: Ediciones Cultura Hispánica, 1965), pp. 225, 227; Gil Fortoul, *Historia*, I, 259-260, 268-269, 459-462.

49. Elías A. Pino Iturrieta, *La mentalidad venezolana de la emancipación (1810-1812)* (Caracas: Universidad Central de Venezuela, 1971), pp. 112-113, 234, 237.

50. Villoro, *La revolución*, p. 109; Breedlove, "Effects of the Cortes," p. 132; Timmons, *Morelos*, pp. 117-123; Hale, *Mexican Liberalism*, pp. 95-96, 112-113, 177, 181.

51. Simon Collier, *Ideas and Politics of Chilean Independence, 1808-1833* (Cambridge: Cambridge University Press, 1967), pp. 147-148, 163-164.

52. Arthur P. Whitaker, "Changing and Unchanging Interpretations of the Enlightenment in Spanish America," in A. Owen Aldridge, ed., *The Ibero-American Enlightenment* (Urbana: University of Illinois Press, 1971), pp. 23-28, 54. For a more extensive discussion of the political ideas of the independence leaders, see Jay Kinsbruner, *The Spanish-American Independence Movement* (Huntington, N.Y.: Robert E. Krieger, 1976), pp. 75-99.

## 13. The Problem Revisited

1. John Lynch, *The Spanish-American Revolutions, 1808-1826* (New York: W. W. Norton, 1973), p. 1, and generally ch. 1.

2. Néstor Meza Villalobos, *La conciencia política chilena durante la monarquía* (Santiago: Universidad de Chile, 1958), p. 226. See also Jaime Eyzaguirre, *Ideario y ruta de la emancipación chilena* (Santiago: Universitaria, 1957), pp. 84-86.

3. José Valero Silva, "Proceso moral y político de la independencia de México," *Estudios de historia moderna y contemporánea de México* 2 (1967): 72.

4. For a discussion of the same problem in other contexts, see Warren F. Ilchman and Norman T. Uphoff, *The Political Economy of Change* (Berkeley: University of California Press, 1971), pp. 136-149; Aristide Zolberg, *Creating Political Order: The Party-States of West Africa* (Chicago: Rand McNally, 1966), pp. 75-87; Aristide Zolberg, "The Structure of Political Conflict in the New States of Tropical Africa," *The American Political Science Review* 62, no. 1 (March

1968): 74-77; Myron Weiner, *The Politics of Scarcity: Public Pressure and Political Response in India* (Chicago: University of Chicago Press, 1962), pp. 34-38, 56-72.

5. See Alan K. Manchester, "The Transfer of the Portuguese Court to Rio de Janeiro," in Henry H. Keith and S. F. Edwards, eds., *Conflict and Continuity in Brazilian Society* (Columbia: University of South Carolina Press, 1969), pp. 148, 160-163, 169-173; and Emilia Viotti da Costa, "The Political Emancipation of Brazil," in A. J. R. Russell-Wood, ed., *From Colony to Nation: Essays on the Independence of Brazil* (Baltimore: The Johns Hopkins Press, 1975), pp. 51-53. See also María Odila Silva Dias, "The Establishment of the Royal Court in Brazil," in Russell-Wood, ed., *From Colony to Nation.* For a discussion of the spread of modern ideas in Brazil, see E. Bradford Burns, "The Intellectuals as Agents of Change and the Independence of Brazil, 1724-1822," in Russell-Wood, ed., *From Colony to Nation,* pp. 211-246.

6. Quotation from John Norman Kennedy, "Bahian Elites, 1750-1822," *Hispanic American Historical Review* 53, no. 3 (August 1973): 435; see also pp. 431-432. For a discussion of slave resistance in Bahia, see Stuart B. Schwartz, "Resistance and Accommodation in Eighteenth Century Brazil: The Slaves' View of Slavery," *Hispanic American Historical Review* 57, no. 1 (1977): 69-81. For a more general discussion of the fear of social upheaval among Brazilian elites, see Kenneth R. Maxwell, *Conflicts and Conspiracies, Brazil and Portugal, 1750-1808* (Cambridge: Cambridge University Press, 1973), pp. 213-229.

7. Stuart B. Schwartz, "Elite Politics and the Growth of a Peasantry in Late Colonial Brazil," in Russell-Wood, ed., *From Colony to Nation,* pp. 137-138; quotation p. 142. For a similar argument about Bahia, see Kennedy, "Bahian Elites," pp. 415-416, 437. For a discussion of economic trends, see Harold B. Johnson, Jr., "A Preliminary Inquiry into Money, Prices and Wages in Rio de Janeiro, 1763-1823," in Dauril Alden, ed., *Colonial Roots of Modern Brazil* (Berkeley: University of California Press, 1973), pp. 262-264.

8. Viotti da Costa, "Political Emancipation of Brazil," pp. 55, 77-82, 86.

9. A. J. R. Russell-Wood, "Preconditions and Precipitants of the Independence Movement in Portuguese America," in Russell-Wood, ed., *From Colony to Nation,* pp. 26-29, 32-33, 36.

10. Viotti da Costa, "Political Emancipation of Brazil," p. 70; see also pp. 66-69.

11. Lynch, *The Spanish-American Revolutions,* pp. 37-57; see also Tulio Halperín-Donghi, *Politics, Economics, and Society in Argentina in the Revolutionary Period* (Cambridge: Cambridge University Press, 1975).

12. Rubén Vargas Ugarte, *Historia general del Perú* (Lima: Carlos Milla Batres, 1966), V, 22-25, 29.

13. Leon G. Campbell, "Recent Research on Andean Peasant Revolts, 1750-1820," *Latin American Research Review* 14, no. 1 (1979): 3-37. Daniel Valcárcel, *La rebelión de Túpac Amaru* (Mexico: Fondo de Cultura Económica, 1947); Vargas Ugarte, *Historia,* V, 50-59; Oscar Cornblitt, "Levantamientos de masas en Perú y Bolivia durante el siglo 18," *Revista latinoamericana de sociología* 70, no. 1 (1970): 100-141.

14. J. R. Fisher, *Government and Society in Colonial Peru: The Intendant*

*System, 1784-1814* (London: Athlone Press of the University of London, 1970), p. 229. See also Vargas Ugarte, *Historia*, V, 249-262; and John R. Fisher, "Royalism, Regionalism and Rebellion in Colonial Peru, 1808-1815," *Hispanic American Historical Review* 59, no. 2 (1979): 232-257.

15. Fisher, *Government and Society*, p. 236; Vargas Ugarte, *Historia*, V, 162-164; and John Fisher, "Silver Production in the Viceroyalty of Peru, 1776-1824," *Hispanic American Historical Review* 55, no. 1 (February 1975): 26-27, 41-43.

16. Quotation from Leon G. Campbell, "A Colonial Establishment: Creole Domination of the Audiencia of Lima during the Late Eighteenth Century," *Hispanic American Historical Review* 52, no. 1 (February 1972): 1; see also pp. 2-3, 6, 10, 18.

17. Leon G. Campbell, "The Army of Peru and the Túpac Amaru Revolt, 1780-1783," *Hispanic American Historical Review* 56, no. 1 (February 1976): 32, 56-57.

18. Quotation from Mark A. Burkholder, "From Creole to Peninsular: The Transformation of the Audiencia of Lima," *Hispanic American Historical Review* 52, no. 3 (August 1972): 414; numbers from pp. 398, 402, 406, 408, 410, 415. See also Mark A. Burkholder and D. S. Chandler, *From Impotence to Authority: The Spanish Crown and the American Audiencias, 1687-1808* (Columbus: University of Missouri Press, 1977), app. V.

19. Fisher, *Government and Society*, pp. 206, 214, 218-225.

20. George Kubler, *The Indian Caste of Peru, 1795-1940*, Smithsonian Institution, Institute of Social Anthropology, no. 14 (Washington: U.S. Government Printing Office, 1952), pp. 3-5.

21. Vargas Ugarte, *Historia*, V, 201, 224, 267, 273-274; VI, 38, 43, 145-149, 250, 278, 294-295.

22. Ibid., VI, 23, 126, 128, 231, 237, 269, 282, 286, 306, 314, 317, 385.

23. Computed from ibid., VI, 334, 340.

24. For a general interpretation, see Heraclio Bonilla and Karen Spalding, "La independencia en el Perú: Las palabras y los hechos," in Heraclio Bonilla et al., eds., *La independencia en el Perú* (Lima: Instituto de Estudios Peruanos, 1972), pp. 23-24, 31-32, 36, 43, 45, 53-54.

25. Charles W. Arnade, *The Emergence of the Republic of Bolivia* (New York: Russell and Russell, 1970), pp. 1-31; see also Cornblitt, "Levantamientos," p. 37; Campbell, "Recent Research on Andean Peasant Revolts."

26. Arnade, *The Emergence of the Republic of Bolivia*, pp. 32-56.

27. Ibid., pp. 80-138, 152, 152-153, 162-165. For a discussion of economic aspects of Bolivian independence, see Luis Peñaloza, *Historia económica de Bolivia* (La Paz: El Progreso, 1953), I, 250-263.

28. For parallels between the experiences of Puerto Rico and Cuba (both loyalist), see René de la Pedraza, "Politics and the Economy in the Hispanic Antilles, 1789-1820" (Ph.D. diss., University of Chicago, 1977), pp. 196-206. For parallels between the experiences of Mexico and Central America (both leading to a conservative independence), see Mario Rodríguez, *The Cádiz Experiment in Central America, 1808-1826* (Berkeley: University of California Press, 1978), pp. 103, 109, 149, 160, 205, 234-235.

# Index

# Publications of the
# Center for International Affairs,
# Published by
# Harvard University Press

Created in 1958, the Center for International Affairs fosters advanced study of basic world problems by scholars from various disciplines and senior officials from many countries. The research at the Center focuses on economic, social, and political development, the management of force in the modern world, the evolving roles of Western Europe and the Communist nations, and the conditions of international order.

*The Soviet Bloc*, by Zbigniew K. Brzezinski (Sponsored jointly with the Russian Research Center), 1960. Revised edition, 1967.

*United States Manufacturing Investment in Brazil*, by Lincoln Gordon and Engelbert L. Grommers, 1962. Harvard Business School.

*The Economy of Cyprus*, by A. J. Meyer, with Simos Vassiliou (sponsored jointly with the Center for Middle Eastern Studies), 1962.

*Communist China 1955-1959: Policy Documents with Analysis*, with a foreword by Robert R. Bowie and John K. Fairbank (sponsored jointly with the East Asian Research Center), 1962.

*Somali Nationalism*, by Saadia Touval, 1963.

*The Dilemma of Mexico's Development*, by Raymond Vernon, 1963.

*The Arms Debate*, by Robert A. Levine, 1963.

*Africans on the Land*, by Montague Yudelman, 1964.

*Democracy in Germany*, by Fritz Erler (Jodidi Lectures), 1965.

*The Rise of Nationalism in Central Africa*, by Robert I. Rotberg, 1965.

*Pan-Africanism and East African Integration*, by Joseph S. Nye, Jr., 1965.

*Germany and the Atlantic Alliance: The Interaction of Strategy and Politics*, by James L. Richardson, 1966.

*Political Change in a West African State*, by Martin Kilson, 1966.

*Planning without Facts: Lessons in Resource Allocation from Nigeria's Development*, by Wolfgang F. Stolper, 1966.

*Export Instability and Economic Development*, by Alasdair I. MacBean, 1966.

*Europe's Postwar Growth*, by Charles P. Kindleberger, 1967.

*Pakistan's Development: Social Goals and Private Incentives*, by Gustav F. Papanek, 1967.

*Strike a Blow and Die: A Narrative of Race Relations in Colonial Africa*, by George Simeon Mwase, ed. Robert I. Rotberg, 1967.

*Korea: The Politics of the Vortex*, by Gregory Henderson, 1968.

*The Brazilian Capital Goods Industry, 1929-1964* (sponsored jointly with the Center for Studies in Education and Development), by Nathaniel H. Leff, 1968.

*The Process of Modernization: An Annotated Bibliography on the Sociocultural Aspects of Development*, by John Brode, 1969.

*Agricultural Development in India's Districts: The Intensive Agricultural Districts Programme*, by Dorris D. Brown, 1970.

*Taxation and Development: Lessons from Colombian Experience*, by Richard M. Bird, 1970.

*Lord and Peasant in Peru: A Paradigm of Political and Social Change*, by F. LaMond Tullis, 1970.

*The Kennedy Round in American Trade Policy: The Twilight of the GATT?* by John W. Evans, 1971.

*Korean Development: The Interplay of Politics and Economics*, by David C. Cole and Princeton N. Lyman, 1971.

*Development Policy II — The Pakistan Experience*, edited by Walter P. Falcon and Gustav F. Papanek, 1971.

*Studies in Development Planning*, edited by Hollis B. Chenery, 1971.

*Political Mobilization of the Venezuelan Peasant*, by John D. Powell, 1971.

*Peasants Against Politics: Rural Organization in Brittany, 1911-1967*, by Suzanne Berger, 1972.

*Transnational Relations and World Politics*, edited by Robert O. Keohane and Joseph S. Nye, Jr., 1972.

*Latin American University Students: A Six Nation Study*, by Arthur Liebman, Kenneth N. Walker, and Myron Glazer, 1972.

*The Politics of Land Reform in Chile, 1950-1970: Public Policy, Political Institutions, and Social Change*, by Robert R. Kaufman, 1972.

*The Boundary Politics of Independent Africa*, by Saadia Touval, 1972.

*Becoming Modern: Individual Change in Six Developing Countries*, by Alex Inkeles and David H. Smith, 1974.

*Big Business and the State: Changing Relations in Western Europe*, edited by Raymond Vernon, 1974.

*Economic Policymaking in a Conflict Society: The Argentine Case*, by Richard D. Mallon and Juan V. Sourrouille, 1975.

*New States in the Modern World*, edited by Martin Kilson, 1975.

*No Easy Choice: Political Participation in Developing Countries*, by Samuel P. Huntington and Joan M. Nelson, 1976.

*Storm over the Multinationals: The Real Issues*, by Raymond Vernon, 1977.

*Insurrection or Loyalty: The Breakdown of the Spanish American Empire*, by Jorge I. Domínguez, 1980.